War's Logic

Antulio J. Echevarria II reveals how successive generations of American strategic theorists have thought about war. Analyzing the work of Alfred Thayer Mahan, Billy Mitchell, Bernard Brodie, Robert Osgood, Thomas Schelling, Herman Kahn, Henry Eccles, Joseph Wylie, Harry Summers, John Boyd, William Lind, and John Warden, he uncovers the logic that underpinned each theorist's critical concepts, core principles, and basic assumptions about the nature and character of war. In so doing, he identifies four paradigms of war's nature – traditional, modern, political, and materialist – that have shaped American strategic thought. If war's logic is political, as Carl von Clausewitz said, then so too is thinking about war.

Antulio J. Echevarria II is Professor at the US Army War College and former Elihu Root Chair of Military Studies.

CAMBRIDGE MILITARY HISTORIES

Edited by

HEW STRACHAN, Professor of International Relations, University of St Andrews and Emeritus Fellow of All Souls College, Oxford

GEOFFREY WAWRO, Professor of Military History, and Director of the Military History Center, University of North Texas

The aim of this series is to publish outstanding works of research on warfare throughout the ages and throughout the world. Books in the series take a broad approach to military history, examining war in all its military, strategic, political and economic aspects. The series complements *Studies in the Social and Cultural History of Modern Warfare* by focusing on the 'hard' military history of armies, tactics, strategy and warfare. Books in the series consist mainly of single author works – academically rigorous and groundbreaking – which are accessible to both academics and the interested general reader.

A full list of titles in the series can be found at:

www.cambridge.org/militaryhistories

War's Logic

Strategic Thought and the American Way of War

Antulio J. Echevarria II
US Army War College

CAMBRIDGE
UNIVERSITY PRESS

CAMBRIDGE
UNIVERSITY PRESS

University Printing House, Cambridge CB2 8BS, United Kingdom

One Liberty Plaza, 20th Floor, New York, NY 10006, USA

477 Williamstown Road, Port Melbourne, VIC 3207, Australia

314–321, 3rd Floor, Plot 3, Splendor Forum, Jasola District Centre, New Delhi – 110025, India

79 Anson Road, #06–04/06, Singapore 079906

Cambridge University Press is part of the University of Cambridge.

It furthers the University's mission by disseminating knowledge in the pursuit of education, learning, and research at the highest international levels of excellence.

www.cambridge.org
Information on this title: www.cambridge.org/9781107091979
DOI: 10.1017/9781316135730

© Antulio J. Echevarria II 2021

This publication is in copyright. Subject to statutory exception and to the provisions of relevant collective licensing agreements, no reproduction of any part may take place without the written permission of Cambridge University Press.

First published 2021

A catalogue record for this publication is available from the British Library.

Library of Congress Cataloging-in-Publication Data
Names: Echevarria, Antulio J., II, 1959– author.
Title: War's logic : strategic thought and the American way of war / Antulio J. Echevarria II.
Other titles: Strategic thought and the American way of war
Description: Cambridge ; New York, NY : Cambridge University Press, 2021. | Series: Cambridge military histories | Includes bibliographical references and index.
Identifiers: LCCN 2020036434 (print) | LCCN 2020036435 (ebook) | ISBN 9781107091979 (hardback) | ISBN 9781107465015 (paperback) | ISBN 9781316135730 (epub)
Subjects: LCSH: Strategy–United States. | United States–Military policy. | Military planning–United States–History. | United States–History, Military. | Military art and science–United States–History.
Classification: LCC U162 .E36 2021 (print) | LCC U162 (ebook) | DDC 355.020973–dc23
LC record available at https://lccn.loc.gov/2020036434
LC ebook record available at https://lccn.loc.gov/2020036435

ISBN 978-1-107-09197-9 Hardback
ISBN 978-1-107-46501-5 Paperback

Cambridge University Press has no responsibility for the persistence or accuracy of URLs for external or third-party internet websites referred to in this publication and does not guarantee that any content on such websites is, or will remain, accurate or appropriate.

To all those who have been, are now, or will be, part of the American way of war.

Contents

Acknowledgments	*page* ix
Introduction	1
Part I First Principles and Modern War	11
1 Alfred Thayer Mahan and Sea Power	13
2 Billy Mitchell and Air Power	32
Part II The Revolt of the Strategy Intellectuals	57
3 Bernard Brodie, Robert Osgood, and Limited War	59
4 Thomas Schelling and War as Bargaining and Coercion	82
5 Herman Kahn and Escalation	93
Part III The Counterrevolution of the Military Intellectuals	111
6 Henry Eccles and the Reform of Strategic Theory	113
7 J. C. Wylie and Strategy as Control	130
8 Harry Summers and the Principles of War	143

Part IV The Insurrection of the Operational Artists 167

9 John Boyd, William Lind, and Maneuver Theory 169

10 John Warden and Air Operational Art 193

    Conclusion 207

    Notes 228

    Select Bibliography 267
    Index 294

Acknowledgments

This book could not have been completed without the inspiration and assistance of many people. My friends and colleagues at the US Army War College Library were incomparably diligent in finding the numerous obscure articles and speeches analyzed in this work: Chief of Research and Instruction Adria P. Olmi; Research Librarians Gail (Jenny) C. Silkett, Megan L. Casey, and Mona J. Kwon; Reference Historian Rodney C. Foytik; and Interlibrary Loan Administrators and Acquisitions Assistants Stephen M. Bye, Paul A. Huerta, and Shannon S. Schwaller. I am also indebted to several people who performed invaluable archival services for me: Julianna Jenkins, Library Special Collections, University of California, Los Angeles; Abigail Gardner, Special Collections, Archives, and History, National Defense University; Stacie M. Parillo (Director), Elizabeth M. Delmage (Archivist), and Elysia Hamelin (Archives Technician), Naval Historical Collection Archives, Hattendorf Center for Maritime Historical Research, US Naval War College; Julie Zecher, Reference Librarian, US Naval War College Library; Alisa M. Whitley, Branch Head and Archivist, US Marine Corps History Division; and James Stimpert, Senior Reference Archivist, Special Collections, Sheridan Libraries, Johns Hopkins University.

Special thanks must go to professors Todd Greentree, Sarandis (Randy) Papadopoulos, and Wallace (Andy) Terrill for reading and commenting on select chapters of the draft manuscript. The time they invested surely contributed to a better final product, notwithstanding whatever imperfections might remain. I am also grateful to my students and colleagues at the US Army War College who, without necessarily knowing it, were sounding boards for some of the analyses in this work. Also Michael Watson and his editing team at Cambridge University Press deserve immense credit for their patience and attention to detail throughout this project, which extended well beyond its anticipated timeline. Most of all, I am profoundly grateful to my wife, Laurie, and our four children: Rachel, Grace, Matthew, and James. Without their support and quiet sacrifices, this book simply could not have been written.

Introduction

> Is war not just another form of expression employed by peoples and governments? Indeed, war has its own grammar but not its own logic.[1]
> —Carl von Clausewitz, *On War*

War's Logic provides a fresh perspective into twentieth-century American strategic thought. More to the point, it offers unique insights into how several of America's prominent strategic theorists conceived of armed conflict. The title stands for a general way of thinking about war. It refers to the reasoning that underlies a theorist's critical concepts, core principles, and basic assumptions regarding the nature and character of war. As Carl von Clausewitz observed, war's logic is invariably political in nature. Similarly, readers of this book will note the American way of thinking about war was frequently political in nature. While *War's Logic* covers ground similar to that of Russell Weigley's classic, *The American Way of War*, it differs from his work in three important respects.[2] First, it draws from archives unavailable to Weigley, thereby providing a richer analysis, albeit covering one century rather than two.[3] Relatedly, it carries its analysis beyond the early 1970s, where his book ended, to address the strategic theories of the 1980s and 1990s, and the American rediscovery of operational art. Finally, it delivers a broader interpretation of US strategic thought by situating it within its various sociocultural contexts across the twentieth century, thus avoiding the narrowly focused "tunnel" histories typical of Weigley's day.[4]

Specifically, *War's Logic* examines the ideas of twelve major US strategic theorists: Alfred Thayer Mahan, William (Billy) Mitchell, Bernard Brodie, Robert E. Osgood, Thomas C. Schelling, Herman Kahn, Henry E. Eccles, Joseph C. Wylie, Harry G. Summers, Jr., John Boyd, William S. Lind, and John Warden III. While their concepts and theories cannot capture the full sum of the American way of thinking about war, they represent a reasonable cross-section of military and nonmilitary perspectives: two from the US Army, including Mitchell; three from the US Navy; two from the US Air Force, one of whom (Boyd) became an honorary member of the US Marine Corps; and five civilians. Their collective ideas cover more than seven generations of US strategic thinking.[5] Admittedly, not every author listed here qualifies as a strategic theorist. Mitchell and Summers were military critics and commentators more than theorists. Boyd, Lind, and Warden concerned themselves with refining operational art rather than theorizing about military strategy. Each thinker, nonetheless, attempted to transform the American approach to war, and each succeeded at least partially.

To be sure, war's nature and its character are closely related concepts. After all, the words nature and character have been synonyms in English since at least the early eighteenth century. The terms were used interchangeably in US military literature until the early 1990s, when, as Part IV shows, interservice debates made it necessary to distinguish between the two. For purposes of this study, the nature of war denotes an author's sense of what armed conflict, at root, was; whereas the character of war refers to the procedural aspects of armed conflict, or a way of fighting; it includes types of conflicts, such as a revolutionary or civil war, in addition to types of warfare, such as naval warfare or air warfare. Context provided a reasonably sure guide as to whether an author meant war's nature or its character, as defined in this study. For instance, Mahan's debate with the pacifist Norman Angell over whether killing in war could ever be morally justified, reveals what the naval strategist believed armed conflict essentially to be, namely a violent extension of the competitive side of human nature. Mahan's lectures on the principles of naval strategy, in contrast, clearly refer to war's character, meaning the special features of naval warfare. It is possible, moreover, for two theorists to have a similar understanding of war's nature but a very different sense of its character. Mahan saw sea power as decisive; while Mitchell considered sea power to have been eclipsed by air power.

By comparison, twenty-first-century military professionals use the term nature of war to refer to those characteristics all armed conflicts have in common. All wars involve a "clash of opposing wills," for instance, as well as the elements of chance and uncertainty which make it impossible to reduce war to a predictable science.[6] War's nature is viewed as unchanging because those forces, though dynamic and variable, are always present, even if minimally. In contrast, the phrase character of war refers to the many types of armed conflicts, including the kinds of participants and their fighting methods, which naturally vary across time and cultures. By this reckoning, irregular warfare has the same nature as regular warfare but not the same character. This dichotomous construct of war's nature and character, though flawed, enables military professionals to study warfare systematically.

As this book shows, at least four distinct models or paradigms of war's nature underpinned US strategic thinking in the twentieth century: traditional, modern, materialist, and political. Mahan and Mitchell typified the traditional model, which saw armed conflict as the natural outgrowth of the competitive instincts of human nature. To be sure, any number of theories of human nature exist. Mahan was raised according to Episcopalian values and believed human nature had a "fallen" or corrupt quality about it. Mitchell, though raised in an Episcopalian boarding school, was, by comparison, more agnostic. Nonetheless, both believed negative behavior was inseparable from the human condition, which in turn made war inevitable but deplorable. The traditional paradigm, which held sway through the Second World War, applied equally well to regular and irregular conflicts. Nor was it uniquely American, as attempts to explain armed conflict as an outgrowth of human nature can be found among classical European military writings, such as Marcus Aurelius' *Meditations*.

The second, or modern, paradigm expanded and refined the traditional one with the help of the English translation of Clausewitz's *On War* by Michael Howard and Peter Paret. The publication of that text, which also contributed to a Clausewitzian renaissance of sorts, provided America's military and policy practitioners with a ready framework for articulating the central role of chance and uncertainty in warfare. War was still a violent extension of human nature. But the debilitating factors of chance and uncertainty received additional attention. By the 1950s, Eccles and Wylie had begun to incorporate those elements into their theories; these naval officers, along with US Army Col. Harry Summers, helped set the conditions for the shift to the modern paradigm of war's nature. That model was enthusiastically embraced by Boyd, Lind, and a host of other maneuver theorists during the 1980s. Boyd's thoughts also exemplified the model's increasingly secular turn. He was born into a Roman Catholic family but came to believe human nature's competitiveness was biologically determined, an essential impulse rather than a spiritual flaw.

The third, or materialist, model of war's nature considered armed conflict largely through a technological lens. This paradigm began to form in the early 1990s in the wake of Operation Desert Shield/Desert Storm, which debuted some long-range, precision-strike capabilities, albeit in limited numbers. It regarded the debilitating influences of chance and uncertainty as largely mitigatable through information technology, and it criticized the modern paradigm for being hidebound and hostile to innovation. The model's materialist quality came from its twofold presumption that destroying a party's material capacity to resist would suffice to destroy its willingness to fight, and that tangible solutions could be found for most of war's dilemmas, specifically, that information technology could "lift the fog of war."[7] In short, the materialist paradigm sought to ignore war's intangible nature in favor of its tangible character. After all, military practitioners were meant to deal with the physical world, not its metaphysical counterpart. Warden's theories laid the groundwork for this paradigm, while other airpower theorists and precision-strike specialists developed it further. Notably, Clausewitz's trinity omitted the influences of technology and economic might; however, historian Michael Handel suggested "squaring" the trinity by augmenting it with a material dimension.[8] That suggestion could have created the requisite conceptual space for the modern and materialist paradigms to merge. Nevertheless, most Clausewitz scholars saw the addition as unnecessary and never supported it sufficiently for it to gain traction.

The fourth, or political, model likens war's nature to a coiled spring. It considers political purpose to be the chief determinant of war's nature, and the only meaningful element in the Clausewitzian trinity. It believes a small accident or error in judgment could lead to a ruinously violent escalation, not only because of the mechanistic character of nuclear warfare, but also because military instincts and public passions were considered explosive. This paradigm achieved its sharpest articulation with the rise of limited war theory in the 1950s, though one can find evidence of it well before then. It still influences much of US strategy, as revealed by the fact that contemporary decisions to limit military actions are largely reflexive rather than calculated. Brodie, Osgood, Shelling, and Kahn – Weigley's strategy intellectuals – actively promoted this model, arguing, not unjustly, that only policy had the broad perspective necessary to ensure the instincts of the military and the passions of the populace were properly managed. The flaw inherent in this paradigm, of course, is its presumption that policy itself is a priori rational, whereas history offers numerous instances in which the opposite is true.

These four paradigms show little evidence of having "shifted" in the sense popularized by historian of science Thomas Kuhn in his 1962 work, *The Structure of Scientific Revolutions*. Kuhn defined scientific paradigms as: "universally recognized scientific achievements that for a time provide model problems and solutions to a community of practitioners," which, in turn, influence rules, expectations, and education to form the "basis for the practice of science."[9] In a similar vein, the strategic paradigms discussed were derived from recognized military achievements (successful uses of force) that for a time provided model problems and solutions (doctrinal concepts and procedures) to the military and policy communities, which in turn shaped rules, expectations, and professional education to form the basis for strategic practice. For Kuhn, scientific revolutions followed a cycle, the heart of which was the paradigm shift, which occurred when the number of observations (anomalies) the previous theory or model could not explain reached the level of a crisis. In contrast, the only paradigm shift that occurred in American strategic thought was from the traditional model to the modern one, and it was closer to an augmentation than a revolution. The other three paradigms remain in fierce but not necessarily overt competition with one another. Kuhn's theory of paradigm shifts is useful, nonetheless, for illustrating what has not happened in the American way of thinking about war.

The modern, materialist, and political paradigms, moreover, continue to contribute to shaping and reinforcing service perspectives, as evidenced by seemingly endless battles over the US defense budget and the country's national military strategy. Conceptions of war's nature are, therefore, of central importance, contrary to what some academics or practitioners have argued. Each community prefers its paradigm, however imperfect, over other models, even though the services may make some concessions in the interest of jointness. Accordingly, the American approach to strategy has become, more or less, what the German émigré and military historian Herbert Rosinski described in 1959, as an "*anarchy* of the most differently conceived military strategies."[10] While anarchy is lamentable in some respects, it is preferable to autocracy or to hegemony; the dominance of one paradigm over the others would stifle creativity and preclude alternative solutions. In addition, autocracy is unnecessary since the "ends-ways-means-risk" model of strategy introduced by Arthur Lyyke, Jr., for all its flaws, prevents anarchy from sliding into chaos by providing a conceptual framework for interservice and interagency debates.

Weigley's *American Way of War*, though pathbreaking for its time, ultimately amounted to a tunnel history of US strategic thinking. It left the social and cultural lanes of the US history underexplored and, thus, failed to include "America" in its story of the American way of war. Any analysis of the American way of thinking about war over the twentieth century should include how America itself changed over that timeframe. With few exceptions, in fact, each of America's key strategic thinkers thought and wrote in a different America. Mahan's America, for instance, was "at war with itself" in sociocultural terms, a fact that sheds additional light on his conviction that sea power could unify and strengthen a people culturally and socially. Mitchell's America, by comparison, was as "reckless and confused" as was his solution to the country's future defense challenges, namely, creating a national air service headed by a single chief. His solution was, thus, less anomalous in character and more in tune with the times than one might think.

In contrast, the America of Brodie, Osgood, Schelling, and Kahn coincided with that of Eccles and Wylie. It began in the 1950s, the "golden age" of the American middle class, and it ended with the political and social violence of the 1960s. The Watts riots of August 1965, which resulted in nearly three dozen deaths and $40 million in damage, unfolded within twenty miles of Brodie's RAND office in Santa Monica and his home in Pasadena, California. It should hardly be surprising, therefore, that Brodie and the other strategy intellectuals considered the sociocultural dimension of war to be too volatile to be permitted to influence US strategy, either directly or indirectly. Hence, they largely excluded it from, or marginalized it in, their theories. On the other hand, the military intellectuals had served among the public, alongside sailors and soldiers, in the Second World War, and consequently regarded the sociocultural or psychosocial dimension of warfare to be critical; they saw it as the reservoir of a nation's willingness to fight. As a result, their theories, though perhaps less sophisticated in some respects, were more comprehensive than those of the strategy intellectuals.

The America of Boyd and Lind was characterized by a period of "cultural malaise" following the Vietnam War, the Watergate scandal, and the economic downturn of the 1970s. They came to despise how the United States began to embrace multiculturalism in the 1980s and 1990s, which they perceived, through ultraconservative lenses, not as evidence of strength, but as both an error and an Achilles' heel. As operational artists, they explicitly identified a nation's sociocultural or psychosocial dimension as a center of gravity that could be attacked through "soft-power" and various nontraditional ways. While their early operational theories looked for ways to disrupt an opponent's armed forces psychologically, their later theories imagined how America itself might lose its willingness to fight due to the frictions caused by its racial, ethnic, religious, and gender differences. Their theories obviously reflected a certain paranoia. Nonetheless, they also drew from established techniques in psychological and information warfare, including those aimed at political and cultural subversion. In sum, this book endeavors to put America back into the story of American strategic thought, if only partially.

This book is structured as a chronicle of debates involving America's predominant ways of thinking about war. These disputes frequently revolved around sets of core principles, each supported at root by a different paradigm of war's nature. Principles, core principles especially, supplied both the weaponry and the turf for the battles over war's nature. Principles, of course, form an essential part of the grammar of war. They link theory to practice and, in some cases, become a formidable rival to war's logic.

Part I, "First Principles and Modern War," discusses the theories and underlying principles of Mahan and Mitchell. Mahan brought Jomini's three core principles – concentration, offensive action, and decision by battle – from the nineteenth into the twentieth century and applied them to naval strategy. Mitchell fashioned a concept of air or aeronautical strategy around the same core principles. These imperatives, moreover, typified the instincts of US military professionals for much of the twentieth century. An example is Adm. Ernest J. King who, in likening warfare to pugilism, affirmed the traditional model of war's nature, even as he endorsed Jomini's core principles: "No fighter ever won his fight by covering up," he once asserted; instead, the "winner hits and keeps on hitting even though he has to take some stiff blows in order to keep on hitting."[11] Another example is Gen. George C. Marshall who, despite the Allies' deficiencies in training and materiel in the early stages of the Second World War, repeatedly insisted the correct military strategy lay in taking the offensive as soon as possible, delivering a concentrated blow across the English Channel, and defeating the German army in a decisive battle.[12] The US military, like others, would never truly abandon these imperatives, even when it added other principles of war to its official doctrine.[13]

In addition, Part I reveals how Mahan and Mitchell, though separated by a generation, shared the same understanding of war's nature but saw war's character quite differently. Mahan put his faith in surface fleets and found the fledgling but expanding potential of aircraft and submarines unimpressive. Mitchell, in contrast, regarded surface fleets as obsolete and called for the aggressive expansion of airpower as the weapon of the future. In effect, each theorist began advocating a separate way of battle: the former surface-centric and the latter air-centric.

Part II, "The Revolt of the Strategy Intellectuals," describes the crystallization of America's way of policy. Based on misinterpretations of Clausewitz's *On War* and of the First and Second World Wars, the strategy intellectuals assumed armed conflict, by its nature, would escalate almost automatically to the maximum possible level of violence. Ergo, Brodie rejected the notion that military imperatives should ever guide strategy, especially in an era in which "second-strike" nuclear weapons could render concentration, offensive action, and decision by battle suicidal. In his view, the only way to restore the utility of military force was to ensure it served only limited aims. Osgood likewise insisted America's political leaders had to contain the aggressive instincts of the military as well as the explosive passions of the populace. His solution involved replacing the military's imperatives with a set of principles that emphasized political control and close circumscription of all parameters of conflict.

Similarly, Schelling's principle of bargaining – which presupposed a shared process of arriving at tacit and explicit agreements – offered an antithesis to traditional military imperatives. The bargaining principle implied commanders might need to exercise restraint just as they were gaining the upper hand, an idea that military leaders like Ernest King would have found ridiculous. Ironically, the bargaining principle also introduced greater uncertainty into strategic thinking, even as it sought transparency and stability, because tacit agreements can be broken without warning, or might never have existed in the first place. For his part, Kahn agreed military instincts needed to be curbed, and he attempted to counter uncertainty by arguing, largely in vain, that escalation itself was also a bargaining process with systematic waystations or steps imbedded along its path. Due to the fact their revolt struck at the US military's foundational strategic principles, therefore, the strategy intellectuals were anything but irrelevant to the American way of thinking about war, as some scholars have claimed.[14] Unfortunately, over time, America's way of policy allowed its grasp of the intricacies of military technique – the essential linkage of concepts and capabilities – to slip, and thus it increasingly struggles to maintain credibility.

Part III, "The Counterrevolution of the Military Intellectuals," explains how Eccles, Wylie, and later Summers, all combat veterans, endeavored to mitigate the strategy intellectuals' rejection of military principles. In addition to urging more rigorous analysis in deciding what to remove and what to retain in the way of guidelines for military strategy, Eccles and Wylie also actively contributed to filtering the vacuous concepts and empty slogans then filling the US defense establishment's lexicon. For his part, Summers exposed the harmful effects of applying academic (and untested) strategic theories in Vietnam. Eccles and Wylie agreed the advent of nuclear weapons had altered the character of war sufficiently to necessitate establishing new guidelines for the use of military force. But Summers believed most armed conflicts would be fought below the nuclear threshold and, hence, he maintained the principles of war, which he regarded as timeless, were still sound guides for crafting military strategy. Eccles, Wylie, and Rosinski also developed a theory of "strategy as control," a concept that had the potential to synthesize America's two antithetical perspectives: its ways of battle and its way of policy. Regrettably, the theory's potential was and remains underappreciated.

Part IV, "The Insurrection of the Operational Artists," considers how interest in operational art increased with the steady progress of denuclearization during the post-Cold War era. Boyd, Lind, and

Warden constructed operational theories that returned to Jominian first principles, though in modified form. Each operational concept concentrated on disrupting the enemy's psychological and physical capacity to resist, collapsing them swiftly through offensive action, and doing so regardless of the political objective. Policy itself was not necessarily an evil. But it was ambiguous and often fickle – two qualities operational art found difficult to accommodate. In truth, operational art never "devoured" strategy, as some have argued.[15] It did, however, stage an insurrection of sorts that attempted to bring military strategy back to its core principles, and which effectively created a "policy free zone" wherein military professionals could hone their operational planning and decision-making skills without distraction. In the process, this insurrection opened the door to an anarchy of operational methods, each of which has been independently refined without considering the possibility of integrating it into a larger synthesis. That anarchy includes the various approaches to counterinsurgency – which themselves are not always inimical to the core principles of concentration, offensive action, and decision by battle – and which are also a form of operational art. Nevertheless, the "new counterinsurgency era" only emerged during the first decade of the twenty-first century and its relevant archives are not yet available; hence, it lies outside the scope of this study.[16]

The chapters that follow describe the ideas of each of these theorists in more detail. They identify the core principles that defined an individual's major concepts as well as the assumptions about war's nature that supported those concepts. For most of the twentieth century, readers will note, the debates among the traditional, modern, materialist, and political models of war's nature made up the American way of thinking about war, even as they divided it.

Part I

First Principles and Modern War

As described in the two chapters that follow, Alfred Mahan and William Mitchell brought the core principles of nineteenth-century warfare into the twentieth century and applied them to conflict at sea and in the air, respectively. Each, therefore, had a hand in universalizing traditional military imperatives across the US armed services. Unlike Mahan, however, Mitchell had personally applied some of those principles in combat, first in small unit actions during the Philippine Insurrection, then while planning and orchestrating several of the largest air operations of the First World War. By comparison, Mahan, who served but reluctantly on the Naval War Board, provided "principled" advice that may have influenced US naval strategy during the Spanish–American War.

The lives of Mahan and Mitchell overlapped for a period of thirty-four years but they wrote their most important works in two vastly different Americas. Both enjoyed privileged social backgrounds shaped by Episcopalian values. Both were also egregiously imperialist and racist. Each also wrote works that put them in the public's eye and drew the ire of their respective presidents. Both attempted to shape US defense policy according to their own visions and for that reason became dubious, yet indispensable, heroes to their branches (or would-be branches) of the US armed forces.

Beyond those similarities, the two were quite different. Mitchell was younger than Mahan by thirty-nine years, an entire lifetime for some. In terms of literary styles, Mahan was Charles Dickens to Mitchell's Jack London. Mahan became a naval officer despite having been raised in an Army family at West Point. Mitchell became an airpower enthusiast and wanted to be appointed head of America's air services, despite beginning his career in the US Army as an enlistee. Perhaps most importantly, each author regarded distinct components of the character of war as more important, though they agreed, for the most part, on its essential nature.

1 Alfred Thayer Mahan and Sea Power

Alfred Thayer Mahan, arguably America's most prolific military writer, adapted the essential principles of nineteenth-century land warfare – concentration, offensive action, and decision by battle – to war at sea. In doing so, he assisted in enshrining a set of "first" principles for naval warfare that derived from war on land and thus unified both conceptually. While he borrowed heavily from the work of the Swiss military theorist Antoine Jomini, he also drew directly from the military imperatives of the US Civil War, which were inelegantly captured in the phrase "getting there first with the most." Mahan's biographers have described him as a philosopher, a prophet, and a propagandist for sea power.[1] He was indeed all of these. But it may be best to think of him as a proselytizer; for he sought to convert his readers, not merely to persuade them and, unlike most propagandists, he believed he had been chosen for this purpose by Providence. This belief fed a certain arrogance in his behavior and outlook. To Mahan, conversion meant internalizing right knowledge in the form of correct principles and then professing or living them.[2] Throughout his professional life he endeavored to convert the public to right knowledge of sea power, to show that it mattered, and that it could influence all dimensions of national life. Among his many converts were two US presidents, Theodore and Franklin Roosevelt, as well as Britain's Queen Victoria, Germany's Kaiser Wilhelm II, and Japan's influential diplomat Kaneko Kentarō.[3] And the list continues to grow.[4]

Mahan's definition of sea power, the ability "to use and control the sea," differs little from how modern air- and land-power theorists have defined power for their respective domains. Contrary to some interpretations, moreover, Mahan's definition remained remarkably consistent over his literary career.[5] It varied only when his proselytizer's impulse drove him to rhetorical excess, or when he desired to accentuate sea power's transformative significance. Sea power, as his four major works – *The Influence of Sea Power upon History 1660–1783*; *The Influence of Sea Power upon the French Revolution and Empire 1793–1812*; *The Life of Nelson*; and *Sea Power in Its Relations to the War of 1812* – attempted to show, could generate a psychological or moral momentum that could enhance national prestige, raise public confidence and morale, and promote security and prosperity.[6] Conversely, the absence or loss of sea power could lead to national stagnation or decline. To be sure, Mahan often insisted the first step to controlling the sea was to build a navy capable of defeating other navies. More fundamentally, however, he believed sea control required establishing a triad of interdependent means – ships, bases, and other critical resources (including markets).[7] All of these were to be rationalized under a rightly principled national or grand strategy.

1.1 Neither Genius nor Fraud

Mahan was neither a genius nor, as Russell Weigley and other scholars have implied, a fraud.[8] His intellect was exacting and precise, but seldom innovative or daring. He could devote several pages to a disquisition of the word "compromise," but he could not synthesize the particulars of naval power – submarine capabilities, advanced communications, and gunfire technologies – into a comprehensive conception of modern naval warfare.[9] While he frequently employed history to illustrate strategic principles, he assiduously avoided commenting on the potential merits of emerging technologies during a period of tremendous technological change. Even more egregiously, he deliberately decoupled strategy from tactics in order to focus on developing principles for the former; that in turn encouraged a bifurcation in the American way of thinking about war, though he was not entirely to blame for it.

Although Mahan's disquisitions were eloquent, they involved a discursive writing style that often obscured just how little he had to say. He cultivated this style partly because publishing outlets at the time paid by the word, but also because he belonged to the nineteenth-century tradition of demonstrating one's sophistication and refinement through extended and elegant prose. "Style is the man himself," he proclaimed, and he wanted his major works, especially *The Life of Nelson*, to be precise, but also "picturesque," "vivid," and "artistic."[10] Unfortunately, American literature had already begun to reject nineteenth-century artifices in favor of greater concision and directness. Even scholarly writing was becoming more direct. Mahan's style, in other words, marked him as something of a relic in an age of innovation and reform.

Despite these shortcomings, Mahan's intellectual gifts sufficed to put naval warfare on a par with some of the budding sciences of the day – particularly economics, psychology, and sociology. These sciences considered principles to be a prerequisite for theory and scientific advancement. Mahan's era was, in fact, an age of principles, and his enthusiasm for them not only paralleled that of his times, it also contributed to legitimizing the educational program of the Naval War College by equating it to a science. In the words of Stephen Luce, the first president of the US Naval War College, Mahan did for naval warfare what Jomini had done for land warfare – he "elevated it to a science."[11] In the process, Mahan also enhanced the aura of professional expertise of US naval officers. At the same time, however, he also personified American social scientist Samuel Huntington's model of the military expert whose level of knowledge posed a threat to civilian control over defense policy.[12]

Alfred Thayer Mahan was born on September 27, 1840, into an anti-abolitionist family. His father, Dennis Hart Mahan, was the dean and a professor of civil and military engineering at the US Military Academy. Despite his father's army background, Mahan evidently came to love romantic stories of the sea. He received an appointment to the US Naval Academy in 1856. Since he had already completed two years of education at Columbia University, Academy officials permitted him to skip his plebe (freshman) year. He apparently did not put much effort into his studies, but still managed to graduate second in his class in 1859.

Mahan served in the American Civil War, but mostly on blockade duty and without seeing any combat worthy of the name. He and his crew earned something of a red badge of courage, however, when their ship, the screw steamer USS *Pocahontas*, sustained minor damage to its upper rigging during the battle of Port Royal on November 7, 1861. During the late 1860s, Mahan had several inconsequential maritime tours that evidently cured him of his boyhood love of the sea. He also experienced what one biographer characterized as a spiritual crisis, and eventual renewal.[13]

In the 1870s, Mahan joined the ranks of reform-minded officers who wanted to rebuild the post–Civil War US Navy along modern lines.[14] In 1877, he was discharged from the service as part of an effort to downsize the Navy. But he was reinstated in 1878 and assigned to the US Naval Academy as an instructor. From 1880 to 1883, he served as an inspector at the Brooklyn naval yard. He was then assigned to the sloop-of-war USS *Wachusett* and sent to South American waters during the War of the Pacific (1879–83), which involved Chile and Peru–Bolivia. In 1884, he received a letter from Luce inviting him to join the faculty of the US Naval War College, which he eagerly accepted. Notably, for all the praise Luce heaped upon him later, Mahan was not his first choice, though he proved to be a remarkable one. Mahan began lecturing in 1886 and succeeded Luce as president of the Naval War College, serving two terms: 1886–89 and 1892–93.

Mahan's *Influence of Sea Power upon History* was first published in May 1890, one year after Britain formally announced its two-power standard, meaning the Royal Navy would maintain a fighting strength at least equal to that of "any two other countries."[15] The ideas of France's *Jeune École* (Young School) were also gaining ground in Germany, Austria-Hungary, Italy, Spain, and Japan at the time. The *Jeune École* held that underwater mines, coastal artillery, and torpedo boats rendered expensive battleships obsolete for purposes of maritime security, and that sea power now meant returning to the practice of *guerre de course* or commerce raiding.[16] Mahan's *Influence of Sea Power upon History* and *Influence of Sea Power upon the French Revolution* instead argued for the superiority of battle fleets. But his next volume, *Sea Power in Its Relations to the War of 1812*, admitted that *guerre de course* had utility under certain circumstances.

In 1895, Mahan received orders placing him in command of the cruiser USS *Chicago*, an assignment he initially resisted, but which gave him an opportunity to visit several European ports where he received numerous honors for his publications (including honorary degrees from Cambridge and Oxford). He retired in November 1896 to devote himself to writing. When war broke out with Spain in the spring of 1898, however, he was recalled to active duty to serve on the Naval War Board, which had been established to provide strategic advice to the Secretary of the Navy. Mahan reportedly criticized the Board as "an absurd institution for directing military movements," arguing a single individual should be in charge.[17] Nevertheless, he remained its vice president until the war ended.

By the turn of the century, Mahan's stature had all but validated Huntington's warning that the real threat to the modern state was not a military coup, but the ascendance of the military expert over the politician.[18] President Theodore Roosevelt prevented Mahan's star from rising that high, however. The two agreed on the need for a battle fleet rather than one optimized for commerce raiding, and on the importance of overseas bases, though Mahan favored expanding into East Asia and the Pacific while Roosevelt inclined toward further involvement in Latin America.[19] But they disagreed on whether the US Navy should consist of ships with "mixed-caliber" guns or "all-big" guns, and on the utility of dreadnought-class battleships.[20] Mahan argued for mixed-caliber guns and smaller ships due partly to spiraling costs, but also because he believed numbers mattered more than size. Roosevelt, however, disagreed and facilitated, if not orchestrated, Mahan's "dethroning" at the hands of former presidential aide William S. Sims, a US naval gunnery officer.[21] By comparison, President Woodrow Wilson chose to handle military expertise by ordering officers not to offer their opinions about the war, as he did in the early years of the Great War. Mahan may well have taken Wilson's order too personally, for his daughter Ellen Kuhn and his son Lyle Evans attributed their father's death to the anxiety it caused him.[22]

In any event, Sims, along with the officer-inventor Bradley Fiske, exemplified a new type of military expert, one that would push US naval thinking in the 1920s and 1930s in the direction of technological and organizational reform.[23] Fiske, for instance, had almost as many inventions to his credit as Mahan had publications. These experts, perhaps too infatuated with technological novelties, found little inspiration in the great proselytizer's expositions of war's core principles but did not dismiss them either. Whereas Mahan unwisely separated strategy from tactics to focus on the former, the new generation of naval experts compounded this error by concentrating on the latter. They did so, moreover, despite the urgings of some of their colleagues and fellow reformers, such as Commodore Dudley Wright Knox, who maintained one foot in each camp by arguing officers could develop expertise in managing modern warfare while also learning about strategy through the systematic study of history.[24]

Decoupling strategy from tactics enabled Mahan to navigate the epochal transition from sail to steam by concentrating on timeless principles that, by definition, must transcend both eras.[25] But it prevented him from arriving at a holistic conception of modern warfare at sea. In 1907, just as innovations in sea- and airborne technologies were accelerating, he admitted to being "too old and too busy to keep up."[26] He was more a theorist of the preceding era than of the next one. Nevertheless, he had contributed more than most to the intellectual grounding of the US Navy and perhaps its sense of professionalism. In 1912, the renowned naval and aeronautical authority Frederick T. Jane listed the US Navy as the third most powerful in the world. The navies of Britain and Germany stood at first and second, respectively, while Japan held fourth and France fifth place.[27] America's navy was neither the largest nor most powerful maritime force on the planet when Mahan died. But it had risen from insignificant to competitor, and its modern crop of technologically oriented officers would take it further.

1.2 Mahan's America – at War within Itself

The America that existed at the time of Mahan's birth in 1840 barely resembled the one he saw near the end of his life. The quarter century or so before the Great War has become known as an age of "Progress" in which revolutionary changes took place in almost every dimension of national life. Most notably, slavery had been abolished. Second,

America's economy had grown exponentially: its gross national product had increased thirteenfold, from $7 billion in 1840 to $91.5 billion by 1920 ($210 billion to $2.75 trillion in 2020).[28] America's per capita income in 1914 was $346 ($9,000 in 2020), the highest in the world; that of its nearest competitor, Great Britain, was nearly 30 percent lower, at $244.[29] That growth was all the more remarkable since the population of the United States had risen from 17 million to nearly 100 million over Mahan's lifetime. The country's standard of living had climbed steadily as well; literacy rates in the United States were higher than any other Western society.[30] New mechanical devices and inventions, such as typewriters, telephones, and washing machines, were reducing life's tedium. By 1902, subways and electric streetcars had largely replaced horse-drawn carriages in major urban areas; after 1910, modern conveniences such as electricity, running water, and central heating began appearing more regularly in American households, even in working-class homes.[31] In addition, the country's political geography had also transformed. The America of 1840 consisted of twenty-six states and a handful of territories; the America of 1914 included forty-eight states and more than a dozen territories and possessions. The country's so-called manifest destiny had been realized and its frontier effectively closed by 1912, though a fictionalized identity based on a romanticized image of the "West" was still young. In effect, America had acquired an empire of dubious virtue, one that challenged its espoused values of liberty and equality.

Of course, outward signs of progress belie the fuller story. When Woodrow Wilson accepted the Democratic Party's nomination for president in 1912, he openly proclaimed the United States was a "nation unnecessarily, unreasonably, at war within itself."[32] Mahan dismissed the speech as little more than campaign rhetoric. But the idea of an America at war rang true in important ways for Mahan's generation, as memories of the Civil War were still sharp.[33] By "war" the Virginia-born Wilson meant the efforts of the moneyed classes to influence the US government and to resist its oversight, a clash that usually benefited those with capital. Nonetheless, American society was at war with itself in other ways as well.

To be sure, slavery had been abolished. But violence against Black Americans and other racial minorities continued: a reported 2,522 Black Americans lost their lives through lynchings from 1889 to the end of the Great War.[34] Racial hate groups such as the Ku Klux Klan (KKK) also gained in both size and influence. In 1896, the same year in which Mahan retired from the Navy, the US Supreme Court granted Black Americans "separate but equal" status in the case of *Plessy* v. *Ferguson*.

Many states, however, simply implemented race codes and Jim Crow laws to circumvent the Supreme Court's ruling. For his part, Mahan came to abhor slavery even though he had been born into an anti-abolitionist family. Like many of his contemporaries, however, he clung to a rigid racial and ethnic hierarchy, a "natural order," in which the peoples of the world were not equal, though some of them were moving "upward."[35]

Mahan's generation experimented with a process of forced assimilation for Native Americans: "killing the Indian to save the man." Just weeks before Wilson's acceptance speech, Jim Thorpe, an erstwhile enrollee in the Carlisle Indian Industrial School, won gold medals in the 1912 Olympics for the decathlon and pentathlon (only to have them stripped months later). The Carlisle School was one of twenty-five institutions across the country aimed at forcibly assimilating Native Americans.[36] By 1918, such efforts had plainly failed; Carlisle, much like the other schools, only managed to graduate one in eight of its students. For his part, Mahan held firm to his belief that some racial and ethnic groups were impervious to assimilation. As he wrote to *The Times* in 1913, "America doubts her power to digest and assimilate the strong national and racial characteristics which distinguish the Japanese," which he feared would remain a "solid homogenous body, essentially and unchangingly foreign."[37] Legalized exclusion of Chinese immigrants began in 1882, and was reinforced over Mahan's lifetime.

It was also the era in which America's "Melting Pot" image emerged, popularized by Israel Zangwill's 1908 play of the same name. The drama debuted to rave reviews in Chicago and Washington, DC, but it was panned as hopelessly naïve in New York City the following year.[38] During the years Mahan and his family frequented it, New York City's population nearly quadrupled, from 1.2 million to 4.7 million, at least two-thirds of which were first- or second-generation immigrants.[39] These immigrants kept many of their ethnic identities and customs alive; few ventured far from self-defined neighborhoods (little Irelands, little Italies, little Polands, and the like) due to fear or the lack of wherewithal. The same was true in other metropolitan centers such as Philadelphia and Detroit. In effect, socioeconomic life in Mahan's America came closer to a zero-sum game than a melting pot: one group's upward mobility was often resisted by, or came at the expense of, another even amidst an expanding economy.

Although America enjoyed a per capita income higher than any other modern society, that statistic was misleading. The US Congressional Commission on Industrial Relations reported that 2 percent of Americans owned 60 percent of the nation's wealth in 1912. Moreover, nearly one-third of American workers earned a yearly income of less than $500, well below the minimum of $700 ($18,900 in 2020) the Commission considered acceptable for a family.[40] Mahan, by comparison, could earn $50–$500 for a single article.[41] In short, an elite class of plutocrats including James Piermont Morgan, Andrew Carnegie, Henry Ford, Daniel Guggenheim, and John D. Rockefeller controlled America's capital. Theories concerning how, or whether, to close the wealth–poverty gap abounded. Some of those, such as the ideas of the political economist Henry George, who believed wealth derived from the land should be divided evenly, inclined toward socialism. In contrast, William Graham Sumner, perhaps America's first social scientist and an authority whom Mahan quoted more than once, argued the poverty gap was not evil but natural; he called it evidence of the principle of "survival of the fittest" at work.[42]

In 1840, America's economy was based on an agrarian-entrepreneurial system. By 1914, it had all but transformed to an industrial-corporate one. Company "shares" had become, almost literally, the new coin of the realm. In some locales, companies controlled entire towns, such as Pullman, Illinois, where the Pullman Railroad Car Company owned the dwellings and stores and conducted most transactions in company script.[43] Little of a company's profits went toward improving conditions for workers, however. Laborers typically worked six or seven days per week in shifts lasting twelve to sixteen hours. Accidents in the workplace were a matter of routine; an average of a hundred laborers were killed daily in workplace accidents.[44] Consequently, unrest in the labor force ran high and American workers went on strike more often and in greater percentages than their European counterparts; at least 15 million US workers went on strike between 1894 and 1914. Many of these strikes, such as those in Pullman (1894) and in Ludlow, Colorado (1913–14), ended in ways that benefited capital, and cost scores of workers their lives.[45] Despite the partial success of the Roosevelt administration in breaking up trusts and monopolies, America's labor wars would continue. For Mahan, the gains of the working classes came at the expense of US national security.[46]

By 1914, scores of skyscrapers, symbols of the new corporate America, dominated urban landscapes; at least a dozen such buildings were within eyesight of two of Mahan's New York City addresses (75 East 54th Street and 160 West 86th Street). He welcomed the subway system, which he said cured the "great restlessness" of his family by making it possible to visit friends on the east side as well as shopping and amusement centers downtown.[47] Like so many of America's privileged upper and middle classes at the time, Mahan's family actively participated in a blossoming culture of art, leisure, and consumerism.[48] Mahan's son recalled his mother counting pennies every month to ensure they had enough money to meet the family's needs.[49] But with an annual salary of roughly $3,000 ($85,000) as a US Navy captain in the 1890s, they had more pennies to count than most American families – enough, in fact, to afford a servant or two.

America's rising standard of living also provoked anxiety over the evils of modern living. The renowned American neurologist George Beard contributed to this concern with his study of *American Nervousness* (1881); Beard suggested the faster pace of modern life had created an epidemic of nervousness, a "loss of vital life force," among the public.[50] While Mahan's daughter Ellen claimed the "crowds in New York City stimulated" her father, she also admitted he had "an intensely nervous disposition," and Mahan himself confessed the "din" and "restless atmosphere" of modern life filled him with unease.[51] His heroic-romantic biographies of Admiral David Farragut (1893) and Lord Nelson (1897) fit within the fading but still prevalent tradition that glorified historical figures – such as George Washington, Napoleon Bonaparte, and Abraham Lincoln – said to have been singular individuals who embodied the transformative movements of their times.[52] Their stories served as a heartening tonic against the era's brewing anxieties. Mahan's Farragut embodied the "soundest" of military virtues, while his Nelson acted in more complex terms: honorable but infelicitous, bold but calculating, strong-willed but flexible. The latter's key to success was his moral certitude, and his ability to hold true to Mahan's favorite first principles: concentration, offensive action, and decision by battle.

These artistic biographies contrasted sharply with other bestselling stories of the period: Stephen Crane's *Red Badge of Courage* (1895), Jack London's *Call of the Wild* (1903), Edith Wharton's *House of Mirth* (1905), and Upton Sinclair's *The Jungle* (1906).[53] Crane's protagonist, Henry, received his wound, an external sign of his courage, not from the enemy but from an anonymous soldier on his own side, an accident of circumstances rather than an act of bravery. London crafted a tale of survival of the fittest as seen through the eyes of a dog that had to adapt to savage conditions. Wharton's protagonist, Lily Bart, lost her love, her identity, and ultimately her life due to the duplicitous values of New York City's high society. Sinclair's Jurgis Rudkus, a Lithuanian immigrant, only escaped the ruthlessly exploitive circumstances of his life as an American laborer by turning to socialism.[54] In contrast, Mahan's *Harvest Within* (1909), written for the express purpose of addressing "modern 'difficulties,'" rejected the notion that circumstances inevitably triumphed over principles.[55] A truly Christian life was an ordered one based on the "acceptance of principles" from which one derived imitable "habits and methods" of conduct.[56] One did not surrender to circumstances, one transcended them – unless of course one was a woman or a racial minority, for whom living a principled life meant accepting one's place in the natural order.[57]

By 1900 some 90 percent of Americans could read, which in turn fueled a modern publishing boom. Publishing magnates such as Joseph Pulitzer (*New York World*) and William Randolph Hearst (*New York Journal*) sought after, or invented, increasingly scandalous stories in a fierce competition for readers.[58] In 1898, Hearst offered Mahan one dollar per word for anything the naval expert cared to write about the crisis with Spain, an offer that far exceeded Mahan's normal rate of 5 cents per word.[59] But the naval expert stuck by his principles and refused to be associated with Hearst's *New York Journal*, which he found distasteful. Instead he sought publishing outlets in the new monthlies and weeklies, including *Collier's* and *McClure's*. Mahan disapproved of modern journalism, however, which he described as a "system of organized gossip" that frequently misrepresented the facts and created myths and misunderstandings.[60] He wanted the press more tightly controlled, but that did not apply to his own opinions. It was the era of Yellow journalism, and its crimes against reason and human decency have been well documented.[61]

America was also at war with itself over its nascent empire. Mahan, who became converted to imperialism in the early 1890s, argued modern conditions made "anti-internationalism" and "isolationism," his labels for anti-imperialism, impossible.[62] He engaged in literary battles with prominent members of the American Anti-Imperialist League, such as Andrew Carnegie and the literary genius Mark Twain (Samuel Clemens). Established in the spring of 1898 as tensions mounted with Spain, the league eventually exceeded 25,000 members, many of whom were leading academics and politicians.[63] "The Peace and Arbitration people – above all Andrew *Carnegie* – get on my *nerves*," Mahan complained.[64] He met America's literary genius, whose books Mahan said he "never admired," at a dinner party in 1894, and described him as a "most remarkable personage."[65] Twain saw the Filipinos as a "poverty-stricken, priest-ridden nation of children," and he openly criticized the US government's efforts to crush the Filipino insurrection after the Spanish–American War.[66] Mahan, however, urged the US military to subdue the Filipinos just as it had Native Americans, and he rejected the idea of applying the principles of self-government to a "people in the childhood stage of race development."[67] For all its economic growth and rising prosperity, therefore, Mahan's America was an embattled one in which he was not merely an observer but an active participant.

1.3 An Age of Principles

If Mahan was a man of principle, as his life and writings suggest, so too was the age in which he lived. Principles were evident in nearly every walk of life, from the rules of fair play that guided the first modern Olympic games in 1896 to the tenets of Taylorism that made factory production more efficient.[68] Principles moved into the home as well with the purpose of raising housework "to the plane of Scientific Engineering," while also allowing the home to serve progressively "as an efficient Unit of the State."[69] A leading proponent of the period's self-help movement, Dale Carnagey (later Carnegie), produced a pamphlet in 1913 that reduced the art of public speaking to a handful of easy to remember principles.[70] Even President Wilson purportedly used principles to steer his foreign and domestic policies, though scholars have since uncovered an unprincipled side to his policies.[71]

Academe, too, embraced principles, which it upheld as the fruits of inductive and deductive reasoning that made theory possible. Theories stood or fell on the strength of their underlying principles. Theory, in fact, was nothing more than principles arranged in a defensible statement or, as Mahan suggested, a "scheme of things."[72] Perhaps the foremost example of the nineteenth-century notion of the relationship between science and principles was the positivism of British philosopher Herbert Spencer. His synthetic theory of evolution was underpinned by the principle of "survival of the fittest," and evolved into the notion of Social Darwinism. Spencer treated psychology, economics, and sociology as if they were natural sciences, and attempted to derive fundamental laws or principles applicable to them.[73]

In 1890, the same year in which Mahan's *Influence of Sea Power* was published, Harvard University's William James fired back at Spencer with *Principles of Psychology*, taking the positivist's data to task for "vagueness and improbability, and even self-contradiction."[74] In the same year, Cambridge University's Alfred Marshall published his classic *Principles of Economics*, which discussed at length the limits of Spencer's positivism, including its want for a vigorous "comparative method" to augment one's observations.[75] In 1896, Franklin Giddings of Columbia University delivered an extensive critique of Spencer's ideas in *Principles of Sociology* while advancing his own theory. More crucially, Giddings admitted that science "could not get on without speculation," that is, guessing. All "true induction," he said, "*is* guessing, ... the swift intuitive glance at a mass of facts to see if they *mean* anything."[76] The scientific method, in other words, consisted in the formulation of hypotheses, or guesses, which in turn coalesced into principles via some combination of induction, deduction, testing, and revision.

Military writers in the nineteenth century essentially held the same attitude toward principles – the products of applying inductive and deductive reasoning to the "data" of military history. Henry Halleck's *Elements of Military Art and Science* (1846), James Mercur's *Elements of the Art of War* (1889), and James Pettit's *Elements of Military Science* (1895) each described strategy as both a "*science* based on a few well defined *principles*" and an "art" that entailed adapting principles "to the ever varying circumstances of war."[77] By the second decade of the twentieth century, US Navy officers like Dudley Knox had defined "doctrines" as bodies of principles, and principles themselves as fundamental truths used as the "basis of reasoning."[78] Indeed, Mahan and Luce would have belonged to what one historian called the US Army's "guardian" tradition, which saw war as both an art and a science.[79] Guardians protected the science of war, its fundamental truths and principles, and attempted to pass it along to other generations. Principles were at once immutable and variable; they were constant, but alterable according to the situation and to one's experience and judgment.[80] By linking the science of war to its art, principles made military theories, counter-theories, and doctrines possible.

In 1891, British Admiral Philip Colomb published *Naval Warfare*, a collection of naval principles derived initially without knowledge (so he claimed) of Mahan's *Influence of Sea Power upon History*.[81] Despite an obvious similarity in their espoused principles, the two could not agree on the meaning of the concept of a "fleet in being."[82] In 1906, Frederick Jane's *Heresies of Sea Power* used an odd but increasingly popular principle to challenge Mahan's definition of sea power.[83] Jane rejected the definition as too vague, and he doubted the wisdom of using history to prove anything, since it can offer as many examples for something as against it. His *Heresies*, therefore, presented an alternative theory that claimed naval battles, just as battles on land, were won not because of sea control but because one side possessed greater physical or moral "fitness to win." But this theory also borrowed from history, in addition to revealing the extent of Jane's Social Darwinism.

In 1911, Britain's erstwhile lawyer and accidental military theorist, Julian Corbett, put forth his own *Principles of Maritime Strategy*.[84] These qualified, if not corrected, albeit politely, many of those Mahan had advocated two decades earlier: the two had a cordial relationship, though they subscribed to different philosophies about the use of military force. Drawing heavily from Clausewitz, Corbett exposed the battle-centric, military-force orientation of Mahan's scheme for establishing sea control. The war's political objective, argued Corbett, ought to be the first consideration in maritime strategy, which was nothing more than "the principles that govern a war in which the sea is a substantial factor."[85] Corbett had a point because Mahan's first principles – concentration, offensive action, and decision by battle – appeared more appropriate for unlimited rather than limited wars. To be sure, one can sometimes annihilate an enemy's entire military force in pursuit of limited objectives, as in the Franco-Prussian War of 1870–71. But doing so might set in motion an escalation requiring more effort or resources than one's leadership is willing to expend or entail greater risk to its political capital than it is willing to take. Mahan eventually came to acknowledge the importance of political considerations, going so far as to describe war in Clausewitzian terms, that is, as a continuation of political intercourse. Yet the proselytizer Mahan never modified his first principles to reflect that turn in his thinking. Not unlike Germany's famous Helmuth von Moltke the elder, Mahan believed policy ought not to interfere in war beyond establishing its overall purpose and main objectives.

Similarly, Fiske's *Navy as a Fighting Machine*, published two years after Mahan's death, first praised his predecessor, then buried him. Fiske argued modern commanders certainly needed sound principles, but even more than that they required expert knowledge in the practical aspects of the US Navy as a functioning system. The work of strategy is threefold, said Fiske: "first, to design the machine; second, to prepare it for war; and, third, to direct its operation during war."[86] His book essentially placed organizational and technical expertise above theoretical knowledge, where they would remain until Henry Eccles and J. C. Wylie sought to restore the balance in the 1950s and 1960s by making theory respectable again. In short, as with the academic sciences, military science (including naval science) also began with speculations, guesses. Naturally, guesses reflect the biases of those who make them; even so, military science could move forward with guesses, so long as it were possible to acknowledge and adjust for bias.

When Mahan began developing principles for sea power, therefore, he was completely in step with the spirit of the times. His method, at least partially inspired by Luce, differed little from academics such as James, Marshall, and Giddings.[87] It nonetheless had several important weaknesses. First, because Mahan's data were generally limited to the age of sail, they were not readily deployable to answer questions asked by naval thinkers in other eras. Second, while he came to learn the value of primary sources, Mahan seldom distinguished between history, as something historians wrote, and the past, the incomplete data they had available to write it. He conflated history and the past without appreciating the subjective nature of the former, which can be thought of as a running argument among historians. Third, he believed history needed the suborning influence of a presentist agenda to prioritize what truly mattered, which in turn meant he willfully excluded details that might have altered his argument.[88] Finally, Mahan availed himself of the comparative method only infrequently, and usually to contrast military principles with those of morality or religion. He saw these disciplines as superior to the natural sciences because they spoke to higher truths. Even with its faults, however, the military science of Mahan and Luce could lay almost as much claim to legitimacy as any academic science of the day.[89]

This legitimacy was important for the US Naval War College because, while war was both an art and a science, only the science could be taught. One could illuminate the art through historical examples, but not teach it. Mahan, much like his contemporaries, saw the relationship between history and principles as dialectical: history played the role of practical reason against the pure reason of principles in an interaction that, in accord with Immanuel Kant's teachings, exercised the mind and elevated one's judgment. Combining history with principles made the "perfect instructor," said Mahan.[90] He had his own judgment elevated while writing *The War of 1812*, for his research caused him to reverse his previous position and to admit the United States had benefited more from privateering and commerce raiding than it could have from engaging in conventional battle tactics.[91] But Mahan's influence at the US Naval War College and on the Navy itself would be greater than the influence of history on Mahan.

1.4   Mahan's First Principles

Mahan developed a list of "general conditions" for sea power and these, for better or worse, have become part of his legacy.[92] He did not create a similar list of principles for naval strategy; nevertheless, he referred to three of them – concentration, offensive action, and seeking a decision by battle – frequently in his lectures. Mahan called concentration the "A, B, C of strategy" and naval warfare's "first principle." He defined it as "keeping a superior force at the decisive point," and he considered it the foremost consideration in military planning. In this way he drew almost verbatim from Jomini, who described concentration as the "fundamental principle of war," and defined it as massing one's forces upon the "decisive points of a theater of war" and upon the "communications of the enemy."[93] But Mahan also admitted to having drawn the principle of concentration from the American Civil War, from the idea of "getting there first with the most."[94]

Concentration consisted of both physical and psychological elements. Physically, it referred to ships, bases, and other resources arranged within supporting distance of one another. By way of illustration, Mahan pointed to the war against Spain in which the United States achieved concentration by positioning squadrons near Havana and Cienfuegos, two of only four coaling stations within the theater.[95] Psychologically, concentration meant focusing one's "mental and moral outlook" and maintaining a "singleness of aim."[96] Moreover, concentration applied to the use of a navy in peacetime as well as wartime. The purpose of a peacetime naval strategy was to protect a nation's maritime interests: its bases and coaling stations, its access to markets, and its sea lines of communication. The United States, he later suggested, should establish alliances, or partnerships, with other seafaring peoples; as a result, he has been given credit for inventing grand strategy.[97] But his lauded notion of grand strategy was merely a projection of his concept of naval strategy onto a global framework.

The principle of offensive action meant maneuvering aggressively to seize the most important positions within a theater of war. "War," claimed Mahan, was a "business of positions," which one either controlled or otherwise denied to the enemy.[98] Failing to do so could mean forfeiting an opportunity for victory or paying too high a price for it. The Russians were correct to defend Port Arthur during the Russo-Japanese War, for instance, because it forced the Japanese to withhold some of their numerically inferior forces to lay siege to it, thus protecting their lines of communication. The Russians erred, however, in not positioning a strong reserve within striking distance of Port Arthur (the "D, E, F" of strategy was to position a reserve within range of the decisive point). The land and sea battles that took place around Port Arthur, in fact, not only "modified the whole tenor of land operations," according to Mahan, they also demonstrated the importance of sea power in modern warfare.[99]

Furthermore, Mahan saw the defender's task as simpler than that of the attacker; he thus disagreed with Clausewitz's dictum that the defense was stronger than the attack. Mahan repeatedly insisted a defensive war "must be waged offensively and aggressively." The enemy "must not be fended off, but smitten down," he argued; until the foe is down it "must be struck incessantly and remorselessly."[100] But he did not see attack and defense as mutually exclusive concepts: "mobile offensive power" (a fleet) and "stationary defensive power" (fortified coastal defenses) must complement one another; a sound naval policy should strike a balance between them.[101]

The principle of decision by battle meant destroying the enemy's fleet, normally by combat, but also by seizing bases or by disrupting sea lines of communication. Only an opportunity to destroy an opponent's fleet could override the principle of concentration, for "control of the sea, by reducing the enemy's navy, is the determining factor in a naval war."[102] Naval strategy must aim to achieve the best results at the least cost, which can only be accomplished by applying the principles of concentration, offensive action, and decision by battle.

In addition to his core principles, Mahan also espoused several noteworthy secondary principles – namely, central position, interior lines, and lines of communications – all drawn from Jomini's *Art of War*. Central position simply meant being situated between hostile formations. It usually yielded shorter lines of communication, or interior lines, which in theory enabled one to shift forces rapidly from one hostile front to another. But in practice, the ability to shift forces swiftly also depended on factors like geography, terrain, and infrastructure – so the advantage might be lost due to circumstances. Lines of communication were the lifelines that kept military forces supplied and "in living connection with the national power."[103] But they also required a certain amount of combat power to protect them.

Principles, therefore, equated to advantages, and naval strategy was simply a plan of action based on proven principles that offered more or better advantages than one's adversary. To his credit, Mahan warned his students that merely applying principles did not guarantee victory.[104] But his proselytizer's instinct generally caused him to dwell on a principle's advantages at the expense of its disadvantages. Central position, for instance, essentially meant one was fighting on two fronts, a serious disadvantage against competent foes.

1.5 War's Nature as Human Nature

Mahan saw war's nature as a violent extension of the competitive instincts of human nature. He believed humanity possessed an innate desire to expand, to colonize, to acquire whatever one desired but did not have.[105] For that reason, the world had as much chance of ridding itself of armed conflict as humanity had of divesting itself of its aggressive instincts. Aggressive action, in any case, was essential to progress; for some evils simply could not be resolved by arbitration.[106] States, like individuals, had a moral obligation to intervene with force to correct wrongs, such as slavery and tyranny. Christian teachings, he maintained, did not condemn war absolutely, only wars fought for base motives. "War is the employment of force for the attainment of an object, or for the prevention of an injury," he argued; "If the object be wrong, the action is also wrong."[107] In short, war was painful and costly but not always avoidable and not always immoral or inhuman. Furthermore, proper "military organization" (his euphemism for military expansion) did not provoke war, but rather contributed to deterring it by showing that one was well prepared.[108]

Mahan frequently described war, the violent side of human competition, in economic terms. But he flatly rejected the arguments of economic pacifists, specifically Norman Angell, who maintained, "nations go to war for material gain chiefly."[109] He could not bring himself to admit the political and moral motives behind the American Civil War were also intertwined with economic interests. Nevertheless, he later came to see politics as an essential component of war's nature. Armed conflict was a "political movement," a "violent and tumultuous political incident" that occurred within the "great political drama of progress." Not unlike Clausewitz, therefore, Mahan came to see armed conflict as both an outgrowth of politics and an instrument of policy. Its political aspects made it both certain and uncertain: one knew with absolute certainty war would occur, but not exactly where, when, or among whom. In this way, war resembled a Clausewitzian game of chance or, in Mahan's words, a "game of wits with many unknown quantities," a game that required "brains" as well as "guns."[110]

Like the Prussian, therefore, Mahan acknowledged the politically competitive dimension of war's nature. Yet he drew a sharp distinction between the responsibilities of the politician and those of the military professional. The former decided whether war was permissible, the latter determined how to win it. Policy, Mahan eventually conceded, had every right to dictate military and naval affairs in peacetime. Nonetheless, it must never intrude into the conduct of wartime operations, where it was "especially ignorant."[111] The duty of military and naval strategists was to achieve victory by doing right by the nature of war, not the wishes of their political leaders.

Mahan gave less attention to war's psychosocial dimension than he did to its military and economic ones.[112] Some useful insights can be gleaned by comparing his ideas to those of US Army Captain John Bigelow, whose *Principles of Strategy* appeared in the 1890s, coincidental with Mahan's first sea power classic. Bigelow discussed a special element, "political strategy" (not to be confused with George Kennan's concept of "political warfare"), which referred to those strategies and techniques aimed at hostile governments and their civilian populations rather than military forces. In short, political strategy meant "bringing the war home to the people," thereby making it "unpopular" or "hateful" to them; he also explained how that concept could apply to conventional conflicts as well as insurrections.[113] Bigelow neglected to address how such a strategy might put neutral populations at risk. Nonetheless, he warned against subordinating political strategy to "regular" strategy because the former would never receive the attention it required. Bigelow's case studies consisted of the American War of Independence, the War of 1812, and the American Civil War – conflicts certainly familiar to Mahan. The US Navy's chief proselytizer certainly saw *guerre de course* and blockading as techniques useful in damaging civilian morale as well as inflicting economic harm; he also appreciated the psychosocial dimension of sea power. Yet he never developed a formal concept of political strategy.

1.6 Conclusion

Mahan's theories of sea power and naval strategy helped enshrine an American way of thinking about war at sea. They also contributed to solidifying the traditional model of war's nature. As discussed, that model believed war was essentially a violent extension of human nature. Political intercourse, which theorists like Corbett saw as the principal driver of armed conflict, was little more than a manifestation of the competitive side of human nature. Ergo, Mahan could acknowledge the role of policy or politics in directing war, while also insisting naval strategy must always aim at outcompeting one's foes. Many of America's outstanding military personalities – including George Marshall, Douglas MacArthur, Dwight D. Eisenhower, George S. Patton, Ernest King, Chester Nimitz, Patrick Leahy, Curtis LeMay, and William Mitchell – shared Mahan's model. They did so even though they belonged to another generation, served in other branches of the US armed forces, or viewed the character of war differently than Mahan.

For America's foremost naval scientist, the character of modern war was theoretical. He easily grasped war's character during the age of sail. But as that age transformed to one of steam and continued to change due to the advent of novel weapons, such as aircraft and submarines, he avoided making the intellectual investment necessary to grasp the newly emerging character of armed conflict. Yet what Luce said of Mahan was correct: he elevated naval warfare to a science, or what had qualified as a science at the time, and with it the prestige of the naval profession. Unquestionably, Mahan brought the imperatives of the nineteenth century into the twentieth and used them to construct a dual theory of sea power and naval strategy. Still, Mahan's legacy is mixed. By concentrating on naval science – as the founding of principles through induction, deduction, and comparison – rather than art or the application of such principles, he routinized the decoupling of strategy from tactics, a practice that has persisted into the twenty-first century. To be sure, he was not solely responsible for that habit, but he set an example that is still applauded.

Mahan's theories both reflected and reacted against the spirit of the age in which he wrote. His America remained at war with itself, even decades after the Civil War. He participated in its battles, albeit as an ultraconservative, particularly through his religious lectures and writings. These battles also helped raise his awareness of war's psychosocial dimension, and the influence sea power could have on it. Of course, sea power could bring a people material goods through maritime commerce. But it could also enhance national prestige and serve as a cultural salve to heal the wounds of disunity. A nation's power at sea, in other words, spoke to its psychosocial strength and resilience, which in turn made it formidable in wartime and influential in peacetime. Landlocked countries, therefore, were fated to remain inferior to seafaring ones, save to the extent they allied themselves with maritime powers.

Although Mahan had something of grand strategic vision, it ought not be overrated. He did little more than elevate his framework for naval strategy to the level of grand strategy. Furthermore, his ideas about which nations the United States should seek partnerships with had more to do with his religious and cultural biases than with an objective assessment of what the world's powers could or would accomplish diplomatically, economically, or militarily. Mahan's template for naval strategy was partly derived from both Jomini and Clausewitz. Yet debates over whether Mahan was influenced more by former or the latter, whether he was doctrinaire (Jominian) or nondoctrinaire (Clausewitzian), have missed the point. The weight of history has exaggerated the differences and suppressed the similarities between the Swiss and the Prussian. In any case, in Mahan's day, as in others, it was not uncommon for someone to hold seemingly contradictory positions without perceiving them as such, as in believing principles to be simultaneously immutable (scientific) and mutable (requiring artful application). As will be shown in subsequent chapters, it was the art that drew more attention as ideas about what science was began to change. By way of tacitly recognizing Mahan's principled contribution to US naval strategy, his erstwhile colleagues Fiske and Sims, concerned more with the intricacies of application, threw themselves into mastering the devil's favorite abode, the details.

2   Billy Mitchell and Air Power

Perhaps America's most outspoken advocate for an independent air arm, Billy Mitchell made a case for air power that essentially built on the same core principles Mahan used for sea power. Mitchell defined air power as the "ability to do something in or through the air," and he consciously linked its civilian and military aspects as a way of selling the latter.[1] Not unlike Mahan's first principles, those Mitchell advanced for air power came down to the simple imperative of "getting there first with the most," that is, bringing more of the right aircraft wherever they were needed before one's opponent could. Overall, however, Mitchell's theories lacked originality; they drew heavily from those of the British air commander Hugh Trenchard and the Italian air power theorist Guilio Douhet, both of whom he met during his career. In fact, as Weigley noted, one could speak of "two Billy Mitchells."[2] The first, the Mitchell of 1917–26, can be described as a student of Trenchard, who advocated using air power in a strategically offensive role and who agitated for an independent air arm. The second, or post-1926 Mitchell, can be thought of as a disciple of Douhet, whose conception of strategic bombing aimed at compelling adversaries to surrender by destroying their vital industrial and population centers.[3] High explosives, incendiary munitions, and poison gas figured large in Douhet's reckoning. But the apocalyptic images associated with such weapons made his theory a tough sell for an American public enjoying an unprecedented economic boom, and whose "chief business," as President Calvin Coolidge affirmed on January 17, 1925, "was business."[4]

Weigley neglected to account for two other Billy Mitchells, however. One of these was the heroic personality portrayed in the 1955 motion picture *The Court Martial of Billy Mitchell*, starring Gary Cooper.[5] Coincidentally, the film *Rebel Without a Cause*, starring James Dean, appeared the same year, making it easier for the American public to imagine Mitchell as a rebel with a noble cause, namely, the task of forcing a harsh, negligent, even criminal, bureaucracy to see the error of its ways. That image was aided by two waves of hagiographies, one that came in the aftermath of Pearl Harbor, when America sorely needed heroes, and one that surfaced after the establishment of the US Air Force in 1947, making that event a prominent feature of Mitchell's legacy.[6]

The other Mitchell whom Weigley overlooked was an extremely ambitious and self-centered one. This Mitchell pursued a personally aggrandizing reform agenda, often played fast and loose with the facts, and willfully poached others' ideas, sometimes to the point of plagiarism. This Mitchell was indeed a rebel with a cause, largely his own, though parts of it contributed to enlightening the public and strengthening US national defense. This cause also created the misleading impression that US air power had only one true champion throughout its early years. In truth, quieter reformers, such as Major General Mason Patrick, managed to accomplish more for US air power than Mitchell had.[7] Nonetheless, he is significant for attempting to change US defense policy and thereby alter the American way of war.

2.1 Egoistic Rebel

As military authorities such as Clausewitz have affirmed, ambition, or the desire for personal glory, is an essential quality for a military commander.[8] Under the right circumstances, the desire for personal glory can change the course of a battle or a campaign. Under other circumstances, it can undermine good order and discipline, especially in peacetime. Mitchell's ambition, which exceeded that of his peers and, evidently, many of his superiors, served him well for the first twenty years of his military career. But the precipitous demobilization that followed the Great War relegated him to a subordinate position in the air arm that both disappointed and frustrated him. Consequently, Mitchell repeatedly and publicly criticized, if not ridiculed, the policies of his superiors, both military and civilian. Like Mahan, therefore, he became the type of military expert Huntington warned could challenge civilian authority in the modern state; yet the social scientist's *Soldier and the State* barely mentions the outspoken flyer. As noted in the previous chapter, President Theodore Roosevelt dealt with the self-assured Mahan by orchestrating a public debate that undermined the naval strategist's credibility; President Coolidge, however, handled the irrepressible Mitchell more firmly, by means of a general court martial.

William Lendrem Mitchell was born on December 29, 1879, into an affluent and politically well-connected family living temporarily in Nice, France. His father, John, had served in the Civil War in the 24th Wisconsin Volunteer Infantry Regiment until mustering out in 1864. His experiences taught him to abhor war. The elder Mitchell instead turned his energies to rebuilding the family business, ultimately making it resilient enough to survive the sharp economic downturns of the mid-1880s and mid-1890s. Throughout most of the 1870s, John served in the Wisconsin state senate. In 1891, he was elected to the US Congress, serving until 1899, first as a representative, then as a senator. During this time, John also acquired a reputation as a staunch opponent of America's military adventurism, a position his son would not share. Despite his anti-war and anti-imperialist leanings, he intervened more than once to advance William's military career.

It has been said Mitchell enjoyed a closer relationship with his mother, Harriet, than his father. But that was not unusual for the times. Two of his contemporaries who rose to high ranks, George Marshall (1880–1959) and Dwight D. Eisenhower (1890–1969), were also closer to their mothers than their fathers. While attending Racine College, an Episcopal boarding school south of Milwaukee, Wisconsin, William wrote frequently to Harriet, and he often did so in unvarnished prose that reveal his budding egoism. He rarely spared her the gory details of death and war. At the age of ten, for instance, he reported, in colorful language, how he had bashed in the head of a skunk.[9] In Cuba he described to her how some of the *trochas* (fieldworks) were "spattered with blood while inside the block house there is blood all over the walls."[10] In the Philippines, he wrote to her in graphic detail of the atrocities committed against American troops by Filipino guerrillas.[11] Again, when his younger brother, John, died in a plane crash in France in the spring of 1918, he relayed to his mother how "The back of [John's] head had been crushed by the impact."[12] For her part, Harriet encouraged any and all communications from her son regardless of their tone or content. "My Dear Boy," she wrote on April 18, 1899, "Gen. Greely [chief of the signal corps] said you were showing a great deal of ability in your work and they were very much pleased with you, that you seemed to get on well with the men and that you made an excellent officer. You may know how happy it makes me to hear [this]. If you will come back to me the same in heart and character as you went away, I can ask nothing more. ... A heart full of love from Mama."[13]

In 1896, Mitchell graduated from Racine College, where he had been enrolled since 1888. His letters to Harriet during this period reveal his anguish about being separated from the rest of the family. But they also convey a growing acceptance of his de facto independence. School officials said he was an intelligent and "very satisfactory boy." He was, however, never more than an average student; he ranked fourth of seven students in the spring of 1891, fourth of eleven students in the autumn of 1892, and third of six students in the autumn of 1893.[14] Rather than spending his time with academic pursuits, William preferred to engage in competitive sports and outdoor activities such as hunting and fishing, for which he developed a lifelong love. Letters from the school's administrators repeatedly assured Harriet her son's behavior was "perfect," as in perfectly normal.[15] They clearly wished to dissuade her from withdrawing him from the school, a threat William occasionally threw at his teachers.

From 1896 to 1898, Mitchell attended Columbian College (now George Washington University) in Washington, DC, which allowed him to be closer to family. But he dropped out at the onset of the Spanish–American War and enlisted in the 1st Wisconsin Infantry. Due largely to his father's political connections, Mitchell received a commission as a second lieutenant in the Signal Corps in about one week and was assigned to the regiment's signal company. The 1st Wisconsin did not arrive in Cuba until December 1898, well after the major fighting had ended. Mitchell expressed extreme disappointment at not being able to experience combat. He threw his energies, instead, into laying some 136 miles of communication cable in Santiago Province, which he accomplished in record time.[16]

The major fighting in Cuba was over, but tensions still ran high among the evacuating Spaniards, Cuban insurgents, and American soldiers. Mitchell had little sympathy for the insurgents, and he judged the native Cuban population ill-equipped for self-government. He believed insurgent activities were responsible for ruining much of the natural beauty of the countryside. As he reported to his mother, "Last night a large number of [Spaniards] went down to the wharf and a whole mob of Cubans followed them, throwing stones, yelling, shooting, and so on. They stopped it, however, after a while without killing many." He went on to say, "It makes one laugh every time one sees the insurgents, they think themselves very fierce when around Spaniards, but when the American privates come along they have nothing to say to them in any open way. But every day or two they stick a knife in one."[17] His attitude toward native peoples softened somewhat over time, as they showed themselves to be brave, though he always considered the white race superior.

In 1899, Mitchell was posted to command a signal company in the Philippines, an assignment he had pressed his father and mother to arrange. It was here he had his first taste of combat, though it was not of the type or scale his father experienced in the American Civil War. It consisted of small raids, ambushes, and skirmishes fought in close quarters, and always with a nagging uncertainty as to the trustworthiness of the local inhabitants. Mitchell claimed to have captured some seventy insurgent flags and seven official seals. He also captured Captain Mendoza, a key insurgent commander, and purportedly facilitated Colonel Frederick Funston's arrest of Emilio Aguinaldo, first president of the Philippines and leader of the insurrection.[18] Not surprisingly, Mitchell despised the Filipino guerrillas as much as he had the Cuban insurgents. Like Mahan, Mitchell saw the Filipinos as too primitive to govern themselves, a view not uncommon among US troops at the time. Soldiers' letters referred to the Filipinos with derogatory racial epithets, or used patronizing expressions such as "poor ignorant devils."[19] Many US soldiers believed the islands, even if multiplied "ten hundred fold," would not be worth the American lives that would be lost in a war between the Philippines and the United States.[20] Mitchell, however, remained convinced America's interventions, because they brought civilization and progress with them, would only improve the lot of native peoples.

Mitchell returned stateside in 1900 and attended the US Army's new signal school in Fort Myer, Virginia. Afterward, he was assigned to Alaska, where he laid communication lines for the Army under extreme conditions. His article, "Building the Alaskan Telegraph System," which reported the experience, resembles a Jack London short story.[21] In Mitchell's story, however, the protagonist (himself) was white and possessed an intellect superior to that of the superstitious "Indian character," as well as the survival skills and savvy necessary to triumph over nature's extremes, quite unlike the character in London's story who died for lack of survival skills. In 1903, Mitchell was promoted to captain. On December 2 of that year he married his first wife, Caroline Stoddard, who had graduated cum laude from Vassar College the year before. They had two daughters and a son together: Elizabeth (1906), Harriet (1909), and John (1918). Mitchell was then posted to Fort Leavenworth, Kansas, in the autumn of 1904 to serve as an instructor at the Infantry and Cavalry School, an assignment Caroline found lonely and intellectually stifling. One of his lectures advised officers to look upon new technological developments, such as wireless telegraphy, with some caution; only a few innovations, such as the automobile, have come through trials of experimentation to make them practical, he warned.[22] He then served as chief of the US Army's First Relief Station after the 1906 San Francisco earthquake and subsequent fire (the dual disaster caused more than 3,000 deaths, $400 million in damage, and displaced over half the city's population of 400,000 people).[23]

In 1909, Mitchell attended the US Army's staff college at Fort Leavenworth and graduated with distinction. In 1912, he was assigned to the General Staff in Washington, DC. He and Caroline lived as if they belonged to America's privileged classes, maintaining two servants and three horses, joining elite social clubs, and hosting dinner parties for rising officers and political figures. They could not have managed the high costs of such a lifestyle without considerable financial support from relatives on both sides of the family, however.[24] From his position on the General Staff, he followed the course of the Great War as it unfolded from August to December 1914. But he wrongly predicted a German victory. In 1915, he wrote a paper for the General Staff entitled, "Our Faulty Military Policy," which warned against the folly of putting one's faith in technological solutions. Like many at the time who worried whether human beings could handle the rigors of armed conflict, he railed against the "tendency to exaggerate the importance of materiel in modern war and to underrate the personnel."[25] The following year, after recovering from a blood clot in his eye and a bout with rheumatism, he became the temporary head of the aviation section and took 1,470 minutes of flying lessons at a civilian aeronautical school in Newport News, Virginia, at his own expense at $1 per minute (a total of approximately $32,000 in 2020).[26]

In the spring of 1917, Mitchell was sent to France, appointed the principal air officer of the American Expeditionary Force (AEF), and promoted to lieutenant colonel. There he met Hugh Trenchard, Britain's chief of the Royal Flying Corps, who introduced him to the idea of an air offensive and the concept of an independent air arm.[27] For his part, Mitchell agreed the first mission of an air offensive must be to destroy the adversary's air power. But he also acknowledged air power's limitations; destroying factories was a "tremendously difficult thing" and the effects of doing so might not be felt for up to a year. Air power alone, he concluded, "cannot bring about a decision," but must instead support the collective operations of all arms.[28]

In October 1917, he was promoted to colonel. By this time, his egoism had made him as many enemies as friends among the senior officers of the AEF. In September 1918, he planned, organized, and executed an air attack – involving more than 1,400 planes – against German positions in the St. Mihiel salient. As a result of the operation's success, which Mitchell greatly exaggerated in an article the following year, the commander of the AEF, General John J. Pershing, approved his promotion to brigadier general.[29] Just a few weeks after the St. Mihiel operation, Mitchell organized and executed another massive air attack against German positions in support of the Meuse-Argonne offensive. His account of it was triumphal rather than critical, which is perhaps understandable given the public's readiness to see something in return for the costs it had borne.[30] The war ended before the practical capabilities and limitations of air power had become clear, though events to that point provided plenty of grist for speculation.

Mitchell returned to the United States in the spring of 1919 to find military demobilization, part of US President Warren G. Harding's policy of returning to "Normalcy," in full and irresistible swing. On Armistice Day, November 11, 1918, for instance, some 195,000 officers and men were assigned to the US Air Service; however, by mid-1919 this number had dropped to 15,875, a reduction of 92 percent.[31] Demobilization took place so hastily, in fact, it put some two million former service personnel into the work force just as most industries were beginning to retool from wartime to peacetime production. As a result, some one million veterans suddenly found themselves unemployed, and the US economy slipped into a short but sharp recession between 1919 and 1921. In the budgetary battles that ensued, the War Department and the Department of the Navy sought to strengthen their positions by proposing new organizations or expanding the purview of existing ones. In 1920, Bradley Fiske, now a rear admiral, urged the US Navy to establish a Bureau of Aeronautics: "let's get a Bureau of Aeronautics pdq [pretty damn quick] – as pdq as possible ... [otherwise] Gen'l Mitchell and a whole horde of politicians will get an 'Air Ministry' established, and the US Navy will find itself lying in the street, and the procession marching over it."[32] Furthermore, the spirit of the age, which still retained the optimism of the Progressive era, saw bureaucracy as a cure rather than a problem: bureaucracies helped rationalize policy by channeling resources toward solutions. This optimism began to fade in the 1950s and 1960s, when bureaucracies came to be seen as inefficient and obstructionist.

Mitchell became the deputy director of the Air Service with responsibility for training and operations, though he had wanted and expected to become its director. But Pershing selected Major-General Charles T. Menoher to be the director. Mitchell's disappointment aside, his new position enabled him to retain his flag-officer status at a time when many senior offers were being either discharged or demoted to their prewar ranks. Additionally, unlike most of his peers, his public image approached celebrity status in the years following the war. That status gave his incessant criticisms of the existing bureaucratic leadership greater punch and brought him into conflict with his superiors, including President Harding's successor, Calvin Coolidge. Moreover, Mitchell's proposals – which included construction of two aircraft carriers, several long-range bombers, a fleet of dirigibles, and a new department modeled on the British Air Ministry – required an increase in military spending, which ran counter to the government's policy of returning to normalcy and reducing the defense budget.[33] Nonetheless, as his letters to his mother reveal, he continued to agitate for the establishment of a unified air service as part of his legacy, "the one project that I most want to leave behind."[34]

Two years after the war, the US Navy began conducting experiments involving the aerial bombing of obsolete and captured warships. Mitchell, contrary to Britain's Air Marshal Hugh Trenchard, had openly declared contemporary aircraft could sink modern battleships.[35] On July 21, 1921, the outspoken flyer's First Provisional Air Brigade succeeded in sinking the target ship *Ostfriedland*, a former German battleship. Both the Navy and Mitchell violated the rules of the tests, but the press played up the event as a victory for the outspoken aviator. The *New York Herald* even called upon the Navy to convert some of its ships still under construction to aircraft carriers.[36] By 1922, the Navy had done exactly that, converting the collier *USS Jupiter* into the carrier *USS Langley*, while also improving the air defense capabilities of its capital ships; by 1927, two other ship-to-carrier conversions had been completed.[37] But these conversions had less to do with the flamboyant flyer's "victory" over the *Ostfriedland* than with the Navy's decision in 1919 to attempt to keep pace with Japan for maritime influence in the Pacific.[38]

In late August 1921, slightly one month after the sinking of the *Ostfriedland*, Mitchell was ordered to deploy elements of his First Provisional Air Brigade to West Virginia to help restore order in a standoff between coal miners and local authorities. He displayed as much sympathy for the coalminers as he had for Cuban insurgents two decades prior. The situation was obviously a volatile one that required diplomatic skills. The outspoken Mitchell, however, decided to tout the capabilities of air power by boasting he could end the disturbance in short order by dropping tear gas on the strikers; should that fail, he would escalate to artillery fire.[39] Fortunately, Brigadier-General Henry H. Bandholtz, Commander of the Military District of Washington, handled the situation more tactfully, and Mitchell, for his trouble, was ordered back to Washington. The situation was finally defused after a brief clash between coalminers and local authorities that resulted in sixteen dead, mostly miners.[40] Mitchell quickly claimed air power had made the difference, though fully a third of the aircraft sent to quell the disturbance had either failed to take off due to mechanical problems, crash-landed at some point during the operation, or had gotten lost.

During the winter of 1921–22, Mitchell, now legally separated from Caroline, toured Europe on an assignment to assess the state of air power in England, France, Germany, and Holland.[41] He purportedly met Douhet during this tour. On November 22, 1922, Mitchell delivered a lecture to the US Army War College in Washington, DC, which reflected the essential points of his assessment.[42] Unlike his report, which was strictly technical in nature, Mitchell's lecture included a summation of the political climate in each of the European powers he visited. It confirms that, for many officers of Mitchell's generation, military thinking did not always divorce itself from political circumstances, but rather took them into account.

His marriage to Caroline ended legally on September 22, 1922. Their intense rows had become legendary and provided much grist for the gossip columnists and paparazzi of the day. On one occasion Caroline was shot in the chest (evidently a glancing wound) by a small-caliber revolver; however, authorities ultimately believed his claim that she had attempted suicide over her accusation that he had attempted to kill her.[43] In October 1923, barely thirteen months after his divorce, Mitchell married Elizabeth Trumbull. From December 1923 to July 1924 the two toured several countries in the Pacific region, while Mitchell conducted another strategic assessment.[44] His subsequent report portrayed Japan as a strategic rival to the United States. But this claim was neither unique nor especially prescient. Conflict with Japan had become a routine scenario after the Russo-Japanese War, as evidenced by the number of Army War College and Naval War College studies and war games dedicated to it.[45]

In September 1925, an angry Mitchell publicly accused the US Navy of negligence and incompetence in two major air incidents: the aborted flights of a pair of PN-9 aircraft destined for Hawai'i on September 1, and the crash of the airship *Shenandoah* two days later.[46] Coolidge had finally had enough, and initiated court martial proceedings against Mitchell, correctly interpreting the flamboyant flyer's rants as attempts to force the hand of the US government. But the aviator evidently welcomed the court martial, believing, narcissistically, he could win the case in the court of public opinion. The trial lasted from October 28, 1925 to December 17, 1925, and he was found guilty of all charges. Notably, he admitted to presenting his optimistic opinions as established facts; nor could he refute charges of plagiarism when confronted with the fact he cribbed several pages of *Winged Defense* from a classified lecture on German submarines delivered at the General Staff College in 1919 by USN Captain and future Admiral and US Senator Thomas C. Hart.[47] Accordingly, the court sentenced Mitchell to suspension of rank, command, and duty, and to forfeiture of all pay and allowances for five years.[48] Six weeks later, however, Coolidge reduced the sentence, allowing him to receive half-pay and full subsistence allowance. Mitchell nonetheless resigned from the US Army on February 1, 1926. He then went on a public speaking tour that earned him nearly $40,000 (approximately $580,000 in 2020), more than six times his annual colonel's salary, before the end of the year.[49] The media began to distance itself from him not long after the trial, however, and the public, too, began to lose interest in his message, which had become gloomy and repetitive.

In May 1927, a new American air hero named Charles Lindberg eclipsed Mitchell's popularity and captured the public's attention. A daring stunt pilot who had received some aviation training while in the US Army, Lindberg made the first non-stop, solo flight from New York City to Paris (3,600 miles) to win the Orteig Prize ($25,000 or $362,000 in 2020). Six others had died attempting to accomplish this feat, but "Lucky Lindy," as the papers called him, managed to do it in 33.5 hours. Young and self-effacing, Lindberg was the perfect foil to the embattled Mitchell, who was almost twice his age. The youthful aviator's story was a much happier one, to this point at least, and as yet untainted by scandal or his fascist leanings.[50] Lindberg's exploit helped boost interest in civilian aviation in a way Mitchell's rants could not; investments in aviation stocks tripled from 1927 to 1929, and the number of air passengers increased from 6,000 in 1926 to nearly 173,000 in 1929.[51] Other air heroes such as Amelia Earhart and aerial acrobats such as "Ethel Dare" (Margie Hobbs) and Bessie Coleman kept interest in civilian aviation alive into the 1930s.[52]

Over the next ten years Mitchell cultivated a relationship with FDR. He actively supported Roosevelt's 1932 bid for the presidency, and in return he fully expected to receive a high-level position in the new administration's reorganization of America's defense establishment, which presumably would have included a sizeable aeronautical department. Roosevelt had a knack, however, for listening to the schemes of others and gaining their support without explicitly committing himself to any specific courses of action or to granting any awards. In the end, Mitchell's egoism undermined his chances. His Congressional testimony on March 1933 condemned the Navy's further construction of battleships and aircraft carriers, but it also unnecessarily lashed out at the American Legion for supporting the Bonus marchers.[53] Mitchell's histrionics continued well into 1934, and eventually became too much of a liability for FDR who, among other things, needed Congressional support for his New Deal.[54] Indeed, 1933 was the worst year of the Great Depression; America's GDP had fallen 46 percent, unemployment had climbed to 25 percent, while the number of people who were underemployed had reached 50 percent.[55]

On February 19, 1936, the aviation visionary died due to a worsening heart condition combined with a severe bout of influenza, though his chronic alcoholism may also have contributed. Notably, his death occurred six months before the outbreak of the Spanish Civil War (July 1936–March 1939), which, had he lived to draw observations from it, might have augmented his views regarding the utility of airpower. Several of Europe's major powers used the conflict to test their respective military organizations, especially their air arms; Germany and Italy, for instance, provided arms to the Fascists under Franco, while Soviet Russia backed the Republicans. Above all, the war demonstrated the value of strategic airlift, about which Mitchell had written comparatively little. The results of the conflict also cast doubt on the effectiveness of strategic bombing, however, which would not have pleased him. While German aircraft had bombed Madrid and Barcelona during the conflict, the bombing seemed to have strengthened civilian morale rather than breaking it, as both Douhet and Mitchell predicted.[56] Whether the American air theorist would have revised his predictions based on the results cannot, of course, be known. In 1941, the B-25 aircraft was named the "Mitchell" bomber in his honor. In 1942, shortly after Pearl Harbor, FDR posthumously promoted Mitchell to major general. Initiatives were also undertaken to award him the medal of honor, but these were blocked. Instead, a special gold medal was created on his behalf.

2.2   Mitchell's America – Careless and Confused

Mitchell was born in 1879 in the early years of America's "Gilded Age," a phrase Mark Twain coined in 1873 to satirize the contradiction between America's espoused values and its preoccupation with wealth, and the appearance of wealth.[57] What Americans took for genuine treasure was simply fool's gold, Twain seemed to say. It was a message that would bear repeating in almost every decade thereafter. In the year of Mitchell's birth, the population of United States numbered nearly 50 million people, and the country consisted of thirty-eight states and eleven territories, including the District of Columbia and 60,000 square miles of "Indian Territory."[58] The US federal government had recently withdrawn its troops from occupation duty in the South, officially ending the all-too-disappointing Reconstruction era. The Carlisle Indian Industrial School had just been founded, and the era of forced assimilation was underway; one of Mitchell's teachers at Racine had previously been an instructor at the Indian boarding school at Keshena, Wisconsin.

By the end of Mitchell's life, the United States was six years into its worst economic catastrophe to date, and waves of "black blizzards" (windstorms) were turning the Midwest and Southern plains into a desolate "Dust Bowl."[59] The country's population had grown to 128 million people, and it included forty-eight states and eight outlying territories and possessions.[60] Its gross national product had risen almost eightfold and its per capita income had more than tripled since 1879.[61] A disproportionate amount of that growth occurred in the 1920s, especially in the half-decade from 1922 to 1927 – Mitchell's most productive years as a military writer. His America, therefore, was the America of the 1920s, a decade author F. Scott Fitzgerald aptly described as "careless and confused."[62] Fitzgerald's novel *The Great Gatsby* appeared six months before Mitchell's trial, and it, like Twain's *Gilded Age*, highlighted the discrepancies between what America allegedly stood for, and how it actually behaved; Jay Gatsby himself, as it turned out, was both more and less than he appeared to be, and so was Mitchell and his America.

In January 1925, when President Coolidge remarked, with benign frankness, "the chief business of the American people is business," US productivity had already soared to unprecedented levels.[63] In 1922, for instance, the Ford motor company could make one Model T, or "Tin Lizzy," every two hours; in 1924, it could produce one every ten seconds.[64] By 1927, automobile productivity had put some 20 million cars on US roads and, by the end of the decade, 60 percent of American families owned automobiles.[65] The surge in output also extended to household items such as vacuum cleaners, washing machines, refrigerators, electric ovens, electric irons, and radios. In 1920, only 9 percent of American homes owned vacuum cleaners, just 8 percent owned washing machines, and only 2,000 households had a radio; by the end of the decade, those numbers had jumped to 30 percent, 24 percent, and 12 million respectively.[66] By early 1929, the gross domestic product of the United States had climbed to $105 billion ($1.5 trillion in 2020), unemployment hovered below 3.7 percent, and the Dow Jones Industrial Average had tripled in value.[67]

The booming economy of the 1920s also reinforced a blossoming consumer culture that prized luxury, or its appearance. Magazines, newspapers, and the new "silver screen" (motion pictures) carried images of everyday items rendered elegantly. The Gilded Age had become the era of Art Deco, a style that put a touch of glamor on everything from household appliances, to automobiles, to aircraft, to skyscrapers such as the Chrysler building in New York City, to business clothing, and to dining- and eveningwear. Mitchell's penchant for flamboyant, nonregulation uniforms during the First World War was only half a decade ahead of its time. Unfortunately, genuine luxury, by design, remained just beyond the reach of most middle- and working-class families – unless they bought goods on credit in "buy now pay later" schemes, as millions of consumers did.[68]

In important respects, however, America had failed to make much progress beyond its Gilded Age. Real wages for middle and working classes had risen about 33 percent since 1914, which led to greater satisfaction; but the gap between the supremely wealthy and everyone else had increased even more.[69] The brief but sharp economic depression of 1919–1921, moreover, gave rise to a series of labor strikes across the country, as well as to America's first "Red Scare," which reflexively attributed Bolshevik beliefs to the leaders of labor unions. The Emergency Quota Act of 1921 and Immigration Act of 1924 not only restricted the flow of immigrant laborers, they were also meant to keep out radical economic notions. Suddenly, to strike had become un-American, as the writer Sinclair Lewis revealed in his novel *Babbit* (1922). The influence of labor unions declined in the 1920s for several reasons, including rising worker satisfaction. Unfortunately, this decline meant labor reforms – such as making workplaces safer – slowed considerably. One consequence was that working classes were paying for America's productivity in high mortality and accident rates. Labor authorities estimated 23,000–25,000 labor-related deaths occurred annually, making the workplace cumulatively "more dangerous than the battlefield," a phenomenon one author referred to as the "carnage of peace."[70] Precise numbers for the 1920s remain elusive, however, because, until the late twentieth century, employers were not required to report labor-related accidents. Consumers were not immune either. In 1920 some 12,000 people were killed by motor vehicle accidents; by 1929, the number of annual fatalities had risen to 30,000.[71] The climax of *The Great Gatsby*, after all, involved an automobile accident. When Mitchell argued that air force personnel needed to be of a special quality because their casualty rate was higher than any other branch of military service, he would have done well first to compare his numbers to injuries suffered on the job and on the highway.[72]

The mass production of consumer goods, especially the radio, offered tangible symbols of Americana. Radios provided news, advertisements, sports events, music, and other entertainment, all of which persuaded listeners of diverse racial, ethnic, and gender backgrounds to accept a common, if superficial, American identity.[73] Radio personality Will Rogers, who attended portions of Mitchell's trial and lent him moral support on the air by poking fun at the War Department, assisted in laying a groundwork of culturally unifying norms through his folksy brand of humor, which reached some 60 million listeners. At one point in Mitchell's trial, Rogers purportedly put his arm around the outspoken aviator and said: "The people are with you Billy. Keep punching. You'll rope 'em yet."[74] Born the same year as Mitchell, the two had flown together over Washington DC in 1925; Rogers died in a plane crash near Point Barrow, Alaska, on August 15, 1935, six months before Mitchell's death.[75] Despite the trappings of a unifying culture, in other words, Mitchell's gilded America was deeply riven with divisions and at war with itself socially and culturally nearly as much as Mahan's had been.

Racial animosities still ran deep, for instance. The failure of Reconstruction and the institution of race codes and Jim Crow laws in the South, combined with the rise of racially motivated hate groups such as the KKK, prompted millions of Black Americans to relocate north in what became known as the Great Migration.[76] Cities such as Chicago, Detroit, New York, Philadelphia, Tulsa, and Washington, DC expanded in size as Black communities grew. A deplorable example of racial violence occurred on May 31, 1921, in the town of Greenwood, in Tulsa, also known as "Black Wall Street" because of its bustling microeconomy. A white woman accused a Black man of assaulting her, and mobs of angry whites descended upon the town and razed it; at least 300 people were killed.[77]

Three years later, as Ford's factories were producing record numbers of Model T's, some 40,000 members of the KKK marched on Washington, DC. At the time, the KKK claimed to have nearly 4 million followers nationwide, and prominent industrialists such as Ford sympathized with them.[78] Ford's genius for mass production concealed an astounding ignorance of US history, and his racist beliefs found an outlet in *The Dearborn Independent*, a newspaper he owned. Mitchell, whose racism rivaled Ford's, referred to the National Association for the Advancement of Colored People (NAACP) as a "communist organization financed from abroad," and he frequently described in racist terms the looming struggle for mastery of the Pacific region he foresaw. In 1923, he warned: "We are faced with a problem much greater than it appears on the surface, that of maintaining not only the political supremacy but also the very existence of the white race."[79] Mitchell still held the same views in 1935: "Whether the culture of the white race is to continue as the world's greatest force, or whether Asiatic culture will dominate, will be determined from the American continent, by air power."[80] Indeed, racial and ethnic tensions had fewer opportunities to improve in the 1920s due largely to the aforementioned Emergency Quota Act of 1921 and Immigration Act of 1924, which placed heavier restrictions on immigration. In 1921, some 805,000 immigrants were allowed into the United States; however, in 1929, only 280,000 foreigners were admitted under the belief that controlling the influx of immigrants would keep unemployment low and real wages high.[81]

Gender discrimination remained a problem as well. Whereas the Suffrage movement had succeeded in gaining women the right to vote in 1920, the movement soon split into multiple factions in what one scholar described as the "feminist crash of the 1920s."[82] The enfranchisement of women had not translated into political solidarity, to greater access to public offices, to progress regarding women's reproductive, marital, or legal rights; or to upward mobility in the workplace.[83] In fact, several of the super-corporations that appeared during the economic boom of the 1920s implemented hiring and promotion practices based on unwarranted assumptions about the "natural roles" of men and women. Consequently, various firms established "marriage bars" that discouraged the hiring of married women and required single women to leave the workplace once they married.[84] While the "flapper" culture emerged partly as a rejection of such norms, it also reflected the fashion preferences of a generation concerned as well as confused about its future.[85] As one eloquent flapper affirmed in 1922, "We are the Younger Generation. The war tore away our spiritual foundations and challenged our faith. We are struggling to regain our equilibrium. The times have made us older and more experienced than you were at your age. ... Work with us!"[86]

Mitchell's America was also the America of Prohibition, of "speakeasies," and of the rise of organized crime. The Temperance (anti-alcohol) movement realized a victory with the passage of the 18th (Volstead) Amendment, which made it illegal to buy, sell, or transport alcohol. Yet the law may have unintentionally contributed to the emergence and expansion of organized crime. While that possibility is still debated, most evidence suggests organized crime, as it is known today, did not exist in the United States until the Prohibition era.[87] Even under the Volstead restrictions, US citizens who wanted alcohol could obtain it, though it might be expensive. In any event, Prohibition failed to curb Mitchell's alcoholism, which evidently worsened over the course of the 1920s. He was seen frequenting night clubs in Washington, DC, and he openly admitted to occasionally drinking too much.[88] A home movie filmed in February 1925, before Mitchell was assigned to San Antonio, shows him at an outdoor party with dozens of friends.[89] Alcohol flowed abundantly from unlabeled jugs, and all women, young and old, sported flapper-style haircuts, tight-fitting caps, and short skirts. In a word, from alcohol consumption to attire, from public jokes to public enemies, rebelliousness had become fashionable.

More a gambler than an investor, Mitchell lost heavily when the stock market collapsed in late 1929. The causes of the crash are still a matter of debate. But the weight of opinion inclines toward the overproduction of goods, the overextension of credit, the miscalculation of risks, and the absence of programmed restraints; in short, carelessness and confusion. The market's eight-year astronomical climb had made many investors, including the gambler Mitchell, uneasy. After all, while even novice investors knew what went up often came down, the crucial question was when. Warning signs of a downturn were already evident in 1928 when automobile sales dropped by 30 percent, construction declined almost as severely, and the prices of farm goods fell. Finally, on October 24, 1929, the stock market dropped 11 percent; five days later, on "Black Tuesday," it fell even further, erasing $25 billion in stock portfolios and $140 billion in savings ($375 billion and $2.1 trillion in 2020).

The collapse of the economy was one thing, as most investors recalled the sharp economic decline of 1919–21. But the duration of the depression, which persistently defied remedy, was another matter. Fortunately for Mitchell, the Boxwood Estate Elizabeth owned was largely paid for; she also had a separate source of income that suffered little in the market's collapse.[90] Unlike hundreds of thousands of Americans, therefore, Mitchell's standard of living slipped little during the Great Depression. He and Elizabeth retained the wherewithal to maintain membership in elite social clubs, to travel, and to entertain up-and-coming officers such as Colonel George S. Patton, Jr. They did not share the plight of commoners, even though Mitchell went to some lengths to present himself as an "everyman" in the media.

The former aviator, in fact, rarely associated with any but the social and political elites of his day. He was, therefore, Jack London in his writing style only. In every other way, he was the antithesis of the common person, the popular theme of the literary works of the period. As if in rejection of the high-sounding rhetoric of the Great War, the literature of postwar America rejected lofty morals and elitism to celebrate the quiet heroism of everyday life. Willa Cather's *One of Ours* (1922) marked the end of the romanticists' love affair with war and military glory, conveying the story of a farm boy who set off for the Great War to fulfill his desire for adventure. Gertrude Stein's brilliant *Making of Americans* (1925) revealed an entire world alongside that of affluent families in the complex and hitherto unexamined lives of their servants. Ernest Hemingway's *A Farewell to Arms* (1929) depicted, somewhat autobiographically, the experiences of a common ambulance driver on the Italian front in the First World War. Pearl Buck's trilogy – *The Good Earth* (1931), *Sons* (1932), and *A House Divided* (1935) – eloquently described peasant life in China. John Steinbeck's "Dust Bowl Trilogy" – *In Dubious Battle* (1936), *Of Mice and Men* (1937), and *The Grapes of Wrath* (1939) – celebrated the nobility of America's unheralded, yet undefeated, common folk. Whereas Mitchell had made a name for himself with his accomplishments in the war, his brand of heroism contrasted sharply with the unrewarded courage of the average person.

2.3   Mitchell's First Principles

Ironically, for all Mitchell's rhetoric concerning the revolutionary changes wrought by the aeronautical era, his first principles for air power differed little from those Mahan had advanced more than three decades earlier for sea power: concentration, offensive action, and decision by battle. While Mahan had scoured history for timeless principles, Mitchell dismissed history as irrelevant. Air power was new and it had changed everything. It had demolished the old frontiers – rivers, mountains, deserts, and coastlines – and now "no place" on the planet was "immune from influence by aircraft." The world had grown smaller, and all distances were now measurable "in hours and not in miles."[91] Travel to any location was, literally, but a function of time.

Advances in aviation technology had demonstrably transformed warfare, Mitchell maintained, by elevating control of the air to an "absolute principle."[92] Henceforth, a "new set of rules" and a "new set of ideas of strategy" would be needed to address the fact that armed conflict now took place in three dimensions: land, sea, and "above."[93] Armies and navies were essentially "helpless without obtaining and holding supremacy in the air."[94] Indeed, Mitchell later referred to armies and navies as little more than museum pieces.[95] The early Mitchell, however, usually assigned armies the role of defending bases. Surface navies, on the other hand, he rejected as utterly obsolete because of the expense necessary to maintain them and since they had no defense against air attack. Even "airplane carriers" (aircraft carriers) were a waste of defense dollars because they could never compete with land-based air power. Only subsurface fleets (submarines) remained cost-effective because they could evade detection from the air. Accordingly, the modern strategist now had to reckon in terms of "*air power, air bases*, and *aircraft*," rather than, as Mahan would have said, sea power, sea bases, and naval vessels.[96]

Echoing Douhet, Mitchell argued air power's principal objective in wartime was to paralyze hostile parties so they could no longer wage war. The most effective method by which to achieve that objective was aerial bombardment of the foes' "vital centers." Destroying or neutralizing them would deprive one's enemies of the means to resist, leaving them with little choice but to concede.[97] For instance, a concerted air attack with poison gas on New York City would "interrupt communications, stop the forwarding of supplies," prevent the use of ports, "kill and disable numbers of the population, cause a general exodus and evacuation of the city, and otherwise interfere with this great strategic centre."[98]

With paralysis as the goal, the governing principle for air power was to gain air supremacy, that is, control of the air. This principle has remained vital for decades; for while definitions of "air supremacy" or "air superiority" have varied over the years, all have entailed some form of control of the air, that is, achieving freedom of action relative to one's enemy. Accordingly, the principles of concentration, offensive action, and decision by battle have remained essential in air warfare. "All the air strength which a nation possesses," Mitchell insisted, "will have to be concentrated at the decisive point."[99] "The nation that gets in the first great air blow amidst the enemy," he added, "is the one that will win."[100] Any party caught by surprise by an opponent with significant air power was finished from the outset: "To sit down on one's own territory and wait for the other fellow to come, is to be whipped before an operation has even commenced."[101] Indeed, "national offense will be more important than national defense," he warned, "because the first smack will be the last."[102] To achieve control of the air, moreover, one would need to fight air battles. Air combats were the only effective form of air defense, according to Mitchell, as antiaircraft capabilities would never have the power to stop a determined air attack. Mitchell prized speed; it always gave aircraft the initiative over seagoing vessels, he said.[103] But he, like Mahan, did not put speed above firepower. Superiority in numbers counted for more in air battles. In sum, "getting there first with the most" was as important in the aeronautical era as it had been during the American Civil War.

Despite the obvious importance of air power, the United States was criminally unprepared, the former air commander argued. The problem was not a lack of enthusiasm for aviation among US citizens, for "Americans make remarkable pilots." They had what it took to create an air force, namely, a "strong national morale, a patriotism and love of country," capable of bearing the high costs of war; and a proper industrial infrastructure and raw materials.[104] Rather, America's lack of progress had to do with the conservative minds in the government that thwarted air power's development. The War Department and the Department of the Navy were, in his words, completely "psychologically unfit" to develop US air power because they lacked vision and could only see what aircraft could not, or should not do.[105] America, therefore, needed a single air representative with the authority to control both civil and military aviation and with the vision to organize an "entirely different system of training, education, reserves, and replacements, from that of the other services."[106] Naturally, Mitchell himself was supremely qualified to be that representative.

Mitchell's 1922 lecture to the US Army War College distilled his main ideas regarding the organization of America's air power. The country needed two aeronautical elements, he said, an air force and an air service. The function of the former was to attack hostile air and ground formations and to protect friendly ones; air service units, on the other hand, acted as "aides to ground troops by doing reconnaissance; regulating artillery fire; conducting infantry liaison, etc." Unlike surface components, air force units had to operate in three dimensions: "up and down, front and rear, and on the same plane." Furthermore, they had to be organized around three functions: pursuit, bombardment, and attack. Pursuit aircraft (an element that distinguished his ideas from those of Douhet and Trenchard) sought out and destroyed enemy aircraft; they needed to maximize speed, maneuverability, and firepower.[107] Bombardment aircraft attacked an adversary's troop concentrations, supply depots, trains, transportation networks, or any target considered worthy of attack; they needed to be capable of carrying heavy payloads and their principal weapons were to be high explosives, gas, phosphorous, and other chemicals. Finally, attack aircraft supported ground operations by engaging targets just behind enemy lines; these aircraft were to be designed to withstand machine-gun and light antiaircraft fire. "With an air force properly organized, equipped, and trained," said Mitchell, "it would be possible to break up all concentrations, prevent train movement, and attack troops on the road so persistently that any contemplated offensive would be broken up before it could start."[108]

Despite having experience as a counterinsurgent, Mitchell neglected to discuss how air power would deal with an enemy insurgency. Perhaps it would have dropped poison gas across the countryside; however, that solution would have killed or injured a great many noncombatants as well. He assumed, like Douhet, that destroying an opponent's means to resist would break the willingness to resist. However, the Morrow Board, which Coolidge commissioned, released a report just days before the announcement of the verdict of Mitchell's trial that explicitly challenged this assumption. "Wars against high-spirited peoples never will be ended by sudden attacks upon important nerve centers," it said. "The next war may well start in the air but in all probability will wind up, as the last war did, in the mud."[109] The report went on to recommend the establishment of an air corps for the Army, but not the independent air service Mitchell desired.

Mitchell frequently claimed the airplane had evolved, and was continuing to evolve, more rapidly than any other technological innovation.

But he often undermined his case by exaggerating the progress of airplane technology. "I can say now, definitely," he once said, "that we can encircle the globe in a very short time on a single charge of gasoline."[110] In fact, even in the late 1920s, it typically took less time to travel across the country by train than by air. Aircraft still had to stop frequently to refuel, could not fly reliably at night, or in stormy weather, and had to skirt significant obstacles or mountains rather than flying over them due to insufficient lift capacity.[111] He also discounted the possibility that countermeasures and defensive technologies, such as radar and antiaircraft guns, might develop quickly enough to reduce the effectiveness of airpower, as they did in the Second World War. While airpower's influence on the war should not be underestimated, countermeasures at times forced bombers to fly at high altitude, or at night, which adversely affected the accuracy of their bombing runs. Rather than regarding aircraft as part of a dynamic measure–countermeasure competition, Mitchell insisted on the invincibility of airpower. The idea that antiaircraft artillery could ever ward off air attacks, for instance, he dismissed as "absolutely not in keeping with the facts."[112] Such overstatements were unnecessary, built resentment among those who knew the facts, put in jeopardy progress toward an integrated defense, and undermined his credibility. Similarly, he published a series of articles in *Women's Home Companion* from 1930 to 1932 that thoroughly romanticized air travel while making unsupportable claims about the imminent progress of aeronautical technology.[113] Some exaggeration inevitably comes with selling a product. But Mitchell was guilty of overselling airpower and himself as its best visionary.

2.4 War's Nature

Like Mahan, Mitchell saw war's nature as a violent extension of the competitive side of human nature. The former aviation commander's definition of war, a "condition which results when one nation attempts to impose its will on another by physical means," would have been acceptable to Clausewitz, as well as to Mahan's and Mitchell's contemporaries.[114] Luce, for instance, went so far as to equate such struggles among nations to a "fixed law" of nature, and he believed no party could suspend this "battle of life" for even a moment without risking defeat and possibly death. By comparison, Fiske put a more materialist spin on the law of nature, arguing the "competition for money or its equivalent" lay at the root of conflict between persons as well as nations.[115] In 1935, less than three months before Mitchell's death, former US Marine Corps (USMC) Major-General Smedley Butler added an earthy touch to this assumption by admitting he had spent most of his time as a marine "being a high-class muscle man for Big Business, for Wall Street and the bankers ... a racketeer for capitalism."[116] War, for Butler, was more about economic than political interests, more about the United Fruit Company than the United States.

To be sure, Luce's words evince more than a trace of Social Darwinism. Yet Social Darwinism was both preceded and strengthened by the sense that war was fundamentally a violent extension of humanity's competitive instincts. By the mid-1930s, moreover, that doctrine had faded, being replaced by the preoccupation with materialism that characterized the era that followed the First World War. In short, whether one saw armed conflict chiefly as a sociopolitical contest, as Mitchell and Luce did, or primarily as an economic one, as Fiske and Butler did, war's nature was still an extension of human nature. What was at odds was how one saw human nature.

Mitchell, moreover, appreciated the political dimension of war's nature, but subordinated political concerns to strategic principles. Whereas Mahan sought to divorce policy from strategy, claiming policy was "especially ignorant" of how to conduct war; Mitchell wished to have a decisive hand in shaping policy. The aviator did not disdain policy as such, though he repeatedly criticized specific defense policies. Mitchell leveraged politics, more specifically political affairs, for the purpose of coercing the US government into expanding its airpower capabilities. His lectures and the official reports of foreign aviation capabilities published while he was the Assistant Chief of Air Service reveal a reasonable awareness of postwar political developments in Europe and the Far East. He believed, like many at the time, the Great War had not ended Europe's troubles and another war was only a matter of time, as was a conflict with Japan. His understanding of politics as a concept lacked sophistication, and was weighed down with racist sentiments; however, he clearly kept himself informed well enough to engage influential political and military figures. Politics was, ultimately, for Mitchell as well as for the politicians of his day, a means to an end.

The flamboyant flyer rarely mentioned the experiential elements of war's nature, such as friction, or the cumulative effects of chance and uncertainty, in his writings. As an experienced soldier he was undoubtedly aware of them. They were also beginning to appear more routinely in the US military's instructional material. In 1936, the year of Mitchell's death, the US Army's Staff College at Fort Leavenworth published *Principles of Strategy for an Independent Corps or Army in a Theater of Operations*, which referred directly to the "fog of war," meaning the element of uncertainty, and what commanders would have to do to overcome it.[117] Two years later, the US Army War College published an English translation of German Major-General Freytag-Loringhoven's classic *The Power of Personality in War*, which expounded in great depth upon the elements that made up the atmosphere of war, to include friction and uncertainty.[118] To admit to such influences, and their possibly adverse effects on the utility of airpower, however, would not have served Mitchell's purposes.

2.5 Conclusions

Mitchell defined airpower not unlike Mahan defined sea power, with simplicity and durability.[119] Since the two were born almost forty years apart, it should not be surprising that each saw warfare differently. Mahan obviously viewed it through the lens of a naval officer; while Mitchell considered it, ultimately, from the perspective of an aviator. Both authors actively promoted the interests of their own branches of service (or would-be service). For Mitchell, airpower had displaced sea power and would drive world affairs; he assigned himself the task of creating a pathway for airpower's further expansion, one that, incidentally, also placed him at its forefront, as its chief pathbreaker. For Mahan, of course, sea power had always influenced the affairs of states; he made it his life's mission to show how and why. Mahan refrained from technological speculation, though scientists in his day routinely engaged in conjecture to advance their fields. Instead, he kept war's changing character at arm's length. Mitchell, in contrast, all but invented a new character of war by engaging in aggressive speculation to the point of misrepresenting possibilities as actualities.

Although such exaggerations were surely intended to showcase Mitchell's proficiency as a visionary, they obscured how much of his own rhetoric he believed. Speculating about the future of airpower or sea power was essential, and to be encouraged. But it also had to be responsible, given the lives and treasure potentially at stake; speculations needed to be compared periodically to unexpected developments and to new information. By the early 1930s, wargaming at the US Naval War College revealed aircraft carriers would be the new queens of the chessboard, especially in the Pacific theater; while other information showed movement of massed formations of any sort, whether at sea or on land, would be extremely difficult without air cover. Unfortunately, responsible theory was not Mitchell's chief concern.

Despite their dissimilar perspectives, he and Mahan embraced the same set of core principles. Mitchell merely modified Jominian principles to suit the aeronautical age; for instance, concentration became on controlling the air and gaining air supremacy, offensive action aligned with striking first, and seeking decision by battle was essentially the same but the battles took place in the air. However, while the naval captain believed military science had validated these principles, the flamboyant flyer internalized the principles while at the same time disassociating them from military science, which he considered obsolete compared to the new aeronautical sciences. Mitchell's combat experience was broader and more extensive than that of Mahan. The former served with distinction in both the Spanish–American War and the Great War, in which he commanded a large formation of aircraft in relatively complex and unprecedented operations. Mahan, on the other hand, had commanded nothing more complex than a ship and its crew. Again, despite their different degrees and types of combat experience, both regarded Jomini's core principles as tantamount to military imperatives.

As noted earlier, these principles underpinned much of the military strategy and campaign planning that took place during the Second World War, and not only for the United States. For Butler and others, they also proved useful in America's small wars.[120] Butler, who incidentally had little regard for Mitchell's boasts regarding airpower, participated in all but a few of those wars, winning the medal of honor twice (in Veracruz in 1914 and Haiti in 1915).[121] His wartime accounts, though edited and tailored for a general audience, read like a doctrine for concentrated, swift, and decisive action in the face of danger and uncertainty – regardless of the size of the foe.[122] It was true, however, that Mitchell concerned himself with major conflicts rather than small wars. Both the airman and the marine, nonetheless, shared at least one thing – the dubious honor of having inspired their respective presidents (Coolidge for Mitchell and Herbert Hoover for Butler) to initiate court-martial proceedings against them. Butler's charges were dropped after two weeks of public outcry. Mitchell's court-martial elevated him to the status of a hero-martyr. While he certainly belonged to the Guardian tradition in so far as he approached war as an engineering problem to be solved, he also typified Morris Janowitz's hero-manager.[123] Mitchell's career followed the path of hero, manager, then hero-martyr, or more accurately hero-self-martyr.

As noted, Mitchell held to the traditional model of war's nature, believing it was simply a violent extension of human nature. That assumption underpinned his belief that defeating one's foes meant rendering them incapable of taking any further competitive actions, a condition he and subsequent airpower theorists referred to as paralysis. Yet while Mitchell had enough knowledge of industrial economies to believe destroying a country's centers of production would disrupt its capacity to resist, he lacked a corresponding empathy for everyday citizens – what bound them together, their strengths and weaknesses – to know how to demoralize them. He was surrounded by evidence of division and rebellion – of ethnic, class, gender, and racial conflicts – in an America that was no less at war with itself than it had been in Mahan's day. Nevertheless, he presumed it was connected and monolithic – that striking one severely enough would generate the desired effect on the others and on its governing institutions. Mitchell's writings show little evidence he considered the possibility that bombarding an adversary's vital centers might inadvertently strengthen its willingness to fight, rather than breaking it; nor do they indicate that he pondered how the relationships among elites, and middle and working classes might function; or whether those relationships differed in significant ways in fascist and democratic societies. In short, Mitchell was as much disposed toward his America, in step with its elitism, its carelessness, and its attitude of rebellion, if not revolution, as he was divorced from it.

Part II

The Revolt of the Strategy Intellectuals

Russell Weigley ascribed a certain "efflorescence" to American strategic writing in the period from the 1950s to the middle of the 1960s. During these years, a small cadre of theorists whom he called the "strategy intellectuals" – Bernard Brodie, Robert E. Osgood, Thomas C. Schelling, and Herman Kahn – developed novel approaches to thinking about war and strategy.[1] Other scholars have since come to view this era in much the same way, upholding it as a golden age in US strategic thinking, which developed a corpus of "distinctive, influential, and conceptually powerful" ideas.[2]

The strategy intellectuals, however, did more than create a distinctive body of thought. By accepting and building upon Brodie's argument in 1946 that the atomic bomb, the "absolute weapon," had altered the fundamental nature of armed conflict, they initiated a revolution in the American way of thinking about war.[3] Like him, they believed the core strategic principles of Mahan's day – concentration, offensive action, and decision by battle – were now patently and ludicrously self-defeating. Yet these imperatives still underpinned the US military's official doctrine and seemed instinctively correct to a generation of senior officers from Ernest King to Curtis LeMay, who assisted in developing and executing US military strategy during the Second World War.[4] As Brodie once recalled, he could make little headway against LeMay, who repeatedly insisted "the 'principles of war' required concentration of effort in time as well as in space."[5]

As evidence of the revolution's success, the precepts of limited war doctrine, which amounted to a "way of policy," began appearing in US Army field manuals by the late 1950s and early 1960s. Limited war doctrine also influenced US strategy, many critics would say unfavorably, during the Vietnam War.[6] The central theories of the strategy intellectuals, however, also provoked something of a counterrevolution involving a select group of "military intellectuals" – US Rear Admirals Henry Eccles, Joseph C. Wylie, and US Army Colonel Harry Summers. This group detected inconsistencies and contradictions regarding some of the concepts being advanced at the time. It responded by advocating rigorous critical thinking and analysis to identify redundant or vacuous notions and, in Summers's case, for a return to using the principles of war as strategic guidelines. Eccles and Wiley were aided by the able mind of Herbert Rosinski, a German émigré and strategy intellectual whom Weigley overlooked.

Chapters 3–5 analyze the substance of the revolution launched by the strategy intellectuals, to include Brodie's and Osgood's theories of limited war, Schelling's concepts of bargaining and compellence, as well as Kahn's unsettling explorations of escalation. Chapters 6–8 then examine the core ideas of the counterrevolutionaries, as propagated by Eccles, Wylie, and later Summers.

3 Bernard Brodie, Robert Osgood, and Limited War

Few strategic theorists did as much to initiate a revolution in the American way of thinking about war than Bernard Brodie. He was not only among the first of Weigley's strategy intellectuals to make an argument for a distinct way of thinking about limited war, a way that bears the imprint of British military theorist B. H. Liddell Hart, he also launched a sustained assault against the US military's first principles. By all accounts, Brodie was a formidable intellectual duelist who brought considerable analytical depth to any topic he addressed. Unfortunately, he often obscured the points he wished to make by employing a discursive and rhythmic writing style that at times rivaled Mahan's own. Despite his obvious success as a strategy intellectual, he remained largely dissatisfied with the amount of recognition he received in his lifetime. Partly, he blamed the lack of recognition on the Research and Development Corporation's (RAND's) lengthy procedures for clearing manuscripts; however, he also felt he had several peers but few equals. Some of his peers evidently agreed; as Thomas Schelling noted, "Bernard Brodie was first – in both time and distinction" among American academics who concerned themselves with military strategy in the 1950s.[1]

3.1 Self-Assured Intellectual

Bernard Brodie was born on May 20, 1910, in Chicago, Illinois, to Jewish-Russian emigres. He married Fawn McKay in 1936, author of several acclaimed biographies and one of the first women to become a tenured professor of history at the University of California Los Angeles.[2] Bernard and Fawn coauthored *From Crossbow to H-Bomb*, an examination of the application of science to warfare, which first appeared in 1962, at a time when interest in the relationship between history and technology had risen sharply due to the space race between the United States and the Soviet Union, as well as increased attempts to harness nuclear energy.[3] The book judged the state of military history at the time, perhaps correctly, as "sentimental" rather than analytical.[4] It also defined science in a manner Mahan would have understood, as the use of principles to describe nature, though all principles were also to be verified through experimentation and observation. In 1932, he received a bachelor of philosophy degree (PhB) and in 1940 a doctorate in international relations from the University of Chicago. He served on the faculty of Dartmouth College from 1941 to 1943, during which time he also held a commission in the US Naval Reserves. He wrote two primers on naval strategy, *Sea Power in the Machine Age* and *A Layman's Guide to Naval Strategy*, both at the behest of the US Chief of Naval Operations.[5] While Schelling hailed the latter work as "some of the best early 'systems analysis'" he had ever seen, Herbert Rosinski, the manuscript's principal reviewer, provided extensive comments that ultimately made the work a success.[6] Brodie duly acknowledged his debt to Rosinski, explaining he knew of no other person in America with a "surer comprehension of the whole field of naval strategy."[7] While Brodie sometimes corrected Schelling's use, or rather misuse, of history, his own usage had failings as well. Nonetheless, the strategy intellectual's research for *A Layman's Guide to Naval Strategy* gave him an understanding of Mahanian first principles and contributed to his impression of the habits of mind, the instincts, of military thinking.

After the Second World War, Brodie resigned his commission as a first lieutenant in the US Navy, and joined the International Relations Department at Yale University, and its Institute for International Studies. In 1946, he became a member of the first resident faculty group at the National War College and began annual lectures at the US Air War College the following year. Soon thereafter he began lecturing at the US Naval War College and the US Army War College. Shortly after the outbreak of the Korean War, Brodie was appointed to be a special assistant to the US Air Force Chief of Staff. In the autumn of 1951, he became a full-time consultant at RAND, and he and Fawn relocated to southern California, near Los Angeles. The year before they moved, their house in Bethany, Connecticut, was featured in *Your House and Home* magazine as a model of taste and decorum. With that, the Brodies essentially stepped firmly into the "golden age" of the American middle class. Brodie worked for RAND until 1966, producing a number of special reports, as well as his larger *Strategy in the Missile Age* (1959) and *Escalation and the Nuclear Option* (1966).[8] The former became required reading in civilian and military educational institutions across the United States.

Brodie also taught at the University of California, Los Angeles, from 1963 until he retired in 1977. In 1973, he published *War & Politics*, which he regarded as his most important work.[9] The book confirmed his legacy as the leading proponent of America's way of policy. In 1976, the year before his retirement, Brodie contributed two crucial essays to the Howard and Paret edition of *On War*: "The Continuing Relevance of *On War*" and "A Guide to the Reading of *On War*." Both contributions shaped, for both better and worse, Cold War interpretations of Clausewitz, especially the two interrelated ideas that war is the continuation of policy by other means and that, without policy's direction, war would escalate to its maximum extent.[10] Incidentally, Brodie, by his own insistence, received only a modest percentage of the royalties for his contributions to the Princeton edition of *On War*, preferring instead to take his reward in the "glory of the thing."[11] He died in 1978 after an unsuccessful battle with cancer.

3.2 Brodie's America – a Golden Age?

Brodie's America, which was also the America of the strategy and military intellectuals, was far removed from that of Mitchell, both in time as well as in character. It began with the "golden age" of the middle class in 1950 and ended with the slaying of four Kent State students in 1970. It saw the rise and fall of materialism and ultra-patriotism, of idealism and optimism. America's GDP more than doubled during this period, growing from $2.3 trillion to $4.9 trillion (in 2012 dollars). Its per capita income increased by nearly 60 percent during the same timeframe; while its population expanded by more than 70 percent, from 151 million in 1950 to 203 million in 1970.[12] The political geography of the United States had also changed, as it granted independence to the Philippines in 1946 (after suffering more than 85,000 casualties fighting to retain it). In addition, Hawaii and Alaska became states in 1959, bringing the official number of states to fifty.

The country climbed out of a short but severe depression caused by a postwar demobilization that put 10 million service personnel into the labor force, the cancellation of government contracts, industrial retooling for peacetime production, and waves of labor strikes involving some 5 million workers.[13] As employment rose, so did the demand for new goods: automobiles, televisions, refrigerators, stoves, washing machines, dryers, and dishwashers became the cherished commodities of the middle class.[14] Automobile sales increased 87 percent from 1950 to 1955, for instance, and by the following year Americans owned three-quarters of the world's automobiles.[15] In addition, suburbanization increased the demand for houses. America's domestic landscape changed as more people moved away from the cities to satellite communities like Levittown, Pennsylvania, named after William Levitt, a former

US Navy engineer. Homeownership climbed as premanufactured houses (prefabs) appeared at an astounding rate, nearly one per day in each of the Levittown locations, or some 38,000 homes per year.[16]

Although this period saw a rise in patriotism with the onset of the Cold War, that sentiment was also offset by sundry abuses of it, such as Senator Joseph McCarthy's relentless search for "un-American" activities which reached the State Department, academe, the media, Hollywood, and eventually the Army.[17] Few Americans approved of his methods. But few did much to curtail them either, perhaps due to fear. His charade of a crusade continued from early 1950 to the Army hearings of May 1954, in which he was finally discredited publicly. Shortly after McCarthy's downfall, Eccles expressed his regret that more officers had not spoken out against the senator sooner.[18]

Racially, the golden age of America saw every bit as much tension and divisiveness as in Mahan's day. President Truman issued Executive Order 9981 (July 1948) which mandated the desegregation of the armed forces.[19] America's armed forces generally resisted integration, however, insisting the services "had to follow, not precede, the integration of American society."[20] Black veterans of the Second World War and Korean War returned home believing they had contributed to a better life for themselves and for other Black Americans; however, in many areas they found little or no change. In March 1955, two years after the armistice that ended the Korean conflict, Brodie opened one of his Army War College lectures, "The Influence of Mass Destruction Weapons on Strategy," with a racist joke.[21] Five months later, on August 24, 1955, a fourteen-year-old Black youth named Emmitt Till was brutally murdered in Money, Mississippi, for allegedly whistling at a white woman; his murderers, two white men, were acquitted by an all-white jury, though they later admitted to being guilty. Less than four months after that, on December 1, 1955, Rosa Parks took inspiration from Till's death and refused to give up her seat on an Alabama bus to a white man, which in turn sparked a state-wide boycott of the bus company.

Thereafter, racial tensions in the United States escalated. In September 1957, President Eisenhower ordered federal troops to escort nine Black students, "the Little Rock Nine," to school in Little Rock, Arkansas. In the autumn of 1959, author and civil rights activist John Griffin darkened his skin for three months to experience life in "Black America"; he published his account of that experience in *Black Like Me* (1962).[22] On February 1, 1960, four Black students staged a sit-in at a drug store in Greensboro, North Carolina, that had refused to serve them.[23] In September 1962, President Kennedy sent US troops to restore order at the University of Mississippi when a riot broke out over the admission of a Black student, US veteran James Meredith; two people were killed and several hundred were injured.[24] In April 1963, civil rights leader Martin Luther King, Jr. was arrested in Birmingham, Alabama, and wrote his memorable "Letter from a Birmingham Jail," declaring "Injustice anywhere, is a threat to justice everywhere." In June of that year, President Kennedy federalized Alabama's National Guard to compel Governor George Wallace to allow two Black Americans to attend the University of Alabama, Tuscaloosa. In August 1963, King gave his memorable "I have a dream" speech in Washington, DC to an estimated 250,000 marchers.[25] From 1964 through 1967, waves of riots broke out in Chicago, Detroit, Harlem, Memphis, Newark, Philadelphia, and Rochester. In early 1965, five weeks after the assassination of activist Malcom X, Martin Luther King, Jr. led a series of demonstrations in Selma, Alabama, to protest practices that prevented Black Americans from registering to vote. Brodie could not have missed the riots that erupted in the Watts neighborhood of Los Angeles, barely twenty miles from his house in Pasadena. Smoke from the devastation was visible for twice that distance. Before the violence subsided, thirty-four people had been killed, more than 1,000 injured, and some 3,500 had been arrested.[26] Yet he refused to do anything more than marginalize the psychosocial dimension of strategy.

The invention of the television introduced a culture of its own during this period, one that quickly eclipsed the impact of the radio on public opinion.[27] All the major US networks covered Soviet leader Nikita Khrushchev's tour of the United States in September 1959, for instance, and by 1960, more than 90 percent of American households owned a television. Visual cues, such as physical bearing and body language, now counted as much as what was said; the network coverage of the 1960 debate between presidential candidates John F. Kennedy and Richard M. Nixon suggested as much; it tipped the scales toward the former presumably because he projected more confidence and vitality. Popular shows such as "Father Knows Best" (1954–60), "Leave It to Beaver" (1957–63), and "The Dick Van Dyke Show" (1961–66) presented America's middle class in idealized settings.

Although such shows generally portrayed women as happy in their roles as wife and mother, that image was challenged by Betty Friedan's *The Feminine Mystique* (1963).[28] Frieden revealed the fact that many women were essentially despondent because they were attempting to fulfill roles they had not chosen for themselves; she described it as the problem with "no name."[29] She and other women went on to help found the National Organization for Women (NOW) in 1966, and assisted in exposing harmful norms, such as paying women less than men for the same jobs, formal and informal quotas on the number of women who could be admitted into advanced degree programs, legal structures that prohibited married women from borrowing money in their own names, and which denied them control over their bodies.[30] This era also saw women begin analyzing the effects of sexist language in mainstream culture and literature.[31] It was knowledge Brodie, Kahn, and other US nuclear strategists of the period ought to have heeded; for they frequently used sexist language to explicate their theories.

But television also brought hits from Broadway and the silver screen into living rooms across the country, presenting images of vastly different Americas. Examples included playwright Lorraine Hansberry's award-winning drama *A Raisin in the Sun* (1959), which depicted the struggles of a Black family, the Youngers, attempting to realize a portion of the American dream; and *Guess Who's Coming to Dinner* (1967), which challenged middle-class assumptions about interracial marriages and exposed conflicting generational attitudes toward race. It was against this backdrop that Thomas Schelling attempted to gain a better understanding of the phenomenon of segregation by applying the tools of game theory and systems analysis.[32] But his models, though illustrative, failed to capture the complexity of the problem.

As Brodie began making his case for a revolution in America's way of thinking about war, he did so against the backdrop of commercial exploitation of public anxieties about nuclear warfare and Armageddon. Low budget science-fiction movies, such as *The Thing from Another World* (1951), *The Day the Earth Stood Still* (1951), and *The Day the World Ended* (1955) – which was released the same year American television sets depicted the first live detonation of an atomic bomb near Las Vegas, Nevada – and *Invasion of the Body Snatchers* (1956) capitalized on such fears.[33] For some viewers, the latter film warned against the insidious inhumanity of McCarthyism; for others, it cautioned against accepting the soulless doctrines of Communism. While the author and directors later denied coloring their work with any political messages, the public had little difficulty finding such meanings given the anxieties of the day.

America's golden age of the middle class also saw the emergence of the "cult of the rebel" in literature and entertainment. In 1951, author J. D. Salinger's *The Catcher in the Rye* was published, and quickly became a bestseller; the public embraced his iconoclastic character, Holden Caulfield, the "catcher," who claimed he only wanted to save innocent children, while at the same time condemning most establishment symbols as "phony." Films like *The Wild One* (1953), starring teen-idol Marlon Brando, and *Rebel without a Cause* (1955), with James Dean and Natalie Wood, also fueled the rebel spirit.[34] Dean died in an automobile accident one month before his movie's release, which all but made the film an instant sensation. Movies such as *Blackboard Jungle* (1955) countered the rebel theme by portraying classrooms as battlegrounds for America's youth, the enemies of which were gangs, alcohol, drugs – and a new style of music called Rock-and-Roll. The cult of the rebel gained additional momentum two years later with Jack Kerouac's *On the Road* (1957), which captured the dying jazz subculture of the 1940s through the book's main character, Dean Moriarty, an unrepentant rebel who remained obsessed with jazz and finding the next high. Also, in the fall of 1957, Elvis Presley debuted his talents in the blockbuster movie *Jailhouse Rock*. Trailers for the movie billed Presley as a "Rebel with a Voice" and a "Blackboard Jungle Kid," though he served honorably in the US Army a few years later, as did many of his peers.[35]

But the year 1957 was also one of notable contrasts. Against the rising popularity of the cult of the rebel, the publication of three hallmark works of US political and social science also took place: Osgood's *Limited War*, Kissinger's *Nuclear Weapons and Foreign Policy*, and Huntington's *Soldier and the State*. Not one displayed a sense for the undercurrents in American culture at the time. Indeed, even with the launching of Sputnik I and II by the Soviets in October and November of that year, which undoubtedly heightened anxieties, the United States clearly did not have a "culture of war." Nor did its youth, which would have to do the fighting, want one. In fact, it did not need one to fight Communism and carry out containment, despite later arguments to the contrary.[36] Instead, Brodie, Osgood and the other strategy intellectuals ought to have adjusted their theories and policy recommendations to account for the culture America did have, not the one they wished it had.

The sentiment of rebellion increased rapidly in the 1960s with the growth of America's counterculture movement, which was marked by a rejection of the values of the establishment, particularly the notion that war was a legitimate extension of politics by other means. Extremists, such as former Harvard professor and psychologist Timothy Leary, advised thousands of young Americans to "turn on, tune in, and drop out," and to use "mind expanding" drugs such as LSD.[37] But even mainstream teens could find little of their parents' generation worth preserving; the British music "invasion" of 1964, with bands like the Beatles, Kinks, and Rolling Stones offered novel sounds and styles, and the possibility of a new generational identity.[38] While some 250,000 Americans were drafted for military service in 1965, others publicly burned their draft cards, an act of civil disobedience and in open defiance of established authority.[39] The end of the decade saw the horrible culmination, though not the end, of these movements with the assassinations of King in Memphis, Tennessee, on April 4, 1968, and Robert F. Kennedy two months later, on June 6, 1968.[40] Hours before King's assassination, he had delivered his prophetic "I have been to the mountaintop speech." Kennedy's assassination was followed by riots at the Democratic National Convention in Chicago, which were televised globally.

To be sure, the counterculture movement came together peacefully in August 1969, at "Woodstock," a three-day concert that took place on a dairy farm near Bethel, New York. However, an effort to replicate Woodstock on the West Coast ended in bloodshed, thus crushing the optimism of a generation. Less than one year later, on May 4, 1970, four students were killed during a rally at Kent State University, and public support for the war declined further. Beforehand, America's strategy intellectuals had allowed themselves to dismiss the counterculture protestors as fringe elements without real political influence. But after the Kent State incident, the importance of the psychosocial dimension of strategy ought to have been abundantly evident to them.

3.3 Brodie's War on Traditional First Principles

In June 1946, Brodie's edited volume entitled *Absolute Weapon* was published.[41] It had only been nine months since the United States had dropped atomic bombs on the Japanese cities of Hiroshima and Nagasaki. While the bombing of Tokyo, Dresden, and other Axis cities during the war was horrific, atomic weapons meant entire cities could be destroyed by means of a single bomb delivered by a single aircraft. Loading such weapons on each bomber in the US arsenal meant entire continents could be wiped out in an afternoon. In short, atomic weapons had transformed warfare in unprecedented and as yet underappreciated ways.

By the time Brodie's *Absolute Weapon* appeared, talk of the revolutionary impact of the absolute weapon was already in the air, so to speak. The academy-award-winning movie *The Best Years of Our Lives* had finally been released in November, after being banned for a time in the United States. It treated realistically the return of three veterans from the Second World War – a bombardier, an Army noncommissioned officer, and a sailor – to their prewar lives, and gave voice several times to what newspapers and magazines had already suggested, the idea that atomic weapons had made war impossible. The movie's tone was at once hopeful and doubtful, however. Indeed, the hopeful side of the public's attitude may have been the main reason *Absolute Weapon* received favorable reviews. Of the book's 203 pages, only page 76 has been singled out by scholars as significant, and on it Brodie declared: "Thus far the chief purpose of our military establishment has been to win wars. From now on its chief purpose must be to avert them. It can have almost no other useful purpose."[42] These three sentences, which academics have since rightly interpreted as a call for a revolution in strategic thinking, may have done more to alter the course of American strategic thinking than the others combined.[43]

Specifically, Brodie's revolution would make the avoidance of escalation a principal aim of strategy. Even US Foreign Service Officer George Kennan, who had authored his famed Long Telegram just four months earlier, took approving note of the volume. "Best way to avoid atomic war," wrote Kennan, capturing the book's core message, "is to avoid war; best way to avoid war is to be prepared to resort to atomic warfare."[44] His comment conspicuously echoed Vegetius' ageless warning: "If you want peace, prepare for war."[45] But it also fell in step with the times. The end of the Second World War was followed by the rapid downsizing of conventional forces, which further underscored the idea that major wars had become things of the past. Rising unemployment, waves of labor strikes, and a short but sharp economic depression marked America's initial postwar years; hence, many US citizens had more to worry about than Kennan's call for a foreign policy aimed at containing Soviet expansion.

America's first strategy intellectual would indeed get his revolution, but not until the end of the 1950s. Throughout the ten years that followed the publication of *Absolute Weapon*, Brodie delivered lectures and wrote articles that attacked the assumptions underpinning what he deemed to be America's traditional way of thinking about war. Between 1946 and 1952, his lectures to the US military's war colleges challenged the priority the services typically assigned to operational thinking.[46] On March 17, 1950, he gave a presentation to the US Air War College entitled "The Problem of Integrating the Factors of National Strategy" in which he openly doubted whether war was ever the "continuation of diplomacy by other means," as Clausewitz had once said it was. Instead, Brodie asserted, armed conflict, "by its mere outbreak," demolished the diplomatic objectives of the preceding peace and replaced them with its own.[47] He then reversed his position some six months later, as he explained, because he had come to realize Clausewitz had meant to say war was an activity that was inseparable from diplomacy.[48] For Brodie, the issue was not just whether diplomacy should control war, which it obviously did, but whether war's grammar – its strategic rules and principles – should ever be allowed to channel policy's logic. In other words, military leaders could not continue to regard war's grammar as inviolable.

Brodie made similar points in a RAND report dated September 4, 1951, in which he explicitly demolished the rationale for the principle of concentration. He turned the expression "getting thar fustest with the mostest" on its head by reminding his readers the Confederate general who purportedly uttered the phrase was on the side that lost.[49] Similarly, in January 1954 he published an article in *Foreign Affairs* entitled "Nuclear Weapons: Strategic or Tactical?" In it, he both anticipated and questioned the logic of the Eisenhower administration's doctrine of "massive retaliation," as any small conflict could explode into a larger one if the White House had only one military response and unless the United States "placed certain restraints upon ourselves and of using our formidable atomic power to force the enemy into observing similar constraints."[50] The doctrine, announced by Secretary of State John Foster Dulles on January 12, 1954, hewed closely to the US military's traditional imperatives.[51] It was intended to be ambiguous and thus to allow US policymakers to choose a level of response appropriate to the situation; as Eisenhower attempted to explain, massive retaliation "did not mean there was only one US response. That is just nonsense."[52] In fact, the country's thirty-fourth president exercised quite a bit of strategic flexibility in his use of force, as evidenced, for instance, in his "third option," that is, CIA-led operations. By the end of 1954, the former Supreme Commander of Allied Forces in Europe had exercised the third option in Indonesia, Tibet, Laos, the Congo, Iran, and Guatemala. Eisenhower also knew at the time the Soviet Union lagged behind the United States in nuclear-capable missiles and bombers; massive retaliation amounted, therefore, to little more than a nuclear version of the "gunboat diplomacy" of the nineteenth and early twentieth centuries by which larger states cowed smaller ones into acquiescence. Questions, nonetheless, quickly arose as to what circumstances the United States might deem sufficient for the employment of atomic weapons; the strategy intellectuals were not shy about offering their perspectives.

In the spring of 1954, Brodie delivered another lecture at the US Army War College, which, like the others, underscored the need for a shift in the American way of thinking about war. During the era of "total war," he said, traditional strategic principles had practically turned armed conflict into an "end in itself"; now, however, wars had to be fought with greater levels of self-imposed restraint.[53] In addition, in November 1954, *The Reporter* published Brodie's article entitled "Unlimited Weapons and Limited War," which dismantled the accepted argument for preventative or "blunting" wars. The concept of preventative wars clearly derived from the core principles of concentration, offensive action, and decision by battle; however, the concept and its principles would fail in practice, the strategy intellectual warned, because it was not possible to be sure of eliminating all the enemy's atomic weapons. That fact, in turn, would leave the United States vulnerable to a devastating counterstrike; ergo, America needed the capability to fight "limited wars for limited objectives. Fighting within such parameters, Brodie concluded, need not necessarily mean waging "war without victory."[54]

The point concerning victory was an important and timely one. Only a few years had elapsed since the public hearings that followed Truman's relief of General MacArthur for insubordination in April 1951. (Incidentally, rising Republican leaders, such as Richard Nixon, had advocated for the reinstatement of MacArthur, though for reasons having more to do with enhancing their own political profiles than agreeing with his side of the controversy.) The hearings revealed at least two conflicting concepts of victory among US military leaders. One of these was MacArthur's by now well-traveled statement that there can be "no substitute for victory," though it was often taken out of context. The other was General Omar Bradley's testimony that victory could be a matter of degree and need not be absolute, as MacArthur's expression implied.[55] Thereafter, the problem of defining victory would reappear frequently in US military doctrine. Even in the age of Mahan, the meaning of victory was mutable and susceptible to political manipulation. The idea of absolute victory was the exception rather than the rule; yet military and policy practitioners readily believe otherwise even in the twenty-first century.

In 1955, Brodie published an article in *Harper's Magazine* arguing that "most of the military ideas and axioms of the past are now or will soon be inapplicable."[56] In 1956, in lectures delivered first at the US Naval War College then at the US Army War College, Brodie outlined how the nature of "modern" (atomic-age) limited war differed from past concepts.[57] In previous eras, armed conflicts were constrained mainly by the want of resources; in the present day, limited wars required belligerents to accept voluntary restraints. Each party must restrict itself willingly, "for the sake of inducing the enemy to hobble himself to a comparable degree." Accordingly, a "revolution" was required in the way Americans typically thought about war and peace, the aim of which must be the rejection of some cherished beliefs, such as the notion there was "no substitute for victory."[58] In fact, many of the classic axioms of strategy, Brodie said, had to go, though, as ever, he was conspicuously stingy with specifics.

Among the few principles he mentioned, however, were those Mahan had brought into the twentieth century, namely, striking first and with the greatest amount of force. First-strike capabilities, as he repeatedly insisted, only fostered insecurity. Second-strike capabilities, on the other hand, reduced anxiety and instability, and promoted deterrence by assuring any opening strike would be met with an overwhelming retaliation. Likewise, in 1957, the year in which two crucial limited-war treatises appeared (Osgood's *Limited War* and Kissinger's *Nuclear Weapons and Foreign Policy*), America's foremost strategy intellectual delivered a lecture to the Staff College at Fort Leavenworth entitled "The Worth of Principles of War." Brodie described how military principles were once viewed as constituent elements of a "body of knowledge" and later evolved into "rules of correct action."[59] Neither perspective, he explained, appreciated the fact that differences in historical contexts can render knowledge and rules invalid. Dogmatic adherence to any given principle, as is the habit of the military mind, said Brodie, created a manner of thinking that hindered the ability to understand when circumstances had changed such that the principle itself was worthless or, worse, self-defeating.

In the summer of 1958, coincidental with the release of the US Army's operational manual FM 100-5, which contained references to limited war, Brodie drafted a working paper for RAND entitled "The Meaning of Limited War."[60] In it, he criticized the doctrine of massive retaliation for its lack of flexibility. He also continued to hammer home his earlier messages regarding the nature of modern limited wars – which required conscious self-restraint in terms of means, open communications with the foe, and the willingness to pursue limited objectives. The "limitations on warfare are nothing to be taken for granted," he wrote; "on the contrary, they will require great care, effort, and sacrifice to achieve and maintain."[61] It was unfortunate, he said, that limited war had become synonymous with proxy war, as that only confused the issue; likewise, the public's reaction to the MacArthur hearings had unnecessarily cast limited war in a negative light. While total war had not disappeared, practically every military principle or slogan had to be rethought, he argued, including "Clausewitz's classic definition that the object of war is to impose one's will on the enemy."[62] This kind of thinking underpinned "unlimited" rather than limited wars, he said. Brodie's argument also broached a question the Clausewitz scholar Michael Handel would address later, specifically whether it would be useful to "square" Clausewitz's trinity by adding a dimension that accounted for the potentially transformative effect of new technologies.[63]

All told, Brodie's lectures to the US military's senior service schools did more than lay the groundwork for a theory of limited war. They hammered away at the military's traditional imperatives, its instincts, which he believed, with justification, underpinned the American way of thinking about war. His lectures reached more than a dozen year groups, half a generation of officers, who varied in rank and experience: from captains and majors at the staff colleges to lieutenant colonels and colonels at the war colleges. To what extent he influenced them, however, is impossible to say. Influence is notoriously difficult to trace, and its effects can prove fleeting. Many of the officers whom Brodie lectured, moreover, had participated in the limited war that unfolded in Korea. From a tactical perspective, that conflict differed little from the Second World War, save for certain rules of engagement. While veterans of those two conflicts might have accepted Brodie's argument regarding the inappropriateness of Jominian core principles, they would have doubted whether his claims also held for the other principles of war: objective, economy of force, security, unity of effort, and simplicity. Those guidelines appeared valid still. In any case, America's first strategy intellectual rarely discussed those basic guidelines. Instead he aimed for a fundamental turnaround based on one core principle, the primacy of policy. In Brodie's words, this was the "single most important idea in all of strategy."[64] Only policy could save war from becoming an end in itself because only policy could give war intelligent, rather than impulsive direction. Of course, Brodie's imperative presumed policy's IQ was up to the task.

3.4 A Doctrine of Limited War

Robert Osgood's *Limited War: The Challenge to American Strategy* was published in early 1957, just as controversies over nuclear weapons testing, the dangers of radioactive fallout, and fears of an inadvertent nuclear war were intensifying.[65] Osgood's book suggested American strategists had to find a way to live with the bomb, namely by submitting to a doctrine of limited war. In the volume's introduction, the German émigré and doyen of realist international relations theory Hans Morgenthau said Osgood had set for himself a herculean task in trying to resolve a twofold problem for American strategy: first, to develop a workable alternative to massive retaliation, which by now had become a catchall for the collective anxieties related to nuclear war; and, second, to win approval for that alternative by exposing the deficiencies in America's evident preference for waging unlimited wars.[66] This latter task, however, derived from the subjective interpretations of Morgenthau and Osgood, who not surprisingly understood the American way of war through the refractive lens of the Second World War.

A native of St. Louis, Osgood enlisted in the Army of the United States in February 1943, at the age of twenty-two, and served stateside throughout the Second World War. He was thus acquainted with the regimentation of military life. But he had no direct combat experience. After the war, he attended Harvard University, and eventually received a doctorate in political science. In 1953, he published *Ideals and Self-Interest in America's Foreign Relations*, which was well received and, according to one scholar, left an enduring and constructive legacy in the field of political science.[67] By 1956, Osgood had become an assistant professor in political science at the University of Chicago. Five years later, he received an appointment to a professorship in the School of Advanced International Studies (SAIS) at Johns Hopkins University. From 1965 to 1973, he held the position of Director of the Washington Center for Foreign Policy Research; in 1969, he was selected to serve on Henry Kissinger's advisory staff. From 1973 to 1979, he served as the Dean of SAIS and published *Limited War Revisited* in his final year there. He was also selected to be an advisor to Ronald Reagan during the 1980 presidential campaign, and three years later was appointed to George Schultz's policy planning council. He was thus both a political theorist and a policy advisor. He was not the intellectual powerhouse that was Brodie; however, he managed to achieve more influence as a policy advisor than did America's foremost strategy intellectual.

Although American diplomacy clearly needed an alternative to massive retaliation, Osgood's attempt to deliver one in *Limited War* met with mixed reviews. One of those reviews came from Brodie, who described the work as "impressive" and "often incisive," but ultimately "disappointing." He found its "scholarship" wanting since it ignored most of the "better specimens" of secondary literature on the subject (especially his own); the "author surveys the material in each chapter almost as though he were the first to arrive on the terrain."[68] The criticism was accurate: Osgood had barely mentioned any of the secondary literature. Another reviewer suggested, presciently, that Osgood's proposal for an American foreign policy based on limited war was "an unsatisfactory focus" for the times because the strategic situation was far too complex for it.[69] Others found the doctrine itself to be little more than an uninspired "restatement of basic postulates."[70] Rosinski once asked Osgood to give him proper credit for the ideas he borrowed from his research on war and strategy, but the limited war theorist declined.[71] To be sure, new ideas almost always encounter negative reactions. Nonetheless, the criticisms also raised valid points: Osgood had not synthesized the existing literature, had not given credit where it was due, and had not presented a wholly original doctrine.

Like Brodie, Osgood believed the advent of nuclear weapons required a thorough rethinking of the "traditional American attitudes concerning the nature of war and the relationship between force and policy." Americans, he thought, typically disassociated power and policy, or war and diplomacy, thus making it difficult to wage limited wars. Unfortunately, Osgood's historical examples were inadequate, and he never considered any of America's small wars, its use of "gunboat" diplomacy, its many interventions in the Latin America, or whether some degree of separation was healthy for a democracy. He was right, however, to criticize America's rather short-sighted mobilization–demobilization cycle: "unpreparedness, mobilization, overwhelming offensive, total victory, and demobilization."[72] While the cycle enabled America to win wars, it did little to deter them because it took US military power "off the table" in foreign policy terms. It also deprived America's political leaders of experience in leveraging military power. Nonetheless, Osgood overstated his case. This cycle has adversely affected military readiness, which has resulted in a mixed record for "America's first battles."[73] Yet the cycle persisted for powerful reasons having to do primarily with avoiding the costs of maintaining large military forces, as well as with remaining unencumbered by Europe's internal struggles for power.[74] Osgood, therefore, assisted in furthering the sense that Americans do not know how to use military power wisely; yet history suggests the inability to employ military force wisely is not an uniquely American trait. Nor can he be faulted for not considering Huntington's theory of "objective control," which presupposed some separation for the sake of civilian control of the military, as the concept had just been published in *Soldier and the State* in the same year.[75] Nevertheless, Osgood's argument failed to consider the possibility that the merging of power and policy would result eventually in the militarization of US foreign policy, and thus the elimination of policy's primacy.

By mischaracterizing the American way of war as employing the utmost military power to achieve victory, Osgood revealed the extent to which his thinking had been influenced by the world wars, especially the Second World War. "Americans," he asserted, "think of every conflict as an unlimited war," and believe "restricting the use of force is morally and emotionally repugnant," even though it would accord with "democratic and Christian principles."[76] Admittedly, the United States mobilized for the Second World War as if it were an unlimited war. Yet a longer historical perspective, from the end of the Civil War to America's golden age of the middle class, suggests Washington's preferred style was to intervene "on the cheap" and then to require its military leaders to improvise.

Osgood's appreciation for the "Communist way of war" was as impressionistic as his interpretation of the American way of war. He believed

"Bolsheviks" regarded every armed conflict as a war of national liberation, which thereby freed them of moral dilemmas and made their uses of force at once "just" and "necessary." The Communist approach to war, he added, was well suited to the realities of the nuclear age since the writings of Marx, Lenin, and Mao, among others, considered armed conflict as nothing more than the continuation of political intercourse by other means. Osgood's simplistic views, which painted the Soviets and Chinese as more ideologically monolithic and militarily adept than they were, certainly aligned with the times. After all, the Communists appeared to hold the upper hand with the loss of mainland China to Mao in 1949, the Sino-Soviet treaty the following year, Ho Chi Minh's victory over the French in 1954, the establishment of the Warsaw Pact in 1955 (albeit in response to the founding of NATO in 1949), and the Soviet intervention in Hungary in 1956.

Given such events, it was obvious the United States needed an alternative to the Eisenhower administration's official doctrine of massive retaliation (and unofficial "third option"). But it was not obvious the alternative should be limited wars, which Osgood defined as conflicts fought for "concrete, well-defined objectives that do not demand the utmost military effort."[77] If the objective was foremost to avoid war and secondarily to blunt or impede Soviet influence, then Kennan's "measures short of war" offered a better option. The Korean conflict, which halted (rather than ended) with an armistice, served as Osgood's model for a doctrine of limited war. "One can hardly overestimate," he wrote, "the importance of the United States' achievement in containing the Communist attack on South Korea without precipitating total war."[78] Historians have since debated, however, how limited the Korean conflict actually was.[79] In Osgood's mind, though, the American public and its leaders had adapted to the strategic situation and pursued concrete, clearly defined objectives short of unconditional surrender. He also listed several of the conflicts of the eighteenth century, most of the nineteenth-century wars, and the struggle in Indochina as limited wars. This last example was unsustainable, since it was a civil war in which the objectives of the Vietminh were not limited. To strengthen his case, Osgood went so far as to mischaracterize unlimited wars, describing them as conflicts fought for "no well-defined objectives" other than "destruction of the enemy," or for goals which threaten values "so important as to be beyond compromise and which, therefore, compel the belligerents to exert their utmost military capacity toward breaking the enemy's will to resist and securing an unconditional surrender."[80] But it is difficult to imagine clearer goals. He also misrepresented unconditional surrender as "antipolitical," or at best "apolitical," ascribing an instinctive rather than rational character to it; in fact, survival is the highest of political stakes.[81]

Two other essential works appeared within months of Osgood's *Limited War*; both strengthened his argument while also drawing attention away from him. The first of these was Henry Kissinger's comprehensive and eloquent *Nuclear Weapons and Foreign Policy* (1957).[82] Kissinger, at the time the Associate Director of the Center for International Affairs at Harvard University, insisted, not unlike Brodie, that nuclear weapons had revolutionized strategy. As the "power of modern weapons grows," he warned, "the threat of all-out war loses its credibility and therefore its political effectiveness." Nor had America's "capacity for massive retaliation" averted crises such as the Korean War, the loss of northern Indochina, the Soviet–Egyptian arms deal, or the Suez crisis.[83] On the other hand, a coherent limited war doctrine could restore the political utility of force. Limited wars, moreover, were not merely small-scale, all-out wars; rather, they attempted "to *affect* the opponent's will, not to *crush* it," a distinction that also appeared in Thomas Schelling's *Arms and Influence* a decade later. "The purpose of limited war," Kissinger declared, "is to inflict losses or to pose risks for the enemy out of proportion to the objectives under dispute."[84] This statement, in fact, foreshadowed how he would direct the Vietnam War; and, as he discovered, this approach cut both ways. A doctrine of limited war, he also stressed, should not eschew the use of nuclear weapons, since to do so invited an opponent to use them first and thus to catch the United States offguard. Moreover, a doctrine that included the potential use of nuclear weapons would likely give belligerents reason to pause and to consider each escalatory step carefully before taking it. Only by fully integrating such weapons into a comprehensive doctrine of limited war could the threat of their use be made credible; only with such credibility could deterrence have its best chance to work.[85]

In contrast to Osgood's book, reviews of *Nuclear Weapons and Foreign Policy* were openly positive. Most congratulated its author for the "magnitude of his effort and the depth and power of [his] analysis."[86] Also, Mike Wallace interviewed Kissinger on *60 Minutes*, affording the would-be diplomat an opportunity to state his case more clearly to the public. But several reviewers disagreed with Kissinger's conclusions. Morgenthau, for one, believed it would be almost impossible to keep a conflict limited once nuclear weapons had been used.[87] Another exception came from Brodie. Kissinger's bibliography had not included Brodie's "Unlimited Weapons and Limited War," published in *The Reporter* in November 1954. Brodie confided in Max Ascoli, editor of

The Reporter, that he suspected the omission to be "deliberate and for petty motives."[88] Kissinger was never above being petty, but the problem was also his style. The book was only sparsely footnoted, not an uncommon practice for the time. Just as he had done in his Harvard dissertation, Kissinger had made liberal use of, and built upon, others' ideas, which invariably obscured where their thoughts ended and his began.[89] It also dovetailed with his later reputation for distorting the truth. In any case, Kissinger listed several of Brodie's works in the bibliography of *Nuclear Weapons and Foreign Policy*, and later admitted his book had been "very much influenced" by Brodie's ideas.[90] The bibliography also referred to Osgood's *Limited War* favorably, as a "very good study of the problems of limited war both historically and in relation to contemporary strategy."[91]

The second important work that promoted Osgood's argument for the doctrine of limited war was former US Foreign Service Officer Robert McClintock's policy paper, "National Doctrine for Limited War."[92] The document was deliberately light on theory; however, McClintock, who had experience in Vietnam and Lebanon, had drafted it for the express purpose of moving the doctrine closer to practice. He applauded the principle of exercising restraint, of having the "courage not 'to push the button,'" and he repeated the general fixation with moving away from Eisenhower's massive retaliation – which ironically Eisenhower had already done. In 1967, McClintock expanded the paper and published it as a book, *The Meaning of Limited War*, which offered a thin, encyclopedia-style analysis of contemporary limited wars: the Greek Civil War (1946–49), the Korean War (1950–53), the Arab–Israeli War (1947–49), the Suez Crisis (1956), the American Intervention in Lebanon (1958), the Indo-Chinese conflict (1962), the French Colonial War in Vietnam (1946–50), and the French-Communist War in Vietnam (1950–54). The volume is significant, however, for carrying forward a critical error in not appreciating "'wars of national liberation'" as consisting of potentially powerful motives, instead of being sham revolutions that gave the West "no reason to be less confident of victory."[93] In fact, genuine revolutions required the West to examine the psychosocial staying power of the societies involved, including its own. McClintock's dim view of wars of national liberation was emblematic of the US approach through most of the 1960s. Put differently, instead of asking themselves what kind of war they were about to embark upon, as Clausewitz suggested, America's chief policy and military practitioners told themselves what kind of conflict they needed to have, as the US involvement in Vietnam began to escalate.

3.5 Limited War's Missing Dimension

The psychosocial dimension of war was conspicuously absent from limited war theory, except with respect to managing public opinion. Nonetheless, contemporary works addressing the topic of social motivation were abundant. Some, such as George Tanham's *Communist Revolutionary Warfare* (1961), described in detail the motivational methods typically employed by "Communist revolutionary warfare."[94] Likewise, in 1962, Peter Paret's and John Shy's *Guerrillas in the 1960's* explained how local recruits were "enrolled not only by administrative machinery, but also by some powerful idea – love of country, hatred of the foreigner, envy of the rich landowner." To be sure, social pressure and terror played roles as well; however, such pressure required an element of "individual conviction" to compel participation in this "most punishing kind of combat." All the better if the conviction were rooted in "real problems, real hopes and fears."[95] Two years later, the CIA's Major-General Edward Lansdale published "Do We Understand Revolution?," in which he described the Vietnam conflict as a "people's war." Lansdale urged the US government to adjust its strategy accordingly.[96] Despite the overwhelming amounts of troops, money, materiel, well-meant American advice, and the impressive statistics of casualties inflicted on the Viet Cong, the "Communist subversive insurgents have grown steadily stronger," argued Lansdale.[97] The West needed a counter-idea, a "heartfelt *cause*," such as independence, if it hoped to rally the Vietnamese people against Communism. The writings of Professor Douglas Pike, a US Army veteran of the Second World War and later a Foreign Service Officer with an impressive record of assignments in Asia, documented Hanoi's commitment to the goal of national reunification, while using Communist techniques and principles as instruments toward that end.[98] While Pike's works came under criticism from experts such as Tanham for portraying the insurgency as stronger than sources indicated, Pike and his critics certainly agreed the Communists were highly motivated.[99]

Similarly, John J. McCuen's *The Art of Counter-Revolutionary War* (1966), later counted among the classics of counterinsurgency theory, put a fine point on motivational factors.[100] McCuen proposed countering revolutionary warfare by inverting its key principles. Much of counterinsurgency doctrine was, he said, based on the inverse of the principles of a people's war. Counterrevolutionary warfare required concerted and sustained political and social efforts, not just military measures.[101] The support of the indigenous populace would not suffice, he added; the people had to be recruited, trained, and fully integrated into the state's counterrevolutionary effort. In other words, successful counterinsurgency efforts required measures that challenged the rules and conditions Osgood had developed for limited war. A problematic assumption underpinned McCuen's recommendations, however, namely, that the populace would naturally grasp the wisdom of supporting the government over the revolutionaries. In sum, though imperfect and perhaps too late in some cases, information pointing to the psychosocial dimension of the nature of the wars at hand was amply available to America's leading strategic thinkers.

3.6 Osgood's First Principles

Like Clausewitz, Osgood defined armed conflict as an instrument of policy. Accordingly, he considered the "primacy of political ends over military aims and means" to be war's most essential principle; he regarded minimal force, applying "no greater force than is necessary," as war's second principle.[102] These principles, which coincided with those of Brodie, effectively described an American way of policy. In addition, Osgood outlined three "conditions" that must obtain for limited war: (1) the fighting should involve only a small number of major participants, preferably two; (2) hostilities should be contained geographically and attacks should be restricted to military targets only; and (3) the war should require only a minimal commitment of the belligerents' human and material resources, and it should not disrupt their economic, political, and social patterns of life. He also added three "rules" for limited war: (1) heads of state had to restrict the nature of their political objectives, and clearly communicate those objectives to their opponents; (2) open communications had to be maintained throughout all stages of the conflict to enable negotiations to commence at the earliest possible time; and (3) the physical dimensions of the conflict had to be restricted insofar as doing so was compatible with the political objectives.[103]

Although some of these principles, conditions, and rules obtained in the Korean conflict, Vietnam was a different story. The primacy of policy was maintained, with some exceptions, in Vietnam, though the US military struggled to reconcile its Jominian instincts with policy's druthers. The idea of minimal force became almost meaningless: nuclear weapons were not used, but the United States dropped a greater tonnage of bombs on Hanoi and its environs than in all of the Second World War. The fighting involved more than two parties, and hostilities were not containable geographically, as they often spilled over into Laos and Cambodia; the war was, moreover, enormously disruptive of belligerents' patterns of life in both North and South Vietnam, and as antiwar protests escalated in the late 1960s, for the United States as well.

Communications remained essentially open throughout the conflict; however, Washington only slowly appreciated how committed Hanoi was to reunification. In addition, the White House had difficulty communicating its goals to the American public clearly enough to sustain its support.

Osgood's *Limited War Revisited*, published in 1979, four years after the North Vietnamese Army captured Saigon, offered no new principles for limited war.[104] The book essentially amounted to an apology, admitting the doctrine of limited war had failed in Vietnam, but asserting it was nonetheless the "mainstay of containment" due to its "inherent elasticity."[105] Osgood acknowledged the costs had exceeded the benefits of the US involvement in Vietnam; he also conceded that the domino theory ought to have been examined more thoroughly.[106] He refrained, however, from concluding it meant policy could not be likened to reason or intelligence without substantial caveats.

Osgood went on to describe three categories of limited war: (1) local, that is, potential conflicts that might involve conventional forces and possibly limited nuclear weapons; (2) unconventional, including revolutionary and counterrevolutionary conflicts, insurgencies and counterinsurgencies, as well as the techniques of guerrilla warfare, terrorism, insurrection, or subversion; and (3) central limited wars, those that might involve a nuclear exchange at the outset.[107] While Osgood attempted to impart an "elasticity" to limited war theory by extending it across these categories, his effort fell short; for, as the Vietnam War demonstrated, if even one belligerent were to pursue unlimited aims in any category, the conflict would not be limited in the sense Osgood desired.

For Brodie, Osgood, and Kissinger, limited war was, of course, also about signaling one's intentions in advance. As such, it permitted parties to play the old game of great power competition with self-imposed restrictions, in a word, to play chess without putting the other player's king in check. Accordingly, neither the US military nor the American public could be allowed anything more than a nominal role in the formulation of something so delicate and yet powerful as military strategy. Putting the theory into practice, nonetheless, raised difficult questions: if fighting and dying decided nothing, but merely allowed the game to continue, why not stop the game altogether? Or, if it must be played, why not play it only with measures short of war?

The Americans of Mahan's and Mitchell's eras would not have asked such questions. But the Americans of the 1950s and 1960s, the Americans of the so-called golden age of the middle class and of the social turmoil of the 1960s, did ask them. The fact that they did so underscores the essentiality of the psychosocial dimension of armed conflict. Many of these Americans served selflessly in Vietnam and elsewhere and opted to put their faith in the country's political and military leadership; however, many more came to believe measures short of war, arms control agreements, and peace overtures offered better solutions for their world. Their answers ultimately prevailed.

The failure of the United States to wage a successful limited war in Vietnam, however, created a powerful myth to the effect that any conflict less than an all-out war was somehow antithetical to the American character.[108] That was not the case. As the history of US armed conflict into the twenty-first century shows, Americans have frequently used military force in limited ways, and for limited aims. But the point of failure was the particular doctrine of limited war espoused by Brodie, Osgood, Kissinger, and later others. It failed, moreover, because it presupposed a tacitly, if not explicitly, cooperative enemy willing to operate within agreed-upon parameters. It compounded that error by excluding an entire dimension of conflict from the crafting of strategy; whereas that dimension was integral to the wars at hand.

3.7 Conclusions

Neither Brodie, nor Osgood, nor Kissinger thought to ask themselves whether, in the spirit of Clausewitz, they understood the nature of the war they were about to undergo. Rather, they attempted to turn the war in Vietnam into what they wished it to be. They approached war's psycho-social dimension largely as an educational problem: the public was to be educated in the rationale for the war in Vietnam and the need to fight it in a limited manner. As Kissinger explained in 1957, "The American people must be made aware that, with the end of our atomic monopoly, all-out war has ceased to be an instrument of policy, except as a last resort, and that for most of the issues likely to be in dispute our only choice is between a strategy of limited war and inaction."[109] He was wrong, of course; for, as Kennan had made clear a decade earlier, inaction was not the only option the United States had besides limited war.

Brodie, Osgood, and Kissinger did not consider human nature to be the driver of war's nature in the way Mahan and Mitchell had. Warfare itself had become more mechanistic, more process driven, more techno-centric. Reflecting the era's infatuation with systems analysis, which had influenced each of them, they viewed armed conflict as a system. But in so doing, they divested war's nature of its human element. Their model also derived, in part, from superficial analyses of military escalation as it unfolded in the world wars, a misunderstanding of which they were all guilty; their narrow reading of Clausewitz's *On War* reinforced that view.

But it mostly derived from the entirely reasonable fear that something could go wrong in the atomic age that would trigger a mutually devastating escalation to an all-out war. War, by its nature, seemed poised to escalate, to uncoil almost automatically, despite humanity's desire to intervene on its own behalf.

Ironically, this paradigm developed less from actual changes in war's character than from perceived ones. The Soviet Union initially had nothing comparable to the nuclear arsenal US intelligence estimates claimed it had. But the perception grew that its arsenal was significant and expanding, which provided the impetus necessary for the emergence of the coiled-spring paradigm. In any case, material reality eventually caught up with perception, and escalation increased from a possibility to a probability.

4 Thomas Schelling and War as Bargaining and Coercion

Harvard economist and Nobel laureate Thomas Schelling, undoubtedly the most academically successful of the strategy intellectuals, proposed two seminal concepts during the golden age of American strategic thinking that paired well with limited war theory. These concepts were the bargaining model of war, which saw every aspect of warfare as the product of active if not always conscious consent; and strategic coercion, which involved compelling or deterring adversaries rather than subduing them. The purpose of limited war, after all, was to arrive at a settlement short of total submission, while also avoiding unwanted escalation. Those aims presupposed a willingness, by all parties involved, to bargain. Likewise, bargaining implies some degree of coercion. Each of these foundational concepts gave rise to multiple subdisciplines in international relations, some of which employ the bargaining model to explain how and why warring parties settle when they do; others push Schelling's binary construction of compellence and deterrence further, converting it into a formula almost despite themselves.[1] Schelling's two seminal concepts, moreover, reveal a model of war's nature akin to that of Brodie and Osgood. But in Schelling's model armed conflict is inherently more unstable because of the intrinsic dynamism of bargaining itself.

4.1 Idiosyncratic Game Theorist

Despite his renown as a twentieth-century strategic theorist, Schelling's many writings ultimately contributed more to pure reason, in the form of game theory, than to practical reason, as something strategic practitioners could use. Brodie, for instance, once endorsed Schelling's *Arms and Influence*, somewhat ambivalently, as a book of "great value, especially to people who are relatively newcomers to the field, though it has, like everything of Schelling's, some quite novel and original ideas."[2] The blurb could just as easily have described Schelling's works in general; for they represent a vexing but sometimes rewarding mixture of the pedestrian and the brilliant, and the original and the idiosyncratic. While Schelling elicited Brodie's assistance in broadening the thrust of *Arms and Influence* so it would appeal to the general reader, the book's overall perspective remained invariably that of the game theorist. As a result, Brodie was largely "dissatisfied" with it, as Schelling later surmised.[3]

Thomas Crombie Schelling was born into a navy family on April 14, 1921, eleven years after Brodie and four months before Osgood. Unlike them, he did not serve in the Second World War, even in a reserve capacity, though he tried. Both the US Army and US Navy found him physically unfit for military duty. He had no military experience to speak of, therefore, and would later attempt to compensate for it by reading military history and memoirs.[4] Those substitutions, however, never sufficed. During the war, Schelling worked as an analyst for the US Bureau of the Budget, and in 1944 he received a bachelor's degree in economics from the University of California, Berkeley. After the war, he assisted in administering the Marshall Plan along with serving as a foreign aid advisor to the Truman administration. In 1951, he completed a doctorate in economics through Harvard University and, by 1956, had joined the faculty at Yale University. Within a year, he had published two important articles: "An Essay on Bargaining" and "Bargaining, Communication, and Limited War."[5]

The latter essay appeared in print almost simultaneously with Osgood's *Limited War*. It is said to mark the beginning of Schelling's transition from an economist to a strategist, a transition that critics contend, with some justification, he never fully accomplished.[6] He sent a prepublication copy of "Bargaining, Communication, and Limited War" to Brodie, who responded by saying he had published similar ideas half a decade earlier in several classified RAND documents, and in two publicly accessible journals. Brodie ended the letter by highlighting a discrepancy in Schelling's reference to the nonuse of gas warfare in the Second World War.[7] Inaccurate or incomplete historical references would plague Schelling's works throughout, however. In 1958, Schelling, influenced by advances in game theory made by mathematician John von Neumann and economist Oskar Morgenstern, connected his concept of conflict behavior to game theory. He is said, thereby, to have revolutionized the field of strategic competition along the lines of his bargaining model; perhaps, however, he merely created a parallel path for it.[8] In 1960, he joined the faculty at Harvard University and shortly thereafter took up employment with RAND as a senior researcher. By 1965, he was sought out by Assistant Defense Secretary John McNaughton to assist in developing the strategic concept for the Vietnam conflict, especially as regards the ill-fated bombing campaign known as "Rolling Thunder."[9] Schelling himself admitted his theory and the campaign were connected, though the full extent of his involvement remains unclear.[10] In 1970, Schelling had a public falling out with fellow Harvard alumnus Henry Kissinger over the Nixon administration's expansion of the war into Cambodia.[11] The economist-turned-strategist then terminated his role as an advisor and was unable to influence US defense policy, as he "no longer had an audience."[12]

Schelling plausibly denied his theories directly influenced America's Cold War policies. Influence is difficult to trace, in any case, and policy-makers rarely give credit to outside sources. Nonetheless, the core principles of bargaining and coercion have obviously shaped contemporary US military strategy, in both theory and practice. Moreover, many of the terms he invented, such as tipping points and collateral damage, have become widespread among defense and security professionals. In addition, Schelling's two major works, *Strategy of Conflict* (1960), which represents human behavior in conflict as a bargaining process, and *Arms and Influence* (1966), which explores how to leverage that process through the threat of harm, continue to inform research into strategic theory.[13]

In fact, Nobel Laureate Roger Myerson referred to *Strategy of Conflict* as a "masterpiece that should be recognized as one of the most important and influential books in social theory."[14] Schelling's contemporary, Osgood, once hailed him as the "most influential exponent" of those theorists who linked limited war and game theory.[15] Even Brodie, though older by almost a dozen years, held Schelling's intellect in high regard. "One is bound to feel when one finds oneself disagreeing with you," Brodie once wrote, "that one is wrong."[16] Despite an awkward start in the late 1950s when the two first met, they developed what Brodie described as a "rugged friendship" reflective of their mutually candid rapport.[17] For his part, Schelling welcomed Brodie's frank and detailed comments as "the kind of thing I need."[18]

4.2 War as Bargaining

Schelling's *Strategy of Conflict* focused predominantly on the decision logic, or bargaining process, individuals used when deciding whether to concede or to continue to compete. A bargain was a "final, sufficient concession," Schelling explained; a bargain was struck when someone made a rational decision to stop unfavorable things from happening, or to enable favorable things to begin happening. Ergo, the strategy of conflict was basically the process of modifying a rival's behavior through "threats," or "threats and promises," until a desired concession was obtained. It thus applied to most non-zero-sum games, not merely war; that is, to those competitions in which more than one favorable outcome were possible. In such competitions, which outnumbered zero-sum games just as limited wars have historically outnumbered unlimited ones, a competitor has both space and incentive to bargain. Schelling, in any case, linked his concept of bargaining directly to limited war theory.

The bargaining process, moreover, was interactive and interdependent, meaning the "ability of one participant to gain [its] ends," depends on "decisions the other participant will make."[19] Nonetheless, Schelling viewed that process only in binary terms, as a series of yes's and no's, or 1's and 0's, suitable for game theory: competitors concede because they think the others will not. "I must concede because he won't. He won't because he thinks I will. He thinks I will because he thinks I think he thinks and so [on]."[20] But binary constructions fail to account for more complex relationships and for exogenous factors. Leaders of gangs might not concede to a rival's demands, not because of what their competitors did or did not do, but because conceding might make the leaders look weak in the eyes of their gangs. Thus, the relationship is triangular not binary, and the most important one is that between leader and led, rather than between the rival leaders. In addition, parties might not concede due to reasons outside their control. In America's war against Mexico (1846–48), for instance, the Mexican army had been defeated. But its government did not concede for some time because it had disintegrated and could not form a consensus. Finally, even concepts like limited and unlimited wars do not fit neatly into binary frameworks. As in the Vietnam conflict, whether one had engaged in a limited or an unlimited war could be a subjective call, a matter of perspective or a question of degree, making it unclear whether, or when, the bargaining model might apply. Put differently, Schelling's binary frame of reference oversimplified the types of situations that confront military strategists.

Schelling divided bargains into "tacit agreements" and "explicit negotiations," arranging them into six categories: (1) the conduct of the war itself, which included agreements over what types of weapons could be used, who could participate in the fighting, and how, and so on; (2) the details of the armistice or surrender document that specified the conditions for halting the war; (3) the status of the enemy regime, or regimes, and their fates after the fighting; (4) the disposition of the territories involved, directly or indirectly, in the fighting; (5) the long-term agreements, such as disarmament or inspection protocols, to preserve the peace; and (6) the postwar status of countries, nations, and alliances and coalitions necessary to satisfy the conditions of peace.[21] Essentially, the bargaining model covered every aspect of war and warfare. It was not only how most wars ended, in other words, it was also how their parameters were defined.

Schelling duly admitted the bargaining process itself might be imperfect. It might be replete with ambiguity and uncertainty, unfolding in fits and starts, carried out by individuals with insufficient experience, or under time constraints, or other pressures, or who despised it as a form of "appeasement," or "collaboration with the enemy."[22] But in his mind none of these conditions negated the fact that bargaining itself took place. Unfortunately, he neglected to consider the second- and third-order implications of such frictions; for if ambiguity and uncertainty prevent one or more of the participants from believing a bargain is in place, and they therefore act as if it were not, then at best the model could describe only a slender portion of reality. Furthermore, war itself appears to be as much about breaking old agreements as establishing new ones. Napoleon was initially successful partly because he demolished the tacit and explicit agreements that went with the traditional methods of warfare. The bargaining model also offered a necessary illusion during the Cold War, namely, that armed conflict, if directed by rational leaders, may be a coiled spring but a relatively stable one since hostilities can end in a negotiated settlement. The possibility that several tacit agreements might not exist when one party believed they did, however, could make the spring less rather than more stable.

4.3 War as Coercion: Deterring and Compelling

Schelling's *Arms and Influence* was published in 1966, as US military's efforts in Vietnam were escalating. The book offered an alternative to brute force, that is, using military power to *take* something from someone, as in seizing another party's territory outright. Schelling's alternative was something he called coercive violence, which meant *making* someone give up something, as in inducing a party to give up its territory by threatening to kill some of its members. In theory, coercion relied on intimidation, or the potential to inflict harm; whereas brute force involved inflicting actual harm. Coercion enabled one to modify an adversary's behavior rather than rendering it irrelevant. Coercive violence was part of the bargaining process; brute force was presumably outside that process. Schelling believed the harm already inflicted on an opponent had less coercive power than the threat of harm to come: "Brute force succeeds when it is used," he added, "but the power to hurt is most successful when it is held in reserve." Moreover, the power to hurt was "bargaining power." Exploiting it was diplomacy, "vicious diplomacy," but diplomacy nonetheless.[23] As he explained in more detail, "To hunt down Comanches and exterminate them was brute force"; whereas "to raid their villages to make them behave was coercive diplomacy, based on the power to hurt." While the pain and suffering to the Indians was much the same either way, the deciding factor in Schelling's mind was "purpose and effect." If Native Americans were killed because "authorities despaired of making them behave that was pure unilateral force." But if *"some* Indians were killed to make *other* Indians behave, that was coercive violence – or intended to be, whether or not it was effective."[24]

The binary distinction Schelling made between brute force and coercive force has been generally accepted. Nonetheless, it, too, is problematic. In practice, both cases require the consent of the victim. If a competitor has seized another's territory by brute force, the victim must decide whether to concede and accept the situation or to resist. Admittedly, the odds of a successful resistance might not be high; however, the resistance could take any number of forms, such as an insurgency which, as the first two decades of the twenty-first century have shown, can level the odds. Thus, the use of brute force is not always outside the bargaining process. Moreover, since consent is required in both cases, Schelling's qualitative distinction between the two types of force disappears. While he was clearly a leading proponent of America's emerging way of policy, his binary framework reflects the telltale signs of a way of battle because it focuses on the climax of war without seeing the contest of wills as potentially continuous.

Schelling also found it necessary to distinguish between active coercion (compellence) and passive coercion (deterrence). Compellence, a term he in fact coined, meant inducing an opponent into taking an action, such as withdrawing its forces from an area, or agreeing to negotiate; it entailed administering punishment "*until* an adversary acted rather than *if* it acted."[25] Deterrence, by comparison, meant intimidating an opponent into *not* taking an action, such as not invading an area, or not launching an attack; it required administering punishment only *if* an opponent took the undesired action.[26] Indeed, warfare can be regarded as a combination of compellence and deterrence, of forcing one's adversaries to take certain actions while depriving them of opportunities to take others.

Contrary to Schelling's binary construct, however, deterrence is not always passively coercive. Prudently digging a moat around one's castle or reinforcing the thickness of one's coastal fortifications are passively coercive actions. On the other hand, some deterrence measures are both actively and passively coercive. Constructing long-range nuclear missiles to retaliate against a rival's possible first strike, for instance, is potentially both, depending on the specific capabilities of the missiles. Likewise, many so-called defensive capabilities – planes, tanks, ships – occupy the middle zone between compellence and deterrence because they can be used offensively or defensively. In sum, once again, oversimplification of the problem eliminates complexity and nuance and drives a wedge between theory and practice.

Similarly, the qualitative distinction Schelling drew between the greater persuasive power of potential harm vis-à-vis actual harm was problematic. Schelling applied this principle in arguing "countervalue" targets (cities) should be held in reserve to maximize one's persuasive potential because cities were ultimately more valuable to an opponent than counterforce (military) targets.[27] Brodie, for one, agreed with Schelling's distinction, as did many of the nuclear strategists, since it appeared imminently logical from a theoretical standpoint.[28] But in practical terms, it is possible to arrive at a point, as the United States did with its strategic bombing program in Vietnam, where the most valuable targets have been destroyed and further bombing only "moves the rubble around," so to speak. At that point, potential harm falls below actual harm.

Schelling's drive for simplicity, his repeated employment of binary distinctions, is understandable; his overriding perspective was that of the game theorist, after all. But such simplicity can lead to any number of false positives for a theory. Some of these outcomes stem from what experts refer to as the "analytical paradox," the impossibility of breaking down something into its component parts without destroying that which makes it what it is.[29] It is impossible, for instance, to determine which factor, or combination of factors, assuming all of them can be known, was decisive in coercing Native Americans to leave their homelands for the Reservations. The known factors include such things as loss of loved ones and of charismatic leaders, fear for the future of the tribe, physical and psychological weariness, lack of food and shelter, promises of relief, and so on; but there could be others that may never be known. In any case, isolating each one, or a specific group of them, distorts their relationship to the others and obscures their collective effectiveness. As a result, while the difficulty of proving whether deterrence worked – thus proving a negative – is well known, proving why compellence worked – thus proving a positive – may be just as difficult. But it has yet to be fully acknowledged.

Schelling's method of strategic analysis, it is worth noting, represents both a step forward and a step backward from that of Mahan's day. Schelling's method, which he called "deductive, vicarious problem-solving," consisted in inserting himself into a situation to understand an individual's decision logic in that situation; he then deduced observations drawn from that situation and applied them, at some risk, to similar situations.[30] The method advanced strategic theory because it relied less on induction than did Mahan's approach; but it also set back strategic theory because it relied too much on deduction. An overreliance on deduction, of course, does not offset an overreliance on induction. Both lead to errors, though the errors are different in nature. Social science, in any case, was about to take a postpositivist turn inspired by Karl Popper.

That turn, however, would not save strategic theory from another of Schelling's errors, one that was not uniquely his but rather common to most strategic thinking, namely, the presumption of rationality on the part of involved parties. For Schelling, rationality meant all parties make decisions based on their best interests – the sum of aims, values, and objectives – within any given situation. By extension, acting rationally meant not acting randomly or haphazardly; but rather after weighing one's interests against the costs and benefits of all actions available within a given situation. But values, obviously, are difficult to gauge. As Schelling once said of the Viet Cong, "We wanted to convince them that we could tolerate more pain than they could, but they weren't rational."[31] Yet the Viet Cong did act rationally given the value they placed on reunification and overthrowing the government in Saigon.

4.4 Schelling's First Principle

Schelling identified four prerequisites for successfully using coercion, and these offer insights into his overriding strategic imperative. The first prerequisite was that the situation should allow both sides space to negotiate. Second, the conflict had to be a non-zero-sum game in which the parties had a common interest in avoiding escalation. Third, the threat of harm had to be both credible and severe enough to affect one's calculation of costs versus benefits; the costs of noncompliance had to be demonstrably higher than its benefits. Finally, an adversary had to be given a specific but an adequate timeframe in which to comply.[32] Assuming these preconditions were met, the use of military force was most likely to be effective and least likely to cause unwanted escalation, if it were applied gradually. Accordingly, graduated pressure, which allowed for the monitoring of each precondition, became Schelling's core strategic principle.

This imperative obviously ran counter to the traditional first principles of concentration, offensive action, and decision by battle. Under these principles, opponents were to be attacked quickly and with as much force as possible to preclude them from implementing countermeasures or from developing a greater resilience to harm. The initial application of harm may also have the undesired effect of strengthening an adversary's willingness to resist. Consider a contest between two boxers: each continues fighting after receiving the initial blow (unless it results in a knockout) even though each knows more pain is coming.

4.5 War's Nature

Schelling's paradigm of war's nature differed slightly from that of Brodie and Osgood. Like them, he essentially saw war's nature as a tightly coiled spring. Nevertheless, whereas a coiled spring is nominally stable, Schelling's theory of bargaining suggested nothing about war was stable. Bargaining meant armed conflict was a process of negotiation – but the uncertainty of politics and warfare makes it difficult to know if a tacit agreement is truly in place, or if an explicit agreement will be honored. One party might misinterpret the actions of another as an implicit agreement; another party might accede to an explicit agreement preparatory to launching a surprise attack later. To be sure, as his biographers have noted, Schelling desired to make the strategic environment of the Cold War more stable; however, the bargaining model pointed in the opposite direction. All told, it underscored the supreme importance of policy's role in war and thus represented a refinement of the model of Osgood and Brodie.

Newton's assumption that the natural state of the universe was one of balance, of equilibrium, had already been challenged by this time. But the full effects of that challenge were not yet appreciated. Nor had complexity theory, chaos theory, and the nonlinear sciences – which articulated the failings of linear models such as Newton's so-called clockwork universe – achieved the popularity they would enjoy in the 1990s.[33] Yet Schelling's bargaining model already contained insights as to the improbability of achieving stability, even if he did not want to admit it to himself. The bargaining model showed strategic environments were naturally unstable; however, it offered a comforting illusion by suggesting opposing parties could negotiate themselves into a new custom or convention, one that agreed to move away from all-out wars toward limited ones. But, again, a bargain was not a guarantee. Perhaps for that reason, Schelling continued to push energetically for explicit arms control agreements; for however imperfect they may be, so long as the process of arriving at them was in place, there was hope.[34]

4.6 Conclusions

Unlike Brodie and Osgood, Schelling's strategic theories concentrated on the psychological dimension of war, on the mental decision processes of heads of state. As such, they had more to do with the human mind than human nature. Personality types and their limitations were completely removed from his calculations; he presumed all minds would act on a rational basis, though he attempted not to define that basis too tightly. He essentially lifted the Clausewitzian "fog" of war for each of his subjects and assumed all of them could perceive and evaluate the relevant factors within their environments, and they could do so with equal competence. These were risky assumptions, and they have contributed to the failure of his theories in practice. Ironically, that failure has not been fully appreciated by the larger strategic community which continues to reference Schelling's theories as if they have been validated. Those concepts have, however, worked well in game/decision theory. The framework of game/decision theory is essential in understanding Schelling's ideas – he informed game theory as much as he was informed by it – and his concepts made little sense outside that framework. Nor did he necessarily intend them to.

Accordingly, Schelling's strategic perspective remained binary, focused on two dimensions, political and military. His theory of coercion and its core principle of graduated pressure speak to conceptions of war's nature and character that were fundamentally bidimensional. That restricted focus was justifiable when the discussion concerned the potential use of nuclear weapons. Beyond nuclear strategy, however, as in situations involving insurrections and counter-insurrections, a three-dimensional focus was necessary. Despite Schelling's albeit limited involvement in the strategic direction of the Vietnam War (in particular Operation Rolling Thunder) and witnessing its military, political, and sociocultural failure, including waves of antiwar protests, he never incorporated the psychosocial dimension of war into his theory of coercion. Instead, coercion – whether of the deterrence or compellence variety – amounted to little more than an exercise of the mind.

Even before the Vietnam War ended, Schelling had expanded his portfolio of interests beyond military strategy and applied what he called "strategic analysis" to several of America's social challenges, including segregation and crime. In 1965, for instance, he published an article outlining the ways in which his brand of strategic analysis could aid in understanding psychosocial decision-making in situations ranging from nonviolent resistance to racial integration.[35] Two years later, he published the results of his research into the relationship between crime and economics, a rising public concern at the time.[36] By 1971, he had expanded that research into a more systematic analysis of organized crime, which he defined as "monopolized crime," the drive for exclusive control over an area or an activity and which by and large provided goods and services consumers could not get elsewhere.[37] His timing could not have been better, as the blockbuster movie *The Godfather* appeared the following year and broke records at the box office. Even in these and his later studies, some of which branched into global warming, he followed a format and methodology beneficial to game theory.[38] Little of that research, however, found its way back into his theory of strategic coercion. Ultimately, his transition away from strategic theory was more successful than his transition into it.

5 Herman Kahn and Escalation

Perhaps America's most maligned strategy intellectual, Herman Kahn dared to think the unthinkable – to consider analytically what a nuclear war might look like if one were to occur. His most significant works include *On Thermonuclear War* (1960), *Thinking about the Unthinkable* (1962), and *On Escalation* (1965).[1] All three made constructive points about the character and nature of nuclear war; however, they failed to inspire the sober dialogue and reflection Kahn intended and, instead, provoked hysteria and derision. His tactic of using rhetorical excess to excite his audiences backfired in the heightened anxiety of the Cold War, particularly during perilous moments such as the Cuban Missile Crisis in 1962. Rather than being lauded for going beyond the conventional wisdom, reviews condemned his works and the film industry satirized his thinking in such movies as *Dr Strangelove* (1964) and *Fail Safe* (1964). Unless the gestures and language of his ample body were visible, Kahn's message lost its mask of irony and came across as naked insanity, as the ruthless calculus of the mathematician crushing the protests of common sense. It was not until the late twentieth century, when the threat of thermonuclear war had faded, that Kahn's works could be seen in a different light – as an indispensable challenge to the underlying assumptions of America's other strategy intellectuals.

5.1 Neither Supergenius nor Strangelove

Herman Kahn was born in 1922, in Bayonne, New Jersey, into a family of Jewish émigrés from Litovsk, but he grew up mainly in the Bronx, New York. From an early age he excelled at any task requiring memorization. He attended the University of California, Los Angeles (UCLA) but was drafted into the US Army in 1943, though he never saw combat. After scoring 161 of 162 on the Army's general classification test, Kahn was assigned to the University of West Virginia to study electrical engineering.[2] Despite achieving a near-perfect score, the highest recorded to that point, he was somehow overlooked for the Manhattan Project, and was detailed to the Army's signal corps. The Army posted him to a detachment in northern Burma responsible for maintaining open lines of communication and supply to Allied troops fighting in China. He was still in Burma on August 6, 1945, when the Enola Gay dropped its atomic bomb on Hiroshima. Decades later, he confessed the horror of the incident had "depressed" him, though he appreciated the rationale for it.[3] Kahn graduated from UCLA in 1946; he received a masters' degree in physics from the California Institute of Technology one year later, and soon thereafter went to work for the RAND Corporation.

In 1953, at the height of McCarthyism, Kahn married Jane Heilner.[4] The FBI began investigating Heilner due to her previous associations with the Communist Party. The investigation subsequently brought Kahn under suspicion as well, though it turned up nothing and the allegations were eventually dropped. Kahn later recalled the psychological exhaustion from the experience had cost him a year of productivity. Afterward, he began writing exploratory studies of game theory and systems analysis for RAND.[5] He soon began employing quantitative analysis to challenge assertions by such organizations as the Federation of American Scientists, which argued nuclear war was not winnable and would destroy humanity.[6]

Undoubtedly, these challenges had much to do with Kahn's desire to attract more support for America's civil defense program, a highly controversial topic at the time. Even if nuclear war were unthinkable, he reasoned, it is the responsibility of government officials and policy advisors to analyze it regardless. In the autumn of 1961, Kahn and several colleagues broke with RAND to establish their own think tank, the Hudson Institute, in Croton-on-Hudson, New York. Whereas RAND served as the "loyal opposition," Kahn told *Newsweek* somewhat sardonically, the Hudson Institute was different in that it was "not necessarily loyal."[7] In 1962, just a few years before Timothy Leary advised America's youth to "Drop Out, Tune In, and Turn On," Kahn sampled LSD as part of the US government's efforts to experiment with the drug and he subsequently completed lengthy questionnaires regarding the hallucinogen.[8]

In the late 1960s, Kahn attempted to establish an advisory office in Saigon whereby he could serve as an advisor on US military strategy in the Vietnam War. He made several trips to Military Assistance Command (MACV) headquarters. Nonetheless, he failed to make headway with the top brass, including US Army's General Creighton Abrams and his aides, many of whom could not get beyond Kahn's arrogance, unkempt appearance, or the media's caricatures of him as the doomsday prophet.[9] But several of his writings also carried the tinge of plagiarism, perhaps due to the loose footnoting practices of the period, which in turn gave some of his ideas an air of unoriginality that may have contributed to their lack of reception. While Kahn became best known for his works on nuclear strategy and escalation, he also researched nonmilitary subjects ranging from urban development to demographics to culture to futurology.[10]

Kahn's health declined rapidly in the early 1980s. For a time, therefore, leadership of the Hudson Institute passed to Colin Gray, a professor of international relations who later authored a scathing critique of RAND's unproductive influence on US strategic thinking during the Vietnam War. Kahn passed away from a stroke in 1984.

5.2 On Thermonuclear War

In 1960, Herman Kahn published *On Thermonuclear War*, a study he began at RAND but completed while on leave at the Center of International Studies at Princeton. The book sold over 14,000 copies in three months, despite (or because of) being panned by the majority of its reviewers. The *Scientific American*, for instance, referred to it as a "moral tract on mass murder" and the *New Statesman* called it "pornography for officers."[11] Enough readers saw the work in the same light as did the director of foreign policy studies at the Brookings' Institution: that is, as an attempt "to awaken the American people to the problem [of nuclear war] and to urge them to take their head out of the sand and do something about it."[12]

Many of his RAND colleagues, in fact, felt Kahn had cribbed their ideas without giving them credit. This was especially true of Albert Wohlstetter, Kahn's erstwhile mentor, who apparently had instructed his understudy to "burn" the manuscript so as to avoid having his own ideas bowdlerized.[13] Other RAND analysts, such as the mathematician Richard Bellman, immediately contacted the major media outlets of the day such as *Fortune*, *Harper's*, *The New Republic*, *Newsweek*, *The Reporter*, *Time*, and *The Washington Post* and expressly denied that Kahn's book represented in any way the sum of their hard work and considered opinions.[14] Pride of authorship seemingly counted for a great deal at RAND in those days.

The structure of *On Thermonuclear War* paralleled, albeit loosely, that of Clausewitz's *On War*. Kahn's work opened with a discussion of the nature of thermonuclear war just as the Prussian's magnum opus began with a discussion of the nature of war in the age of Napoleon. The similarities ended there, however. Clausewitz had identified the chief elements that comprised the nature of war in his day and offered it as a framework for analyzing the nature of the war at hand. In contrast, Kahn explained that the nature of thermonuclear war was unknown partly because it had not happened yet, which was a good thing, but mainly because it was too horrible for most people to contemplate. After living with "nuclear bombs for fifteen years," he said, "we still have a great deal to learn about the possible effects of a nuclear war."[15] Not enough thought had gone into what might happen if such a war did occur, he asserted, or whether the policies in place were the best ones for preventing it.

The second part of the book included a hypothetical formulation of US objectives and plans, and how these could be served better by more thorough analysis. The third and final section consisted of analyses of the world wars, as well as six hypothetical present and future wars. This section highlighted the conditions under which deterrence had succeeded or failed in the past, and their implications for contemporary US defense policy. Kahn classified deterrence into three types: (1) deterrence of a direct attack, (2) deterrence of extreme provocations, and (3) deterrence of less aggressive moves by increasing the costs to the aggressor in graduated or controlled ways.[16] According to him, US defense analysts generally subscribed to the concept of "finite deterrence," the dual idea that an enemy can be killed only once and that overkilling by any factor was, thus, a waste of resources.[17] In January 1959, for instance, the Pentagon provided US Secretary of State John Foster Dulles with a "finite" list of targets, the destruction of which would prove fatal to the Soviet Union.[18] Theoretically, once enough nuclear weapons had been built to guarantee destruction of those targets, whether countervalue (cities) or counterforce (military sites) in nature, construction of the weapons could cease. Of course, how many and what types of munitions might be needed to guarantee such destruction, given improvements in anti-missile defenses and other factors, became matters of debate; an example is the controversy that lasted from 1958 to 1961 over the US Navy's submarine-launched Polaris missiles versus the US Air Force's Minuteman missiles. Finite deterrence was, therefore, more an aspiration than a practice. Additionally, certain scenarios, such as a massive Soviet assault in Europe, might force the West to consider using its nuclear weapons in a first-strike mode, which would make most deterrence calculations irrelevant.

Although the common belief was that thermonuclear weapons had changed the "character of an all-out war in such a way that if both opponents are prepared, the old-fashioned distinctions between victory, stalemate, and defeat no longer have much meaning," Kahn argued this view had too many unexplored assumptions.[19] It had not yet been proven that a country could not recover from a nuclear exchange. Much depended on what measures a nation had taken beforehand to protect its citizens and their local economies, farmlands, and livestock. Much also depended on how many nuclear weapons would be exchanged. One could conceive of any number of scenarios in which each party used only a small portion of its nuclear weapons; hence, the resultant devastation might be manageable. The facts regarding nuclear fallout, Kahn insisted, were still being examined and affirmed; perhaps proper planning might enable a population to mitigate the effects of fallout, and to recover from them. Others, however, took him to task on this point.[20]

On Thermonuclear War concluded with a call for better planning and analysis. The United States could ill-afford to be anything but sober about deterrence, he said. "Reliable deterrence of a war is much more difficult than has been supposed in the past," and the "quality of our deterrence can make a great deal of difference in our position and policy."[21] Policymakers had to think beyond deterrence to defense, and to the allocation of resources accordingly. If nations were not to be inevitably annihilated in a nuclear war, then its aftermath required greater attention. In addition, the West had to maintain a "balance of terror" and a flexible defense posture so as to enable military intervention when and where necessary.

After reading Kahn's *On Thermonuclear War*, Albert Wohlstetter publicly complained he had been plagiarized, and that complaint was not unjustified. Many of Kahn's points, in fact, amplified those Wohlstetter had made in a 1958 RAND study and in a 1959 *Foreign Affairs* article, "The Delicate Balance of Terror."[22] Wohlstetter had asked three critical questions: Was deterrence now automatic? Was all-out war nearly obsolete? Was mutual extinction the only outcome to be expected of a general war? Wohlstetter's and Kahn's answers were the same: no – on all counts. The thermonuclear balance was not stable but "precarious," said Wohlstetter, and this fact had serious implications for US defense policy. Kahn's analysis essentially made the same point but offered several details that revealed just how precarious that balance, indeed, was. Deterrence could work, said Wohlstetter. But it would become more difficult in future decades if policymakers continued to misunderstand the nature of nuclear deterrence. This nature consisted not in matching, or overmatching, the first-strike weapons of one's opponents, but rather in maintaining survivable second-strike capabilities, an idea Brodie believed had originated with him.[23] Wohlstetter went on to argue the accelerating pace of technological change would render deterrence more difficult by upsetting the balance of economic and military power. Deterrence was, therefore, at once inadequate and yet indispensable. It required a larger framework of strategic agreements, as well as a sustained commitment to them, and the willingness to accept a lower level of security than one might like: both parties have to accept some vulnerability in order not to feel inclined to attack.

To his credit, Kahn did more than purloin some of Wohlstetter's points; he took many of them further. Kahn, for instance, recommended conceiving of the delicate balance of terror in three periods or intervals: near-term survival to 1961; mid-term survival to 1965; and long-term survival to 1975.[24] The role of policymakers was then to ensure decisions made in the first window did not adversely affect survival in the second, or that decisions made in the first and second windows did not undermine the chances of survival in the third. Kahn also advocated the development of stronger conventional capabilities, as well as improved active and passive defense systems, such as missile defenses and shelters. In some ways, Kahn and Wohlstetter had staked out overlapping but ultimately dissimilar positions.[25]

Among the more controversial themes in *On Thermonuclear War*, was Kahn's "Doomsday Machine," a concept that would provide fuel for satire and serious criticism. This "extinction-level device" came to the American public's mind primarily through Stanley Kubrick's film *Dr. Strangelove: How I Learned to Stop Worrying and Love the Bomb*, a dark satire of the logic, or lack thereof, that underpinned nuclear strategy. In the movie, one American bomber cannot be recalled after responding to a false alarm triggered by a paranoid US Air Force general named Jack D. Ripper, a character presumably patterned on Curtis LeMay; the Soviets then activate a Doomsday Machine that destroys the world.[26] Kubrick later admitted he had based the character of Strangelove on the combined personalities of Kahn and (former) Nazi scientist Wernher von Braun.[27] Kahn attempted to spin the allusion by claiming Strangelove resembled Kissinger more than himself.[28] But he failed. It was Kahn after all, not Kissinger, who had introduced the concept of a Doomsday Machine.

A caricature of Kahn also appeared in the movie *Fail-Safe*, a somber account of a technical malfunction that requires a tit-for-tat nuclear exchange. Once again, an American bomber penetrates Soviet air space, despite robust defensive measures and active cooperation between the White House and the Kremlin. The bomber destroys Moscow, and the US President, played by Henry Fonda, must reciprocate by destroying New York City. Kahn's personality is represented by Professor Groeteschele, who makes a nakedly quantitative argument to launch a massive first-strike against the Soviets to take advantage of the situation.[29] The tit-for-tat exchange, in fact, pointed to a step in the latter versions of Kahn's Escalation Ladder.[30] *Fail-Safe* both captured and exploited the public's growing concern that a nuclear war might start accidentally, that the elaborate system of precautions put in place to protect US citizens might instead put them at greater risk.

Both films appeared less than two years after the Cuban Missile Crisis. Both also portrayed Kahn's analytical thinking as grotesque. Nuclear strategy was, even at this stage, so coldly mathematical as to be irrational, despite the intentions of the strategy intellectuals. Even high-ranking officials, such as US Chief of Naval Operations Admiral Arleigh Burke, could acknowledge most US and Soviet military installations were too close to cities to make distinctions between counterforce and countervalue targeting workable. "When those missiles start coming over," Burke informed the US Senate Armed Services Committee in 1962, "you do not know whether the intent of the enemy was to hit, or not to hit, a city if he hits it."[31] The signaling strategies of Schelling, too, did not accord with practical realities.

Kahn's "Doomsday Machine" actually represented three devices in *On Thermonuclear War*: the Doomsday Machine, the Doomsday-in-a-Hurry Machine, and the Homicide-Pact Machine. Each machine was programmed to destroy the planet if any party violated specific rules or made certain threats. All served the same purpose for Kahn, namely, to act as foils against "a good deal of current strategic thinking."[32] The underlying point, for instance, was to expose the specious logic of massive retaliation, and to reveal how mindlessly counterproductive the development of increasingly destructive nuclear weapons would be. Any such Doomsday Machine, he believed, would prove ultimately unacceptable to the US Congress, a decision that perhaps implied two things: "either some of the weapons systems currently being proposed are also unacceptable, or that the way we talk about these weapons systems is wrong – very likely both."[33] It was up to the US defense establishment and the White House to prove to Congress that any planned weapons were not in effect Doomsday Machines; for weapons that appeared too effective might provoke an attack rather than deter it. The Homicide Pact, said Kahn, symbolized the official deterrence policy between NATO and the Warsaw Pact, since its failure would lead to "automatic mutual homicide."[34] This rationale was, of course, the same as that which would underpin the policy of Mutual Assured Destruction (MAD), and Mutual Assured Agreed Destruction (MAAD), two ironic but sadly apposite acronyms. Nonetheless, Kahn's use of the Doomsday Machine as a metaphor exemplifies his habit of being too clever by half; for it frightened rather than forewarned.

In addition, *On Thermonuclear War* introduced an early version of Kahn's Ladder of Escalation. Table 46 "Nonmilitary Deterrents" and table 47 "Military Deterrents" illustrate the rudiments of this ladder, which would evolve and merge over the course of his other major works into its ultimate form of forty-four steps. He developed the steps to facilitate analyzing the nature of deterrence and bargaining, an inspiration clearly drawn from the works of Schelling, though Kahn did not attribute it to him. Nonmilitary deterrents consisted of seven effects, which today would be referred to as costs: (1) negative internal reactions; (2) losing friends or antagonizing neutrals; (3) creating or strengthening coalitions of enemies; (4) lowering the reaction threshold of potential opponents; (5) diplomatic or economic retaliation; (6) an increase in the potential opponent's military forces; and (7) "not going to heaven."[35]

If these nonmilitary effects failed to deter a foe, military deterrents would come into play. There were eight of these: (1) temporizing military measures – alert, mobilization, etc.; (2) direct military support for the threatened area; (3) a small controlled reprisal; (4) a small controlled war; (5) a large controlled reprisal; (6) a large controlled war; (7) a spasm war; and (8) a countervalue war.[36] These deterrents, like Kahn's other lists, derived from his penchant for systems analysis, a method of regarding any activity as a system to be broken down into individual steps or components. Ever a lover of enumeration, Kahn presented them for purposes of discussion and for the benefit of game theory. They did not indicate escalation could only proceed according to these steps; however, they did represent escalation as a binary process. Despite ample fear of escalation, few studies by 1960 offered an anticipatory analysis of its component parts. Kahn's was the boldest and most detailed to date.

5.3 On Escalation

In 1962, the same year as the Cuban missile crisis, Kahn published *Thinking about the Unthinkable*, which featured an Escalation Ladder of sixteen steps – roughly a third of the final version of the Ladder.[37] The book opened with a chapter that provided a rationale for thinking about nuclear war, how it might happen and the course it might take. The problem of escalation, Kahn insisted, was not easily reducible to the either–or choices of game theory, though he represented it that way regardless. Nor would avoiding the problem make it disappear, he said. Nonetheless, he failed to address the destabilizing effect that might occur if one side, in thinking about thermonuclear war, concluded it was survivable, which then might encourage it to strike first.

Kahn's *Thinking about the Unthinkable* outlined four categories describing how a thermonuclear war might commence. The first category was an "Inadvertent War," in which the conflict began due to mechanical or human error, which included false perceptions and expectations. The second was "War by Miscalculation," in which one side misjudged its chances for success and thus initiated a conflict it mistakenly thought it could win. Included in this category was escalation from a limited conflict that appeared controllable at the outset, but then led to an all-out war. The third category was "War by Calculation," in which one party chose armed conflict as the lesser evil. Preventive wars and preemptive attacks fell into this group. The last category was "Catalytic War," in which a third party drew, either deliberately or unintentionally, the world's superpowers into a major conflict. "World War I," Kahn reminded his readers, "was a catalytic war, set off by Serbia and Austria."[38]

Thinking about the Unthinkable also reiterated Kahn's argument for a civil defense program, the chief advantages of which were that it would save lives and facilitate postwar recovery. It also augmented the three categories of deterrence he discussed in *On Thermonuclear War* with three additional strategic objectives: (1) improved war outcome, limiting the damage inflicted on the United States and its allies and improving the military outcome of the conflict; (2) stability, reducing the likelihood of an inadvertent thermonuclear war; and (3) comprehensive arms control, limiting arms races and the use of force in settling disputes.[39] Unfortunately, he also believed the Defense Department's endless tendency to divide and subdivide categories had already made the discussion of nuclear deterrence unwieldly.

Kahn's most significant contribution in *Thinking about the Unthinkable*, however, lay in his merging of Schelling's concept of bargaining with the Escalation Ladder. Indeed, Kahn's notion of escalation remains vague and immature unless one sees it as a form of tacit and explicit bargaining. "As the balance of power becomes more firm and the consequences of a misunderstanding more serious," he wrote, "it is likely that explicit and implicit bargaining, negotiation, and a crude kind of adjudication by 'world opinion' will become the rule."[40] Kahn added a summation of Schelling's seven bargaining positions, or tactics: (1) it is in your interest to concede; (2) somebody has to be reasonable; (3) my partner won't let me; (4) this is my last demand; (5) your friends do not agree with you; (6) it is unfair to complicate (or oversimplify) the problem; and (7) put yourself in my place. Accordingly, escalation resulted when disputing parties applied pressure, step by step, to move one another beyond their initial bargaining positions and closer to an agreement. The basic steps, in his opinion, were:

16 Aftermath
15 Some kind of all-out war
14 Complete evacuation
13 Limited nonlocal war
12 Controlled local war
11 Spectacular show of force
10 Super-ready status
9 Limited evacuation
8 Intense crisis
7 Limited military confrontations
6 Acts of violence
5 Modest mobilization
4 Show of force
3 Political, diplomatic, and economic gestures
2 Crisis
1 Subcrisis disagreement.

"We wish to study Escalation Ladders," Kahn went on to explain, "because each rung is important by itself as an alternative or possibility, and partly because every action must be considered in a context of what may have preceded it or followed it."[41] The purpose, therefore, was to consider how one's opponents, one's allies, one's domestic populations, and neutral parties, would react to each rung. The influence of game theory is evident here. The rungs were not necessarily immutable, but their arrangement did reflect Kahn's assumptions and expectations. One's opponent might make different suppositions, which could lead to a situation in which two or more ladders were operative at the same time.

A related failing in this and Kahn's subsequent escalation ladders was the assumption of strategic clarity or, put differently, the lack of opacity or ambiguity. When *Thinking about the Unthinkable* appeared in 1962, it found its natural contradiction in the award-winning *Pearl Harbor: Warning and Decision* by Roberta Wohlstetter (neé Morgan).[42] The book became a foundational reference for much of Cold War strategic theory because it was the first study to deal seriously with ambiguity, the difficulty of determining precisely what an adversary's signals meant. Roberta analyzed the Japanese attack on Pearl Harbor through the lens of communications, and intelligence gathering, analysis, and dissemination. Put simply, *Pearl Harbor* asked what the United States knew before the Japanese attack, when it knew it, and how it had responded as a result. While two decades of technological development had occurred since the attack, Roberta rightly concluded ambiguity was unavoidable. "We must be capable of reacting repeatedly to false alarms," she argued, "without committing ourselves or the enemy to wage thermonuclear war."[43] Three years later Roberta published an article in *Foreign Affairs* that analyzed the Cuban Missile Crisis.[44] One would not want to carry historical analogies too far, she admitted, but it seems clear the "problem of warning" was "inseparable from the problem of decision."[45]

Kahn's response, which he presented in *On Escalation* in 1965, while not admitting wholly to the incapacitating influence of strategic opacity, nonetheless attempted to address it by arguing ambiguity itself could be reduced by increasing one's knowledge of escalation, and by gaming its various branches and sequels. In this way, one could gain a better understanding of the relationship between an escalatory warning and an escalatory decision.[46] By this time, the Escalation Ladder had grown to forty-four steps, and it was completely wedded to Schelling's concept of bargaining, and to its attendant notion that escalation was a "competition in risk-taking," or in resolve.[47] Kahn defined escalation at this time as an "increase in intensity or scope of a conflict," and he built on the construct employed in 1963 by defense analyst Morton Halperin, who said it typically took the form of either a "sudden *explosion*" or a "gradual *expansion*."[48] Kahn, again ever the enumerator, added three possible ways in which escalation might occur: through an increase in intensity, through a widening of the area of the conflict, or by compounding the clash of arms through an attack on an adversary's allies or partners outside the conflict area. Notably, none of these accounted for temporal escalation, prolonging a conflict such that it gradually consumes resources disproportionate to the value one's adversary places on its goals. In any case, an escalation ladder, Kahn warned, was little more than a metaphor, a conceptual vehicle for visualizing the processes by which the intensity of a conflict might increase. Its actual utility derived "partly from its provision of a convenient list of some of the options available, and partly from its ordering of escalatory activities in a way that facilitates examination and discussion."[49]

Kahn discussed each of the rungs of his final Escalation Ladder in detail. "The unthinkable all-out war," he noted, "is becoming 'thinkable,' even possible."[50] He grouped the Ladder's forty-four rungs into seven regions or brackets, each of which indicated the crossing of a threshold or "firebreak." At each firebreak, "very sharp changes in the character of the escalation take place."[51] The regions were (1) subcrisis maneuvering – the don't rock the boat threshold; (2) traditional crises – the nuclear war is unthinkable threshold; (3) intense crises – the no nuclear use threshold; (4) bizarre crises – central sanctuary threshold; (5) exemplary central attacks – central war threshold; (6) military central wars – city targeting threshold; and (7) civilian central wars – which was the final region and thus without a threshold. He likened the thresholds to the seven floors of a department store, each of which offered a new set of options to the buyer. Incidentally, Brodie examined and rejected the firebreak concept as nonsensical the following year.[52] The term "bizarre crises" requires some explanation; it covered situations in which the use of nuclear weapons was "very limited and restrained."[53] The term was not uncommon among defense intellectuals at the time; Schelling, for one, had considered including a chapter on bizarre wars in his *Arms and Influence*, but in the end did not.[54]

Despite whatever light it shed on critical decision points regarding escalation, the Ladder, Kahn admitted, had several defects. The first of these was that any metaphor oversimplified and even distorted the process it represented. One should not infer, for instance, the "escalation distance" or reaction interval between rungs would be the same in each case. The order of the rungs might also change according to such factors as the imminence of all-out war, or the strength of political commitments, and so on. Nor could the model capture the effects of simultaneous moves. Differing national outlooks or "strategic cultures" (to borrow a problematic term coined in the late 1970s) posed an additional problem. Soviet military behavior, Kahn opined, might "differ extensively, in kind and degree, from the probable American style of war."[55] Ergo, the Soviets might follow an entirely different escalation ladder, such as the one developed by his colleague at the Hudson Institute, Edmund Stillman.

Kahn also acknowledged other defects in the Escalation Ladder. These included the assumption that the parties involved were rational actors, the failure to account for ambiguity and uncertainty, the absence of workable alternatives particularly in the upper rungs of the ladder, and the model's inability to account for long-term instability; that is, the frequency with which one resorted to certain rungs on the ladder would alter their relative value and importance. In short, the Escalation Ladder reflected most of the "pitfalls" of systems analysis he identified in 1957, especially "modelism," or a preoccupation with the model itself and with answering "overidealized questions" about it rather than addressing practical policy concerns.[56] In effect, Kahn admitted that his Escalation Ladder suited practical reality less than it did game theory because it reduced complex decisions to simple binary, yes or no, questions. Nonetheless, Kahn's definition of escalation – an "increase in intensity or scope of a conflict" – has survived into the twenty-first century, informing scholarly research and defense policy choices, and influencing professional military education.[57] His underlying assumption, that escalation can be managed even if not entirely controlled, remains operative alongside the fear that it is inherently uncontrollable.

5.4 Disengaging from Vietnam

Kahn's theories on thermonuclear war and escalation were by no means the sum of his contributions to the American way of thinking about war. Indeed, he showed a well-developed talent, as any research director must, for shifting his research efforts to accommodate the sundry interests of prospective clients. For instance, in July 1968, just months after the failure of the Communists' Tet Offensive and while the presidential election campaigns were underway, *Foreign Affairs* published Kahn's interpretation of the strategic situation in Vietnam, presciently entitled "If Negotiations Fail."[58] Not only would the many supporters of the US intervention suffer in the event of a Communist victory, he argued, but also recriminations and disillusionment would abound at home. "A 'stab-in-the-back' legend on the right," he predicted, "would compete with 'military-industrial-complex' theories on the left." The incompetence and immorality of the "establishment" would have been demonstrated, and a Goldwater-style conservative backlash would undoubtedly ensue.

Echoing counterguerrilla expert Sir Robert Thompson's *Foreign Affairs* article published only three months earlier, Kahn estimated the North Vietnamese and Viet Cong could put some 250,000 troops into the field every year.[59] These numbers meant Hanoi could easily replace the 50,000 or so casualties the National Liberation Front suffered annually, as well as a similar number of losses on the part of the North Vietnamese Army. Therefore, the war was not yet at the stage where serious negotiations might commence, which meant the fighting would have to continue until it reached such a point. However, given the change in US leadership that had followed in the aftermath of the Tet Offensive – Clark Clifford had replaced McNamara as Secretary of Defense, General Abrams had replaced General Westmoreland as commander of MACV, and President Johnson had chosen not to run for reelection – the timing was right for Washington and Saigon to shift their strategies. Accordingly, Kahn proposed a program that foreshadowed the Nixon administration's policy of "Vietnamization," gradually turning the war over to the government in Saigon and its army, while concomitantly reducing US forces.

Likewise, in August of the following year, two months after US forces had begun to withdraw and three months before the policy of Vietnamization was officially announced by Nixon (November 3,

1969), Kahn and Hudson's colleague Garrett Scalera presented a discussion paper that articulated a three-part strategy for the program. Part I entailed standing up a rural police force of some 100,000 personnel. Part II consisted of establishing area security for the South Vietnamese population. The third part involved the "full professionalization" of American and South Vietnamese efforts, which meant eliminating or reducing the day-to-day bureaucratic practices that so obviously hampered the execution of the war by creating additional friction. Among these practices were the twelve-month rotation policy for officers, personnel policies that prioritized career development over winning the war, an overemphasis on conventional operations, along with the establishment of large fixed military camps that discouraged the interaction of US troops with the local peasantry.[60] Indeed, Kahn seemed to have tapped into the public's sentiments, as polling data showed nearly two-thirds of Americans had already indicated they supported a policy of "full professionalization" in 1966, and 77 percent said the same in 1967.[61]

As with most think tanks, the Hudson Institute had to shape its research agenda according to the interests of its clients, both prospective and active. By the 1970s, therefore, Kahn began broadening Hudson's research profile to attract clients outside US defense circles. In 1974, for instance, the Institute completed *American Values: Past and Future*, a study that examined some significant trends in US society.[62] National morale had hit a low point, and it was still declining, the study said. The downturn had begun in the 1960s and had accelerated. Assassinations, attempted assassinations, race riots, student protests, the failure of American foreign policy, controversies over the Vietnam War, the Watergate scandal, rising inflation, a broadening economic recession, and worsening energy and ecological problems were just some of the concerns contributing to the depth of the public's malaise. The nuclear family, too, was thought to be threatened. Divorce rates were on the rise; almost 20 percent of the adult population was either divorced or legally separated – all of which suggested the family was no longer the dependable transmitter of values it once was, though it remained an important one.

Americans had evidently lost confidence in their government, even as they wanted that government to take notice of, and to make greater efforts to resolve, the larger economic and social problems of the day. The public still believed in the American way of life, but it saw few prospects for economic growth and progress.[63] The idealistic youth of the early 1960s had become disillusioned; individualism and self-fulfillment had begun to replace political and social activism. The nation seemed to lack direction and purpose; it wanted strong leadership, but not necessarily strong (autocratic) leaders. American values, the study went on to say, would remain in a "state of flux and strain" through the 1970s, and likely for some years to come. Traditional values were still the dominant ones, the study claimed, though such values were in the process of eroding.

In some ways, the malaise was a byproduct of macrotrends such as the rise of a postindustrial society and deurbanization. As such, it might not have been preventable. But its effects might have been mitigated by, among other things, an educational system that did not foster idealism or inflate youthful expectations of the American dream. A more realistic expectation might have been to anticipate the need for tradeoffs between traditional and emerging values, especially during periods of dramatic change.

In other ways, however, the growing sense of malaise laid bare the fact that few US theorists conceived of strategy in more than two dimensions. The trends impacting American society had not emerged overnight; they had been in the making since the middle of the 1960s, and as early as the 1950s in some cases. Yet mainstream US strategic thinking took little account of them. To be sure, economic and psychosocial development theories were not scarce at this time. Walt Rostow's *Stages of Economic Growth*, though almost pathologically flawed in its efforts to represent an "anticommunist" model, was an example of the former.[64] The "Program for the Pacification and Long-Term Development of Vietnam" (1964–65) attempted in Vietnam was an example of the latter.[65] Nonetheless, a fully integrated view of war and of strategy remained elusive. Instead, America's way of war had begun to assume the characteristics of a "way of policy," one that, in important respects, was just as narrow as its "way of battle."

5.5 Kahn's First Principles and War's Nature

The core principles of Kahn's theories of escalation differed little from those of the other strategy intellectuals. Policy must come first. Indeed, the strategy intellectuals saw their way of policy not only as necessary, but as superior. Consequently, they denigrated the importance of war's other nonmilitary dimensions, its economic and psychosocial ones. Kahn, for his part, attributed more agency to policy than did they; policy, he believed, would be involved in every step of an escalation, and it had the capacity to slow or even halt it. As discussed earlier, Brodie, Osgood, and Schelling likened war's nature to a coiled spring precisely because of its explosive properties. But the strategy intellectuals considered human instincts and passions to be imminently more volatile and thus a greater threat to policy itself. Such irrational forces, as Osgood explained, "find their outlet in the blind, unreasoning destruction of the enemy. They are antithetical to the political control of war, because political control would restrict the use of force."[66] Importantly, however, the strategy intellectuals also attributed a mechanistic aspect to war's nature, meaning it could uncoil automatically, at the push of a button or because of a mistake that sets the apparatus in motion. Kahn challenged that view, suggesting it was both too simplistic and too pessimistic. Aside from an accidental launch, policy could cause escalation to pause or to cease altogether, except in extreme cases. But his arguments failed to convince either Brodie or Schelling.

5.6 Conclusions

Kahn's theories were at once synthetic and simplistic. He borrowed Brodie's and Osgood's imperative of the primacy of policy, leveraged Schelling's concepts of bargaining and graduated pressure, applied the tools of systems analysis, and with the aid of all of these produced a cognitive map of escalation useful primarily, if not solely, to a game theorist. Importantly, however, his map, or ladder, of escalation suggested the coiled spring of armed conflict might not unload all at once, that belligerents were just as likely to avoid instant Armageddon by employing nuclear weapons in accretionary but violent bargaining processes designed to coerce each other. For that reason, nuclear warfare itself could no longer remain unthinkable: governments needed to devote more resources to understanding it as well as the conditions under which it might be survivable, if not winnable. Ultimately, the same instability that haunted Schelling's bargaining model also compromised Kahn's escalation ladder – namely, that it was always too easy to assume a bargain was in place when it was not. War, after all, is as much about making bargains as breaking them.

Kahn's understanding of war's nature paralleled that of the other strategy intellectuals, but especially that of Schelling. Ideologies and the automatic, machinelike aspects of armed conflict displaced human nature as war's principal driver. War was still, at root, a coiled spring. But the ability of politics to interrupt the uncoiling of that spring, he believed, was greater than Brodie and Osgood allowed. The only human characteristic common to his four causes of thermonuclear war – inadvertent, miscalculation, calculation, and catalytic – was that of error. But unlike the human propensity to sin in Mahan's day, error could be corrected within the spring, and thus without appealing to a higher power. Accordingly, war's nature was antithetical to human nature.

While Kahn challenged the assumption that nuclear warfare was not survivable, his work was too derivative to claim any original core principles. Initially, he saw the character of war chiefly through the lens of nuclear warfare. The aperture of that lens widened as he examined the course of the Vietnam War and the military strategy guiding it. It widened again in the 1970s when he began considering the sociocultural causes and consequences of the US failure in Vietnam. Still, his findings and recommendations typically built on others' conclusions, and thus fell more into the category of synthetic rather than original. In any case, one often sacrificed originality to remain relevant to the fast-moving debates of the day. Not surprisingly, spinoffs of existing research could attract more attention in the policy world, and do it more frequently, than new research; the Hudson Institute, like many think tanks, needed that attention to survive.

By the end of America's golden age of strategic thinking, the revolt of the strategy intellectuals (buoyed as it was by RAND's ample resources) had prompted a rethinking of the presumed dynamics and denouements of war. To be sure, Brodie's constant attacks on Jomini's core strategic principles had not resulted in their removal from the military lexicon. But it had caused a generation of officers to rethink them. His and Osgood's principles of limited war began appearing in US operational doctrine by the late 1950s and early 1960s as alternatives to the traditional imperatives. Unfortunately, military and policy practitioners seem not to have understood the conditions and rules necessary for limited war to succeed. None of those prerequisites were sufficiently present in the Vietnam conflict, yet the theory was applied anyway. To have believed it would work beyond its acknowledged scope, as Kissinger and several of the theory's other proponents did, was both unreasonable and irrational.

Part III

The Counterrevolution of the Military Intellectuals

As America's strategy intellectuals set about revolutionizing US strategic thinking, a few military "intellectuals" began to think critically about course of that revolution. Their efforts, which included developing several original concepts, amounted to something of a counterrevolution. The most important of these concepts came from two naval officers, Rear Admirals Henry E. Eccles and Joseph Caldwell Wylie, both of whom had considerable combat experience in the Second World War. More significantly, they took advantage of the access and time afforded by their assignments at the US Naval War College to engage the strategic issues of the day, and to analyze and debate them. Combat experience can provide practical insights to the benefit of military theory, but it can also obstruct other, potentially useful perspectives. Fortunately, Eccles and Wylie followed the spirit of Clausewitz's advice and employed their wartime experiences to enrich rather than to entrench their thinking.

To be sure, RAND became a formidable analytical powerhouse in the early years of the Cold War, pouring its ample resources into solving the problems of nuclear deterrence and arms control, and into underwriting the research of the strategy intellectuals. But a rather modest triumvirate of Eccles, Wylie, and the German historian Herbert Rosinski managed to develop a new concept centered on the idea of strategy as the art and science of control. It did so, moreover, at much less cost to the US defense budget than typical of RAND. Rosinski laid the initial groundwork for the theory of strategy as control; Eccles situated it within a comprehensive framework, and Wylie developed a scheme for operationalizing it.

In the late 1970s, another combat veteran, US Army Colonel Harry Summers, availed himself of an opportunity to write and to reflect at the US Army War College. Summers came on the scene in the latter stages of the counterrevolution. His ideas, nonetheless, paralleled those of Eccles and Wylie. Like them, he repeatedly stressed the importance of Clausewitzian critical analysis and of returning to strategic fundamentals. His main contributions to military theory, however, came principally in two forms. First, he exposed the fallacy of assuming the winning of battles always led to the winning of wars. Second, he revealed the folly of conceiving of and implementing military strategy without an established set of guiding principles. Collectively, moreover, the military intellectuals shared an understanding of war's nature that hewed closely to the traditional model, but which also anticipated the experiential features of the modern paradigm.

6 Henry Eccles and the Reform of Strategic Theory

Rear Admiral Henry Eccles was the first of the military intellectuals to participate in the counterrevolution in military theory, though he might have preferred to describe it, less dramatically, as correcting the ship's rudder. After the Second World War, he became the US Navy's leading expert on logistical issues and laid the foundations for the modern science of logistics. He also became one of the US military's most important intellectual reformers and educators, redefining military theory along Clausewitzian lines to promote critical analysis over prescriptive action. Eccles's approach to theory reinforced a broad and much needed reexamination of strategic principles and concepts generated during the expansion of the military-industrial complex under the Eisenhower administration. In short, it swept away errors in thought and expression.

Eccles's approach led, furthermore, to his construction of a comprehensive framework reflective of the purpose of the comparative method in vogue at the Naval War College in Mahan's day. As readers will recall, the comparative method assessed a concept's limits by contrasting it against other concepts and in different contexts. For Eccles, a concept also had to be situated within an accepted framework or structure. His approach bridged the gap between concept and doctrine, and furthered military education by dividing theories from slogans during a period of transition, if not anarchy.[1]

6.1 Logistician and Structuralist

Henry Effingham Eccles was born in 1898 into a family with Episcopalian values, and raised in Bayside, Long Island. He was home-schooled until the age of ten. He entered the US Naval Academy in 1918, at the age of twenty, and graduated four years later. Eccles attended a preparatory school that trained him to pass the Academy's entrance examinations with some efficiency. He described himself as a "non-regulation" midshipman due to his "continual minor disciplinary trouble."[2] He had several ship assignments in the early 1920s and attended the Navy's submarine course in 1925. By 1930, he had earned a master's degree in engineering from Columbia University.

Eccles served multiple tours on battleships, submarines, and destroyers before the Second World War. When the Japanese attacked Pearl Harbor, he was in command of the destroyer USS *John D. Edwards* in the Philippines. He was wounded in the early stages of the conflict. After convalescing, he served in the US Office of Naval Operations coordinating logistics for forward bases across the Central Pacific. This experience provided the foundation for much of his later theories of logistics. Eccles served the final two years of the war in the Pacific Fleet headquarters as the director of advanced bases. After the war, he commanded the battleship USS *Washington*, and was subsequently assigned to the newly established Department of Logistics at the US Naval War College, where he served until 1951.[3] Afterward, he became the Assistant Chief of Staff for Logistics for US and NATO naval forces in the eastern Atlantic and Mediterranean. He retired in 1952, but he remained affiliated with the US Naval War College as a consultant until 1985.[4] His intellectual legacy was recognized in 1985 by the US Naval War College, which named its library in his honor.[5] He passed away the following year.

6.2   War's Changed Nature

In Eccles's view, two impediments stood in the way of developing a comprehensive theory of war: the anti-intellectualism of the military, which prided itself on its "practical" point of view and devalued scholarship; and the "electronic-nuclear phase of the industrial revolution, which had cast doubt on the classic theories of war."[6] To achieve the counterrevolution, or correction to the ship's rudder, he thought necessary, Eccles had to wage a war of ideas on at least two fronts: one that encouraged military professionals to think beyond "slogans," a pejorative reference he may have borrowed from Brodie; and the other that entailed a systematic stripping away of the thick clouds of semantic confusion that hindered strategic thinking at the time.

Eccles's early lectures, which culminated in his first substantive publication *Operational Naval Logistics* (1950), explicitly stressed the importance of understanding the winnowing effect of logistics on national policy.[7] Logistics restricted tactics, which in turn restricted strategy, which in turn restricted, or ought to, rational policy. Put metaphorically, the farther the arm of policy must reach, the weaker will be its grasp – unless the lifeblood of logistics can be made to flow with enough vigor to maintain policy's grip. He advanced this thought, incidentally, at the very time the idea of momentum was becoming increasingly important in US naval strategy. Eccles's early writings concentrated mainly on describing the basic structural aspects of logistics, and their vital nature. They also reveal his decidedly structuralist bent: all actions, theories, and concepts required an organizing framework or structure into which they could be integrated in order to realize their full meaning. Many of his later writings introduced structures, from the spectrum of conflict to the elements of national power, for precisely that reason.

Eccles's second book, *Logistics in the National Defense*, first published in 1959, set out, albeit in an elementary textbook fashion, to define the fundamental structure and principles of logistical support. It also situated those elements within a modern typology of war. It began by acknowledging that the "nature of war" had changed. "A generation ago," said Eccles, with echoes of Mahan, "it was generally considered that war was a specialized [type] of brutal formal contest in which nations or groups of nations frequently engaged after failing to solve differences by negotiation." Peace was the normal state; war was the aberration. But that outlook has changed, he insisted. Competition and conflict were now normal. Conflict, in fact, was "unceasing" and involved violence at all times, including in "political, economic, military, or para-military" forms. It was "simultaneously formal and informal, and ... ideological and physical, and ... within and among nations." War was basically one part of a continuum of unending conflict, and it could be "understood as merely an accentuation or increase in the degree and scope of violence."[8] What Eccles had attempted to describe was the general movement away from an understanding of international relations in terms of Newtonian concepts, such as equilibrium and stability, toward a model that allowed for the possibility that imbalance and instability might be the natural state of affairs. This perspective differed little from that of Schelling, who advocated concepts that promoted a more stable strategic environment.

"War is not necessarily nor inevitably 'total,'" Eccles went on to say, and he described the various ways in which it could be limited, ways that essentially agreed with fundamentals of limited war theory described by Brodie and Osgood. While he did not footnote Osgood's *Limited War*, he listed it in his bibliography, along with Kissinger's *Nuclear Weapons and Foreign Policy*. Eccles's discussion of how wars can be limited – aims, geography, effort, and weapons – certainly paralleled Osgood's own. The United States must be prepared, he concluded, to use military force at any point along a broad "spectrum of conflict" ranging from the romantic dream of "absolute peace" to the ultimate nightmare of "unlimited total war."[9] This concept of a spectrum of conflict, in fact, would become an enduring feature of US military thinking, surviving into the twenty-first century, albeit in greatly modified form.

An effective policy or strategy, Eccles believed, required integrating all the "elements" of power – political, economic, psychological, and military. This organizing concept, known later as DIME (diplomatic, informational, military, and economic), would survive into the twenty-first century. In conjunction with the elements of power, Eccles described various "tools" of conflict; these included "overt armed forces, covert armed forces, subversion, sabotage, economic action and pressure, political pressure, ideology, propaganda, terrorism, mental torture, and physical torture."[10] Overt military action, it was clear, was only one type of coercive force.

Eccles's analysis also employed terms like "brush-fire" conflicts and "broken-back" wars, which had begun to appear more frequently in the defense literature of the period. The fact that he referred to them in *Logistics in the National Defense* reveals a conscious effort to integrate the latest intellectual fashions into a framework useful for modern-day practitioners. It also shows the extent to which the US military, more generally, had begun to accept the validity of forms of conflict besides general and all-out war. In fact, Eccles's *Logistics in the National Defense* explicitly declared the "nature of war," by which he meant the nature of warfare, or the conduct of war, had changed. It would continue to transform, he believed, through the addition of "more and more areas of human relations, activities of people, elements of power, and tools of conflict."[11] At root, war was still driven by human nature. But Eccles and other analysts began to view the social dimension of conflict with greater interest.

Several other distinguished lecturers who visited the Naval War College in the 1950s and 1960s also contended the nature of war had changed. In October 1955, Professor Gordon B. Turner of Princeton University argued, in much the same sense as Clausewitz, the transition from the dynastic wars of the eighteenth century to the national wars of the nineteenth century brought about a fundamental change in the nature of warfare.[12] He went on to describe, in Brodie-like fashion, how the ever malleable nature of war had changed once again with the advent of nuclear weapons, making it necessary to fight wars only for limited objectives and only with limited means. The next day, a lecture entitled "The Nature of Military Strategy" by the Naval War College's own Ernest J. King Chair of Maritime Strategy, Professor Hiram Stout, explicitly addressed Brodie's claim that old concepts of strategy have come to a "dead end."[13] Drawing from Eccles's definition of strategy as the "comprehensive direction and control of power toward the attainment of broad objectives or aims," among other definitions, Stout rejected Brodie's claim, arguing the basic components of strategy – active direction, power, and objectives – were essentially timeless regardless of the strategic environment. The nature of warfare was still a lively topic two years later when Professor J. Huston took it up in his lecture, "The Theory and Principles of War."[14] War was both an instrument and a determinant of policy, declared Huston, and he suggested five guiding principles for waging war that aligned loosely with America's emerging way of policy: primacy of "political purpose," the "indivisibility" of the overall strategic picture, the "relativity" of gains and losses, "flexibility" of mind, and use of "minimum force." Brodie and Osgood both added to the strategic debates at the Naval War College with lectures on "Strategy as an Art and a Science" and "Concepts of General and Limited War," respectively.[15] Brodie largely avoided the title of his talk except to say the art of strategy lay in experienced judgment, while the science was based on the use of the scientific method. Osgood skirted the issue of defining the difference between general and limited war to address what he saw as a dearth of investment in US capabilities for limited war, especially given the acknowledged shortcomings of the Eisenhower administration's doctrine of massive retaliation.

The quest to understand ongoing changes in the conduct of war continued well into the next decade. By the late 1960s, however, the *Naval War College Review* began featuring more articles written by military professionals, thereby adding practitioner perspectives to those of academics. From 1962 to 1969, more than a third of the articles published in the Navy's foremost strategic journal dealt with some aspect of insurgency or guerrilla warfare. This ratio compares favorably that of the Army's *Military Review*. At least 25 percent of the articles published in the *Naval War College Review* during these years addressed how Communist ideology influenced Soviet or Chinese concepts of war and strategy. More than 10 percent of the articles explored the role of naval power in limited war. Another 15–20 percent attempted to come to terms with how new communications technologies might influence US public opinion and the prosecution of armed conflict. Many of the articles, in fact, dealt with more than one of these topics at a time.

A popular theme in professional military literature during this period was the importance of sociopolitical developments, even if intertwined with technological changes, in determining war's character and possibly its nature. Few articles dealt solely with technological change and the conduct of war, save those that addressed nuclear warfare, and those rarely analyzed it in any depth; nuclear warfare was still largely an unthinkable topic. Of the four recognized species of armed conflict a naval officer might encounter – all-out war, general war, limited war, and revolutionary war – the latter two received the most attention well into the 1960s. As one retired US foreign service officer told Naval War

College students in 1969, "I am quite sure that, over the next few years, at least half of you will be involved in some type of insurgency."[16]

Nor was it only the Navy's officers and educational institutions that perceived, and attempted to cope with, the transformation of warfare. The Army's chief educational institutions – its military academy at West Point, its staff college at Fort Leavenworth, and its war college at Carlisle Barracks – also addressed what many perceived to be a fundamental shift in the nature of warfare. Many officers directed their attention to the problems posed by revolutionary wars. As one historian noted, student papers began to feature the names of counterinsurgency experts, such as Robert Thompson, David Galula, and Roger Trinquier, in their notes and bibliographies; they also admitted that effective counterinsurgency strategies required at least some knowledge of the social and behavioral sciences.[17] To be sure, this heightened attention owed much to the aforementioned "big push" in guerrilla warfare the US Army launched in the early 1960s. Yet this push accomplished its goal of raising awareness. In addition, several important changes in doctrinal perspectives had taken place beforehand. Fort Leavenworth, for instance, initiated a rewrite of its curriculum in 1958, well before Kennedy's election and prior to his administration's decision to put greater emphasis on guerrilla and counterguerrilla warfare.[18] By 1961, the curriculum also covered such topics as Field Army Operations in Limited War, Corps Operations in Limited War, Division Operations in Situations Short of War, Division Operations in Limited War, Development and Use of Guerrilla Potential in a Limited War, and Military Operations against Irregular Forces.[19]

In the meantime, the US Air Force also had opinions about how the nature of warfare had changed. Its *Air University Quarterly Review*, founded in 1947, immediately began touting the capabilities of air power. An example was a two-part article by one of Billy Mitchell's ardent supporters, Alexander de Seversky.[20] Seversky argued the United States should have put all its "resources into long-range strategic Air Power" after the attack on Pearl Harbor, and thus "finished the war *by our own strength* ... with complete control of the air all over the globe." Instead, the United States opted to rebuild the Navy and to chain itself to the "obsolete strategy of surface struggle." According to Seversky, this choice was nothing less than a failure of "strategic vision." Interestingly, after surveying the damage Allied bombing had done to Germany, he argued the anticipation of harm to come was not what compelled a people to surrender, as Schelling would later claim; rather it was the "actual destruction of its means of waging war" that made an adversary accept defeat.[21]

Whereas Osgood and Kissinger preached constraint with the use of force in the nuclear age, moreover, Seversky advocated the opposite. On December 28, 1957, the year in which Osgood's and Kissinger's contributions to the theory of limited war appeared, Mike Wallace of *60 Minutes* interviewed Seversky on public television.[22] The airpower advocate insisted a revolution in the nature of warfare was underway, due chiefly to the expanding capabilities of long-range bombers and missiles, both of which had rendered surface control unnecessary. Admittedly, the interview exposed Seversky as a zealot armed with slogans instead of ideas, and prone to spreading conspiracy theories about the American public being kept in the dark to minimize defense spending. But his attitude regarding the capabilities of airpower reflected the general impatience of a new service, now freed of the shackles of conventional thinking, eager to show its mettle. Other air officers dealt with topics ranging from the need for updated air doctrine, to standardized educational requirements, to celebrations of Douhet, to the technical details of emerging missile and propulsion technologies.[23] Some officers provided running commentaries on air operations over Korea, while others addressed air power's role in limited war, in guerrilla warfare, and in counterinsurgency operations; still others considered the impact of advances in space technology on future warfare.[24] Some authors went so far as to agree with Brodie that limited wars after 1945 differed in nature from their predecessors, thus requiring a revolution in strategy.[25] On the whole, while US Air Force literature was self-assertive in its early years, it later came to consider issues regarding the changing character of war. While the US military uniformly acknowledged the character of war was changing, its understanding of that character and its transformations was not uniform.

6.3 Theory as Critical Inquiry

The belief that war's nature was undergoing a profound change was reinforced in Eccles's third book, *Military Concepts and Philosophy*, which appeared in 1965, two years before Wylie's *Military Strategy*.[26] It represented a compilation of ten years of lecturing and thinking about war, and offered a further refinement of the ideas he had advanced in *Operational Naval Logistics* and *Logistics in the National Defense*. It reintroduced familiar concepts such as the spectrum of conflict, which he claimed, essentially correctly, had been embraced by the Pentagon. The book's chief purpose, however, was to elevate Eccles's Clausewitz-like conception of theory as a "clarifying discipline" to the level of a philosophy for the study of war. Concepts may come and go, but theory, the philosophical study or critical examination of armed conflict, could serve military professionals throughout their careers. Like Clausewitz, Eccles believed theory's role was not to dictate, but to simplify, explain, and illuminate. This role had become even more critical because modern technology had undermined the "classic theory of war," and semantic confusion now ruled in its stead.[27]

As in his previous works, Eccles demonstrated his faith in the ability of rigorous analysis to arrive at the truth. Like so many military professionals of his day, he held positivist assumptions regarding the possibility that analysis could lead to genuine knowledge.[28] Analysis would clear away "semantic uncertainty" and in so doing distinguish sound concepts from empty slogans. Knowledge was both possible and necessary, especially at this point in history because service rivalries in the wake of the Second World War had contributed significantly to the semantic confusion that dominated discussions about military power and defense policy. False strategies, such as "weapon strategy" or the practice of shaping strategy around weapons, had emerged as a result. This practice, he warned, led to a search for weapons with ever more destructive power – without considering the real ends those weapons could serve.[29]

By way of illustration, Eccles quoted extensively from General Maxwell Taylor's *Uncertain Trumpet*, believing the Army officer had aptly portrayed "how the definitions of general war and limited war were formulated and twisted to conform to certain previously formulated concepts of force structure, force balance, and budget allocations." Military theory and doctrine, in other words, had become casualties of the Pentagon's bureaucratic battles. As a result, the military lost control of its "own language" and the "scholars, scientists, and publicists – who were without command experience and responsibility – moved in."[30] Army Colonel Harry Summers would later make much the same claim in his critical analysis of American strategy in the Vietnam War.

Along these lines, Eccles found the intrusion of game theory into US strategic thinking to be of increasing concern. Articles in the *Naval War College Review* distilled the theory into manageable lectures for the benefit of its readers, and illustrated how it could expose the relative value of one course of action over another – given known, and controllable, initial conditions.[31] Other contributions underscored the theory's utility to war gaming, which by this time had become something of an established tradition for the college.[32] Still others addressed how game theory and war gaming could help officers think through the implications of restricting the application of force in the waging of limited wars.[33]

Nonetheless, Eccles's *Military Concepts and Philosophy* urged caution, noting the criticisms of Karl Deutsch, P. M. S. Blackett, and Solly

Zuckerman, who maintained game theory was essentially experimental and not suitable for application to practical matters.[34] Zuckerman, especially, worried that war and strategy involved too many qualitative variables that cannot be quantified, and that change occurred too frequently for the formal logic of game theory to keep pace.[35] Unfortunately, Eccles's warning came too late in the case of Schelling's theories, which had been applied in Operation Rolling Thunder earlier that year with disappointing results.

Eccles also believed theory had a secondary, integrative purpose that involved relating the components of armed conflict to each other – such as military might to political and economic power – so that they formed a comprehensive whole. A complete and coherent structure was a prerequisite to a comprehensive theory of modern conflict and, hence, to an appropriate national strategy. To be comprehensive, a theory had to include the following elements: an understanding of the nature and structure of modern conflict and the essentials that comprised it, the manner in which the essentials relate to one another, the manner in which war relates to other parts of society, and the nature of the forces that act throughout the whole structure.

In addition, a comprehensive theory of war required a general theory of modern conflict, a theory of strategy, a theory of logistics, a theory of tactics, a theory of command decision, and a theory of military organization that included intelligence, communications, and weapons' capabilities. Such a theory, in turn, had to be integrated into additional theories of government, of economics, and of the rationales for one's foreign and domestic policies. While the task of accomplishing so extensive an integration presented a "staggering challenge," Eccles insisted it was necessary for officers in positions of high command – who have the responsibility not only of employing combat forces, but of creating and supporting them.[36] Command meant addressing the concerns of all three tasks simultaneously, which naturally required considerable discipline. Otherwise, one might get drawn into what Eccles described as the "snowball effect" in which the demands of maintaining one's forward-operating bases drain significant resources from the frontlines. Furthermore, he urged his readers to view logistics as a system, and not merely as a collection of technical functions. Logistics formed the "bridge" between a nation's economy and the tactical operations of its combat forces. Accordingly, three corollaries were worth keeping in mind: a logistic system had to be in harmony with the national economic system and with the diverse tactical requirements of the field; economic factors will limit the kinds of forces that can be created, while logistical factors will limit the types of forces that can be employed;

finally, command organizations will transform war potential into combat power by the ways in which they use and control the logistics system.[37] Collectively, these were the reasons economic power was not an accurate gauge of a nation's military power.

Surely anyone in high command would benefit from a comprehensive perspective such as the one Eccles outlined; however, the challenge he had created was not so much "staggering" as it was impossible. Few practitioners would have the time for such an exhaustive level of analytical inquiry and synthetic integration, unless of course they became instructors at one of the nation's war colleges. Ironically, being assigned to an academic tour of that sort severely reduced one's chances of rising to a position of higher command. For that reason, it was a sacrifice not everyone was willing to make. Nonetheless, by default, it fell to the war colleges to perform the difficult analytical and integrative work needed to erect such a comprehensive theoretical structure, to revise it as conditions warranted, and include it as a formal part of professional military education.[38]

6.4   Strategy as Control

As mentioned, Eccles, Wylie, and Rosinski collaborated to establish a theory of strategy as the art of control. Indeed, both officers credited Rosinski for introducing them to the initial concept, "comprehensive control."[39] Rosinski was born in East Prussia in 1903. He emigrated to Great Britain in 1936, to escape Nazi persecution. He moved to the United States in 1940 and accepted an appointment at the Institute for Advanced Study in Princeton, New Jersey. Throughout the 1940s, he published several works on military affairs and foreign policy, including a revised edition of his 1939 book, *The German Army*. During the 1950s, he became a frequent lecturer at the US National War College and US Naval War College, where he obviously influenced the thinking of Wylie and Eccles, among others. Unfortunately, he succumbed to a heart attack in 1962, at the age of fifty-nine, and left behind far too many unpublished manuscripts.[40]

By most accounts, many of Rosinski's colleagues found him unreliable and unable to meet deadlines and contracts. He often failed to meet the terms of his writing contracts. At times, he delivered manuscripts that varied greatly from what editors and publishers wanted and expected. Partly this failure was due to Rosinski's habit of overcommitting himself to writing projects, which caused him to submit incomplete or inappropriate manuscripts to meet deadlines.[41] The result was a legacy of intellectually probing manuscripts which, for one reason or another, were inconclusive, unfinished, and unpublishable. His histories amounted to theories presented as historical narratives. His article, "Scharnhorst to Schlieffen: The Rise and Decline of German Military Thought," for instance, set purely theoretical terms for what constituted military thought, as well as its rise and decline, regardless of historical context.[42] It also revealed Rosinski's elevated opinion of Clausewitz's work, an appreciation he clearly passed on to Wylie and Eccles.

In two unpublished papers, the "Evolution of Warfare and Strategy" and "New Thoughts on Strategy" (1955) to which both Wylie and Eccles had access, Rosinski defined strategy as the "comprehensive direction of power" and tactics as "its immediate application." This definition, presumably derived inductively from Rosinski's study of war, implied that strategy was more than the mere direction of action. It must also account for the "multitude of possible enemy counteractions and thus it becomes a means of control. It is this element of control," Rosinski continued, "which is the essence of strategy: Control being the element that differentiates true strategic action from a haphazard series of improvisations."

Strategy thus aimed at the control of a "field of activity, be it military, social, or, even intellectual," including "every possible counteraction or factor." Comprehensive control, in turn, meant a "concentration upon those minimum key lines of action or key positions from which the entire field can be positively controlled."[43] The concept applied equally well to the offense, where the aim was to break down the enemy's control, and to the defense, where the goal was to thwart the enemy's attack while retaining as much control for oneself as possible while avoiding collapse. Control, he added, was perhaps easiest to achieve on land, more difficult at sea, and most difficult in the air.

Eccles subsequently modified Rosinski's concept, defining strategy as the "comprehensive direction of power to control situations or areas in order to attain broad aims or objectives." Strategy must begin with a thorough "analysis of objectives," and it must select the "tactics and weapons" most appropriate to the type and duration of control desired, rather than allowing the tactics or weapons to dictate strategy. Strategy should use "destruction" only when no other method was available for achieving control. Deterrence, for example, was not a valid strategy because it was only "partial and negative," but it could serve as an integral component of an overall strategy.[44]

The idea of strategy as the art of control was not entirely new; nor should it come as a surprise that two veterans of the Second World War should have developed it. After all, the twentieth century's most cataclysmic war required fighting for some degree of control over, and within, the domains of land, sea, and air to compel the surrender of the Axis powers.

This was the case even if Allied doctrine itself obscured the idea of control, or arbitrarily distinguished different degrees of it through the use of such indistinct terms as "command of the sea" or of the air. For instance, Brodie's wartime primer, *A Layman's Guide to Naval Strategy*, defined sea power in Mahan-like fashion, as the totality of warships, installations, and geographical circumstances which enable a nation "*to control transportation over the seas during wartime.*" Correspondingly, the party that could "carry on its own commerce and stop that of the enemy is said to be in 'command of the sea.'" Command, however, had never meant absolute control, Brodie stressed, only the successful control of one's own "sea-borne communications over certain areas."[45]

Control of the land, sea, air, even if temporally or geographically constrained, clearly contributed to winning battles. Yet control remained important after the fighting as well. Enemy troops had to be disarmed and moved to internment camps, in other words, controlled. Some degree of control also had to be established over civilian populations in the aftermath of battle in order to restore order. While Axis leaders had been compelled to surrender, many of their institutions had to be dismantled and new ones built in their places – all of which required some degree of control.

As a strategic concept, control was qualitatively superior to compellence and, in fact, is the precondition that makes the latter possible. The need for control in war termination and in conflict resolution was obvious, and this requirement alone rendered it superior, as a strategic concept, to Schelling's notions of bargaining and compellence. As discussed earlier, Schelling's analysis did not venture far from a party's immediate decision to concede; nor did he have much to say about how to prevent opponents from reversing their decisions, or simply feigning compliance to buy time. What his theory also lacked was the idea of control as a precondition – an element that did not destroy the process of bargaining as much as it improved the odds of a favorable one.

Wylie and Eccles argued the concept of strategy as control remained useful throughout the course of an armed conflict, not just in the aftermath of the fighting, and not just for all-out wars, but for limited conflicts as well. The core idea entailed changing the pattern of the conflict in a manner that gave one the upper hand over one's opponent, however temporary, and control over the general course of the war. That amount of control required identifying the center of gravity of the conflict. Schelling dissected the decision dynamics that might take place between warring parties but not the overall framework of the conflict itself. The process might need to be iterative, depending on how the adversary responded. One's advantage might have to be leveraged to gain another, and yet another, for instance, until the war could be concluded.

6.5 Reclaiming War's Missing Dimension

Eccles's final major work, *Military Power in a Free Society* was published in 1979, four years after the fall of Saigon and the agonizing evacuation of the American embassy there.[46] It was also the year in which the Soviet Union invaded Afghanistan and embarked upon a Vietnam of its own. *Military Power in a Free Society* differed from Eccles's other books in two important respects: it examined the US failure in Vietnam through the lens of strategic fundamentals, and it attempted to integrate social factors into the analysis of that failure. Patently right of center in its perspective, its diagnosis of the problem of US strategy was nonetheless refreshingly three-dimensional. *Military Power in a Free Society* vigorously criticized civilian policymakers and military leaders alike, while pointing to evidence of rising racial tensions and uncertainty regarding the morality of war that ought to have signaled to America's chief policymakers the need for a different strategic direction.

America's political and military leaders, said Eccles, had abandoned, or perhaps never understood, the fundamentals of strategy. "It is difficult to dignify US military action in Vietnam by the word strategy … At no time did any course of action which was adopted pass the tests of suitability, feasibility, and acceptability." By mid-1966, it was clear the United States had become trapped in an impossible situation. Ironically, the US Army's Harry Summers was in the process of making a similar argument. By then, "President Johnson had no strategy; all he could do was to improvise in desperation."[47] Yet the White House refused to acknowledge its dilemma, and military professionals, for their part, acquiesced by hiding damaging information, developing misleading statistics, and explicitly falsifying reports.[48] The White House attempted to overmanage operations, and the military, in turn, compromised on its planning fundamentals. As a result, US political and military leaders ceded the initiative and control of the conflict to the enemy, and in the process destroyed the confidence of the American public in its government.

Importantly, *Military Power in a Free Society* claimed a radical shift had occurred in America's social structure and culture. The generations of the First and Second World Wars, said Eccles, reflected a certain "conceptual unity" with respect to the reasons for those conflicts and the methods by which they were waged. The generation of the 1960s, however, was characterized by "wide and bitter differences of opinion" over the merits and means of the Vietnam War. Class and race antagonisms had grown stronger in the 1960s; the "well-to-do" were able to stay in college and avoid combat duty, while racial minorities and the economically disadvantaged shouldered a disproportionate share of the war's burden. This situation was exacerbated by the obsolescence of the draft law of the 1940s, which was in still effect at the time of the Vietnam conflict.[49] That law was designed for a conflict on a scale akin to that of the world wars, but it was completely inadequate for the situation in Vietnam.

America's social divisions did not go unnoticed by other military practitioners. Several officers attempted to assess what the strategic implications might be of society's changing views towards war and military service. One officer, for example, conducted an exhaustive examination of the major theories purporting to explain the phenomenon of student protests in the 1960s.[50] None of the theories was completely persuasive, he concluded; but each offered a partial explanation. His examination drew from the Urban Research Corporation's 1969 report on student protest. The report showed that, for the first half of 1969, less than 10 percent of America's colleges and universities experienced a student protest, and only some 3.5 percent of the nation's 7,000,000 students took part in one.[51] Yet this minority had achieved a degree of visibility and a voice disproportionate to its mass, due largely to the amount of attention the protests received from the media.

Student protests on almost any scale were something new compared to student behavior in the 1950s and in earlier decades. The 1960s had earned a reputation as "The Decade of Protest." Protest itself – which assumed a variety of forms in haircuts, dress, speech, music, and art – became a matter of self-identity for the "counterculture" movement of 1960s. It was an indicator of a sea change in attitude. The pendulum of antimilitarism would not swing back until Americans faced a serious threat, he opined.[52] Nonetheless, "for the nation's leadership to fail to educate the American people that military assistance, in men, money, and material, will be a continuing requirement would be a mistake that could mean the loss of world leadership."[53]

Reflecting a view shared by many of his contemporaries, Eccles referred to the media, history's celebrated Fourth Estate, not as a sub-element of the populace, but as a separate institution.[54] In effect, the media – newspapers, magazines, radio, and television – generally pursued their own interests, and did so nominally, and never entirely, for the sake of the public. Their search for headlines and "good copy" sometimes led to the willful exaggeration or elision of critical facts, which in turn fed the cycle of mistrust and animus that grew among the populace, the government, and the military. The question "What's wrong with the American press?" was a recurring one during this period; and it implied the media ought to have done more to support the government.

Eccles believed the media had distorted the facts about the war – almost as much as the government and the military had. In fact, he regarded the reports of the media as more truthful overall than those of the government and the military. He did not mention whether the release in 1971 of the "Pentagon Papers" helped him form this opinion. But it is likely the many revelations therein played a role, especially since the contents of the Pentagon Papers were discussed at a Naval War College roundtable on "Communications Media," and the proceedings were subsequently published by the *Naval War College Review* in 1972. Neil Sheehan, a reporter with *The New York Times*, an editor of the Pentagon Papers, and an erstwhile White House correspondent, noted the general sense was that the media ought to have done more to speak truth to power.[55]

Military Power in a Free Society considered the role of the media in some detail. After a brief historical survey from the Spanish–American War to Vietnam, Eccles concluded the media perform a "dual role" in the waging of war and the crafting of strategy. On the one hand, they inform and influence public opinion; at the same time, they advise the "government of the state of public opinion," what the public thinks about the direction of the war. The value of this information is that it "can determine what we should try to do," what political objectives the country should seek, as well as "what not to do," whether political leaders should continue the war or seek peace.[56] In short, the government's ability to use force corresponded directly with the rise and fall of public opinion – insofar as opinion was a reliable measure of public support.

This conclusion was certainly not the first time US strategists had pointed to the need for public support in the prosecution of war. Limited war theorists had recognized its importance as well. They generally found it worrisome, however, because they feared the public – perhaps too familiar with traditional notions of war and ignorant of the risks of escalation – would agitate for strategic objectives that were more appropriate for an all-out war; hence, the information released to the public had to be restricted and packaged as positively as possible. This angst was misplaced, though, as some contemporary research showed. The public had not agitated for escalation, but its opposite. One student's research revealed US political leaders had often wrongly assumed American public opinion was unstable, and they frequently blamed it or used it as a scapegoat for their own failed or aborted policies.[57]

US public opinion, while not unstable, did sometimes reflect views that seemed "schizophrenic," in the words of at least one analyst; Americans, he said, were "ideologically conservative, but operationally liberal."[58] Americans wanted a strong military posture, he said, but not an increase in defense spending. In truth, much of this apparent schizophrenia had to do with the way survey questions were asked. Instead of swinging from one extreme to the other, American public opinion seems to have preferred the middle-ground – the very zone opinion polls have difficulty capturing. Americans had simply indicated they wanted sensible tradeoffs between a strong posture and constrained military spending.

For his part, Eccles believed assessing the public's willingness to support military action needed to be formalized in developing strategy. Indeed, crafting strategy within the context of a modern free society was increasingly becoming America's inescapable challenge. Unfortunately, gauging public attitudes, even with "scientific" opinion polls, was far more art than science. It was an art, in fact, wherein US policymakers had yet to demonstrate consistent skill.

6.6 Conclusions

Eccles approached strategic theory as a structuralist; he saw doctrinal structures as necessary to confirm a concept's utility, clarify its relationships with other concepts, and preclude contradiction or redundancy. What's more, doctrinal structures contributed to creating stability in environments characterized by conceptual fluidity and uncertainty. But military professionals, too, had a role to play in reducing instability; Eccles encouraged them to regard new concepts with skepticism and to think of theory as critical inquiry, à la Clausewitz. Indeed, critical inquiry was to be the lifelong companion of the military professional.

During this period of instability, concerns over the transformation of war's character overtook questions about its nature. For his part, Eccles saw war's nature through the lens of the traditional paradigm. He saw armed conflict as a violent extension of human nature, but with a twist: human nature both reflected and influenced the behavior of social groups. Put differently, societies represented an expansion, or multiplication, of human nature: social groups took on the personalities of their leaders, much like a ship's crew assumed the character of its captain. After all, as Clausewitz had said, armed conflict was more a social activity than an art or a science. Eccles took that observation further, however, by equating a society's psychosocial (moral) health to its ability to achieve success in war.

Eccles's conception of war's character was, therefore, three-dimensional, unlike that of the strategy intellectuals: the psychosocial dimension of armed conflict was as important as its military and political dimensions, as demonstrated by the Vietnam War. Accordingly, his thinking did not depart from the traditional paradigm, but rather enlarged and refined it with additional observations. On the other hand, he did engage the Clausewitzian concept of friction more directly than did Mahan or Mitchell. As the theories of the Navy's master logistician reveal, Eccles regarded friction as an attritional force that weakened the reach of policy, an idea that created conceptual space for the modern paradigm of war's nature.

7 J. C. Wylie and Strategy as Control

A naval practitioner with combat experience in the Second World War, J. C. Wylie contributed in three important ways to the counterrevolution of the military intellectuals. The first of these was his concept of strategy as control, which he constructed with the assistance of Henry Eccles and Herbert Rosinski. This concept, expressed in Wylie's classic *Military Strategy*, offered a practical alternative to the abstract theories of the strategy intellectuals.[1] Just as importantly, it provided a joint framework for the development and execution of military strategy within a modern context; as he often stressed, strategic practice required "a good deal of overlap and merging."[2] His concept was integrative at a time when the roles and missions of the services had come under scrutiny due to the impact of nuclear weapons on modern warfare. Thirdly, he raised the critical point that armed conflict might be just as much a break in policy, especially for the defender, as its continuation by other means. That point, though partially recognized by Brodie, was insufficiently accounted for by America's way of policy.

7.1 Pragmatist and Theorist

Joseph Caldwell Wylie was born on March 21, 1911, in Newark, New Jersey. He was not raised in a military family; his father became a chief executive officer of a company that manufactured maritime lighting and signaling equipment. Rather than completing high school, Wylie attended a preparatory school for the US Naval Academy and gained admission in 1928. Since the academies did not grant diplomas at the time, he often referred to himself, with obvious irony, as a "high school dropout who never went to college."[3] Decades later, he was still at a loss to explain why he had applied to the Academy, except that it had always been an ambition of his.[4] Unlike Eccles, Wylie did well both academically and otherwise as a midshipman, graduating near the top of his class in 1932, three years into the Great Depression. He served aboard the cruiser USS *Augusta* for his first assignment, where he eventually had the opportunity to work under then Captain Chester Nimitz. For four years, Wylie toured ports such as Hong Kong, Amoy, Foochow, Nanking, Tsingtao, and Singapore. In 1937, he married Harriette Bahney, and they had two children together. From 1936 through the summer of 1941, he served on the destroyers USS *Reid*, *Altair*, and *Bristol*. Even before the Japanese attack on Pearl Harbor on December 7, 1941, Wylie saw action with the USS *Bristol* as part of US naval forces assigned to protect merchant vessels ferrying supplies across the Atlantic Ocean from Canada to Iceland. Merchant marine sources indicate German U-boats sank at least a dozen vessels from December 1940 to early December 1941.[5]

From 1942 to January 1943, Wylie, a lieutenant commander, was assigned to be the executive officer for another destroyer, the USS *Fletcher*. He participated in naval engagements in the waters around Guadalcanal in November 1942, where US forces suffered heavy losses, and was awarded the silver star. In one incident, Wylie ordered his sailors to fire on Japanese pilots who had parachuted into the water after their planes were shot down. The pilots had refused to surrender and, as he later explained, "I was afraid they would return to attack us again in different aircraft."[6] In another war, his actions might have been grounds for an official inquiry and disciplinary action. But the extreme acrimony that characterized the conflict in the Pacific theater, on both sides, has been well documented. In January 1943, Wylie assumed command of the USS *Trever*, a fast minesweeper, and saw action during the Solomon Islands campaign. He was ordered back to Pearl Harbor midway through the year, where his experience proved instrumental in standardizing command and control procedures aboard destroyers. He drafted the *CIC Handbook for Destroyers*, which was distributed across the Navy and provided a basis for officer training. From January to June 1945, Wylie, now in command of the destroyer USS *Ault*, saw action in operations near Taiwan, the China Coast, Okinawa, and Iwo Jima.[7]

After the war, he was detailed to the Office of Naval Research for a short time. Then, from 1948 to 1949, he attended the US Naval War College as a student. While there the well-publicized "revolt of the admirals" took place wherein senior Navy officers attempted to obstruct the development of the Convair B-36 bomber.[8] US Air Force officials claimed the B-36 had sufficient range and hauling capacity to render aircraft carriers obsolete; while the Navy's admirals saw it, not incorrectly, as a threat to naval aviation and, by extension, the Navy's ability to defeat hostile naval forces at sea and to project power ashore. The Navy had already been reduced by approximately 80 percent, from 4 million personnel to 450,000 and from 1,300 vessels to 238.[9] The planned production of the B-36, therefore, appeared to be another assault on the Navy, especially with airpower zealots such as Seversky repeating Billy Mitchell's assertions regarding the obsolescence of sea power.

Although the revolt of the admirals failed to stop the production of the B-36, the Navy took a hard look at its roles and missions, and Wylie became part of that effort. From 1950 to 1952, he led a working group tasked with explaining the US Navy's raison d'être. He also contributed to reforming the program of instruction at the Naval War College at about the same time. Underpinning the latter effort was the realization among such Navy leaders as Admirals Raymond Spruance and Richard Conolly that historical knowledge was critical to strategic decision-making, but few naval officers had time to learn it. To solve the problem, at least partially, Wylie recommended the Naval War College consider partnering with Herbert Rosinski, who had demonstrated a great breadth and depth of historical knowledge. "There actually is no one else in the world today," Wylie informed Rosinski, "who understands the subject [of sea power] as you do."[10] The partnership of Wylie and Rosinski essentially amounted to a merging of theory and history that exceeded what Mahan had advocated fifty years earlier.

In 1953, Wylie commanded the USS *Arneb*, an attack transport. During that assignment he also wrote most of his manuscript for what would become his major work, *Military Strategy*.[11] The manuscript's original title was "The Military Mind."[12] The "mind" was something of a cultural preoccupation in the United States for the middle decades of the twentieth century, as evinced by such works as Perry Miller's *The New England Mind* (1939), W. J. Cash's *The Mind of the South* (1941), Gung-Hsing Wang's *The Chinese Mind* (1946), and the chapter on the "military mind" in Huntington's *Soldier and the State* (1957). Wylie initially seemed concerned with demonstrating how four different military minds – continental, maritime, air, and guerrilla/revolutionary – approached strategy differently, while arguing for their integration with his strategy of control. His editors nonetheless rescued his book from the possibility of temporal irrelevance and increased its durability in the field of strategic studies.

After commanding the USS *Arneb*, Wylie served as an operations officer in, and later the chief of staff for, Amphibious Group II. From 1958 to 1959, he commanded the USS *Macon*, a heavy cruiser. From 1959 to 1960, he served on the staff of NATO's supreme allied command. He was promoted to rear admiral on December 1, 1960, and commanded Cruiser Division Three. He was assigned to the Joint Strategic Survey Council from 1962 to 1964, which had the mission of providing the joint chiefs with strategic assessments and policy recommendations on any number of critical issues, including the mounting US involvement in Vietnam. As he later explained, the council performed only an advisory function for the joint chiefs and had little impact on US policy.[13]

It was during this assignment that Wylie and US Air Force Brigadier-General Stanley Holtoner drafted "A Strategic Appreciation" of the situation in Vietnam in which they purportedly argued not to increase America's involvement in Vietnam. "Dien Bien Phu," they noted, "had been lost in metropolitan France not in southeast Asia." In their view, rising social turbulence and anti-imperialist sentiments in France made it morally and psychologically impossible for the government in Paris to generate support for the war, and they saw parallel tensions mounting within the United States. Hence, Washington should pursue a more modest policy limited to blockading the coast, mining the harbors, and otherwise disrupting the flow of arms and supplies into North Vietnam.[14] The notion that the French lost the war in Paris not in Indochina was later criticized by Brodie, who attributed it to General Maxwell Taylor's testimony to the Senate Foreign Relations Committee in 1966. "The proper reply," said Brodie, "might well have been: 'Of course; where else should they have made the appropriate decision?'"[15] Brodie's point was correct: conceding defeat was ultimately a political decision. Yet Wylie also had a point: as a democracy, the government in Paris had essentially conceded to the will of the French populace, to pressures from the psychosocial dimension of war.

During April and May 1965, Wylie served as deputy chief of staff for planning and operations to the commander-in-chief, US Atlantic Fleet, for the US intervention in the Dominican Republic. The operation followed on the heels of Operation Rolling Thunder (March 1965) and because of its temporary success likely influenced, if indirectly, the subsequent escalation of US military forces in Vietnam. In 1966, the year before his *Military Strategy* was published, he became the deputy commander in chief of US Naval Forces, Europe. A practitioner turned theorist, Wylie retired from active duty on July 1, 1972, after forty-four years of service; he passed away on January 1, 1993.

7.2 A Rationale for the Navy

In November 1951, Wylie delivered a presentation at the US Naval War College on the "Navy's Reasons for Being" that discussed the need for a navy in the new strategic environment.[16] At that point, the US Navy had not fought a major sea battle in half a dozen years; nor did one appear likely, considering the composition of Chinese and Soviet navies. After destroying North Korea's insubstantial maritime forces, the US Navy shifted to executing critical, but low-profile missions such as protecting allied convoys.[17] If such missions were to be typical of the Cold War, the Navy might need to reexamine its purpose, something it had not done since the era of Mahan. At that point, the Navy's raison d'être consisted of three missions: protecting US maritime commerce, destroying hostile naval forces, and projecting power ashore. Since then, however, the advent of nuclear weapons made it more likely Moscow would, in Wylie's words, "choose to impose its wishes by a series of 'Koreas' throughout the fringes of its present power" than by a decisive confrontation.[18] Ergo, Wylie proposed a military strategy of deterrence in which the Navy, Air Force, Army, and Marine Corps cooperated jointly to provide multiple response packages to any given crisis provoked by Soviet influence.[19] He had described the strategic environment in line with the basic principles of Truman's National Security Council Paper 68 (NSC-68), which defined the Cold War as an ideological struggle that, "from the Soviet side, did not permit compromise," as Paul Nitze, the document's chief architect, later explained.[20] More concretely, NSC-68 called for increased spending on nuclear as well as conventional forces, and thereby gave the Navy new life, a life Wylie aimed to nurture fully. To be sure, Wylie's proposal protected the equities of the Navy by making it central to the country's response options. But it did so without endangering the equities of the other services. Wylie's proposal revealed a nonparochial perspective, also evident in his other works, that would serve him well as he began fashioning the concept of strategy as control.

7.3 Strategy as Control

On September 11, 1952, Wylie delivered a presentation to his Newport colleagues on the topic of "Maritime Strategy."[21] He incorporated Brodie's guidelines for "sound strategy" into his own evolving theory of strategy as a plan of control, rather than a plan of destruction. "The aim of any war," said Wylie, was "to establish some measure of control over the enemy. The pattern of action by which this control is sought is the strategy of the war."[22] While any number of specific types of strategy might exist, all of them fell within three main streams of strategic thought: continental, air, and maritime. Continental strategies were those in which the "major and critical part of the action to establish control over the enemy is directed against [its] armies" with all other efforts in support. Air strategies sought a decision primarily through air action, with "predominant emphasis on strategic bombardment." Maritime strategies exploited seaborne "communications systems" to establish control over one's foes. A maritime strategy normally consisted of two phases: the establishment of control of the sea, and the "exploitation of that control by one or more selected critical areas of decision on land."[23] He underscored the Navy's particular "way of battle," pointing out how naval officers often regarded the first phase as an end in itself. To be sure, maritime strategies must include naval tactics and engagements; however, a preoccupation with phase one, with winning sea battles, tended to restrict the focus of maritime strategies too narrowly.

Moreover, Wylie's argument paralleled Mahan's belief that the fundamentals of strategy, its purposes and patterns, were timeless. Modern developments, or "complications" as he called them, such as mechanization, improvements in explosives, new revolutionary movements, increased logistical demands, enhanced aviation capabilities, and the invention of nuclear energy had certainly altered warfare. But they had not "revolutionized" strategy in the sense Brodie and others had claimed.[24] The purposes and patterns, of course, remained timeless because human nature, the root of war, was also timeless. For that reason, a maritime strategy of control would possess enough inherent flexibility to serve the interests of the United States and NATO for some time to come.

Thirteen years later, Wylie developed these ideas further in a lecture he delivered at the Naval War College on August 17, 1965, three months after his assignment as deputy chief of staff for planning and operations in the US intervention in the Dominican Republic. Wylie's lecture, entitled "Historical and Contemporary Theories of Strategy," précised his book, *Military Strategy*, and added a crucial fourth stream of strategic thought to the three he had described earlier.[25] This one, the "war of national liberation," he referred to as a new phenomenon as it did not follow the classic rules of warfare; it was also usually and misleadingly referred to as guerrilla warfare, and its critical element was "control of the rural peasant power base."[26] A military strategist needed to be able to identify and exploit the weaknesses inherent in each theory, weaknesses that stemmed from each theory's "tacit assumptions." If the rural peasantry could not be brought to the revolutionists' side, for instance, the "'war of national liberation' could not get off the starting blocks."

As an example, Wylie mentioned the "strategic hamlet program," which he considered sound in concept but poorly executed. The program entailed forcibly relocating South Vietnamese peasants to newly erected villages where, presumably, they would be insulated from Viet Cong infiltration and easier to protect. While the British boasted of having used a similar program successfully in Malaya, the idea of transferring it to Vietnam was problematic due partly to the Diem regime's indifference, if not disdain, for the rural peasantry.[27] Wylie offered few suggestions for improving the program's execution; however, he did suggest America's way of battle complicated its ability to identify the problem in the first place: "As a nation we have intuitively recognized that the basic problem in Southeast Asia is a socio-political one, but we really seem unable to apply anything other than our military strength." According to Wylie, the only US military involvement (since 1960) in which the purposes were clearly stated was the intervention in the Dominican Republic: to protect American lives, to protect the US embassy, and to evacuate US citizens and friendly nationals. The opposite was true for debacles such as the Bay of Pigs invasion and the escalating involvement in Vietnam.[28]

In effect, Wylie's strategy of control developed as a practical alternative to America's way of battle. Control, not destruction, was the ultimate goal, and control meant placing an individual *"on the scene with the gun."* That person "is control" and that person "determines who wins." That individual need not be physically present on the scene, but must be available, and be seen to be available. To put soldiers in those positions, however, required strategists to achieve some control over the "pattern of war." That kind of control was to be achieved by manipulating the "center of gravity of war to the advantage of the strategist and the disadvantage of the opponent."[29]

The concept of the center of gravity had been included in the US military's educational texts since the 1920s, which defined it as the hostile "decisive element," usually the enemy's main force.[30] Wylie instead likened centers of gravity to "centers of weight" or "focal points," the manipulation of which could shift the direction or momentum of the conflict. A center of gravity resembled a "national jugular vein" in the sense that attacking it would force the opponent into some form of accommodation. Control of the "strategic weights or centers of gravity in any war, large or small, limited or unlimited, is a basic advantage that should be sought by any strategist. It is the fundamental key to warfare."[31]

Wylie further defined control as the "creation of conditions more favorable to us than would have existed had we not gone to war." One had to achieve sufficient control to "re-settle" the enemy "after the fighting into some acceptable status in whatever may be the postwar scheme of the world."[32] Control provided more flexibility to the strategist than did sheer destruction, moreover, because destroying a foe's armed forces or collapsing its government might not actually meet one's aims. While some destruction certainly would lead to greater control by immobilizing or paralyzing an adversary, Wylie suggested one could also achieve a more positive and more viable form of control through the physical occupation of specific localities or "focal points." Implicit or explicit threats of destruction, he said, echoing Schelling's notions of coercion, could also result in some degree of control. Finally, one could also achieve various degrees of control through "economic, political, social, and psychological pressures."[33]

By way of illustration, Wylie referred to the campaign between Scipio and Hannibal in the Second Punic War (218–202 BCE). When Scipio assumed command of Rome's legions, Hannibal's forces occupied the lower half of the Italian peninsula, and the war had essentially settled into a state of equilibrium. Scipio attacked Hannibal's principal base of supply in Spain, the capture of which gave a significant advantage to Rome. Scipio then landed on the coast of Africa and threatened Carthage, a move that in turn forced Hannibal to withdraw from Italy to defend the city. Scipio then dictated the terms of the final battle at Zama by taking a position within the fertile valley that supplied Carthage the bulk of its food, thereby requiring Hannibal to march his troops there. Similarly, in a second example, US General William T. Sherman had manipulated the center of gravity of the American Civil War when he marched into the heart of the Confederacy.[34] As Wylie pointed out, however, Sherman's "sequential" strategy might not have succeeded had it been attempted two years earlier, before the "cumulative" strategy of the Union blockade had taken effect. Much like Clausewitz, Wylie saw centers of gravity as dynamic, not static or fixed. Centers of gravity emerged in the interplay of the strengths and weaknesses of the combatants. Like two wrestlers, the moves and countermoves of the combatants shifted the pattern of conflict sometimes towards equilibrium and sometimes in a direction more favorable to one party or the other.

Wylie's book also explored "sequential" and "cumulative" methods of control, as well as their combination.[35] He borrowed these methods directly from Rosinski, who in 1951 framed them as "directive" and "cumulative."[36] In sequential strategies control came as a result of a logical sequence of actions or phases, such as the great drives across the Pacific theater in the Second World War or the Allied advance across France in 1944. Control occurred in stages, as one's forces advanced ever closer to an opponent, eventually removing all the opponent's options but compliance or annihilation. By comparison, in cumulative strategies control accrued over time, as in strategies of attrition and exhaustion, until one's opponent passed the "point of no return." Ironically, a victorious party might not realize that its opponent has reached its point of no return; the opponent might not realize it either or be willing to admit it.

Cumulative strategies applied best in psychological and economic warfare, both of which relied on an accretion of effects.[37] Alternatively, wars of national liberation and people's wars used both forms of control. Such wars typically unfolded in three phases: building a physical and psychological base of support among the peasantry, carrying out limited guerrilla attacks to demoralize the adversary, then a full-scale offensive aimed at defeating the enemy's forces and seizing the seat of power. Clearly, the two forms of control operated simultaneously and reinforced each other in this type of conflict. Wylie's point, though, was that cumulative strategies were underappreciated, and thus required more study by America's civilian and military strategists.

7.4 War as a Breakdown of Policy

Although he largely agreed with Clausewitz, Wylie was perhaps the first US military theorist to challenge the assumption that policy directed war. Some of America's more colorful military figures, of course, had already challenged it in practice. Wylie correctly distinguished between policy as a product of a political process, and political intercourse as an ongoing political activity. One might assume wartime purposes were "basically the same as prewar policy purposes except that the means of pursuit of the policies are somewhat more violent." But that was not always the case. Political intercourse might well continue once a conflict had broken out, and an aggressor's prewar policy might initially be the same as its wartime policy; nonetheless, that would not necessarily be true for the nonaggressive party. Most likely, that party would need to formulate a new policy appropriate to the situation, though self-defense was always a standing, if implicit, policy.

North Korea's attacks across the 38th Parallel in June 1950 illustrated Wylie's point: the attack had not been anticipated by the White House, and no policy was in place to respond to it. One was developed in some haste, but only as the invasion unfolded. Truman had received word of the attack on Saturday, June 24, 1950. Yet he did not meet with his advisors until the following Monday evening, June 26, at which time a tentative policy was fashioned, only to be updated repeatedly as the situation developed.[38] "Once war comes," said Wylie, "nearly all prewar policy is utterly invalid because the setting in which it was designed to function no longer corresponds with the facts of reality."[39] From the standpoint of a defender desiring not to be attacked, Wylie was correct. But policies can also anticipate an act of aggression, or a change in circumstances, and prepare for them by developing contingencies. The outbreak of war need not render prewar policy "utterly invalid," in other words. Nevertheless, it is always possible the contingencies do not fit the actual circumstances, thus creating a policy gap.

Limited war theory did not devote enough attention to either the possibility or the effects of an absence or a breakdown in policy. It assumed a policy would always be in effect or formulated quickly enough to avoid a gap in guidance. Moreover, crises can cause hasty decisions that give policy an irrational character. Yet Wylie ought to have explored this issue further. If a nonaggressor must scramble to formulate a new policy, a break ensues, short or long, in which no policy is, in fact, directing the war. In such periods, military forces find themselves either waiting for instructions or following outdated ones, or, as in the case of General MacArthur, taking actions according to military doctrine or tradition; that is, according to war's grammar.

One of those traditions was the belief that defeating the enemy's army was the proper aim in war. While that may be true in many cases, "if we always saddle ourselves with [this] self-imposed restriction," said Wylie, "we have indeed denied to ourselves consideration of a vast span of actions that might more readily and easily achieve the needed measure of control." What was required, therefore, was the "broadest possible conceptual span of strategies for war," of war-planning concepts and strategies that were "flexible and noncommittal."[40] Concepts aimed at establishing some measure of control, over one's enemy or over the situation, Wylie urged, were better than a single strategic approach based on destruction. As he stressed, "we are not talking about battles; we are talking about war." There was, in his view, too little discussion of war in its "totality" – of its multiple dimensions – and too much attention given to the act of winning battles.[41] Unfortunately, he was correct.

Theory itself, Wylie said, in agreement with Clausewitz, was merely a way of ordering one's thoughts, of making sense of events, and of anticipating, as opposed to predicting, the consequences of those events. A "theory," he explained, was "an idea designed to account for actuality or to account for what the theorist thinks will come to pass as actuality. It is an orderly rationalization of real or presumed patterns of events."[42] Put simply, one's expectations – one's assumptions about war's nature – mattered even if they remained implicit. In this sense, Wylie's concept of theory differed in subtle ways from those of Clausewitz or Eccles. While each theorist emphasized analysis, Wylie aimed more directly at exposing the strengths and weaknesses of a theory's "tacit assumptions."

7.5 Wylie's First Principles

Wylie's core principles – summed up as control first, destruction second – built upon and refined the nineteenth-century imperative of "getting there first with the most," as promoted by Mahan. Likewise, Jomini's core principles – concentration, offensive action, and decision by battle – supported Wylie's first core principle and thus demonstrated their value in the nuclear era, though with obvious caveats. But Wylie added greater granularity to Mahan's imperative by joining it with the concept of center of gravity. While that concept was not new, Wylie expanded its definition beyond an enemy's main fighting forces, the common definition, to mean a "national jugular vein," an item that, if properly threatened, should compel the enemy to concede. One could apply it, moreover, in any type of conflict or in pursuit of any kind of political objective. The center of gravity served as the focal point against which one might apply a variety of pressures – military, economic, political, social, psychological, or some combination of them – individually or collectively to achieve a decisive level of control.

Wylie's second core principle meant treating destruction not as an end itself, but as a means. Destruction must lead to greater control, even if by merely thwarting an opponent's efforts to achieve control it was gratuitous and possibly counterproductive. An armed conflict was not simply a battle writ large; ergo, control had to extend beyond the battle into postwar processes, at least to a degree. Nor did that principle contradict decision by battle so much as provide it with a concrete purpose. America's military strategists struggled to make the conceptual leap from thinking about battles to thinking about wars, according to Wylie; that observation represented one of his key takeaways from the armed conflicts in Korea and Vietnam. It would also figure large in Harry Summers's work, *On Strategy*, discussed in the next chapter.

7.6 War's Nature and Society

Like Eccles, Wylie clearly subscribed to the traditional, or Mahanian, conception of war's nature. War was essentially a violent extension of the competitive side of human nature. As such, warring parties acted aggressively to achieve control over the situation, or over each other; hence the importance of getting there first with the most. By pointing out that war was often a break in policy rather than its extension, Wylie had not rejected the idea that policy *should* direct war. Instead, he questioned the assumption that it *did*, pointing out lapses in direction. Unfortunately, the implications of those lapses or gaps have remained underexplored in the American way of thinking about war. America's way of policy, moreover, has barely acknowledged them. One remedy, of course, is to ensure military commanders possess enough political acumen to make on-the-spot decisions which, if not always right, are at least not too far wrong. The strategy intellectuals, in other words, were clinging to an ideal that, though born of necessity, was nonetheless problematic.

7.7 Conclusions

Although strategy as the art and science of control reflected mainly the experiences of two veterans of the Second World War and the knowledge of an émigré historian, it offered a practical framework for military strategy in almost any era. It has not been fully developed, however, and instead has fallen into obscurity, save as an academic curiosity. The military intellectuals bear some responsibility for that outcome because they neglected to address some of the obvious problems of converting the theory into practice. Suppose, for instance, one lacked the time or wherewithal to achieve any real degree of control over a foe or a situation; then what? How, moreover, might one achieve control over a peer without triggering escalation? In short, the military intellectuals made assumptions that limited the appeal of their theory.

Although Wylie's model of war's nature followed the traditional paradigm, he and Eccles also understood armed conflict to be a social phenomenon, as per their study of Clausewitz. But they interpreted the behavior of societies or social groups largely as human nature writ large. Accordingly, the traditional paradigm remained valid even with the additional attention Eccles and Wylie gave to the psychosocial dimension of war. For Wylie, policy's influence over the direction of war was not a given. While he did not dispute policy's right to govern strategy, he laid bare the uncomfortable reality – that policy often cannot exercise its right because the situation has changed radically enough to render previous political decisions irrelevant before new ones can take their places. This observation amounted to a call for two things: policies that were more anticipatory in nature, and military leaders who were more sensitive to political concerns.

For Wylie, war's character underwent two significant turns. First, nuclear weapons threatened to change the entire conduct of war and nearly rendered his service obsolete. Second, the renewed use of guerrilla warfare widened war's character and cast a sharper light on the importance of the psychosocial dimension. Partly in response to these turns, Wylie advanced one major core principle: concentration of multiple forms of power against an adversary's center of gravity for the purpose of achieving control rather than mere destruction. This principle represented a partial synthesis of the clash between America's way of battle, as reflected in the tradition of Jomini's imperatives, and its way of policy, as captured in the precepts put forth by the strategy intellectuals. The synthesis, as such, failed to take hold in the American way of thinking about war, though the idea of applying all available forms of national power in a crisis has ebbed and flowed in US strategic thinking.

8 Harry Summers and the Principles of War

A decorated veteran of the Korean and Vietnam conflicts, US Army Colonel Harry Summers made two important contributions to the American way of thinking about war. Both appeared in Summers's *On Strategy: The Vietnam War in Context*, published in 1981, just two years after Osgood's *Limited War Revisited* and Eccles's *Military Power in a Free Society*.[1] The book fiercely criticized US military strategy, or the lack of it, as conceived and carried out in the Vietnam War, and it spared neither the strategy intellectuals, whom Weigley lauded, nor the many military and policy practitioners in the background, who went unrecognized. Its primary objective, however, was to shame the US Army into taking more responsibility for the debacle in Vietnam and thereby to restore its tarnished image as a profession.

Summers's first contribution was to explode the assumption that tactical victories led automatically to successful wars. As he bitterly noted, "On the battlefield itself the Army was unbeatable; yet in the end, it was North Vietnam, not the United States, that emerged victorious."[2] Secondly, he caused the American way of thinking about war to reconsider the principles of war, which Brodie and Osgood had effectively demolished. Summers insisted the principles of war should occupy center stage as guidelines for crafting military strategy. His argument spurred a brief period of enthusiasm for martial principles. But it eventually ran up against the US Army's AirLand Battle doctrine, built around tenets that echoed the traditional military imperatives of Jomini. Summers's analyses of the Vietnam War also reveal a telling confusion regarding the nature of war and its conduct that was not untypical for the times.

8.1 Soldier and Critic

Harry Glenn Summers, Jr., was born on May 6, 1932 in Covington, Kentucky. He was not a genuine intellectual, military or otherwise, and was not shy about admitting it. He enlisted in the US Army in 1947, at the age of fifteen, without having completed high school. At the time of his enlistment, the Army was still in the process of downsizing under the Truman administration's bid to reap postwar peace dividends to finance the Marshall Plan. The US Army had been reduced from 8 million personnel and eighty-nine combat divisions to fewer than 1 million personnel and ten combat divisions, and several independent regiments and battalions.[3] In the summer of 1950, he saw intense combat in Korea as a soldier in the 24th Infantry Division, whose unit was routed by Communist forces. In 1957, four years after the armistice that ended hostilities on the peninsula, he received a direct commission in the US Army. As readers will recall, 1957 was the year in which Osgood's *Limited War*, Kissinger's *Foreign Policy and Nuclear Weapons*, and Huntington's *Soldier and the State* appeared, the Soviets launched Sputnik I and II into orbit, and Elvis's "Jail House Rock" energized a generation approximately one decade younger than Summers. By then, Summers had also completed equivalency programs for a high school diploma and a bachelor's degree. From 1966 to 1967, Summers served as a battalion operations officer in Vietnam, as waves of social protests and riots swept across America. In 1974, the year in which Richard Nixon resigned as president of the United States, Summers returned to Vietnam to serve as chief of the Negotiations Division of the "Four Party Joint Military Team." The team's principal task was to resolve the status of US service members listed as missing in action.[4]

During this assignment, Summers reportedly reminded a North Vietnamese Army (NVA) colonel: "You know, you never defeated us on the battlefield." The NVA officer allegedly replied, "That may be so, but it is also irrelevant."[5] Historians and others have repeatedly cited this dialogue as evidence of Summers's revelation that battlefield victories do not necessarily suffice to win wars – unless they are integrated into a conscious military strategy. But the NVA colonel's remarks could also have simply meant, "we are where we are, how we got here doesn't matter," thus reflecting an attitude that sees past events as having little bearing on the present. In other words, the tally of battles won and lost will not influence the outcome of the task at hand, the negotiations. The outcome of that task will depend on the skills of the individuals involved in the negotiations. In any case, Summers made other assertions that support the first interpretation and the lesson that wars are not won by battles alone has become an indelible part of his legacy.

In 1975, Summers was one of the last US Army officers to evacuate Saigon as NVA units overran it. Afterward, he was posted to the Army's Command and General Staff College at Fort Leavenworth. In 1979, he was assigned to the faculty of the US Army War College, where he took the opportunity to think analytically and to write critically about war and strategy, and the US military. Two years into this assignment, he published *On Strategy*, which appeared at a time when the US Army was still coming to terms with its Vietnam experience. Arguably, considering the difficulties the Army had in Iraq and Afghanistan in the early decades of the twenty-first century, it still has not done so.

A study published before the Vietnam conflict ended suggested the war had deeply divided the Army's officer corps: "Senior officers are often perceived as being isolated, perhaps willingly, from reality," it said, adding that too many junior officers regarded the integrity of their superiors with suspicion.[6] Captains and majors attending the US Army Command and General Staff College in the mid-1970s were on the "brink of mutiny," reported one general.[7] Students openly challenged senior officers in lecture halls and seminar rooms, sometimes accusing them of being nothing more than "ticket punchers."[8] As one student of the Staff College class of 1975 recalled, "Many of us believed we had been led badly in Vietnam and the war had been badly managed; hence, we treated most visiting flag officers badly, making it clear that their personal ethics were particularly suspect."[9]

Summers became something of a hero to that generation; his argument that the US Army had won all the major battles but had lost the war resonated with it. Copies of his monograph were sent to all major military commands for use in professional development seminars. The commercial edition of *On Strategy* established Summers as an expert on military affairs and raised his profile, as well as that of the Army War College. Although founded three-quarters of a century earlier (1902), the US Army War College had yet to produce its own Mahan, Eccles, or Wylie. While Summers surely was not in their league intellectually, he seemed to personify the Eccles–Wylie ideal of using critical analysis in a lifelong process of professional development. In 1992, one year after the Persian Gulf War, Summers published *On Strategy II*. Unlike its predecessor, and almost as an apology for the frankness of that work, *On Strategy II* struck a triumphal tone and congratulated the US military for "getting it right."

8.2 *On Strategy* and *On War*

Unfortunately, *On Strategy* was neither well written nor well organized. Nor could it conceal its author's emotional disappointment with the outcome of the Vietnam War. But it captured the spirit of critical inquiry that characterized Clausewitz's *On War* (and some of his other works). The working title of the initial manuscript was "On the Vietnam War:

A Strategic Primer," and its origins trace to a directive issued by the US Army's Deputy Chief of Staff for Operations in the late 1970s. The directive instructed the US Army War College to support a project called "Strategic Lessons Learned in Vietnam." Summers became the project manager and its lead author, but he received input from many organizations within the US Department of Defense as well as other experts. Throughout 1980, he circulated draft chapters of the study for comment. One insightful colonel complained a certain chapter read like a "sophisticated version of the stab-in-the-back theory developed in the German officer corps to explain [its] defeat in World War I."[10] Summers eventually eliminated the chapter. Nonetheless, the final version of *On Strategy* retained something of a "stab-in-the-back" tone. Summers, for instance, complained the White House's decision to commit the US Army to war without first committing the American people, through a declaration of war, was not only unwise, it was unforgivable.[11]

A few external reviewers also offered insightful comments. Maneuver theorist William S. Lind, for instance, noted the draft manuscript was two completely different works spliced together: a "quite good one analyzing the Vietnam war in terms of Clausewitz' principles of war, and the other a quite bad one which attempts to give simple answers to some of the war's larger problems and to tell Army officers what they want to hear."[12] According to Lind, the section dealing with the principles of war was well done, though he questioned its lack of emphasis on maneuver. The US military should have conducted more mobile operations to destroy enemy formations, he insisted. Lind thus suggested Summers consider working "Boyd's theory" into the manuscript's analytical framework. Perhaps the larger question was whether the United States ought to have intervened in Vietnam in the first place, an intervention Lind likened to Athens' ill-fated Syracuse expedition. Among other issues, the expedition epitomized the failure to align ends with ways and means; it was simply too ambitious as conceived as a conquest, even for Athens, which was relatively strong at the time. Summers agreed with Lind but avoided raising the question for fear it would give Army officers "too easy an out" and would distract them from examining the Army's many missteps in the war.[13]

Historian Michael Howard also reviewed the draft manuscript and complimented Summers on his application of Clausewitz's principles, a treatment that was "highly perceptive and of the greatest possible value." The problem for the United States, added Howard, was that it had underestimated the will of the North Vietnamese. "They were in fact prepared to pay a far higher cost, and to face a greater degree of improbability in achieving victory than the American government ever gave them credit for." Washington only needed to impose unacceptable costs on Hanoi, said Howard, but sometimes achieving even "a limited objective" requires making "a total commitment."[14] These remarks fit neatly with Summers's view; "psychologically and institutionally," he said, the Army was best suited for a total commitment.[15] Limited interventions were the job of the Marine Corps.

Reviews of the commercial edition of *On Strategy* were overwhelmingly favorable; most applauded Summers, an Army colonel, for having the courage to criticize the Army.[16] Eliot Cohen, then an assistant professor at Harvard University, called the work "fascinating" and "provocative." He praised it for dispelling the two central myths about the conflict, namely that the US military had been defeated, and that the war was lost due to a "failure of will on the part of civilian politicians."[17] While Summers had not explicitly reproached civilian leaders for lacking the will to win, he had blasted their reluctance to mobilize fully and to treat the conflict as a genuine war: actions that did not demonstrate a willingness to do whatever was necessary to win.

On Strategy consisted of two parts. Part I, "The Environment," employed Clausewitz's trinity – which Summers interpreted as the people, the government, and the army – as an analytical device to expose the ultimately crippling friction present in the relationship between the Army and the American public. It highlighted three sources of such friction: the "natural" friction between the American people and its Army, the friction inherent in the national security bureaucracy, and the friction caused by US military doctrine. Part II, "The Engagement," examined how well the United States fought the war. For Summers, the bottom line was "we failed to properly employ our armed forces so as to secure US national objectives in Vietnam."[18] It was unclear, however, whether by "we" he meant the country's political leadership, the US military's senior leaders, or both. He certainly criticized both with equal energy.

In substance, *On Strategy* represented a clear rejection of Brodie's fundamental point that the advent of nuclear weapons negated traditional strategic principles. To be clear, Summers did not dispute the idea that policy must, in all cases, control the instrument of war. But he believed, as Clausewitz advised, that policy must know the instrument it intended to use. Regrettably, America's policymakers had shown they did not. Moreover, according to Summers, they were advised by individuals who lacked practical experience and an understanding of the nature of war. Like the stereotypical political science professor, they could explain why military force should be used, but not how. Of course, this problem is unique neither to the Vietnam era nor to US policymaking.

Furthermore, Summers criticized the strategy intellectuals for collectively dwelling too much on the fear of escalation, a fear that had induced American policymakers to wage war as if they had no choice but to employ force indecisively. "Our fears became a sort of self-imposed deterrent," he complained.[19] The will of the American populace should have been mobilized for the US involvement in Vietnam, and thus the US Congress should have declared war. However, the government shrank from doing so, which put the US military at a disadvantage since the enemy's concepts of "wars of national liberation" and "people's wars" permitted it to mobilize fully. Fear created specific habits of thought, argued Summers, and the United States had slipped into a particularly injurious one.

One consequence of this habit, he noted, was the use of "signaling" strategies in Vietnam rather than war-winning ones. While the employment of military force always sends signals, the chief problem usually lies in determining whether the signal received was the same as the one sent. In Summers's eyes, unless one party took decisive action, signaling might continue indefinitely with little to show for it but mounting casualties. Essentially, relying on signaling strategies alone could lead to open-ended wars. Accordingly, such theories only added to the confusion over what role, if any, military victory should play in limited conflicts. As discussed earlier, limited-war theorists eschewed the term victory because they feared such a military goal would overtake the war's political objective. However, Summers contended that this narrow understanding of victory emerged largely from the experience of the Second World War. The Allies' pursuit of "absolute victory" and unconditional surrender had conditioned the US military into believing anything short of such goals amounted to a kind of failure.[20] Before the Second World War, victory simply meant destroying enough of an enemy's forces to compel it to sue for peace.

As an example, Summers pointed to the 1939 edition of FM 100-5, which stated: "The *conduct of war* is the art of employing the Armed Forces of a nation in combination with measures of economic and political constraint for the purpose of effecting a satisfactory peace." Obviously, a "satisfactory peace" did not require unconditional surrender. The "ultimate objective of all military operations," the manual went on to say, "is the destruction of the enemy's armed forces in battle." But the goal of such a "decisive defeat" was to break the enemy's "will to war" and to force it "to sue for peace, which is the national aim."[21] The aim of victory, in other words, was simply peace not conquest; hence, victory could set the conditions for a negotiated settlement similar to the one that ended the Korean conflict.

Although MacArthur's belief that there was no substitute for victory had become a favorite target for limited-war theorists, Summers argued, it was not the dominant view among America's senior military leaders. During the congressional hearings over MacArthur's relief, for example, General Omar Bradley, then Chairman of the Joint Chiefs of Staff, stated that victory had "many variations," ranging from a "small thing" to "unconditional surrender."[22] Bradley's statement clearly contradicted MacArthur's opinion, though the latter had not said that victory must be *absolute*. In any case, certainly not all senior US military leaders shared MacArthur's views.

The 1954 edition of FM 100-5, continued Summers, missed an opportunity to build on Bradley's idea that victory was scalable. Clearly influenced by the Korean conflict, the manual introduced the term "wars of limited objective," meaning the "destruction of aggressor forces and the restoration of the political and territorial integrity of the friendly nation." Nonetheless, instead of aligning victory with such objectives, the manual's authors removed the term altogether because military victory itself did "not always assure the realization of national objectives."[23] Unfortunately, the 1962 edition of FM 100-5 compounded the error by dropping the concept of wars of limited objectives in favor of "wars of limited means." Limiting one's means was completely appropriate, he acknowledged, so long as one's opponents did the same.

That was not the case in Vietnam, said Summers, where the United States restricted itself much more than did its adversaries. North Vietnamese territory, for instance, was considered "inviolable," while South Vietnam remained "open to attack." Disproportionately limiting the means of war, moreover, resulted in forfeiting the possibility of achieving "escalation dominance," a concept Summers attributed to Edward Luttwak, but that others believed had originated with Schelling and that had gained wide currency by this time.[24] Summers interpreted escalation dominance to mean raising the "level of warfare" beyond an opponent's capacity to respond. In short, Washington's disproportionate, self-imposed limits worked at cross-purposes with its goals, ill-defined as they were. They put the United States into a position where it could not take the actions necessary to compel Hanoi to come to terms and was thus irrational.

In fact, by 1962, Brodie's and Osgood's limited-war revolution had already spread widely, even to the point of penetrating the Army's operational doctrine. General Maxwell Taylor's *Uncertain Trumpet* had stated "only limited operations" could henceforth "serve a coherent purpose."[25] Moreover, as one historian has noted, Taylor energetically "embraced" much of the scholarly literature on limited war.[26] By this time as well, some general officers claimed to be reading Osgood's *Limited War*.[27] The 1962 edition of FM 100-5 greatly expanded the 1954 manual's treatment of limited war, defining it as "any conflict which does not involve the unrestricted employment of all available resources." A limited war, in contrast to an all-out war, involved "conscious restraint on the part of the belligerents" regarding "weapons, locale, or participants. The scope, intensity, and duration of limited war may vary widely." Limited wars were not necessarily "unimportant or little." The point at which a limited war might become a general war was "impossible to locate with precision," as it is determined by one belligerent concluding its survival is "*directly* and *immediately* at stake," and deciding to discard all restraints.[28] The paragraph clearly reflected the main ideas of Brodie and Osgood. The 1962 field manual went on to address the implications of limited war for certain military operations. It also included aspects of Eccles's counterrevolution, discussing the general components of his "spectrum of conflict."[29] At one end of the spectrum was "cold war," all competition short of armed conflict. At the other end was the traditional category of general war. Limited war occupied the vast range between these two extremes. Accordingly, most conflicts now fell into the category of limited wars.

However, Eccles's spectrum of conflict, a copy of which remains in Summers's archives, apparently made the Army colonel uncomfortable. He wished to have it abolished mainly because it blurred the distinction between peaceful competition and war, each of which he saw as governed by different rules. But he also disapproved of it because it conflated the two primary ways in which wars were limited: objectives and means. Limiting one's objectives, of course, did not necessarily preclude maximizing one's means, as Bismarck had shown in the Franco-German War of 1870–71. Nor did limiting one's means rule out pursuing maximum objectives, as the United States had done in Guatemala in 1954 and had attempted to do in Cuba with the Bay of Pigs invasion in 1961. While most wars were obviously limited compared to the extremes of all-out wars, the label obscured which aspects conflict were to be limited.

8.3   War's Traditional Nature (and Vietnam)

Although Summers can hardly be said to have spared American policymakers or their civilian advisors, the burden of his criticisms fell on the US Army. It was the Army's fault, for instance, that limited-war thinking had obscured the meaning of victory in official doctrine in the first place. The Army also shouldered much of the blame for not impressing upon the US Congress the need for a declaration of war.[30] Later, the Army's leaders saw the failure to mobilize the public as one of the critical mistakes of the war. The Abrams doctrine and the Weinberger–Powell doctrine both developed, in part, to compel policymakers to deliberate over the costs and benefits of military action and to make them own the decision to send US troops into harm's way, before sending them.[31]

Summers also faulted the US Army for not grasping the true nature of the conflict, though he, too, struggled to answer Clausewitz's supreme question: "The first, the supreme, the most decisive act of judgment the statesman and commander must make," wrote Clausewitz, "is to recognize the kind of war they are undertaking, neither mistaking it for, nor attempting to turn it into something it cannot be because of the nature of the circumstances."[32] "As military professionals," declared Summers, "it was our job to judge the true nature of the Vietnam War, to communicate those facts to our civilian decision-makers, and to recommend appropriate strategies." But the Army failed to do so. "Almost a decade after our involvement," he said, "the true nature of the Vietnam war is still in question."[33] Some experts wanted to fit it "into the revolutionary war mold," he complained, and to "blame our defeat on our failure to implement counterinsurgency doctrine."[34] The US Army, he said, contributed to this perception by succumbing to the mystique of guerrilla warfare, a fascination prevalent in the early 1960s. At that time, the message was: "If you want to get promoted, if you want to get ahead, you've got to get on board."[35]

Of course, the question of the nature of the Vietnam War was an important one; indeed, the supreme one. But it did not require a metaphysical answer. As noted earlier, the words nature and character can point to types of wars, rather than their inner workings. Summers initially refused to see the conflict as a continuation of Vietnam's long struggle for independence. In his eyes, only the first Indochina War (1945–54) was a revolutionary war; the second one (1959–75) was a war of conquest in which Hanoi attempted to dominate all of Indochina. In that conflict, the Viet Cong were not part of a genuine revolutionary war. Rather, they formed a "simulated insurgency," a strategic distraction, that drew attention away from Hanoi's main effort, the operations of the NVA.[36] After the failure of the 1968 Tet Offensive, which he interpreted as a tactical victory for the US military but a strategic defeat, the Viet Cong faded into insignificance. He later went so far as to say the people's war had failed tactically but succeeded strategically – and it was largely the Army's fault for not reacting appropriately.[37]

Historians have since disputed Summers's interpretation of the Tet Offensive, noting that American reports of insurgent casualties were inflated; whereas their estimates of Viet Cong strength before the offensive were too low.[38] Hence, the Viet Cong had suffered heavy casualties, but had not been smashed and probably could have absorbed even higher casualties. In fact, it is not unusual to have inflated reports of enemy casualties in wartime, and American shortcomings in this regard were not unique, nor should they be surprising. Nevertheless, they have prompted historians to question whether US forces indeed had won all the war's battles, as Summers claimed.

Contemporary counterinsurgency experts were also divided over the true nature of the war. Some, such as Robert Thompson, formerly head of the British advisory mission to Vietnam, argued the Viet Cong's activities were the decisive ones; the NVA's battles were the diversions. Both Summers and Thompson, however, agreed Hanoi had fully committed itself to winning. In 1968, Thompson estimated the Communist leadership in Hanoi could afford to lose as many as 100,000 casualties per year, more than the South Vietnamese and US militaries could reasonably inflict, before its forces lost operational effectiveness. "In its way," remarked Thompson, "this is a Dien Bien Phu except that it does not require victory in battle at one particular place."[39] Hanoi thus had little reason to accept the offer of negotiations unless something changed. Two characteristics described Maoist revolutionary wars, he said: they were relatively immune to the direct application of conventional force and they were wars to the finish.

In contrast, other experts, such as Chalmers Johnson, Douglas Pike, and Denis Warner, inclined toward Summers's interpretation. They detected a shift in Hanoi's strategy, though they believed it took place in 1969, rather than in 1968, and that it was brought about largely by Le Duan, who had eclipsed Ho Chi Minh as North Vietnam's principal strategist.[40] Pike described the change in terms of an increase in "psychomilitary operations," the use of major offensives not to win the backing of the South Vietnamese, as Maoist doctrine prescribed, but rather to weaken the willingness of citizens and policymakers in the West to support the United States.[41] Whether due to casualties suffered by the Viet Cong or simply Le Duan's impatience, Summers was not alone in believing Hanoi's strategy had taken a different turn after the Tet Offensive.

Nor was he alone in seeing that conflict almost exclusively through an American lens, as a military intervention to stop Communism, rather than as another chapter in the long struggle for Vietnamese independence. For Summers, the Communists always created a myth of revolutionary legitimacy, while actually exploiting local peoples, and terrorizing or coercing them into taking actions they would not otherwise have considered. The ability of Ho Chi Minh, and later Le Duan, to co-opt

Moscow and Beijing into supporting them may well have been underestimated at the time. Both Vietnamese leaders managed to obtain critical weapons and other resources in return for promises to keep the war "special," that is, geographically contained and well below Washington's escalation threshold.[42] Put differently, the core mistake US policymakers and strategists made was not looking deeper than the outer skin of the chameleon to examine its inner composition. The government in Hanoi, the populace in North Vietnam, and the NVA, were fused together in a Clausewitzian sense, even if largely through fear. Neither South Vietnam nor the United States cared to match that level of integration, though Summers repeatedly asserted the US military was a "trinitarian" military, an "instrument of the American people rather than of the American government."[43] That discrepancy made the conflict qualitatively more difficult than most of America's other limited wars.

Summers's initial remedy, declaring war to mobilize the US "national will," was as excessive as it was naïve. But it was popular among some senior Army officers. His archives contain numerous letters supporting his views. Still, massive mobilization would not likely have fused the American government, its society, and its military together in the way he wished. Without a direct threat, US interests in Vietnam were not strong enough to bring together an America that was deeply divided along racial, generational, ethnic, and gender lines. Moreover, mobilizing the American public for Vietnam would have done little more than draw attention away from US deterrence efforts in Europe and Korea. Until unifying social and political reforms were implemented in South Vietnam, mobilizing the American public was not likely to make much difference.

A better strategic solution for the United States, therefore, would have been to draw the line of Containment differently, stopping the proverbial dominoes from falling by reinforcing those countries where the West already had significant political, economic, and military advantages. Some of the most obvious candidates would have been South Korea, Japan, Formosa, the Philippines, the Dutch East Indies, Australia, New Zealand, and possibly Malaysia, Indonesia, and Singapore depending on the circumstances. The point is, the strategy had to be such that American society, as divided as it was, could have endured its strains over the long term.

8.4 The Principles of War

Determining the true nature of the war was not the only problem the US military faced. According to Summers, it also had to craft an appropriate strategy based on that nature. Tragically, as he went on to explain, the

US Army no longer knew what strategy was. For too long, the Army had treated strategy as little more than a budget exercise, a bureaucratic pastime properly left to civilians. Consequently, all the major innovations in strategic thinking since the beginning of the nuclear age had come from civilians. Ironically, Summers admitted that he, too, had struggled to find an adequate definition of strategy.[44] He finally settled on the US military's official definition (1979): "strategy is the art and science of employing the armed forces of a nation to secure the objectives of national policy by the application of force, or the threat of force."[45] Even this definition he found wanting in terms of explaining how one might go about achieving the objectives of national policy.

Borrowing a phrase from an Army War College colleague, Summers referred to the principles of war collectively as "military planning interrogatories" because they offered an "analytical framework" that enabled one to reduce abstract concepts to practical realities.[46] In short, the principles required war planners to inquire how best to apply military force in a particular situation. In this sense, Summers's use of principles retreated from that of Mahan. In February 1981, for instance, Summers sent General Donn Starry, Commanding General of the Army's Training and Doctrine Command, a reprint of an article by Major Edward S. Johnston on the "Science of War" (1934), which discussed the relationship between the art and science of war.[47] The article, which Starry evidently did not understand, defined principles in Mahan-like fashion, as "statements of invariable and fundamental truth."[48] As Chapter 1 showed, this definition was based on the positivist conception of science that prevailed at the time. Science aided art rather than supplanting it. Starry and Summers both showed the US military's seemingly ingrained aversion to the idea of applying scientific formulas in war, though both accepted Johnston's proposition that the principles of war had a timeless quality about them.

To his surprise, however, Summers found that the 1962 edition of FM 100-5 only discussed the principles "in terms of their *tactical* application." Their strategic sense had been lost. As he discovered, the US Army first codified the principles of war in 1921, in *War Department Training Regulations 10-5*, which stated, "their application to the preparation for war and the direction of war is called strategy. Their application to specific battles and operations is called tactics."[49] In contrast, US doctrine referred to the principles as "fundamental concepts, the result of centuries of tradition and experience." They had evolved into their present state and for that reason were thought to have achieved a certain unassailable validity, even if their importance varied according to the situation and they required judgment in application.[50]

For Summers, the nine traditional principles of war applied not only to tactics or to operations, but also to strategy. "The first principle of war, The Objective," he said, "focuses our attention on what we are to accomplish. The second principle, The Offensive, tells us in general terms – i.e., the strategic offensive, the strategic defensive – how we are to go about attaining the objective. The next three principles," he went on to say, "Mass, Economy of Force, and Maneuver – elaborate on the second principle by providing more details on *how* to conduct our operations."[51] Surprise can maximize the effect of those operations on the adversary. Security, Simplicity, and Unity of Command describe conditions that reduce one's vulnerabilities to enemy action and to friction.

The objective, as he further explained, is the first principle of war "because all else flows from it." In a strategic context, the principle pointed to the need to conduct a rigorous analysis of the political objective to determine appropriate military objectives. The military must bear the responsibility for insisting the political leadership specify "tangible, obtainable political goals," and describe them in "concrete terms." Even though political leaders eschewed the idea of tying themselves to fixed objectives, and desired instead to preserve "maximum flexibility and maneuverability," the military required firm objectives around which to plan and conduct operations. In short, going to war required a clear "definition of 'victory,'" which should be neither absolute nor rigid.

From the perspective of strategy, the principle of the offensive remained important, Summers insisted, even if one's governing policy was defensive in nature, as was the case with Containment. The offensive simply meant "maintaining initiative and freedom of action" in the face of an adversary. In fact, the term initiative might be the better word to use. He then advocated a power-down approach in the execution of strategy, one that extended maximum latitude to subordinate organizations so long as they operated within the parameters established by the national authority. Not unlike Wylie might have urged, the goal would be to direct maximum efforts against the foe's center of gravity, which is not necessarily its armed forces, by using the principles of mass, economy of force, and maneuver to achieve the objective. Collectively, these principles meant reevaluating priorities in light of America's strategic deterrence missions in Europe and Korea, while maintaining strategic flexibility and readiness. The United States had not used its resources wisely in Vietnam and got itself embroiled without being able to follow through conclusively. Summers's use of these three principles thus pointed, albeit crudely, to the intrinsic flaw of Containment, that it could lead to defending every domino and thus to overcommitment.

The United States lacked unity of command at the highest levels, Summers noted, because the missions of preparing for war and conducting war work at cross-purposes in a limited conflict. The Department of Defense needed to consider how to reorganize its functions to preclude that sort of conflict from happening again. As regards security and surprise, it was not difficult to practice either tactically. Given the open nature of US society, however, they could be maintained strategically only with great difficulty. Future military strategists would have to take the open nature of US society into better account. Finally, Summers found that American policymakers and military planners abandoned the principle of simplicity in Vietnam. Plans were often too complex to be executed as they were intended.

Summers's archives also include an essay by Major-General Herbert E. Wolff proposing public support as the tenth principle of war. A native of Cologne, Germany, Wolff was a US Army veteran of the Second World War, Korea, and Vietnam, who had received a battlefield commission in 1945. He attended the Army War College in 1962 and his fifty-three-page thesis shows evidence of a lively but practically grounded intellect.[52] His essay on public support, originally published in *Infantry* in 1965, began by drawing directly from Clausewitz's trinity – defined as political motivation, operational activity, and social participation.[53] The principles of war, he maintained, must address all three of these dimensions; regrettably, they did not. The political and operational dimensions were well represented, but a void existed with respect to the social dimension. To address that deficiency, the essay proposed adding public support – the "help of the people as a force to strengthen and assist the direction of the effort" – to the nine officially recognized principles of war.[54]

Public support is required for all forms of war, argued Wolff, from limited to general, from conventional to unconventional. Moreover, the support of the home front may well contain "the mechanism which allows the original nine principles to operate" in the twentieth century. "Warmaking potential without determined public support counts for little," he added, but "physical capability coupled with a popular commitment is the surest prescription for success."[55] Curiously, *On Strategy* did not reference Wolff's tenth principle, an odd omission since the book explicitly criticized policymakers and military professionals alike for overlooking the importance of war's psychosocial dimension.

Unfortunately, key US policymakers – especially Johnson, Kissinger, and Nixon – fed information to the American public sparingly. As explained by Walt Rostow, President Johnson's special assistant for national security affairs, the aim was to maintain a "low-key campaign of public information" to generate support but not mobilization. To accomplish that purpose, Johnson had at his disposal a reasonably extensive and responsive apparatus, consisting of the consolidated public affairs offices of the Pentagon, the State Department, and the White House. Together, they implemented a communications program called Operation Maximum Candor that included Johnson's own "Why Vietnam" speech in 1965, later made into a film that mimicked the style of Frank Capra's Second World War *Why We Fight* series.[56] Nonetheless, the administration considered the articulation of its war aims so complex it entrusted only four persons with that task: Secretary of Defense Robert McNamara, Secretary of State Dean Rusk, National Security Advisor McGeorge Bundy, and Johnson himself.[57] The theories of Brodie and Osgood reinforced these prejudices by associating the public with the irrational element of war. Even though the White House made some concessions to public opinion during the conflict, it aimed to preserve rational direction of the war by minimizing the public's influence.

Summers's rationale for rejecting Wolff's recommendation is unclear, though he may have believed the legislative and executive branches of the US government, not the Army, should assume chief responsibility for generating strategic communications. Yet America's "psyop" organizations (US Army, Joint US Public Affairs Office, CIA, MACV-Studies and Observations Group, and US Information Agency) repeatedly endeavored to shape public opinion at home and abroad during the Vietnam War. These organizations achieved considerable successes. But so, too, did Hanoi's propaganda program, which exploited the Johnson administration's "lack of candor on the war," the racial and ethnic tensions in US society, and the antiwar protests by media celebrities.[58] In short, the interrelated topics of psychological warfare and generating public support were hardly unknown; nor were US agencies inept at them. Rather, US strategists treated the psychosocial dimension of war as an item to be managed instead of as something that should have required the strategy itself to be managed.

In 1982, the year in which the commercial edition of *On Strategy* appeared, another Army officer, John I. Alger, published *The Quest for Victory: The History of the Principles of War*.[59] Alger was an assistant professor in the history department at West Point and an erstwhile student of Peter Paret. Alger discovered not only that the number and types of principles had varied over time and across cultures, but so too had the meaning of the word principle itself. He defined the term, inductively, as a "fundamental truth that is professed as a guide to action." While his research revealed some common aspects regarding the principles, he had to admit "consensus regarding their content and form is notably lacking."[60] But a lack of consensus is the fault of the individuals studying an object, not the object itself. Hence, the content and form of a principle would almost certainly vary according to the biases of those describing it. Nevertheless, whereas Summers urged the Army to return to the business of strategy, in part by rediscovering the principles of war, Alger suggested they were mutable. Nevertheless, he did not go as far as Alain Enthoven, one of McNamara's so-called whiz kids, who dismissed the principles as a "set of platitudes that can be twisted to suit almost any situation."[61]

In fact, the US military has maintained a love–hate relationship with the principles of war for most of the modern era, which may explain why it has neglected this section of *On Strategy*. Military educational seminars have portrayed the principles as essential to success in war, even though doctrinal publications usually relegated them to an annex. For his part, Summers insisted the principles were "neither immutable nor causal," but he gave them an importance in *On Strategy* that suggested otherwise.[62] They were not to be used prescriptively, he warned, but rather to stimulate thought and to urge mental flexibility. Yet cadets at America's military academies had to memorize the principles of war to pass their military science courses, and junior officers have had to write seminar papers proving the timeless validity of this or that principle. Instead of merely stimulating thought, therefore, the principles have also become associated with recipes for success. The closing years of the twentieth century saw debates over whether the US military ought to combine its principles of war with its principles other than war, or whether the idea of martial principles had outlived its usefulness altogether.[63] Those and other debates regarding the number and nature of the principles of war continued well into the first decade of the twenty-first century.[64]

Summers's emphasis on the principles of war notwithstanding, he recognized the chief risk of this approach, namely that the US military would lack an appreciation for nonmilitary issues. As Brodie had pointed out, American military leaders had been educated and trained to "win" whatever the cost, even to the point of disregarding the second- and third-order effects of victory. "The whole training of the military," Brodie maintained, "is toward a set of values that finds in battle and in victory a vindication. The skills developed in the soldier are those of the fighter, and not of the reflector on ultimate purposes." The solution, he said, borrowing from a speech Eisenhower delivered at the Naval War College in October 1961, was to ensure all "our officers are growing up to understand the problem of the citizen and the citizen leaders" and not just purely military subjects.[65] The solution did not seem to be working, however, as evidenced by Brodie's mocking references to Thomas Power's *Design for Survival* (1964), Nathan Twining's *Neither Liberty, Nor Safety* (1966), and Curtis LeMay's *America is in Danger* (1968). Instead, the reasoning of the military mind was still dangerously narrow.

8.5 Summers's First Principles

Ten years after the appearance of *On Strategy* and six months after the successful conclusion of Desert Storm, Summers published *On Strategy II: A Critical Analysis of the Gulf War*.[66] The book argued the swift defeat of Saddam Hussein's forces proved the US armed forces had recovered from its Vietnam malaise. "This time we had done it right," he declared. While the president had not asked the US Congress for a formal declaration of war, explained Summers, he had requested an authorization "to the use of 'all necessary means' to drive Iraq out of Kuwait."[67] That authorization restored the critical link between the US Army and the American people, according to Summers. Additionally, a new warfighting doctrine, AirLand Battle, had enabled the Army to rise "like the phoenix" from the ashes "to recapture its soul and reassert its battlefield primacy."[68]

On Strategy II consisted of three parts: the first, "The Remarkable Trinity," summarized the argument of *On Strategy*; the second, "The Remarkable Renaissance," described the doctrinal rebirth of the US military and the foundational role Clausewitz's theories played in it; the third, "The Remarkable War," explained how the US military applied the principles of war to achieve tactical and strategic success against Iraq. For Summers, the end of the Cold War meant the end of the requirement to fight limited wars. He applauded the success of Containment but regretted that it had forced the US military to fight on the strategic defensive and to surrender the "battlefield initiative to the enemy."[69]

Summers attributed most of the success of Desert Storm to the American "renaissance in military thinking in the 1970s and 1980s."[70] But the victory also owed much to reforms within the realms of personnel and materiel. In 1979, for instance, military pay was so low that a third of enlisted soldiers (E-4 and below) qualified for food stamps; moreover, more than 25 percent of all service members ranked in the lowest category for intelligence.[71] In addition, of the ten active Army divisions stationed stateside in 1979, only four were considered capable of deploying overseas in a crisis.[72] In the 1980s, the Reagan administration dramatically increased defense spending, which in turn contributed to better pay for service members, improvements in recruiting and retention, as well as state-of-the-art enhancements in military training and hardware. Equipment upgrades included the Abrams tank, Bradley infantry vehicle, Patriot missile system, Blackhawk helicopter, and Apache attack helicopter.[73] These systems were more than a match, qualitatively, for their Soviet counterparts (T-72 tank, BMP infantry assault vehicle, ZSU-23/4 antiaircraft weapon, and MI-24 Hind-D helicopter) as well as the older models in service with the Iraqi army.[74] In short, whereas the US army of 1990–91 executed Desert Storm with an impressively low number of casualties, the margin of victory for the US Army of the late 1970s would have been tighter.

For all of Summers's earlier emphasis on the need to link strategy and tactics, *On Strategy II* drew a red line between political and military responsibilities. "While 'strategies' – the ends for which wars are waged – are largely political," he said, "'grand tactics' and 'tactics' are the exclusive province of the military."[75] Even though the US military grasped the importance of linking strategy and tactics, the bulk of its reforms took it in the opposite direction, toward Brodie's overprofessionalization. Evidently, the challenges of the modern battlefield were such that US officers now required an unprecedented intellectual commitment to their profession.

The US Army's new operational doctrine, AirLand Battle, first published in the 1982 edition of FM 100-5, reflected some of that commitment. AirLand Battle replaced the previous concept, Active Defense, which was based on decimating Soviet forces while trading space for time. In contrast, AirLand Battle stressed seizing and retaining tactical and operational initiative by attacking the enemy's echelons in depth with integrated air and ground operations, even while on the strategic defensive. It also introduced the concepts of decentralized operations and the "operational level of war," meaning corps' commands and higher. This level of command assumed direct responsibility for some traditionally strategic decisions, such as disposing forces, selecting objectives, setting the terms of the next battle, and exploiting previous successes.[76]

Importantly, FM 100-5 (1982) acknowledged Summers's point that "successful military operations do not guarantee victory."[77] Critically, however, the Army had arrived at a different cure for that problem. It decided tactical commanders needed to be shielded from policy's influence because policy was ignorant of war's nature and had disrupted small-unit actions by attempting to micromanage them. For the Army, the chief purpose of the operational level of war was to filter policy's influence by converting it into actionable military objectives, while also unifying assorted allied formations into a common strategic effort.

FM 100-5 (1986) refined these ideas, while also introducing the concept of operational art, the manner or style of employing military forces. This edition likewise conceded Summers's point that battlefield victories "may not alone" assure the achievement of national security goals, but it also stressed that defeat would "guarantee failure." Accordingly, it gave considerable autonomy to the operational artist, who decided "when and where to fight and whether to accept or decline battle." The purpose of operational art was to achieve "decisive success" by pitting "superior combat power" against the enemy's center of gravity.[78] In important respects, therefore, FM 100-5 absolved tactical commanders of responsibility for achieving political goals, unless those aims were synonymous with decisive success. Put differently, it restored professional autonomy to combat commanders, while purportedly putting a more effective instrument into the hands of policy. The obvious flaw in this logic was that if military practitioners were not taught to work within political considerations as tactical commanders, they would not have learned the skills necessary to convert policy guidance into military objectives as operational-level commanders. The new doctrine posed few problems for the US intervention in Panama (1989) which was fought as a miniature air–land battle; nor did it hinder Desert Shield and Desert Storm (1990–91), since political aims and military objectives essentially coincided. But it fell short in crises such as Bosnia (1995–96) and Kosovo (1999), in which reconciling political and military objectives proved immensely more difficult.[79]

For all their emphasis on new principles and imperatives (adaptability, initiative, depth, and synchronization) the 1982 and 1986 editions of FM 100-5 essentially returned to the core principles of concentration, offensive action, and decision by battle, as advanced by Mahan. All of these, however, required modification to apply to low-intensity conflicts and operations other than war. The US Army's operational doctrine of the 1980s paid too little attention to the need to school military planners in engineering tactical objectives, not from larger operational objectives, which was comparatively easy, but rather from policy goals with all their inherent ambiguity. The Army's doctrine of the 1990s moved in the direction of closing that gap, but perhaps inadvertently established a second grammar of war while failing to emphasize the importance of working *with* policymakers as well as *for* them.

8.6 Conclusions

Like Clausewitz, Summers believed war had its own grammar (in strategic principles) but not its own logic. Nonetheless, by repeatedly stressing the importance of the principles of war, Summers imparted a certain de facto logic to war's grammar. He considered the principles sacrosanct and timeless; whereas Clausewitz regarded them as important but flexible, requiring judgment in application, to include a mature assessment of the nature of the war at hand. While some items of war's grammar – security, simplicity, and unity of command – applied to all types of armed conflict, others – such as the offensive – did not. Summers, however, remained chiefly focused on conventional warfare. He rarely discussed how these "military interrogatories" might apply to unconventional operations, or to what in the 1990s were known as "operations other than war."[80] He certainly did not agree with the CIA's Major-General Edward Lansdale, who maintained conventional military principles were counterproductive in a people's war.[81] By 1995, well after Desert Shield/Desert Storm, the US military added legitimacy, perseverance, and restraint to its official principles of war – all of which pointed, at least tangentially, to war's psychosocial dimension.

Summers answered Clausewitz's supreme question in much the same way as traditionalists like Mahan and Mitchell. But he also acted, albeit unknowingly, as something of a transitional figure to the modern paradigm with his detailed treatment, perhaps overtreatment, of the concept of friction in *On Strategy*. Summers used Clausewitz as a battering ram to crash through the portcullises of what he believed to be wrongheaded ideas. In contrast, Eccles and Wylie, who were certainly not strangers to the concept of friction, put a finer point on Clausewitz's emphasis on theory as critical inquiry.

But Summers also found it difficult to answer the second part of Clausewitz's supreme question; that is, he remained confused about character of the Vietnam War. That confusion, indeed, reflected a larger misunderstanding endemic to the American way of thinking about war at the time. As discussed earlier, US policy and military practitioners in the 1950s and 1960s recognized four categories of armed conflict: all-out war, general war, revolutionary war, and limited war. Yet the type of war Hanoi was waging spanned all four categories (save for the use of nuclear weapons in an all-out conflict). As a result, America's military strategists could see enough of the type of war they wanted to see to confirm their own biases. In short, Summers's confusion was not atypical for the times. Unfortunately, it not only heightened the tensions between America's political and military practitioners, it also undoubtedly contributed to the country's reputation for astrategic thinking.

All told, the revolt of Weigley's so-called strategy intellectuals succeeded. But so, too, did the counterrevolution of the military intellectuals, at least to a substantial degree. The former prompted policymakers and military professionals to think about war differently; the latter urged them to think about war properly. Obviously, these aims need not have been mutually exclusive. Thinking differently can lead to the discovery of unanticipated opportunities; however, it requires a willingness to experiment and innovate and to accept risks when doing so. To be sure, the exigencies of the Cold War required the United States to try new strategic theories, such as limited war and Schelling's brand of coercion, without testing them – not that testing them would have been easy given the state of conflict simulations at the time. Nevertheless, it is not wise for democracies to experiment with new military methods that may put the lives and treasure of their citizens at greater risk, unless the costs are evenly distributed across all sociopolitical levels. With respect to the Vietnam conflict, they were not.

Eccles and Wylie sought, and partially achieved, a workable synthesis between traditional core principles and those of the strategy intellectuals. They also exposed limitations of game theory, renounced the concept of "weapons strategy," and countered air power's claims that navies had become obsolete in the nuclear age. As part of the late counterrevolution, Summers agitated for a revival, rather than a synthesis, not only of Jominian core principles but of the principles of war in general. Fundamentally, the clash between the strategy intellectuals and the military intellectuals also involved conflicting paradigms of war's nature, one derived from a broad understanding of human nature and one centered more on a mechanistic view of escalation.

Ironically, despite their differences, both parties agreed on one critical point: America's policymakers and strategists relied too much on military force. From the Truman administration forward, however, America increasingly employed economic rather than, or in conjunction with, military power. During the Eisenhower era, military power steadily acquired an unconventional character, a combination of CIA operatives and, later, US special forces. This combination of unconventional military power and economic power essentially represented the preferred American way of war until the Johnson administration escalated the US involvement in Vietnam with conventional forces.

Of course, it is not clear that better resourcing of pacification programs or other nonmilitary measures would have saved Vietnam. Drawing Containment's defensive line to include the Republic of Vietnam was a poor choice from a grand-strategic perspective. Indochina should have served as a "trade space," an area ceded to enemy advances but also subjected to subversive or insurgent activities by military advisors reinforced by offshore air and naval power. The actual defensive perimeter should have been drawn back further, roughly along the line running from Japan, South Korea, Formosa, and the Philippines – where the odds favored the United States and the rest of the Free World. To be sure, that course of action, which meant losing Indochina to the Communists not long after the loss of China, would have required a vigorous public information campaign in the face of the specious but seductive logic of the domino theory. But that campaign would have been less difficult than the one White House officials ultimately had to wage to justify additional expenditures of blood and treasure to prop up a corrupt and disdainful foreign government.

The counterrevolution of the military intellectuals created the space for two important changes in the American way of thinking about war after Vietnam. Most importantly, it encouraged the further development of operationally focused military theories. The strategy intellectuals had maintained military strategy was too important to be left to military practitioners. The military intellectuals countered by saying strategy was too important to be left to academics. Operational art, which reflected a commander's style or method of campaigning rather than a distinct level of command, became the sole purview of the military practitioner. It also served as a response to critics, such as Edward Luttwak, who claimed Anglo-Saxon officers did not "think or practice war in operational terms."[82] Without such thinking, concepts such as maneuver warfare (discussed in the following chapters) would run into civilian interference. The general hope, though, was that both the art and the level would facilitate actively linking strategy to tactics, as Summers had advocated, regardless of the strategic theory de jure.

As the preceding chapters showed, interservice rivalries also influenced the content of counterrevolution, particularly Wylie's initial focus. His efforts to clarify the US Navy's raison d'être revealed the need for a framework to rationalize the ways and means of military strategy across the services. In May 1989, Colonel Arthur F. Lykke, Jr., of the US Army War College, published such a framework. Lykke drew from General Maxwell Taylor's conception of strategy as "objectives, ways, and means," and converted it into something of an engineering problem or a mathematical equation: "Strategy," said Lykke, "equals *ends* (objectives toward which one strives) plus *ways* (courses of action) plus *means* (instruments by which some end can be achieved)."[83] A good strategy was one in which the three parts of the equation were in balance: the ends did not exceed the capacity of the ways and means, thereby reducing risk of failure. Lykke's equation brought criticism from those who thought it too simplistic. But it caught on within the US Department of Defense as a tool for justifying operational concepts and force structures, though the author later stated that was not his intention.[84] Of course, balance, as always, lies in the eyes of the beholder, and any service could use the framework to make a case for more resources or, conversely, to claim it could accomplish more than the other services and do so at lower risk.

Part IV

The Insurrection of the Operational Artists

Weigley's *American Way of War* ends its story in the early 1970s, before the withdrawal of America's major combat forces and the ultimate evacuation of the US embassy in Saigon in 1975. The following chapters continue the story of the American way of thinking about war from the 1970s into the 1990s. It is a story, moreover, that reveals a growing focus on winning battles rather than winning wars, though this emphasis came about partly because the major theorists of this period – John Boyd, William Lind, and John Warden – saw a need for conceptual and doctrinal reform within their respective services, and so focused their attention accordingly. The theories of Boyd and Lind provide something of an exception to the general inclination toward winning battles, as their conjectures also encompassed the psychosocial dimension of war. Importantly, however, their works also reveal a darker side to US military theory, one that perceived diversity as threatening.

Although the idea that the next major conflict might involve nuclear weapons had not fully disappeared by the mid-1980s, many US theorists, including Schelling, believed it was unlikely.[1] Indeed, the Arab–Israeli War of 1973, the Chinese invasion of Vietnam in 1979, the Soviet invasion of Afghanistan in 1979, and the Falklands War of 1982, among others, made it increasingly necessary to think about how to fight wars without nuclear weapons. The conditions that justified Brodie's limited war revolution, in other words, had begun to disappear. Whereas Herman Kahn once dared to think the unthinkable, the US military now realized it did not need to, even though some of its operational doctrine, such as FM 100-5 (1976) "Active Defense," still did. In short, the period from the late-1970s into the early 1990s was marked by a rediscovery of operational art and of operational theories.

For better or worse, the theories and the art enjoyed a symbiotic relationship. Historical studies of the operational art appeared as American operational artists looked for successful models to emulate.[2] It eventually became clear that American operational art had developed differently because it faced the special challenges of projecting power across vast distances that included significant bodies of water, and thus required more joint cooperation.[3] By the second decade of the twenty-first century, research into operational art went beyond describing its variations to identifying its chief limitations and risks.[4]

9 John Boyd, William Lind, and Maneuver Theory

By the time Harry Summers's *On Strategy* appeared in print, US Air Force Colonel John Boyd and defense writer William Lind, two of America's most controversial theorists, had launched a concerted effort to reform American military thinking. Reform was necessary, they insisted, because the American way of thinking about war had become ossified. Furthermore, it had become unimaginative, too reliant on attrition models, and overlooked the all-important psychological dimension of warfare. US Air Force Colonel John Warden (discussed in the following chapter) came to a similar conclusion. Boyd and Lind stressed the importance of rapid decision-making and speed of movement to unhinge an enemy psychologically. Their approach evolved into a theory of "maneuver warfare," which quickly gained momentum within the US Army and US Marine Corps. Boyd's contributions to the American way of thinking about war consist not only in his well-traveled, if superficially understood, OODA loop (observe, orient, decide, act) but also his efforts to promote a new way of thinking about competition in general. His ideas have remained particularly influential within the US Marine Corps, which honored him with its insignia, the eagle globe and anchor.[1]

William Lind acknowledged borrowing freely from Boyd's concepts, especially the OODA loop. But he also set forth plenty of his own ideas in *The Maneuver Warfare Handbook* (1985) and *The 4th Generation Warfare Handbook* (2015) as well as a host of articles.[2] A radical conservative driven by an unabashed antipathy for multiculturalism, Lind combined elements of maneuver theory with theories of social decline. In 2015, historian Martin van Creveld said Lind stood out by casting the historical development of warfare in terms of "four stages or 'generations'" instead of weapons and organizations.[3] These generations were manpower, firepower, maneuver, and terrorism and insurgencies. Gone was the idea of hammering a polity into submission through aerial bombardments, in the style of Douhet or Mitchell, or by subjecting it to a relentless stream of propaganda, as during the Cold War. Instead, disintegration was to be achieved by finding the existing fissures within a society and intensifying them.

9.1 Paradoxical Maverick

Much has been made of Boyd's "maverick" qualities.[4] Mavericks are expected to be fiercely independent and recklessly heroic. They can become rebels with a cause who launch crusades against entrenched orthodoxies. Mavericks replace other orthodoxies with their own precisely because they believe theirs is the right way, and the only way. Boyd did that; he bucked the system, thought "outside the box," employed unorthodox methods to accomplish his aims. But to the extent the maverick motif is real, it brings with it a certain paradox; by defying convention, mavericks attract opprobrium and thereby decrease the odds of obtaining the thing they want. While Boyd agitated for conceptual reform, he also openly accused some flag officers of stupidity and wrongheadedness, which in turn alienated him from those with the power to implement reforms. The maverick motif, therefore, sometimes conceals failure, particularly failure to adapt to and work within an existing power structure. Ironically, Boyd came to be known for preaching the need to adapt swiftly to one's environment, though he himself showed little aptitude for doing so.

John Richard Boyd was born on January 23, 1927 in Erie, Pennsylvania. Three years later, in the early months of the Great Depression, his father, Hubert, died from pneumonia. Thereafter, John's mother, Elsie, worked as many as three jobs at a time to keep from losing the house and to provide for herself and five children. In 1933, John and his sister Ann contracted measles, a disease that would cause the deaths of more than 14,000 people in the United States from 1933 to 1935. In 1933, Ann was also stricken with polio, perhaps the most despised disease in America at the time because it typically afflicted young people predominately and because it paralyzed rather than killed. Sadly, in the year Ann was stricken, the rate of polio infection had dropped precipitously – by two-thirds – which made the fact that she had become a victim that much more devastating.[5] In the America of the 1920s and 1930s, almost every disease came with a stigma, which in turn added the burden of shame to a family's suffering.

Given these strains, it is perhaps not surprising that John failed the first grade in 1933, though he passed without difficulty the following year. By his own admission, he was never more than an average student, except perhaps in mathematics; he even claimed to have scored only ninety points (ten points below average) on an IQ test.[6] His fondness for aircraft and the competitive aspects of sports, especially swimming, became evident in his early years. In 1944, his older brother, William, was diagnosed with a form of schizophrenia and died in a mental institution –

yet another affliction that caused marked psychological pain for the Boyd family. On October 30 of that year, John enlisted in the US Army air corps to avoid being drafted into one of the other branches of the Army, and reported for duty on April 16, 1945. However, the war ended before he saw any action, and he thus served out his two-year enlistment on occupation duty in Japan.[7]

From 1947 to 1951, Boyd attended the University of Iowa and enrolled in the newly established Air Force Reserve Officer Training Corps (ROTC) in 1948. Evidently, his maverick tendencies showed during his ROTC flight training, as he repeatedly attempted the riskier aerial maneuvers before he had mastered the basics. After graduation, he was posted to the 51st Wing, 25th Squadron, in Korea, and flew twenty-two missions as a wingman before the armistice was signed.[8] Even though he had no combat kills, his experience in Korea laid the foundation for much of his later thinking about aerial maneuver and tactics, as well as the core of his conception of military strategy. By some accounts, he became especially intrigued with the question of why the American-built F-86 Sabre defeated its counterpart, the Soviet-made MiG-15, by a ratio of 10:1, even though the overall performance characteristics of the US aircraft were inferior.[9] The answer appeared to lie partly in the better quality of training US pilots received, but also in the one characteristic in which the American aircraft had an edge, its ability to transition quickly from one aerial maneuver to another. From 1954 to 1960, Boyd was assigned to the Fighter Weapons School at Nellis Air Force Base in Nevada, where he improved the realism and efficiency of the fighter pilot training program. He distilled much of his knowledge of aerial maneuvering into a 147-page manuscript, the *Aerial Attack Study*, which became the basis for the US air force's tactical doctrine (Air Force Manual 3-1).[10]

From 1960 to 1962, Boyd attended the Georgia Institute of Technology and graduated with a bachelor's degree in industrial engineering. That education helped him develop what would later become known as the energy maneuverability (EM) theory. This theory resulted in uniform criteria for comparing the performance characteristics of unique aircraft designs and showed American combat aviation technology had fallen behind that of its Cold War rival. Put starkly, the Soviet MiG-17, MiG-19, and MiG-21 were, in some categories, competitive with the US F-4 Phantom, F-104 Starfighter, F-105 Thunderchief, and F-106 Delta Dart.[11]

In 1965, he was transferred to the Air Force's Research and Development Program in the Pentagon, where he participated in developing the F-15 Eagle. From 1972 to 1973, he was assigned to

Thailand and took part in US efforts to monitor, through electronic surveillance measures, the flow of enemy vehicles and troops along the Ho Chi Minh Trail. In 1973, he returned to the Pentagon and assisted in developing the F-16 Falcon and later the A-10 Warthog close-air-support aircraft. He also became a champion of the military reform movement of the 1980s, which sought ways to rationalize defense procurement and to incentivize "out-of-the-box" thinking across the US military. The movement included such notables as Senator Gary Hart, and individuals who would become Boyd's trusted associates, among whom were William Lind, Thomas P. Christie, Franklin C. Spinney, and Pierre M. Sprey. In general, the reformers opposed the US Defense department's predilection for buying increasingly sophisticated and expensive combat systems, though the movement gained a reputation for being zealous to a fault.[12]

In 1976, Boyd began developing "Patterns of Conflict," a briefing that sought to reveal the keys to military success. In the 1980s, Boyd assisted in revising the US Marine Corps (USMC) warfighting manual (FMFM 1). He also provided expert (and usually handwritten) testimonies to Congress on topics such as "Reforming the Military." In April 1991, for instance, he testified to the Aspen Committee that three basic elements contributed to success in war, in order of importance: people, strategy and tactics, and hardware.[13] To win in wartime, the military needed to promote talented officers, such as (his friend and co-reformer) USMC Colonel Michael Wyly, over the unimaginative bureaucrats who seemed to populate its flag-officer ranks. Boyd died in 1997 at the age of seventy, leaving a legacy of interrelated briefings and an oral history, but not enough published works to constitute a formal body of knowledge.

9.2 Radical Conservative

An avowed Anglican, William Sturgiss Lind was born in Cleveland, Ohio, in 1947.[14] Unlike Boyd, Lind was fortunate enough to obtain an Ivy league education. He received a bachelor's degree in history from Dartmouth College in 1969 and, two years later, a master's degree in history from Princeton University. Also, unlike Boyd, Lind never served in the military. "By the time I got out of college," he reportedly said, "it was obvious the Vietnam War had been lost, and only an idiot volunteers for a lost cause."[15] From 1973 to 1976, he worked on the military reform agenda of Senator Robert Taft, Jr. (R-Ohio). From 1977 to 1986, he did the same for Senator Gary Hart (D-Colorado). In 1986, he and Hart coauthored *America Can Win: The Case for Military Reform*, which called for widespread changes in US weapons procurement, force structure and organization, and military education and training. According to *America Can Win*, the goal of military reform was to create "conventional forces effective enough to get [the United States] off the nuclear hook."[16] In effect, the book sanctioned the expansion of military capabilities related to conventional warfighting, but with an emphasis on increasing efficiency and reducing waste.

By the late 1980s, Lind had become the Director of the Center for Cultural Conservatism at the Free Congress Foundation. In 1987, he coauthored *Cultural Conservatism* with William Marshner, which put forth a plan for revitalizing traditional institutions.[17] Lind has remained an outspoken critic of multiculturalism, which he has likened to "political correctness" or "cultural Marxism," the goal of which is to destroy "Western culture and the Christian religion."[18] One of its chief weapons was "mass immigration," which he claimed submerged the "native population and their beliefs in a sea of foreigners" until they disappeared.[19]

For Lind, liberal values were unnatural, dishonest, and divisive. The Enlightenment had imbued humanity with patently false ideas concerning cultural equality and the perfectibility of society. The Enlightenment narrative of progress was an illusion, and not even a good one. Humanity needed an alternate historical narrative, one based on facts, not fantasies, and one that appreciated rather than loathed Western culture.[20] Diversity, he maintained, was not a strength, as proponents of multiculturalism claimed, but a weakness. Diversity meant a fragmented culture, the subversion of national identity, and the forfeiture of the will to win.[21] It eroded the sociopsychological counterweights Boyd had said were necessary for preserving initiative, adaptability, and harmony. It not only rendered the United States vulnerable to attack by an enemy's ideological vanguards, it did most of their work for them. Lind used both nonfiction and fiction to convey his ideas. A short story entitled "Victoria," authored by Lind and later published as a novel under the pseudonym Thomas Hobbes, can be found in Boyd's archives.[22] It tells the story of a future America riven by false beliefs and intellectual cowardice. Only by physically eliminating the leaders of cultural Marxism and establishing an enlightened despot could one restore balance and repair a divided America.

9.3   Post-Vietnam America – in Malaise and Decline

Boyd, Lind, and Warden wrote their foundational theoretical works during the last three decades of the twentieth century. Their America was characterized partly by the malaise of the post-Vietnam era, and partly by the optimism and opportunities for growth that came with the dénouement of the Cold War. It is important to note, however, that Boyd spent his formative childhood years in the social and economic uncertainty of the Great Depression; Lind and Warden, in comparison, had benefited from the golden age of America's middle class. Indeed, by the 1950s Eisenhower's economic conservatism had replaced Roosevelt's economic socialism, and America's real gross national product had risen to a prosperous $2.9 trillion.[23] By late 1957, as Sputnik I and II had orbited the globe and Elvis's "Jailhouse Rock" caught on amongst America's teens, Lind was ten years old and Warden fourteen. Lind and Warden were part of the "baby boomer" generation, which had helped increase the US population from 129 million to 172 million by 1957. Furthermore, Boyd's family had agonized over the outbreak of epidemics such as measles and polio, while vaccines for these were readily available in the United States by the time Lind and Warden were teenagers. At the end of the 1960s, in fact, advances in medicine, especially antibiotics, had contributed to an increase in life expectancy by nine years for men and twelve years for women.[24]

Combatting feminism would become a leitmotif for Lind. The 1960s saw the blossoming of what Gloria Steinem referred to feminism's "second wave," which urged women to take greater control over their lives by challenging their traditional roles. In many ways, they were doing exactly that. In 1947, when Lind was born, only 29 percent of college students were women; however, by the time he was of college age, 41 percent of college students were women.[25] When he was in his early thirties, half of married women and two-thirds of single women were working, though they were still being paid 40 percent less than men for comparable jobs.[26] Some basic social mores were changing as well, which conservatives and antifeminist activists such as Phyllis Schlaffley blamed on feminists' "anti-family, anti-children, and pro-abortion" attitudes. About 50 percent of marriages were ending in divorce, as more states began adopting no-fault divorce laws. Also, by the end of the 1960s, the number of people who disapproved of sex before marriage had declined by 20 percent.[27] By the end of the 1970s, purportedly 30 percent of children were born out of wedlock.[28] Lind saw these developments as evidence of social decline. Meanwhile, feminist presses and periodicals were flourishing. New types of feminist fiction, including dystopias such as Joanna Russ's *The Female Man* (1975) and Margaret Atwood's *The Handmaid's Tale* (1985) blossomed in Lind's America as well.[29] Lind countered such works with a dystopia of his own entitled *Victoria* (2014). In the book, Mrs. Kraft, one of his female protagonists of the "Retro-culture Movement," proclaimed "These days, women are told they were oppressed and mistreated in the past, and that they will be happier if they can live in the business world, the world of men. That is another modern lie." "As far as all the nonsense about women being oppressed by being given charge of the home," she added, "I find quite the opposite is true."[30]

When the antiwar demonstrations and racial conflicts of the 1960s began to accelerate, Boyd was in his thirties, and Lind and Warden in their late teens.[31] By the late 1970s, all three authors had experienced the full force of American antimilitarism. For them, the words of General Fred Woerner, a 1939 graduate of Berkeley University, rang true: "Antimilitarism is a constant in American society."[32] The America of the operational artists had witnessed the fruition of Kahn's 1968 predictions concerning the repercussions of the US failure in Vietnam: recriminations abounded, disillusionment had grown. The public had lost confidence in its government; the military had developed a "stab-in-the-back" narrative that blamed politicians for the defeat; and the political left argued the war had been mindlessly prolonged by the military-industrial complex.[33]

All three operational theorists could also identify with the loss of "conceptual unity" Eccles had referred to in *Military Power in a Free Society* (1979); the Vietnam War had, indeed, exacerbated social differences.[34] The major polls suggested national morale had fallen to an all-time low. Worse still, it had not yet hit bottom; drug use was escalating across the country; divorce rates had increased and the nuclear family showed signs of disintegrating; America had slipped into an economic recession, inflation was rising, and oil prices remained at all-time highs due largely to the OPEC embargo of 1973.[35] The fundamentalist revolution in Iran and the overthrow of the Shah in February 1979, the subsequent hostage crisis and the failed rescue attempt (Desert One), as well as the rise of anti-American sentiment across the Middle East more broadly, suggested US political and military leadership remained as patently inept as it had been at any time during the Vietnam era.

Notably, in July 1979, well before the Iran hostage crisis, US President Jimmy Carter admitted on public television he believed the country was in a political and social crisis, one that struck "at the very heart and soul and spirit of our national will." He went on to say: "We can see this crisis in the growing doubt about the meaning of our own lives and in the loss of a unity of purpose for our nation. The erosion of our confidence in the future is threatening to destroy the social and the political fabric of America." Presumably, Carter merely wanted to rally the public behind his energy conservation program. But his "malaise speech," as it came to be called, did not play that way in the press. Instead, the speech came across as confirming the growing apprehension that America had emerged from the

Vietnam War confused, and that it was now in political and social decline.[36] Given such events, Boyd and Lind had little difficulty believing America was experiencing a crisis of heart and soul. Warden, however, did not share their pessimism.

All three had reason to celebrate the fall of the Berlin Wall in 1989, the victory over Iraq in 1991, and the collapse of the Soviet Union shortly thereafter. Like Summers, Warden saw the US military's success in the Gulf War as a vindication of its professional expertise, though for different reasons. By comparison, the early 1990s offered few positive signs for Boyd and Lind. Immigration had increased to an average of 978,000 per year, most of them now Asians and Hispanics rather than the white Europeans of Mahan's day; throughout the 1990s, the immigration average per annum was more than twice what it had been in the 1970s. Also, by the beginning of the 1990s, women outnumbered men in undergraduate and master's programs, and more than 60 percent of women over the age of twenty were in the work force.[37] During this period, as well, many religious conservatives saw the AIDS epidemic of the 1990s as a form of divine retribution against gays and lesbians.

Boyd's archives hold a handprinted manuscript, dated 1992, declaring that America now faced "momentous economic, financial, moral, intellectual, and social tribulations." Corruption was evident at all levels of government; America's cities were in decay; racial gangs were committing murder in the streets; homelessness, poverty, and child and spouse abuse were on the rise; as was "Satanism" and other cultish movements; homosexuality had increased; so had sexual permissiveness and abortion; unemployment and underemployment had become chronic; as had racial conflict. As far as this manifesto was concerned, America had entered into a "process of social disintegration," not unlike that masterminded by Karl Marx and Moses Hess, and which the "governing elite" unwittingly abetted because of its own flawed "theology of equality."[38] The document stopped short of advocating the violent overthrow of the US government. But it did call for revolutionary cultural change. It also provided a preamble to a much longer document, "In the Shadow of Doom: Social Disintegration in America," that described how the "intellectual war plan" that Karl Marx had developed for the social disintegration of Germany was now being carried out in the United States.[39] Curiously, both documents are devoid of any accompanying notes or information regarding their provenance. But the ideas expressed in them will undoubtedly pique the interest of anyone concerned with cultural disintegration as a form of warfare.

9.4 Boyd's Theory of Winning

Boyd's "Patterns of Conflict" endeavored to identify those "ideas and actions" that contributed to "winning and losing in a highly competitive world."[40] But it was superficial at best; its sources consisted mainly of popular histories and memoires such as J. F. C. Fuller's *Conduct of War 1789–1961* (1961) and F. W. von Mellenthin's *Panzer Battles* (1956). However, a smattering of works by scholars such as Michael Handel and Walter Laqueur were also listed. Quite ambitiously, "Patterns" attempted to do four things: (1) to elucidate the "nature of moral–mental–physical conflict"; (2) to discern a pattern for successful operations; (3) to generalize about "tactics and strategy"; and (4) to find a "basis for grand strategy."[41]

For Boyd, the moral, mental, and physical dimensions of conflict were interrelated: competition occurred in all of them simultaneously, and successes (or losses) in one dimension were felt in the others. The pattern for success he discerned was that victory usually went to the party that adapted faster than its opponent; that is, the party that managed to cope with uncertainty, change, and time more efficiently. Greater efficiency, or speed of execution, led to greater effectiveness over the long term. Tactically, success amounted to observing, orienting, deciding, and acting faster than one's adversary. This OODA cycle or loop became the most memorable aspect of Boyd's legacy. As "Patterns" maintained, strategic success came from penetrating the "moral–mental–physical being" of one's rivals to destroy their "internal harmony, produce paralysis, and collapse [their] will to resist."[42] Unless the bonds that enabled the foe to exist as "an organic whole" could be severed, thereby creating multiple "non-cooperative centers of gravity," the enemy was likely to continue to resist.

Human beings, according to Boyd, had a natural hierarchy of desires: first "to survive," second to survive on one's "own terms," and third to improve one's "capacity for independent action."[43] Hence, the essence of grand strategy was to maximize one's ability to realize these desires and, if necessary, to reduce the ability of one's rivals to do the same. Strategy thus required an understanding of war's socio-psychological dimension, which he conceived as the "underlying self-interests, critical differences of opinion, internal contradictions, frictions, obsessions, etc." afflicting the societies in conflict.[44] Critically, therefore, Boyd's search for patterns included not just the military and political dimensions of war but also its socio-psychological dimension, a fact that much of the research into his thinking has overlooked.

By the late 1980s, "Patterns" had become the first part of a larger briefing entitled "A Discourse on Winning and Losing" (known to insiders as *The Green Book*). According to some accounts, "Discourse" might require as many as two days (approximately fourteen hours) to present, and Boyd reportedly refused to shorten it, offering to deliver only the "full brief or no brief."[45] The second and third parts of "Discourse" included briefings entitled "Organic Design for Command and Control" (1987) and "The Strategic Game of ? and ?" (1987). The former made a case for organizing all command-and-control procedures around the OODA loop. Whenever he delivered the latter briefing, Boyd replaced the question marks with the words "interaction" and "isolation." This briefing expanded upon the latter portions of "Patterns," and argued the objective of strategy was to increase, or to sustain, one's ability to interact with the environment, a repository of essential resources, and to decrease the ability of one's adversaries to do the same.

Part four of the "Discourse" consisted of the one noteworthy essay by Boyd, "Destruction and Creation" (1976). The essay attempted to show how concepts were inevitably destroyed and created in a dialectical interaction between one's observations and one's environment.[46] It was an obvious application of the essence of the OODA loop that blended Thomas Kuhn's theory of paradigms, and how they shift, with Boyd's own unbridled passion for conceptual creativity. It used Kurt Gödel's incompleteness theorem to claim no system can be understood within itself; the theorem actually shows only that no single set of axioms can explain natural mathematics. The essay also borrowed Werner Heisenberg's uncertainty principle to argue the act of observing always alters the phenomenon being observed; however, the uncertainty principle only claims one can determine either the velocity of a subatomic particle or its position, but not both simultaneously. "Destruction and Creation" also drew from the second law of thermodynamics to insist internal perspectives never suffice; in fact, the second law of thermodynamics only says disorder, or entropy, increases within closed systems.[47] In other words, Boyd's method involved extracting laws and principles from distinct fields of study and attempting to apply them, quite inappropriately, to other matters.

A later briefing entitled "Conceptual Spiral" (1992) made up part five of the "Discourse."[48] This briefing explored the dialectical interaction between observations and environment more closely. It contended that because any interaction with the environment altered it in unpredictable ways, one required ever newer models or frames of reference to understand the environment. The process of understanding is thus evolutionary. It must evolve to keep pace with changes in the environment, which in turn creates an escalating spiral of concepts. The final part of the "Discourse" was "Revelation," which summarized what many of Boyd's followers took to be his core message, namely, that winners innovated faster and more effectively than losers.[49] Innovators, for instance, could take sundry items – a pair of skis, the motor from a boat, the steering wheel from a bicycle, the treads from a tractor – and build a snowmobile that might enable them to win; whereas losers would only see an assortment of unrelatable parts. This analogy underscores the eclectic character of Boyd's intellect, a trait that endeared him to the reform movement and contributed to an enduring legacy among military officers.[50] Lind went so far as to refer to him as America's "greatest military theorist," partly because of Boyd's eclecticism and his willingness to connect the patently unconnectable.[51]

But Boyd's eclecticism, due in part to the fact that he was an autodidact, also had serious drawbacks. On the plus side, autodidacts either lack or deliberately eschew formal structures or "boxes" that would constrain their intellectual creativity. On the negative side, they also want for mentors who, in the style of Herbert Rosinski, might guide them away from intellectual dead-ends toward more productive goals. A mentor might have recognized Boyd's overriding concern was epistemological in nature. That mentor might have advised him to study more closely the works of Karl Popper, who since the mid-twentieth century was at the epicenter of a methodological revolution in the social sciences. Popper's *Logic of Scientific Discovery* (1959) exposed the limits of inductive and deductive reasoning and suggested replacing them with a "falsifiable hypothesis" in an effort to disprove a theory.[52] Until a theory was disproven, it remained tentatively valid. While Boyd listed some of Popper's works among his sources and may have read them, he appears not to have studied them. Instead, his "Discourse" shows a growing profusion of connections, of intertwining hypotheses and speculations, many of which likely seemed intriguing to his audience, but were ultimately unjustifiable or indefensible.

Although Boyd became notorious for making late-night phone calls to colleagues to discuss his latest "breakthroughs," this practice also meant he left few letters that might have provided more insights into his thinking. His listeners, moreover, generally lacked the educational exposure necessary to challenge or to channel him.[53] Without such guidance, autodidacts can waste precious time developing observations that add little of value to existing knowledge. Boyd drew from several scientific laws, but those laws possessed no special validity outside their original contexts. In "Destruction and Creation," furthermore, he attempted to establish parallels between the path of destruction–deduction–analysis, on the one hand, and that of creation–induction–synthesis, on the other. A mentor might have pointed out that such an effort was flawed from the outset. Deduction resembles creation more than it does destruction, and it has more in common with synthesis than it does with analysis. In any case, the making of such connections had become an intellectual fad in the 1970s and 1980s, most noticeably illustrated by the popular writings and television series of philosopher-scientists such as Jacob Bronowski and James Burke, each of whom rendered complex scientific ideas and developments accessible to the general public. If the 1960s brought about divisions and revolutions, the 1970s stressed connections and stability. Boyd's affinity for connections and parallels, in other words, mark him not as unique but rather as part of the cultural–intellectual mainstream of the period.

Critics have identified problems with Boyd's methodology, which at least one scholar has identified as inductive.[54] Strictly speaking, Boyd's method was neither inductive nor deductive. His personal experience had already taught him which principles (though he eschewed the term) he ought to promote: observing first, orienting first, deciding first, and acting first. In effect, these activities captured a pilot's decision cycle or OODA loop, which Boyd elevated to a theory. Instead, it had more in common with the comparative method, the third step in the scientific approach Luce promoted at the Naval War College nearly seventy years earlier (Part I, Chapter 1). The comparative method permitted him to draw illustrative parallels, to extend his principles beyond the cockpit, and to apply them to human decision-making in any competitive environment. But the connections were asserted rather than proved.

The OODA loop is obviously about adaptation.[55] But it is also about gaining a temporal and psychological advantage by moving more swiftly through what Boyd took to be a common and natural decision-making process. The purpose of adaptation was to win. For Boyd, resolving strategic dilemmas required stepping outside one's habits of thought, one's familiar paradigms, to gain a more holistic and thus more beneficial perspective. In short, the military mind must learn to solve its strategic dilemmas not unlike the way a fighter pilot approached aerial combat, by maneuvering into a position of advantage.

9.5 The Maneuver Revolution

The maneuver warfare school of thought originated in part with the US Marine Corps' efforts to reinvent itself in the late 1970s and early 1980s.[56] However, it also grew from the US Army's efforts to lift the aura of failure that plagued it after Vietnam. As Lind noted: "The problem is that our military establishment has lost sight of the art of war."[57] America's failures in Vietnam and Desert One, as well as its unsatisfactory performances in Lebanon and Grenada, gave considerable weight to his claim. Furthermore, many of the articles published by Marine officers and Army officers during the 1970s and 1980s conveyed a tone not unlike Lind's: Americans were not thinking about war correctly and they would do well to adopt the concepts and techniques of the Germans and Israelis who, with some inevitable exceptions, seemed to have gotten it right. Maneuver warfare, in effect, became the basis for the conceptual rebirth of the US military.

In brief, maneuver theory stressed the importance of out-positioning one's opponents in three ways: (1) physically, (2) mentally or psychologically, and (3) temporally, that is, by maintaining a faster tempo of operations. The latter two dimensions were considered more critical than the first. As Lind explained, the central idea was to move "through repeated cycles of observation-decision-action" faster than one's opponents, which in turn was called cycling "inside" them. As a result, the actions of one's enemies would become increasingly irrelevant and they would come to realize they can do nothing to control the situation; their forces would thus suffer a "mental breakdown in the form of panic" and would essentially be defeated before they were physically destroyed. "The Boyd Theory," proclaimed Lind, "is the theory of maneuver warfare."[58]

Proponents of maneuver warfare quickly elevated the theory to an ideal, a model for the correct way of fighting. They portrayed maneuver as the opposite of attrition, which they saw as ruthless, costly, and manifestly incorrect. Scholars such as Richard Betts likened this enthusiasm to a kind of "doctrinal fetishism."[59] Others, such as Edward Luttwak, fired back, insisting the conceptual reorientation of US ground forces toward maneuver was a clear and present need.[60]

In their enthusiasm, however, maneuverists repeatedly associated their theory with the German blitzkrieg of the Second World War. Yet the Wehrmacht never developed an official blitzkrieg doctrine. Instead, German doctrine referred to two types of land warfare: *Bewegungskrieg*, or a war of movement, and *Stellungskrieg*, or a war of positions.[61] Strictly speaking, the opposite of maneuver warfare was not attrition but positional warfare, a Jominian-like struggle for key positions – such as harbors, transportation hubs, airfields – the capture of which enabled one to dominate the theater of war.[62] A war of positions might involve the techniques of attrition or annihilation, or any combination of them. From the German perspective, moreover, the experience of trench warfare in the First World War presented interwar theorists with a twofold problem: how to achieve a breakthrough swiftly and cost-effectively, and how to exploit it before the enemy could establish another line of prepared defenses. By the Second World War, the ability to combine armored vehicles, wireless communications, and air power to strike at weak points in the defender's lines made it possible to achieve breakthroughs at acceptable costs. Air power, in turn, facilitated the rapid and deep exploitation of a breakthrough by providing a protective umbrella for advancing columns and by interdicting the flow of enemy troops and supplies into the battle area. This air–ground combination generated a relentless momentum, a *"Schlacht ohne Morgen"* (literally "Battle without Morning") that kept the enemy off-balance while also creating any number of options: encirclements, overrunning command posts, or capturing supply depots. This was essentially *Bewegungskrieg* with twentieth-century materiel.

The enthusiasm of the maneuverists also caused them to undervalue the campaign plan. While they repeatedly pointed to the Wehrmacht's triumph over France in 1940 as the ideal application of the principles of speed and focus, they paid little attention to the German plan of attack. Had the Germans followed the original scheme of maneuver, which resembled in concept the attack plan of 1914, they would have run headlong into the main effort of British and French forces. Even the German high command expected only a limited victory with this scheme. The plan was ultimately and grudgingly modified, due in part to the objections of General Erich von Manstein (for which he was subsequently punished) so that a thrust through the Ardennes became the main effort.[63] This approach took the Allies by surprise and led to the encirclement of a large portion of their forces. The German invasion of Norway in April 1940 also succeeded mainly because of the level of planning that went into it.[64] In contrast, Hitler's invasion of Russia in June 1941 was hastily and amateurishly planned, and the vaunted principles of speed and focus yielded a series of encirclements that did not culminate in an overall victory. In short, the one example maneuverists resorted to most often to justify what elevated their theory above its alleged antithesis, attrition, was based largely on a superficial understanding of the most destructive war of the twentieth century.[65]

Maneuver theory had other shortcomings as well. To begin with, maneuverists gave too little attention to the problem of maintaining the flow of logistics in the fluid, nonlinear battles they envisioned. Obviously, without logistics, maneuver, and indeed any type of warfare, quickly becomes impossible. While historical studies showed that Germany's lack of motorized transport led to breakdowns in supply over the vast expanses of the Soviet Union, few maneuverists bothered to study those problems and draw lessons from them. Joint concepts such as "Focused Logistics," published in 1996 as a component of *Joint Vision 2010*, seemingly acknowledged the problem. But solutions capable of working within the chaotic environments envisioned by maneuverists remained elusive. Even the promises of twenty-first-century information technologies fell short in this respect.[66]

Second, maneuver theory tended to overlook the critical role of air superiority. Without it one's forces quickly lost combat power and freedom of movement. Rommel experienced that problem in North Africa in 1942–43, as he later attested: "British and American superiority in the air alone has again and again been so effective that all movement of major formations has been rendered completely impossible, both at the front and behind it."[67] The situation was even worse in France in 1944. By way of illustration, Allied air attacks caused Germany's crack Panzer Lehr Division to lose approximately 12 percent of its combat power while en route to its battle positions near the city of Caen; the division was later essentially wiped out by Allied carpet-bombing on July 25–26, 1944.[68] Few air strategists regard using aircraft in such ground-support roles, as "flying artillery," with anything but scorn. Nonetheless, the carpet bombing of the Allied front along the edges of Normandy opened the way for maneuver warfare in northern France. Moreover, air interdiction missions in the zone beyond friendly artillery range contributed to sustaining the tempo of ground operations.

Outside the concept of AirLand Battle, maneuverists rarely discussed the codependency of air and ground maneuver. Few examined the utility of maneuver principles in situations in which only restricted or degraded movement might be possible. Many rejected the AirLand Battle tenet of "synchronization," the doctrinal term used to describe aligning one's fire and movement either simultaneously or sequentially to maximize their effects. Not only would synchronization limit independence and creativity, they argued, the time and effort necessary to achieve it would adversely affect operational tempo.

A third significant problem was the lack of jointness in the maneuverists' overall vision. Not only did it fail to address integrated air–ground maneuver, as mentioned, it also overlooked integrated sea–ground maneuver. Naval experts such as Wayne Hughes pointedly underscored the challenges of maneuver warfare at sea. As he noted, the 1992 edition of Naval Doctrine Publication 1 (NDP 1) said maneuver warfare existed for the US Navy, which had the timeless and vital mission of delivering goods and services: that is, "Marines, strikes, and sustainment of the ground campaign." To fulfill this function, however, the US Navy had long designed its ships to be "operationally mobile but not tactically nimble."[69] Operationally, the Navy could shift from one hostile shore to another relatively quickly. But once the process of offloading troops and supplies began, parts of the Navy were largely and necessarily immobile until that process was complete. In short, the Navy had to forgo some of the vaunted principles of maneuver warfare in order to perform its primary mission. That choice, said Hughes, was the correct one: that mission mattered more than the principles. By implication, however, Hughes had also rightly criticized maneuver theory for being preoccupied with ground forces and for ignoring the larger context of joint warfare. In the meantime, other naval officers wondered whether the term "naval maneuver warfare" itself might constrain how one thought about applying revolutionary technologies at sea.[70]

Finally, maneuver theory was flawed in another critical respect. Despite its symbiotic relationship with operational art, it was about winning battles rather than wars. Maneuverists and operational artists readily acknowledged Harry Summers's warnings in *On Strategy*. Nonetheless, the crux of their theory rested on the assumption that winning battles, preferably through maneuver, led to the winning of wars. Unfortunately, as history shows, defeating an enemy's armed forces in battle did not always compel its government to concede. In many of the countries Hitler overran during the Second World War, for instance, governments continued to function, if sometimes in exile, and populations continued to resist through partisan activities, if tentatively at first. Put differently, the elements in Clausewitz's secondary or subjective trinity may not be completely interconnected in a given conflict, which certainly underscores the pertinence of Summers's message.

A second wave of maneuver theorists, which appeared in the 1990s, attempted to address some of these criticisms. Its chief claim was that maneuver warfare was a "thought process" not a prescriptive doctrine.[71] However, efforts to prove this thought process could apply to low-intensity conflicts, which the US military conducts at a much higher rate than mid- or high-intensity campaigns, were not persuasive.[72] For example, the US catastrophe in Somalia (1992–94) suggested the maneuverists' model was too inflexible to apply to low-intensity conflicts, though unwise political decisions also contributed to the failure.[73] Secondly, the political conditions surrounding the clashes in Bosnia (1992–95) and Kosovo (1999) largely precluded the use of ground maneuver. Furthermore, the second wave, influenced by Weigley's interpretation of the American way of war as heavily reliant on attrition strategies, continued to hold to the flawed dichotomy of attrition and maneuver, condemning the former while praising the latter. In sum, despite offering a nuanced interpretation of maneuver warfare as a thought process rather than a doctrine, the second wave enjoyed no more success than did the first in giving it a joint flavor and in applying it to the full spectrum of conflict.

9.6 Maneuver and War's Missing Dimension

Most of the literature on Boyd, though insightful, has primarily examined his thoughts related to the psychological dimension of warfare and to innovation and creative thinking. It has not considered his ideas concerning war's social, or psychosocial, dimension to the same degree. But those thoughts, in some ways, were more novel and innovative than his other concepts. By way of illustration, "Patterns" contains repeated references to the importance of rending the enemy's social fabric, the threads that hold the adversary's society together. Boyd discussed conflict *between* social systems but also *within* them, particularly with the rise of capitalism in the nineteenth century and the "periodic *crises*" it caused due to social and economic tensions. Whereas he admitted his analysis had a "Marxist flavor," he avoided using the framework of class warfare. Instead, he concentrated on the role of "guerrilla vanguards," hard-core ideological leaders, who sow discord and amplify internal frictions. The "creation of crises and vanguards . . . make evident the foundations upon which to conduct insurrection/revolution in order to destroy a society from within."[74]

A substantial portion of Boyd's strategic theory, in fact, dealt with destroying an opponent's moral cohesion, while avoiding the destruction of one's own. The aim of moral conflict, he said, was to "pump-up friction via negative factors," such as "menace, uncertainty, and mistrust," in order to "breed fear, anxiety, and alienation." These, in turn, would "generate non-cooperative centers of gravity, as well as subvert those the adversary depends upon, [and] thereby sever moral bonds that permit the adversary to exist as an organic whole."[75] Menace he defined as "impressions of danger to one's well-being and survival"; uncertainty amounted to the "impressions, or atmosphere, generated by events that appear ambiguous, erratic, contradictory, unfamiliar, chaotic, etc."; and mistrust was an "atmosphere of doubt and suspicion that loosens human bonds among members of an organic whole or between organic wholes."[76] Protecting one's own society required strengthening three critical "counterweights" – initiative, adaptability, and harmony – against the negative factors. Initiative meant an "internal drive to think and take action without being urged;" adaptability was the "power to adjust or change in order to cope with new or unforeseen circumstances;" and harmony amounted to the "interaction of apparently disconnected events or entities in a connected way."[77]

Boyd's concern with moral conflict invariably reflected the political and social turmoil of the 1960s and 1970s. He began developing "Patterns of Conflict" the year following America's evacuation from Saigon, and two years after Nixon's resignation as US president. In sum, America seemed to be weaker internally than ever before, save obviously for the period of the Civil War. Boyd's prescriptions for destroying a society from within, in other words, seemed to have all the empirical grounding they needed.

Moreover, his thoughts regarding social vulnerability served as a springboard for Lind's theory of Fourth Generation Warfare (4GW). Initially advanced in the late 1980s, 4GW posited that warfare had evolved through a series of "distinct generations." The first generation – that of massed manpower – reflected the tactics of line and column, which combined the firepower of linear formations with the "élan" of the conscript armies of the revolutionary era. The second generation – massed firepower – remained essentially linear in nature but relied increasingly on heavy volumes of indirect fire. This generation continued to characterize US tactics into the 1980s, according to the authors. The third generation – maneuver – relied on mobility and consisted of bypassing and isolating enemy forces, rather than attacking them head-on. The authors held these to be the first genuinely nonlinear tactics. While the US Army and US Marine Corps concentrated on perfecting this form of warfare, they were already being outflanked by the emergence of war's fourth generation. This generation combined "carryover" characteristics from the third generation, including mission orders, decentralized logistics, maneuver, and "collapsing the enemy internally." Lind and his colleagues speculated that conflict in the fourth generation would be "widely dispersed and largely undefined" and would consist of blurred distinctions between peace and war, no definable battlefields or fronts, and concurrent activities designed to undermine a rival's society and culture. Fourth-generation warfare might also involve advanced or emerging technologies, such as directed energy weapons, electromagnetic pulse (EMP) devices, robotics, remotely piloted vehicles, computer viruses, artificial intelligence, and new media and communications capabilities.[78]

"In Fourth Generation war," Lind added later, "the state loses its monopoly on war." This type of war "is marked by a return to a world of cultures, not merely states, in conflict." In 4GW, "invasion by immigration can be at least as dangerous as invasion by a state army."[79] "Multiculturalism," he declared shortly after the attacks of 9/11, "is death" in 4GW. "Multicultural countries will break apart in very messy, many-sided civil wars," as in Yugoslavia. Accordingly, "America urgently needs to reaffirm its historic, unified culture. It must also drastically reduce the number of immigrants it accepts. At present, we are importing fourth-generation warfare by the boatload."[80]

Conventional militaries were of little use in such conflicts. Solutions could come only from adroitly maneuvering within war's sociocultural dimension. Appropriate measures should include reuniting "Christendom" and creating alliances with Russia, and with Chinese and Hindu cultures to encircle the "main threat, Islamic culture." The countries that survive in a fourth-generation world "will have open political systems and unified cultures," Lind added, but the United States had a closed system (two parties from the same class) and a "formal policy of multiculturalism" that divided rather than unified.[81] Put differently, Lind's theory of 4GW blended the era's growing concern with insurgents and other violent nonstate actors with ultraconservative anxieties regarding the apparent loss of the West's cultural canon and the fraying of its moral fabric.

The theory's various flaws have been discussed at length in numerous publications. In sum, those flaws fall into three broad categories.[82] First, the theory's proponents grossly exaggerated the novelty and effectiveness of 4GW based on a faulty reading of history; they engaged in speculation but represented it as analysis. Speculation is obviously not the same as theory. Second, their exaggerations fueled a subsequent and more critical claim, namely that 4GW was the wave of the future and, thus, that other forms of warfare were obsolete. Their argument, in fact, was not that 4GW would coexist with other forms of war, but that it would eclipse them. Third, they defined 4GW so broadly as to encompass almost every type of irregular war, especially insurgencies. But they neglected to discuss the capacities modern states already possessed to deal with those types of conflicts, particularly paramilitary arms of intelligence organizations such as the CIA, which, along with other kinds of special forces, routinely organize and equip irregular troops to do the bidding of states. Hence, while the theory's proponents claimed they sought only to draw the attention of defense bureaucrats to a worsening problem, they rarely shifted their fire beyond the presumed inadequacy of conventional forces for unconventional warfare.

This last criticism also underscores a rift that developed between the view of 4GW held by T. X. Hammes and that of Lind and, apparently, van Creveld. Whereas Hammes's *The Sling and the Stone* likened 4GW to insurgency, Lind contended it was really about the use of "cultures as weapons."[83] The forces of 4GW "win by pulling the states they are fighting apart at the moral level." Like the United States in Vietnam, states that possess overwhelming physical power can lose a war in the moral dimension if they cannot bring the conflict to a close within a reasonable period and without using force disproportionately. Otherwise, the more powerful state assumes the aspect of a brutal Goliath against the weaker state's David, irrespective of the principles for which either stands. Eventually, "Disgust at [the stronger state's] own behavior spreads and grows within [its] own public and its own armed forces. Morale weakens, dissent from the war spreads and the public comes to desire only an end to whole dirty business."[84] The West's cultural aversion to war, in other words, leaves it vulnerable to a more warlike culture clever enough to take advantage of it. Lind's view drew directly from his ultraconservative cultural and political perspectives, which saw dissention as disunifying and exploitable, an outlook seemingly validated by his first-hand observation of the social violence of the 1960s.

9.7 Boyd's First Principles

Like so many of his professional colleagues in the last two decades of the twentieth century, Boyd considered the principles of war as little more than an amateur's "laundry list." Each of the world's major powers had developed its own, which changed over time and which, he believed, demonstrated their impermanence and inutility. In comparison, the laws and principles of science did not change. Hence, the principles of war were not genuine principles, according to Boyd. Nor did they really assist militaries "to shape and adapt" to the "uncertain and everchanging environment of conflict or war." The solution, in his view, was to set aside the traditional principles in favor of "appropriate bits and pieces" that better described what one needed to do in an armed conflict. He listed six such "bits" or guidelines: (1) compress own time and stretch out adversary time; (2) generate unequal distributions as a basis to focus mental–moral–physical effort for local superiority and decisive leverage; (3) diminish own friction (or entropy) and magnify adversary friction; (4) operate inside adversaries' observation–orientation–decision–action loops or get inside their mind–time–space; (5) penetrate adversary organism and bring about their collapse; (6) amplify own "spirit and strength," drain away that of adversaries, and attract the uncommitted.[85]

Upon closer scrutiny, however, this list had much in common with the traditional principles of war. Boyd's first and fourth guidelines, for instance, differed little from the principle of maneuver, except they pertained mainly to time rather than to space. His second guideline was basically the principle of mass, or concentration, with the addition of moral (psychological) force. Boyd's third principle combined unity of command and simplicity, two well-known measures for reducing friction. His fifth guideline captured the essence of maneuvering in the sociopsychological dimension of war. His last guideline represented a combination of security and the political dimension of maneuver. The traditional principles of offensive, economy of force, and surprise were implied in all of these. In sum, Boyd's "appropriate bits and pieces" amounted to a realignment and perhaps a reprioritization of the traditional principles of war – but hardly a rejection of them.

Similarly, other maneuverists explicitly eschewed developing a list of principles, insisting, not incorrectly, "fighting by lists" was both foolish and dangerous. However, it is impossible to describe a theory and to discuss its merits without identifying its essential verities, its principles. According to Lind and Wyly, if one must identify principles, one need only mention two: focus and speed.[86] In retrospect, these fundamentals amounted to a twentieth-century refinement of the military imperatives advanced by Mahan – concentration, offensive action, and decision by battle.

9.8 War's Nature

Like Mahan, Boyd saw war's nature as an extension of the competitive aspects of human nature. Unlike Mahan, however, Boyd's understanding did not revolve around the existence of a supreme being, who had created the universe. Rather, the human impulse to compete came directly from the survival instinct that every species possessed. "Life," said Boyd, "is conflict, survival, and conquest." A certain biological determinism, married with Darwinian natural selection, thus underpinned his conception of human nature. The desire to survive, preferably on one's own terms, and to enlarge one's "capacity for independent action" were inseparable from the human condition. Accordingly, war was, in essence, a competition for the resources necessary to satisfy these basic instincts.[87] Disorder, therefore, was more natural than order; put differently, Boyd's notion of the state of nature did not assume the universe was governed by Newtonian equilibrium. Instead, he assumed, or attempted to assume, a Hobbesian world of all against all, in which disorder created its own order. Furthermore, he endeavored to describe this world with terminology he borrowed from complexity theory and chaos theory, both of which became popular in the 1990s, and both of which posited a state of nature that was dynamic rather than stable.[88] Both theories fit well with the idea of movement – constant, unavoidable, and relentless – that underpinned Boyd's worldview. His use of them, however, was amateurish and inconsistent.

Lind's understanding of war's nature differed from Boyd's in two key respects. Both saw war as boundless in a manner that resembled the Chinese concept of "unrestricted warfare."[89] Both conceived of war in multiple dimensions, and both considered the moral or psychosocial dimension to be the most critical. But whereas Boyd saw rapid movement and adaptation as the keys to winning in all dimensions, Lind believed victory came by upending an adversary's systems of belief, its unifying values and cultures. Secondly, as an Anglican, Lind imagined a world with a natural order that reflected the work of a divine hand, much as Mahan did. What he found to be familiar and comfortable was, by definition, natural. The goal for Lind, therefore, was to restore, then to strengthen, his notion of the natural order against other, insidious cultural values.

As one marine officer noted, the dispute over synchronization revealed the presence of two incompatible views of the nature of war. The first view believed war's "inherent nature" was "fundamentally, intractably, chaotic and probabilistic." Hence, it saw synchronization as a vain attempt to impose control over the uncontrollable. The second outlook believed the "chaos and uncertainty of the battlefield can be mastered and provided with a governable structure and order." Accordingly, it regarded synchronization as both possible and desirable.[90] Maneuverists generally subscribed to the first view, insisting speed was the quintessential principle of warfare. But this insistence also widened the division between what was and was not war. Speed and focus might well apply to some military operations other than war. Nonetheless, other qualities such as presence and staying power might count for much more.

Maneuverists generally saw war's nature in experientialist terms, marked by uncertainty and other types of friction, to which one must adapt more effectively than one's opponent. These elements were inescapable; one could reduce friction through training and combat experience but never eliminate it entirely. Maneuverists believed friction could be accommodated through minimalist or decentralized control, and they embraced Clausewitz's apparent antipathy for mechanistic systems of war. But they failed to see, or saw but refused to acknowledge, that decentralization reflected and encouraged a tactical mindset. In the absence of higher-level guidance, decentralization led to atomization on the battlefield rather than unity of effort, because individual units tend to regard their own battles as matters of life and death.

9.9 Conclusions

The maneuverists who contributed to the rediscovery of US operational art in the 1970s and 1980s reflect some of the best and worst traits of the American way of thinking about war. They were clearly innovative, having developed new and supplementary concepts with commendable dispatch. Indeed, Boyd, Lind, and many others pushed the concept of maneuver into psychological warfare, into irregular warfare, and into information operations, among other areas.[91] Regrettably, both Boyd and Lind based many of their seminal ideas on wishful thinking and on the selective study of history. They, and their successors, committed themselves to solving, and in some cases solved, the underlying tactical and operational problem of the Cold War, namely, how to fight and win while outnumbered on the modern, highly lethal battlefield. At the same time, as a negative trait of the American way of thinking about war, they refined and proselytized their solutions, rather than integrating them into a synthetic and more comprehensive way of war. In addition, they avoided more critical problems, such as investigating how to convert vague policy aims into something more concrete that military forces could accomplish. Almost despite themselves, therefore, America's modern maneuverists enhanced their country's way of battle at the cost of improving its way of war.

By incorporating the Clausewitzian imponderables, particularly the concept of friction, into their understanding of war's nature, Boyd and Lind, along with other maneuver theorists, contributed to fashioning the modern paradigm of what war, at root, was. Their understanding of war's nature, thus, assumed all wars, regardless of type, were united by common features. Accordingly, as the US Marine Corps doctrinal pamphlet *Warfighting* (MCDP-1) stated, and as the US Army and US Navy agreed, "War is shaped by human nature and is subject to the complexities, inconsistencies, and peculiarities which characterize human behavior." Its essential features were "friction, uncertainty, fluidity, disorder, and danger," in addition to complexity and human will and emotions.[92] Any doctrine or theory that neglected these features and attempted to reduce war to a formula would, on that account, be inherently flawed. The first test of any theory or concept was, therefore, whether it accorded with war's nature.

In sum, under the modern paradigm, the nature of war was more than an extension of the competitive aspects of human nature. It was also a unique experience, shaped by the special features identified above, all of which invariably made the easy more difficult. Since they were assumed to characterize every war, it made sense to associate them with war's nature. However, the assumption itself was problematic: many conflicts have no more friction, uncertainty, fluidity, disorder, or danger than some everyday walks of life. As previous chapters showed, tens of thousands of Americans lost their lives every year and an average of 600,000 more were maimed annually in work-related accidents. Far fewer Americans lost their lives serving in President Wilson's overseas interventions, or in Smedley Butler's so-called Banana Wars; indeed, the Spanish flu of 1918 killed more than half a million Americans, or twice as many as died in the First World War. By the 1970s, conditions had certainly improved in the workplace; nonetheless, more than 40,000 Americans were losing their lives in traffic accidents yearly and hundreds of thousands more were being injured, compared to 58,000 American deaths during the entire fifteen-year involvement of US troops in Vietnam (1960–75). Moreover, where one is located in time of war matters a great deal: Brodie, Osgood, and Kahn, for instance, served in the US military during the Second World War, but they never experienced combat, and thus were all but strangers to war's special features. What Clausewitz described, and the US military adopted as the nature of war, spoke to the experience of being within the immediate zone of conflict. That experience was neither universally nor unequivocally true for every participant in war. Boyd, for instance, was in that zone and tried repeatedly to experience aerial combat directly, but never succeeded.

From the 1980s to the 2010s, military theorists and practitioners began deliberately distinguishing war's character from its nature, referring to the latter as constant and the former as ever changing. The environment in which war was to be waged had transformed from one in which nuclear weapons *may* be used to one in which they *might* be used. The shift was subtle but complete, for it allowed for a level of military–intellectual self-indulgence not found in the era of Eccles and Wylie. It also facilitated the return of the operational level of war as a legitimate arena of professional study, and with it came a host of operational theories.

Without the advance of multiculturalism in the 1990s, however, it is unlikely either Boyd or Lind would have attempted to apply their maneuver theories to war's psychosocial dimension. While their concepts were clearly alarmist, both theorists plunged energetically into a dimension of warfare underexamined since the Vietnam era and its immediate aftermath. Each saw wide-ranging evidence of social decline, driven largely by their ultraconservative worldviews. But their works also suffer from an inability or unwillingness to engage social science to the same degree as they did military science.

10 John Warden and Air Operational Art

In 1988, six years after the appearance of Summers's *On Strategy* and three years before Desert Storm, US Air Force Colonel John Ashley Warden III made a controversial but seminal contribution to air operational art with his publication of *The Air Campaign*.[1] The book aimed to provide a "philosophical and theoretical framework for conceptualizing, planning, and executing an air campaign." But it also laid the groundwork for a series of subsequent concepts, such as effects-based operations, that proved to have much more durability than Warden's original "ring theory," which is explained below. Like Summers's *On Strategy*, Warden's *Air Campaign* addressed, or attempted to, the weak spot in American strategic practice, the critical juncture between the "selection of national objectives and tactical execution."[2] It was within this space, presumably occupied by operational art, that political ends were translated into military objectives and into campaigns to accomplish those objectives. It was also within this space, seemingly, that America had failed in Vietnam. Not unlike Summers, Warden called upon military planners to recognize the principles of war as a military grammar capable of rationalizing policy's logic.

10.1 Entrepreneurial Theorist

John Ashley Warden III was born in 1943 into a military family. His grandfather, father, and uncle had received commissions in the US Army. His grandfather joined the Army in 1908 after completing the reserve officer training program (ROTC) at Texas A&M and served for thirty-nine years, but he never saw combat. His father completed the same program in 1935 and was assigned to the Pacific theater during the Second World War, but he also never saw combat. Warden's uncle, however, logged over two hundred combat hours with the US Army Air Corps during the war. John Warden graduated from the US Air Force Academy in 1965, and served in Vietnam in 1969, recording 266 combat missions.[3] Similar to many of his contemporaries, Warden came away from his Vietnam experience believing overly restrictive policies and rules of engagement had reduced the conflict to an absurdity. His disdain for signaling strategies ran as deep as Summers's own.

In 1975, Warden received a master's degree in political science from Texas Technical University for his thesis, "The Grand Alliance: Strategy and Decision."[4] His core argument paralleled the views of Osgood, namely that the American approach to the Second World War tended to disassociate power and policy. Like Osgood, he believed the goal of military victory had taken precedence over political considerations and, in turn, resulted in ceding key positional advantages in Europe to the Soviets. By the early 1990s, his materialist view of war's nature still shared some of the assumptions of the modern model, which obviously stood in sharp contrast to Osgood's political paradigm. Warden, in fact, explicitly rejected the "whole concept of limited war that had been espoused by the nuclear theoreticians in the 1950s and 1960s"; he went on to say the idea of "fighting not to win was just ludicrous."[5] When queried years later, Warden clarified his position by adding, "there is no problem with having limited objectives for a war as long as you realize that limited objectives have virtually nothing to do with the kind of war you may have to wage."[6]

In 1985, Warden attended the National War College, where he wrote *The Air Campaign*. At the time, the US defense establishment was involved in the buildup of the Reagan years. The US Army was in the process of developing its AirLand Battle doctrine. Record of air power's employment in the Arab–Israeli wars (1967–82) had been mixed due to improvements in air defenses, especially surface-to-air missiles. But by the First Lebanon War (1982) the balance favored aircraft, as the Israeli Air Force's US-made F-15s and F-16s proved superior to Syria's Soviet-built MiG-23s and SA-6s (and some SA-8s and SA-9s). Precision-guided munitions, combined with improved command-and-control systems and electronic countermeasures, made it possible to conduct cost-effective Suppression of Enemy Air Defense (SEAD) missions, and thus open the way for a more comprehensive air attack. Similarly, the inadequacy of shipborne air defenses was noted in the Falklands War of 1982, in which the Royal Navy had six ships destroyed and eleven damaged due to air attacks.[7]

By the time Desert Storm concluded in 1991, Warden had added to his experience as a fighter pilot with assignments on the Pentagon's Air Force staff, including a tour with a planning cell called Checkmate. He had quickly become well known (though not necessarily well liked) within defense circles for his development of "Instant Thunder," his concept for the initial phase of the air campaign against Iraq, which reflected many of the ideas in *The Air Campaign*. Warden chose

"Instant Thunder" as the operation's name to distinguish it from the failure of "Rolling Thunder" in Vietnam. "This *was not Vietnam*," he said, "this is doing it right. This is using air power."[8]

As historians have noted, Instant Thunder flatly rejected the graduated response and signaling strategies of the Vietnam era.[9] Nonetheless, material constraints and logistical limitations make some incrementalism unavoidable in war; plus, while a degree of service parochialism is always to be expected, several of the Gulf War's key decision-makers, such as General Colin Powell, then Chairman of the Joint Chiefs of Staff, saw Warden's plan as too zealous. In a briefing before the start of the air campaign, Warden reportedly told Powell: "This plan may win the war. You may not need a ground attack."[10] Powell nonetheless insisted on a comprehensive plan, one that addressed the final phases of the conflict and accounted for the possibility the Iraqi army might not surrender. In the process of fashioning that plan, Warden developed a productive relationship with then Lieutenant-Colonel David Deptula, who later authored the concept of effects-based operations.[11] Deptula said he had been inspired by his interactions with Warden and their collaborative planning efforts. The air phase of the Gulf War eventually began on January 17, 1991; it involved 40,000 air sorties and lasted thirty-eight days.[12]

From 1992 to 1995, Warden served as commandant of the Air Command and Staff College. While there, he contributed to revising the curriculum, to which he added a course on the air campaign, among other changes. Warden retired from the air force in 1995 and established a consulting firm called Venturist Inc. He soon codeveloped a strategic planning protocol known as the Prometheus Process, which adapted military concepts, such as centers of gravity, to use in the business world.

10.2 Air Operational Art

The Air Campaign provided a philosophical and theoretical alternative to AirLand Battle, which Warden believed had shortsightedly tethered air power to land power. In his view, air power could do more than merely support a surface campaign. But it needed a proper operational concept to enable it to realize its full potential. Air operational thinking, he claimed, had declined since the end of the Second World War largely for two reasons. First, the advent of nuclear weapons had seemingly rendered traditional principles irrelevant. Second, modern operations were complex and more difficult to master than either strategy or tactics. Accordingly, Warden's *Air Campaign* not only proposed to obviate AirLand Battle, it also aimed to halt the decline in American air operational art by treating air power as the arm of decision. In short, not unlike Douhet and Mitchell, Warden proposed relegating surface campaigns to a secondary or tertiary status in which they supported the air effort.

Like the designers of AirLand Battle, Warden defined the operational level of war as the echelon of command responsible for planning and conducting campaigns and major operations. He nonetheless cautioned against the tendency to compartmentalize warfare; the levels of war were to be thought of as a dynamic "continuum" with important "interrelations," rather than as discrete strata.[13] *The Air Campaign* concentrated on theater command, specifically the concepts and principles a theater commander must consider when employing air power.

The first concern of any theater commander was to achieve and maintain air superiority. "Since the German attack on Poland in 1939," Warden asserted, "no country has won a war in the face of enemy air superiority." Indeed, even Hanoi's ultimate success in Vietnam occurred after US air power had been withdrawn. He neglected to admit, however, that the overwhelming superiority of US air power had not been able to bring Hanoi to the negotiating table. Air superiority meant "having sufficient control of the air to make air attacks on the enemy without serious opposition and ... to be free of the danger of serious enemy air incursions."[14] It was, thus, clearly a matter of degree, which might vary from total control of the air domain in a theater to control over certain areas or for specific periods of time. Achieving air superiority, or denying it to the enemy, was not solely the mission of air forces. It was also a function of the capabilities of ground and naval forces.

Since air superiority could not be assumed, air-campaign planners had to consider five potential cases and shape their planning accordingly: (1) both sides have the capability and will to strike each other's bases; (2) one side can strike its foe anywhere, but the other can only reach the front lines; (3) one side's bases can be attacked, but it cannot attack its opponent's bases; (4) neither side can attack its adversary's bases, hence, air combat action is confined to the front lines; and (5) neither side can or wishes to bring air power to bear.[15]

When offensive air operations were possible, Warden continued, military planners must identify the foe's center, or centers, of gravity. He acknowledged Clausewitz as the author of the concept, but his own definition of it differed markedly from that of the Prussian. A center of gravity, said Warden, was the "point where the enemy is most vulnerable and the point an attack will have the best chance of being decisive." The term, borrowed from mechanics, indicated "a point against which a level of effort will accomplish more than that same level of effort could accomplish if applied elsewhere."[16] Warden thus likened the center of gravity to a weakness or a vulnerability; whereas debates in the military literature of the 1980s and 1990s suggested otherwise.[17] By the mid-1990s, US military doctrine defined a center of gravity not as a vulnerability but as a source of strength, though it could have vulnerable aspects. Even with ample room for disagreement, there was enough consensus to suggest centers of gravity were points of high sensitivity, which, if struck with appropriate force, would generate disproportionate effects.

Warden also believed, unlike Clausewitz, that every level of warfare had a center of gravity. Often, these can be found within the categories of equipment, logistics, personnel, or command and control. Sometimes they can be conceived as "concentric circles." The "quickest and cheapest" path to victory, he advised, was to attack directly the "political center of gravity – the capital or the king." If such "ultimate" centers of gravity cannot be struck, Warden went on to say, the commander must identify "reachable" centers of gravity.[18] The primacy he imparted to the concept, however it might be defined, meant air operational art assumed the essential feature of, and became comparable to, operational art on land and at sea.

Less than twelve months after Desert Storm, Warden's reference to concentric circles had crystallized into what became known as the "five rings" model.[19] As he explained, "every state and military organization will have unique centers of gravity – or vulnerabilities" and these can be developed into a general model that facilitates strategic analysis. The center circle was the command element; it was the most critical because it was the only one that could make concessions. If it could not be attacked directly, it must be threatened indirectly by inflicting damage on the surrounding rings. The next vital ring was essential production, which encompassed much more than war-related industry. It included electricity and petroleum products or any industry essential to the functioning of a modern state. Such systems were fortunately few and often quite vulnerable. Damage to essential production systems could lead to concessions if it made fighting difficult or impossible, or if it drove a state's social or economic costs high enough. The third ring was a state's transportation system, its rail lines, airlines, highways, bridges, airfields, ports, and so on. Damage to a state's transportation system reduced its ability to move goods, services, and information from one point to another. Without such movement, a state would cease to function. Transportation facilities were usually redundant, however, and thus more difficult to damage to the degree necessary to compel a state's leadership to concede.

The fourth ring was the population and its food sources. Warden believed this "ring" was the most difficult to attack directly, due to ethical and legal restrictions but also because it could be immense and its pain threshold could be high, especially in a police state. Nevertheless, indirect attacks, as in psychological warfare, against a hostile public could prove effective. The last ring was the hostile state's fielded military forces. In Warden's opinion, the military forces were not the most vital element in war; they were only a means to an end. Their principal function was to defend one's centers of gravity or to attack the those of the foe. This view was not the classical one, he said, because most military theory to date aimed at defeating a foe's military forces rather than coercing, or compelling, the state's leadership to comply with one's wishes. Or rather, it assumed the best way to compel a state was to defeat its military forces. In contrast, Warden, not unlike Douhet, sought to bypass a state's military might in so far as possible and to strike directly at its decision-making body. As he reminded his readers, "It is imperative to remember that all actions are aimed against the mind of the enemy command."[20]

Two things distinguished Warden's thinking from that of Douhet, however. First, as discussed earlier, Warden did not regard the population as a particularly promising target, since attacking it directly was too difficult, in addition to being morally reprehensible. Douhet believed otherwise. Second, Warden attempted to view an opponent holistically, as an integrated system, rather than simply as a polity with some degree of influence over its governing body. "We must focus on the totality of our enemy," he maintained; "if we are going to think strategically, we must think of the enemy as a system composed of numerous subsystems."[21]

10.3 Enemy as a System

By 1995, the year he published what would become his most widely cited work, "The Enemy as a System," the second and third rings of Warden's theory had evolved into "organic essentials" and "infrastructure," respectively. Organic essentials consisted of energy (electricity, oil, food) and money. Infrastructure pertained to roads, airfields, and factories. The article also explicitly expanded the ring theory to include nonstate actors. The criticism that US strategic thinking only concerned itself with states had already gained considerable momentum by the mid-1990s. The enemy, whether a state or a nonstate actor, Warden suggested, can be thought of and analyzed as a system.

The article also admitted the utility of his five-rings model "may be somewhat diminished in circumstances where an entire people rises up to conduct a defensive battle against an invader."[22] If the populace is well motivated, he said, it might fight for an extended period with just the resources naturally available to it. These are special cases, however, in which each individual would become a "strategic entity" unto itself. Such situations can accomplish defensive goals but not offensive ones because the latter require a higher level of coordination. Nor should such cases be confused with Maoist people's wars, he added, as these possess all the attributes the ring theory describes.

Crucially, the "Enemy as a System" also distinguished between two planning perspectives: "strategic war" and "tactical war." The former perspective considered the whole of war; it began by thinking from the top down – that is, it started with objectives; the latter started at the bottom with the basic goal of destroying an opponent's fielded forces. Viewing the enemy as a system, accordingly, facilitated identifying an adversary's strengths and weaknesses in relation to what one wanted, and introduced the possibility of developing strategies that might accomplish one's objectives more efficiently. The obvious implication, therefore, was that if air power could be shown to be an effective instrument of coercion, it would have greater appeal to policymakers.

10.4 Neither Paralysis nor Coercion

The suitability of strategies of coercion to Warden's theoretical framework for applying air power was obvious. But the efficacy of his approach was called into question the following year (1996) by Robert Pape's *Bombing to Win*, which argued that strategic bombing was only marginally coercive.[23] Pape examined thirty-three strategic air campaigns to determine what caused states to concede, and he found that the threat of military failure, or what he called denial of a foe's military objectives, proved more effective than attacks against civilians, also known as punishment. This conclusion ran counter to the belief that inflicting punishment on civilians – by attacking electrical grids, transportation networks, food production, and so on – was more effective than destroying an adversary's military capabilities.

Pape contended instead that, because denial eliminated a hostile party's military capabilities, it also undermined its military strategy, and thus its prospects for victory. The costs of the war would then become increasingly unbearable as the adversary's chances for victory diminished. *Bombing to Win*, therefore, rejected the assumption Douhet and Mitchell made, namely that the populace and the political leadership were linked. By Pape's reckoning, most political leaders would continue to pursue victory, regardless of the preferences of the populace, until they lost the means to do so. Pape, therefore, made three claims with respect to the employment of air power in the first Gulf War. First, he said the campaign proved coercion by means of modern air power could work. Second, he defined Warden's operational concept for "Instant Thunder" as a decapitation strategy. It argued Saddam Hussein was coerced into to abandoning Kuwait by a strategy of denial, not of decapitation. Finally, while Pape admitted advances in military technology had improved the effectiveness of air power, he also insisted those improvements benefited air interdiction, or the disruption of a foe's military strategy, more than strategic attack.[24]

Warden responded by arguing that *Bombing to Win* merely returned to an outmoded tactical approach of destroying an opponent's combat power, rather than acknowledging the possibilities inherent in a strategic-level attack that leveraged new capabilities. "Pape failed to grasp the revolutionary impact of precision weapons," said Warden, and he "thus significantly undermined his already shaky arguments against strategic airpower."[25] Modern air power could not only destroy a foe's weaponry; it could halt a strategic entity's ability to function, he maintained. Success was achieved when the targeted systems were shut down, irrespective of the amount of physical damage inflicted. The air strategy for the Iraq war had not been decapitation, he explained, but rather a parallel attack against the Iraqi state as an integrated system. The goal had been to achieve strategic paralysis and thereby compel Iraq to comply with coalition objectives, and the goal had been achieved.

The debate revealed an important discrepancy between Warden's and Pape's understandings of the concept of strategic paralysis. Warden's sense of the term more or less subsumed Pape's concept of denial by rendering the enemy's entire military strategy, whatever it may be or whatever it might become, impossible to execute. In contrast, Pape equated strategic paralysis to neutralizing the foe's political leadership or eliminating its ability to direct its forces. If taken to an extreme, strategic paralysis could work against compellence because hostile political leaders who were killed or rendered powerless could not comply with one's demands; they could not call off attacks or order withdrawals. To avoid this extreme, strategic paralysis must be carefully defined prior to military planning, lest expectations not be met.

10.5 Effects-Based Operations

Although Warden's five-ring theory did not become part of the official doctrine of the US Air Force, it inspired other operational concepts. The most significant of these was perhaps Deptula's effects-based operations (EBO) mentioned earlier. EBO appeared when the American armed forces had begun to "downsize" by nearly 35 percent across the board, as the Clinton administration sought to reap a "peace dividend" from the denouement of the Cold War. EBO seemed to offer a conceptual tool that could facilitate the Defense Department's strategy of replacing human capital with technology. It was supposed to assist in refining and broadening the options available to policymakers by requiring them to think in terms of the "effects" they wished to achieve, rather than merely reducing an opponent's military capabilities. Joint and interagency planners would then develop optimal combinations of means and methods to achieve the desired effects. Accordingly, EBO promised to provide enhanced precision in planning, execution, and assessment of operations "against enemy systems."[26] If policymakers had difficulty articulating end states or objectives hitherto, this concept, or more precisely this process, would presumably force them to do better. As one think tank noted, nothing about EBO was "new," save that it offered a more "comprehensive mental model, a systematic approach, more emphasis and rigor," and expanded the "traditional solution space."[27] So, in essence, nothing about EBO was new save for the fact it derived from an air warfare mindset of selecting the right munition for the mission. Nonetheless, some groups saw it as nothing short of revolutionary.[28]

EBO soon sparked serious debates within the defense community as it pertained mostly to the US Air Force and thus the US Army, US Navy, and US Marine Corps saw it as a grab for a larger share of the defense budget at their expense. EBO gained momentum because it appeared to offer a clean, relatively low-cost solution to otherwise messy interventions in complex environments. It also had the advantage of being a suitable fit for Admiral Arthur Cebrowski's Defense Transformation program, the offspring of the Revolution in Military Affairs initiative overseen by Andrew Marshall and the Pentagon's Office of Net Assessment. Transformation purportedly eschewed platforms in favor of information-sharing networks, and EBO provided an operational concept around which such networks could be built. Unfortunately, the methods of analysis and modeling necessary to make EBO work were not available at the beginning of the twenty-first century. And, as a RAND report cautioned, it would take years for research-and-development efforts to bear enough fruit for EBO to be useful.[29]

The debates came to a head in 2008, when US Joint Forces Commander General James N. Mattis, USMC, rejected EBO on the grounds that it ran counter to everything that was known about the nature of war. For Mattis, because adversaries were "smart and adaptive" and because operational environments were "dynamic with an infinite number of variables," it was "not scientifically possible to accurately predict the outcome of an action." To suggest otherwise, he said, would run "contrary to historical experience and the nature of war."[30] Moreover, the concept had simply not delivered on its promises to clarify and simplify planning processes and, instead, only caused more confusion. Mattis's comments went viral almost instantly, and other flag officers, such as Lieutenant-General Paul Van Riper, soon voiced their objections as well.[31]

Consequently, the reception of EBO within the US defense community remained divided along surface and air perspectives, though some officers on both sides crossed service lines.[32] The disparity in perspectives went beyond service rivalries and budget shares, and included the question of whether the modern paradigm of war's nature should yield to a materialist one and permit it to become the foundation for future US defense policy. The modern view held that friction was an unavoidable characteristic of war. Military personnel must be trained to work within it, as they would in air or water, and to make sound choices even amid high levels of uncertainty. The materialist view believed, just as Warden and Admiral William (Bill) Owens did, that the "fog of war" could be lifted by applying the proper technology.

Later incarnations of EBO, such as EBAO (Effects-Based Approach to Operations) withdrew somewhat from the bald claim that friction could be eliminated. The official description of EBAO by the US Air Force's Curtis E. LeMay Center for Doctrine Development and Education said the "'human element,' 'friction,' and the 'fog of war,' can never be eliminated." In addition, commanders at all levels would invariably have to deal with "interactively complex problems" that lacked simple solutions.[33] Nonetheless, these admissions were unpersuasive. Effects-based operations and the parallel concept, effects-based approach to operations, required more than minimal degrees of linear predictability. Otherwise, planners could not begin to draw causal linkages between desired effects and the proper methods and means for achieving them. Admittedly, the environments in which military operations take place are not completely chaotic or nonlinear. Otherwise, military operations would have no hope of succeeding and would be pointless. Nevertheless, to achieve the precision of effects they promised, EBO and EBAO needed more "knowns" than typically were known.

Even more regrettably, Defense Transformation and its techno-centric focus led to opportunity costs that hampered preparations for human-centric conflict. In other words, Transformation left US forces poorly prepared, albeit partly by their own choices, to deal with insurgencies or to conduct counterinsurgency operations and stability operations – that is, to close the gap between a way of battle and a way of war. In short, Transformation ought to have covered the entire spectrum of conflict, not just those areas in which US forces had already demonstrated high levels of competence. US strategic thinking by this point had drifted quite far from what it had been in Mahan's day. Rather than attempting to instruct and to inform, it actively sought ways to predict and to guarantee.

10.6 First Principles

Warden's ring theory clearly rested on Jominian first principles. Strategists and operational planners concentrated friendly air (and other) capabilities to strike appropriate targets with offensive action, whether in parallel or sequentially, to achieve a decisive knockout blow. In addition, like Boyd, Warden also emphasized the principle of speed. He continued to stress speed and efficiency through the remainder of the 1990s: speed of decision-making, of procurement, and of reform. He criticized the US government's cumbersome and inefficient procurement model. "The world is a radically different place than it was ten years ago," he declared. "We live in an ultra-fast-time world where the geopolitical environment is without precedent in human history and powerful new technologies are appearing at an accelerating rate."[34] Revolutionary geopolitical and technological changes, he went on to say, were already well underway. These changes, coupled with new social and economic pressures, meant the US government required commensurately radical solutions to ensure its security. In brief, America needed a new military force, one that could succeed in a "fast-time world." Warden, like many others in the defense industry of the 1990s, felt the United States should not only actively participate in the military revolution of the period but direct, if not dominate it. The goal should be to have the "first military force in history designed specifically to impose system-wide shock on an opponent in a time period measured in hours, while making very low loss and casualty rates a primary design feature."[35]

10.7 War's Nature

Importantly, Warden's "Enemy as a System" revealed his view of the nature of war, which he saw as changeable and indeed manipulable. Armed conflict, he argued, had transformed in critical ways since the days of Napoleon and Clausewitz. Most importantly, the relationship between the moral (psychological) and the physical elements of war had shifted. Whereas Napoleon could claim war's moral and physical factors were as three is to one, material factors – tanks, planes, ships, artillery, and so on – had eclipsed moral factors in importance by the middle of the twentieth century. No amount of will, claimed Warden, could make up for an absence of materiel; hence his materialist model of war's nature. "This is not to say that morale, friction, and fog have all disappeared," he explained; rather, it meant one could regard them as separable from, but related to and dependent upon, materiel.

Accordingly, armed conflict could be thought of as an equation: "(Physical) × (Morale) = Outcome."[36] As a strategic entity's physical means to resist were reduced, its morale too was diminished or neutralized. The equation reflected linear or proportional relationships in that it assumed the more a foe's means to resist were reduced, the more one could expect resistance to wane or to become irrelevant. It also accounted for nonlinear relationships such as the possibility that the destruction of certain physical capabilities might cause an opponent's will to collapse precipitously.[37] Unfortunately, it discounted the possibility that a foe's resistance might continue, or increase dramatically, due to the destruction of certain physical means. In Afghanistan and Iraq, for instance, some parties resorted to small arms and ad hoc weaponry, such as improvised explosive devices (IEDs), in the absence of larger conventional means. Ad hoc weapons, moreover, could generate significant strategic effects and yet be extremely difficult for air power to target. Warden had thus attempted to bypass the thorny problem of gauging an opponent's willingness to fight by making morale contingent on material factors. The overriding purpose of destroying materiel was to create a condition of strategic paralysis in which an adversary no longer had the means to resist. The great promise of information technology, furthermore, was that an adversary's physical means of resisting would be identifiable and targetable. That promise, in turn, meant one could reduce the play of chance and probability. If one could simplify the problem to merely destroying material capabilities, war's imponderables could be rendered inconsequential, and the conduct of war, as well as its very nature, could be transformed. One of the great failings of the logic of such materialist perspectives, unfortunately, was that it consistently underestimated or assumed away an opponent's ability to adapt.

10.8 Conclusions

Warden explicitly developed his theories with the aim of maximizing the operational potential of air power. He appears to have done so not merely to promote air power, but because he believed it was superior to, and ought to dominate the other services in the planning and execution of US military operations. While he promoted his branch over the others, he saw himself as redressing an imbalance in operational doctrine that inclined toward surface forces and was not open to new ideas. His bias, however, was obvious and provoked resistance to his ideas. Yet Warden's theories, especially the ring theory, were met with a certain incredulity even within his own service: the ring theory, for instance, which echoes the systems analysis methodology popular in RAND at the height of the Cold War and may have been partially applied in Desert Shield/Desert Storm and later in the campaigns in Bosnia and Kosovo, cannot be said to have proven decisive in practice. Admittedly, American-led air power could turn off the lights in an adversary's capital, decapitate its primary leadership, and disrupt the flow of a country's goods and services. But it could not reliably compel an opponent to take a desired action. To be sure, it could raise the level of pain and discomfort for a foe in a Schelling-like, incremental fashion; for even NATO's combined air forces could not strike every target simultaneously: they needed to rearm and refuel. Also, as readers will recall, Schelling said force held in reserve possessed more coercive power than the force already used. Nevertheless, paradoxically, holding some amount of force in reserve provides an enemy the opportunity to develop countermeasures, and thus to strengthen its resistance to coercive force. One should expect a tradeoff, then, between the coercive value potential force should have and what it may have after a certain amount of time has elapsed. In Vietnam, that tradeoff proved consistently disappointing to US efforts.

Warden's conception of war's nature was materialist and thus, by extension, malleable. In other words, the state of modern technology meant one could employ certain tools and weapons in an armed conflict to reduce, or make irrelevant, the effects of critical elements of war's nature on friendly forces. For that reason, war's apparently physical character became much more important than its seemingly metaphysical nature. For a time, therefore, air power theorists and practitioners answered the question of war's nature by ignoring it. The history of warfare was no longer relevant to what warfare now was or should be. More precisely, they focused on an entirely different question: what effects needed to be achieved to accomplish one's political objective?

Later, proponents of effects-based operations and the effects-based approach to operations accepted, at least rhetorically, definitions that described war as unpredictable by its nature. These definitions, however, did not alter the fact that EBO/EBAO enthusiasts continued to promise low-cost outcomes. The services' opposing attitudes toward the conceit of prediction intensified their rivalries, which were deeply rooted enough to prevent the modern paradigm of war's nature from shifting to the materialist one, and vice versa.

Warden's theories rested on a holistic conception of society; otherwise, its five concentric circles would not necessarily be circles or concentric. He, therefore, assumed modern societies were connected enough that striking targets in one circle would produce the desired effects in another. All around him, however, was evidence of division and disunity, particularly in the wake of his Vietnam experience. His appreciation of modern society reflected a certain textbook simplicity, therefore, that overlooked the extent to which a society's divisions are an essential part of its holistic functioning. As Schelling's research noted, organized crime provides the public with illicit but desirable, perhaps in some cases necessary, goods and services. Ergo, the ways in which societies function depend as much upon their dividing as their unifying elements, and on the interplay among them.

Ironically, while Warden's ring theory was built on the premise of an interconnected society, he consciously decoupled material capacity to fight from psychological willingness to do so. That decoupling simplified the thought process behind strategic coercion, reducing it to a question of destroying physical capabilities. But that simplification also eliminated the need to consider whether destroying some capabilities, or inflicting collateral damage, might inadvertently strengthen a party's willingness to fight. Ultimately, that way of thinking – that an opponent's willingness to resist would diminish as its capacity to fight disintegrated – might have justified investing in air power, but it made his model as binary and linear as that of Schelling. Those characteristics, in turn, rendered his theory susceptible to failure in nonlinear environments. In short, Warden's theories would have benefited from a firmer historical grounding, at least a general familiarity with sociological structures, as well as a greater sense of how culture might affect a party's willingness to fight.

Conclusion

Over the course of the twentieth century, America's strategic theorists drew from at least four paradigms of war's nature: traditional, modern, materialist, and political. The traditional paradigm remained in vogue until the 1950s, even though the expansion of airpower during the 1920s and 1930s qualitatively changed the character of war. For that reason, the same three Jominian core principles – concentration, offensive action, and decision by battle – remained operative. The development of nuclear weapons in the late 1940s and 1950s, however, raised concerns over those principles and the traditional paradigm. As a result, it was strongly challenged by the political model, through the vehicle of limited war theory. By the late 1950s, the political model was in open conflict with the traditional paradigm. By this point, the principles of limited war theory had taken precedence over the core Jominian imperatives. In this case, a change in the character of war, or rather a near-change since nuclear weapons were not used after 1945, had created competing paradigms in the American way of thinking about war.

By the mid-1970s, however, America's failure in Vietnam undermined confidence in both the traditional and political paradigms; neither seemed to have worked. The denuclearization of the character of war over the 1980s and 1990s, in conjunction with the Clausewitzian renaissance, which placed greater emphasis on the role of policy and politics in war, provided an opportunity to convert the traditional paradigm into the modern one, as well as to strengthen the political paradigm. By the beginning of the 1990s, further changes in the character of war, especially in the form of advances in information technologies, encouraged the emergence of the materialist model of war's nature. While both the modern and materialist models have paid lip service to the primacy of the political paradigm, each continued to emphasize Jomini's core principles, albeit more as operational rather than strategic imperatives.

Arguments for a particular American strategic culture typically fail to account for the tensions between Jominian first principles and those of the political paradigm, tensions which have persisted into the twenty-first century. The story of the American way of thinking about war is thus a dynamic one; it is as much about the tensions between its competing ways of battle as between them and its way of policy.

First Principles and Modern War

As discussed in Part I, Mahan brought Jomini's first principles, along with military imperatives popularized during the American Civil War, into the twentieth century. However, it would be wrong to say Mahan's thinking (or Jomini's for that matter) reflected a "scientific approach to war" in the sense the term is understood today.[1] For Mahan and his contemporaries, the word science described any discipline underpinned by induction, deduction, and sometimes a complementary third or comparative process. For Mahan, science enabled individual skill rather than eliminating the need for it. Over the twentieth century, science developed mechanisms and technical processes to reduce, if not eliminate, the need for individual skill and thereby reduce the incidence of error. Today's scientific approach to war is thus an inversion of what it was in Mahan's day.

Nor did Mahan necessarily see war as an engineering problem to be solved, even though numerous engineering tasks, such as building roads, bridges, bases, and fortifications, have always been required in wartime. Rather, Mahan saw war as an individual duel, writ large, in which the imperatives of concentration, offensive action, and decision by battle offered critical advantages. These imperatives fit the presumed nature of war at the time by providing the same advantages in individual pugilism as they did for combat on a larger scale. Moreover, the appearance of an engineering perspective in Mahan's writing at the time was driven largely by the need to establish concrete programs of study at the US military's professional schools, namely its staff and war colleges. Military science and naval science were legitimate topics; however, it was not considered possible to teach art. Furthermore, the preoccupation with science or scientific principles was not unique to the military; as shown, it was common across academe as well as in most walks of life.

Comparatively speaking, military thinking in Mahan's day was more conservative, more reticent to advance novel theories, than its academic counterparts. To a degree this is understandable, as the stakes can be high in wartime. To be sure, Mahan made expansive claims about the influence of sea power. Yet these claims pale in comparison to the assertions of scientists, such as George Beard, for whom "American nervousness" was an established fact, and for advocates of Social

Darwinism who believed, with unblinkingly certainty, that its precepts rested on the methods of science. Whereas Mahan and Luce encouraged due diligence to ensure naval theory did not outpace naval science; American academics actively sought to push their theories to the edge of what the scientific method could support. Academic accolades, after all, are awarded for advancing the body of knowledge in a field, not for consolidating it. As sociologist Franklin Giddings admitted in 1896, American scientists at the time were hardly strangers to speculation.[2]

The scientific conservatism of Mahan and Luce all but disappeared in the era of Billy Mitchell and his relentless advocacy of airpower. Mitchell was clearly more interested in influencing US defense policy than in constructing a theory, and he frequently called upon aeronautical science, such as it was, to support his claims. He openly criticized gradualist reforms, aggressively presented speculation as fact, and patently eschewed the scientific method. Even the battleship tests of the early 1920s, which began under the auspices of scientific experimentation, ended up as public drama. Mitchell's vision of US airpower was based on Mahan's model of war's nature and, as noted earlier, drew from the same set of first principles. But his ideas were largely derivative, or in some cases demonstrably plagiarized, and seldom constrained by facts. He concentrated on selling airpower warfare not unlike the way Mahan had energetically sold the virtues of sea power; in that sense their evangelist impulses differed little – except that Mitchell also expected to be rewarded with a position of influence within the US defense establishment. Both writers desired to convert the public, not merely to persuade it. In the process, both drew the ire of their respective presidents. Both also managed to establish enduring legacies that still have many followers.

Admittedly, Mitchell's writings raised the profile of airpower in the public's eye. But they would have been much less effective without the daring exploits of civilian aviators, such as Lindberg and Earhart, who captured the public's imagination. Aviation became a public sensation in the 1920s and remained such throughout most of the 1930s. More importantly, the Mitchell controversy drew attention away from strategic principles, which made up Mahan's focus, and toward military technique, in the spirit of Admiral Bradley Fiske, who placed organizational and technical expertise above theoretical knowledge. It suggested the key to victory in the next war was to be found in technological and organizational innovations, and less in the artful application of principles per se. The Mitchell controversy, in other words, represented a clash of military techniques within the context of the changing character of modern war. The traditional paradigm of war's nature, however, would remain uncontested until Brodie challenged it in 1946.

Although a temporal synthesis of sorts developed during the interwar years with the emergence of naval and land-based air power, the Mitchell controversy raises questions regarding the influence service antagonisms have exerted on US strategic thinking over the twentieth century. The effects have, in fact, been mixed. On the positive side, interservice rivalries have compelled each service to reexamine its raison d'être, its roles and missions. An example is Wylie's 1951 paper, "The Navy's Reasons for Being," which made a case for a joint, balanced, and flexible strategy for countering whatever crises the Soviet Union might instigate. Such introspection can result in new operational or strategic concepts, or a requirement for another type of military hardware.

But interservice rivalries have also generated counterproductive patterns of behavior, a strategic anarchy of sorts, in which concepts were developed or investments made for the express purpose of preserving budget share (or expanding it). Interservice rivalries have also contributed to America's strategic anarchy by standing in the way of a holistic conception of warfare and by reinforcing parochial, service-specific assumptions about war's nature. Even the Goldwater–Nichols Act and a series of official documents purporting to establish a "joint vision" of the future of warfare have failed to unify service perspectives; they have instead simply linked together each service's vision of its roles and missions.[3] This arrangement has facilitated anarchy rather than resolving it; however, that might be a more beneficial relationship than hegemony.

The Revolt of the Strategy Intellectuals

In 1946, when Brodie argued the advent of atomic weapons necessitated a revolution in strategy, Karl Popper's anti-positivist revolution, which was contingent on the idea of the falsifiable hypothesis, was hardly underway. Nonetheless, Brodie and Osgood had managed to foreshadow Popper by casting doubt on Mahan's and Luce's method of induction. For these two strategy intellectuals, induction could only yield subjective and contextual military principles and not objective or universal ones. Whereas US military doctrine still described the principles of war as timeless, Brodie and Osgood saw such descriptions as evidence of the rigidity of the military mind, a rigidity that could only prove dangerous in an era marked by the unprecedented destructive power of nuclear weapons. In response, the strategy intellectuals, especially Osgood, developed several principles of their own – principles that helped define an American way of policy.

The significance of Brodie's lectures to the US military's staff and war colleges in the early 1950s has been overlooked. These lectures were tremendously important for two reasons. First, they went directly to the heart of the matter (insofar as Brodie ever went directly to the heart of anything) by calling into question the utility of the principles of war. While he did not analyze all the US military's official principles of war, he repeatedly attacked the Jominian imperatives of concentration, offensive action, and decision by battle. Second, the lectures underscored what he saw as the transformation in war's nature as well as its character.

Both strategy intellectuals held similar assumptions about war's nature. Their understanding was based on their observations of the two world wars, which they believed were driven more by military imperatives, inflexible mobilization timetables (First World War) and warlike passions (Hitler and German revanchism, Japanese militarism) than policy, a misunderstanding not uncommon for the times. Policy did, in fact, drive those wars, as diplomacy has its own instinctive and irrational impulses: the Domino theory and the fear of appearing soft on Communism are but two examples. By equating policy to rational decision-making, Brodie and Osgood created an ideal model of war, one that was reassuring on paper to all who might wish to avoid another global conflict, but which could never exist because it would have required policymakers to be absolutely rational.

Unlike their academic colleagues, Brodie and other members of RAND, such as Wohlstetter and Kahn, had a solid functional grasp of military technique, the conceptual and technical aspects of modern warfare. Brodie was conversant in the details of nuclear yields, missile ranges and payloads, and the basic advantages and disadvantages of various armored fighting vehicles, aircraft, and naval vessels. He and Fawn collaborated on a book, *From Crossbow to H-Bomb*, that highlighted the historical importance of technology in warfare, for instance.[4] He also appreciated the central purposes of high-level military organizations, such as Strategic Air Command (SAC), and more than a few of his warnings seemed to have been aimed directly at SAC leadership.

Yet for all his technical knowledge, Brodie did not advance a holistic or tridimensional view of war or strategy. He acknowledged war's psychosocial dimension in some of his works, such as his classic *War and Politics* in which he asserted "good strategy presumes good anthropology and sociology."[5] But his treatment of that dimension did not go much beyond warning his readers against stereotyping one's adversaries. Instead, he concentrated on warfare's political and military dimensions at the expense of its psychosocial and economic ones; he also did so during one of the most socially and culturally turbulent periods in US history. He surely grasped theories that explained the causes of war in psychosocial and economic terms, but he had little use for them.

Presumably, one reason for his disdain was that the psychosocial and economic dimensions of conflict would have been irrelevant in a nuclear war. Conversely, a limited war would have required controlling the public's passions, lest they prove distracting. As he argued in *War and Politics*, the nature of war was essentially political because wars begin and end with decisions made at the highest levels of government. Hence, only the political dimension of war truly mattered and strategy's purpose, therefore, was simply to accomplish policy's objectives.

Consequently, one of Brodie's most important, if regrettable, legacies was the creation of a bidimensional conception of strategy: in short, America's "way of policy." As discussed elsewhere in this volume, this type of policy continues to inform the American way of war, a characteristic that became embarrassingly evident when policymakers needed to rediscover the merits of a "whole of government approach" for the interventions in Afghanistan and Iraq. The rediscovery itself should not have been necessary because the utility of bringing diplomatic, military, economic, and psychosocial power together in an integrated approach ought to have been apparent to American strategists well beforehand. They also should have known not to portray the approach as something unique or revolutionary, as doing so only revealed their incompetence. Much of the strategic literature at the time, which carried versions of Clausewitz's expression that war was nothing but the continuation of policy by other means, essentially depicted strategy as a two-dimensional problem: political and military. It was easy to forget Clausewitz had also warned against ignoring any of war's dimensions.[6] Of course, that is no cure all either; for a whole-of-government approach in which the government is guided by hubris, racism, or confuses ideology for strategy would only exacerbate strategic problems rather than solve them.

Compared to Brodie, Osgood's grasp of political and military history as well as military technique and was much weaker. Osgood was familiar with conventional capabilities but unfamiliar with unconventional ones, the type most needed for the many interventions and "small wars" of the Cold War. His 1957 volume, *Limited War*, attempted to establish not just a theory of limited war but a doctrine, replete with an overarching principle – the primacy of political ends over military aims – and an attendant corollary of employing no more force than is necessary.[7] These two imperatives were intended to override the military's first principles not merely supplement them.

Nevertheless, Osgood's doctrine also included important conditions and rules designed to restrict its applicability: limited wars were to involve only a small number of belligerents, be contained geographically, and require only a minimal commitment of resources so as not to disrupt daily life. They were also to require heads of state to follow three rules: to develop clear, restrained objectives and communicate those objectives to their adversaries; to maintain open communications throughout the conflict to facilitate negotiations; and to restrict the war's physical dimensions. Unfortunately, these conditions and rules also increased the possibility of a military and political stalemate, as in Korea, where US forces have been positioned since the 1953 ceasefire.

Limited war doctrine thus exposed the United States to strategies of "tie-down," or exhaustion as in Vietnam. Tying down US forces in one theater meant they were not available for another. The American political process, with its four-year election cycles and systems of accountability, is particularly vulnerable to strategies of exhaustion.[8] It is worth noting that Osgood's *Limited War* was published in 1957, as Elvis Presley, "rock and roll," and the cult of the "rebel," were taking American youth by storm, and racial tensions in the south were increasing. He paid too little attention to the undercurrents in American society, and the human capital that would have to carry out the doctrine he had outlined. In short, limited war theory underestimated the country's psychosocial "staying power" as well as its willingness to pressure political leaders into withdrawing from overseas commitments.

Osgood also overlooked the opportunity to connect his principles to Kennan's "measures short of war" or to its broader concept of "political warfare," a misnomer to be sure.[9] Osgood's omission is peculiar given his obvious familiarity with Kennan's concept of Containment which he duly analyzed in *Limited War*. For Kennan, political warfare was to be the primary means of executing Containment Measures short of war, as his 1946 lecture of the same name indicates, consisted of the tools available to diplomacy for waging political warfare; that is, below the threshold of a shooting war. Osgood's doctrine should have discussed political warfare as a potential cause of actual war, and what the implications might be of such an event for limited war. Such a discussion might have given the doctrine greater concreteness.

Perhaps the larger problem with Osgood's doctrine, however, was its failure to grapple with the practical constraints of military technique and to incorporate those into his discussion of limited war's conditions, rules, and principles. Rather than the vague, macro-level division between "power and policy" he posited, and for which he offered little cure, a recurring challenge for the modern American way of war has been and remains how to integrate political and military techniques. Establishing a dialogue between political and military leaders is an indispensable first step. But the problem has become more difficult over time, due, in part, to the overspecialization of military technique over the course of the twentieth century. Successful integration has become more a matter of chance – a convergence of the right people at the right time – than it should be.

On the other hand, Osgood's division, though troublesome in the short term, may help protect a democracy in the long term. Popular admirals and generals highly skilled in political technique have openly challenged national policy in the past; had they been able to do so in larger numbers it might well have undermined civilian control over the military. This possibility reflects Huntington's concern over the emergence of the modern military expert which was, therefore, well placed. Oddly, though, Huntington did not include military publicists in this category. Mahan, Mitchell (as well as Butler) became political targets of the White House precisely because they appeared to wield too much indirect influence over national policy. Put differently, if military leaders become more acquainted with political technique without policymakers becoming more familiar with military technique, the military will have the advantage in public debates. Perhaps the safer course, therefore, is for America to maintain a way of policy separate from its ways of battle, and to accept the frictions that result therefrom.

Unlike Brodie and Osgood, Schelling took American strategic thinking into the cognitive-psychological realm. Schelling's theories of bargaining and coercion explored both the conditions and dynamics of conflict and offered hypotheses as to why one party might concede to another. But these hypotheses, because they were paradoxically isolated from real conditions for purposes of study, also came to epitomize the academic perspective. Schelling, like other nuclear strategists, was entirely familiar with the technical capabilities of nuclear weapons and some other forms of military technique. His hypotheses fit better within the context of the former than the latter, which also meant they offered little in the sense of broader utility. While they have long appealed to game theory and decision theory, those approaches to decision-making have become increasingly reflective of pure rather than practical reason.

Schelling's theories of bargaining and coercion were ground-breaking for game theory but incomplete for the practice of strategy. Brodie was right to be dissatisfied with them. They involved risky levels of mirror-imaging and assumed away ambiguity and friction. They also gave rise to second- and third-generation offshoots, such as graduated pressure and escalation dominance, each of which assumed more knowledge of a foe and of a strategic situation than was realistic. Each also failed to account adequately for asymmetric responses. Even though his later thinking shows evidence of Popper's antipositivist revolution, it did not aid in grounding his theories.[10] Their limitations include, most importantly, the fallacy of omission that comes from defining one's hypothesis so narrowly that crucial dynamics of the problem are excluded from the study. This is the same fallacy that prevents a theory from being transferable to the real world. As Brodie insisted in *War and Politics*, strategic theory "is nothing if not pragmatic"; it must be "a guide to accomplishing something and doing it efficiently."[11] Nonetheless, as Brodie's letters reveal, he knew all along Schelling's theories were not pragmatic. Schelling does not seem ever to have grasped how great the gap was between his theories and strategic practice.

Like Brodie, Schelling excluded the social and economic dimensions of war from his conception of strategy, and for the same general reasons as his "rugged" friend. In the end, Schelling's analysis of the cognitive domain, however illuminating, oversimplified the process of decision-making even as it laid the foundations for the academic understanding of what it takes to make strategy work. His concept of war's nature accorded with that of Brodie and Osgood. War was through-and-through a fully charged spring ready to explode; but for Schelling the trigger that could set off runaway escalation lay in the cognitive–psychological dispositions of the opposing leaders. This point of view still obtains in the twenty-first century.

The state of science for Kahn was much the same as it was for Schelling, with the exception that Kahn, influenced more by RAND's affinity for systems analysis, took a more holistic view of phenomena like escalation. Despite their interest in systems analysis, none of the other strategy intellectuals had attempted to consider escalation as a holistic system per se. In due course, Kahn called into question their assumptions about escalation and war's nature. Rather than a tightly compressed spring, Kahn suggested war must also have politically defined thresholds, or waystations, from which policy might pause the process of escalation to assess the situation. Granted, at some point the machinery of war could assume control and escalate to nuclear annihilation. But it was just as likely such a machinelike response could be paused before that happened. While Kahn's escalation ladder has long been criticized for, among other things, mirror-imaging how belligerents would view its steps, this criticism overlooks how the ladder strengthened the political model of war's nature even as it weakened limited war theory's hold on it.

Kahn's theory of escalation changed few minds, partly due to his speculations about the survivability of a nuclear war, and partly because his method of delivery and jarring appearance detracted from his message. It was simply safer for the America of the 1960s, the decade in which the Civil Rights Movement was bringing to light contradictions in official US policies, to believe he was wrong. To trust the US government, or any government, with that much responsibility was, for many citizens, too much of a stretch. Ironically, the Cuban Missile Crisis of 1962, a near-catastrophe indeed, can be said to have validated both Kahn's model and that of the limited war theorists simultaneously. War was ultimately averted due to the active involvement of policymakers and military officers on both sides. But friction in the form of different cultures and languages, as well as psychological stress, could have caused events to play out differently. While Kahn's theory might have been right, the risk was too high and hence his framework has been discarded in favor of that of the limited war theorists. In fact, their assumption that uncontrollable escalation is inherent in war's nature remains virtually unchallenged.

Kahn's grasp of military technique, like that of the strategy intellectuals in general, was sound with respect to nuclear weapons and the major components of military hardware – aircraft carriers, bombers, submarines, and so on. His understanding of operational concepts was less firm but by no means deficient. Of the strategy intellectuals, the breadth of his interests was probably second only to Schelling's. His intellectual range enabled him to reach beyond defense topics to a wider range of clients for the Hudson Institute, his think tank on the Hudson River. By the 1970s, American society and culture had become important topics and Kahn, therefore, explored the causal connections between the social turmoil of the 1960s, America's failure in Vietnam, and the period of social malaise that followed. He did not, however, revise his original view of war's nature. Instead, it remained as two-dimensional as that of Brodie and Osgood, though he attributed more agency to policy than they did.

The Counterrevolution of the Military Intellectuals

As Henry Eccles and J. C. Wylie began writing in the mid-to-late 1950s, most scholars and military analysts had agreed atomic weapons had altered the fundamental nature of war, not just its conduct. If armed conflict was no longer politically useful, that would be an alteration of its fundamental nature. Lectures at the US staff and war colleges, therefore, began advancing Brodie's argument for a revolution in military strategy. Military practitioners, too, had begun to debate whether the change in war's nature would render some branches of the armed forces, particularly the US Navy, less relevant. America's principal Cold War enemies were essentially land powers. Those debates expanded into other dimensions in the 1960s, as American political and military practitioners began to appreciate the significance of "brush-fire" and "broken-back" wars as stages in the larger process of decolonization, though many were not relevant to that phenomenon. War's nature seemed to be changing at

Conclusion

both ends of the spectrum of conflict – at the high end in the realm of all-out war and at the low end with respect to conflicts in which violence was limited. New slogans and catchwords, often tied to a specific military program, began appearing in defense literature. These created conceptual confusion and false expectations.

The accumulation of these developments prompted Eccles and other military instructors to begin subjecting all strategic concepts and terms to rigorous examination. While Eccles has rightly become known for his contributions to the theory and practice of modern logistics, he also deserves credit for having inspired a Clausewitzian-style counterrevolution in military theory. The aim of this counterrevolution was to teach officers to educate themselves through a lifelong process of critical inquiry and reflection. Eccles, in essence, brought the science of Mahan and Luce back into American strategic thinking. As mentioned earlier, that science amounted to a form of philosophical inquiry in which induction and deduction played central roles in enhancing the judgment of a military commander, not providing a substitute for it. Eccles took that goal one step further by attempting to return American strategic thinking to a conceptually defensible baseline. He therefore built a structural hierarchy of concepts designed to promote clarity and to restore order to a situation Rosinski referred to, quite correctly, as strategic anarchy. However, Eccles's message, which needed to go much further than the Naval War College and the Pentagon, had the disadvantage of appearing resistant to new ideas. It is, nonetheless, the purpose of critical inquiry to subject new and old ideas to the same critical standards.

Both Eccles and Wylie possessed a high level of expertise in the naval technique of the 1940s and 1950s. Beyond that, their expertise is difficult to assess, though Wylie was certainly conversant in Maoist people's war. Both also participated in their communities and clearly appreciated the psychosocial dimension of warfare. Their experiences in the Second World War and as instructors at the Naval War College obviously added to their expertise, though not necessarily equally. Their military experience might only have given them a narrow range of expertise, save for the opportunity they received at the Naval War College to broaden their perspectives by engaging with scholars and other officers. In this regard, their interaction with Rosinski proved invaluable to them as well as to him. Without it, the strategy of control advanced by this triumvirate would not have developed.

The strategy of control, in fact, marks a partial return to the model of war's nature that predominated before the nuclear age. If war was essentially a violent extension of human nature, then one ought to endeavor to control both the dimensions and dynamics of that competition. Thus, the first principles of concentration, offensive action, and decision by battle still applied. Admittedly, those principles had to be modified according to the desired type and degree of control. But the strategy of control itself was a logical response to the paradigmatic crisis the traditional model of war's nature confronted because of nuclear weapons. Unfortunately, the theory remained incomplete, as it only explored the military dimension of conflict. The Vietnam War and the social turmoil of the 1960s later drew Eccles's and Wylie's attention to the importance of war's psychosocial dimension. They did not, however, expand their theory of strategy as control accordingly. The reason for that, as noted earlier, may well have been that their theory could be taken as merely formalizing the obvious.

Rather than assume policy needed to contain military instincts and public passions as the strategy intellectuals did, the military intellectuals placed the psychosocial dimension foremost, as something of a center of gravity, especially for a democracy. To be sure, in many respects this was hindsight, rendered perfectly clear in the wake of Vietnam rather than in the conflict's early or middle stages. But the services generally shared the same view, particularly the US Army, which believed the war was lost when public support was lost, along with the Army's link to the American people. Many political and military leaders vowed never to repeat that mistake. The idea behind the Total Force was presumably to ensure the executive branch could not go to war without calling up the reserves, which in turn meant selling the conflict to Congress and the American people before deploying significant numbers of troops. Ironically, this attitude represents a retreat from the US military's initial aim, though contested by historians, to draw LBJ more deeply into the conflict.

Harry Summers came to the counterrevolution late, half a decade after the Vietnam War. But his arguments aligned well with Eccles's sense of theory as critical analysis in the spirit of Clausewitz; for that is what Summers's book, *On Strategy*, was. Summers, however, abandoned depth for breadth: he raised provocative and probing questions: from the Army's lack of professionalism in the Vietnam era to its unwarlike culture to the lack of public support to the neglect of military principles. He then offered these as reasons for America's failure in Vietnam. His critique was far-ranging but superficial; it never offered enough evidence to make a compelling case for either of these causes. *On Strategy* combined several speculations and deductions; however, there its resemblance to the scientific method ended.

Instead of a single fatal wound, Summers suggested the US involvement in Vietnam suffered the death of a thousand cuts, the deepest of which was the US military's failure to use its time-tested principles of war to craft its military strategy. In effect, he attempted to shame the American armed forces, the US Army especially, into returning to its nine officially sanctioned principles of war. These, he argued, should serve as the grammar that channels policy's logic. Logic can overrule grammar, of course; but only if it is willing to risk a disappointing outcome. Interest in the principles of war rose sharply in defense literature for a time thereafter, though at least one practitioner-scholar doubted their presumed immutability since they had varied over time and across cultures.[12] Those variations, however, came to be seen as inconsequential, the result of viewing similar tactical and operational imperatives through different cultural lenses. The renewed interest in principles of war came to be something of a fad. It had the unintended consequence of obscuring the distinction between core and general principles. The former included concentration, offensive action, and decision by battle; the latter consisted of maneuver, unity of command, surprise, simplicity, economy of force, and security.

On Strategy also mounted a dogged defense of the traditional paradigm of war's nature, the model of Mahan and Mitchell. As noted, some of Summers's contemporaries, such as General Edward Lansdale, saw the nature of the Vietnam conflict in an unconventional light and thus agitated for an alternative grammar of war. But nothing Summers observed in Vietnam caused him to doubt the traditional model. In his mind, the Vietnam War was essentially a violent extension of human competition, which meant Mahanian first principles remained valid. He dismissed the revolutionary aspect of the conflict as little more than a propaganda ploy or a strategic diversion. To Summers, the four types of conflict – total, general, limited, and revolutionary – then recognized in defense circles shared the same nature.[13] They varied only superficially, like a true chameleon.

Ultimately, this model of war's nature was insufficient for the Vietnam conflict. But so, too, was the model of the limited war theorists. Henry Kissinger's efforts to apply limited war principles failed, for instance, largely because they prevented him from coercing Hanoi into compliance within tolerable cost thresholds for the United States. While Summers clearly understood the importance of war's third dimension, his solution for strengthening America's willingness to fight came uncomfortably close to militarizing US society. He ought to have known it could never be an unacceptable solution for the United States. Like so many others, however, he also failed to see the Clausewitzian trinity's potential utility in identifying synergies, meaning a party's ability to wage war becomes greater than the sum of its capabilities. Instead, Western policymakers and defense analysts preferred to calculate a party's diplomatic, economic, military, and psychosocial power linearly. That habit, unfortunately, led them to underestimate the willingness of the North Vietnamese to fight and to endure hardship.

Summers, of course, is well known for his remark that winning the major battles in the Vietnam conflict did not suffice to win the war. Battlefield victories may mean little unless they are politically leveraged; even in limited conflicts small successes can mean gaining just enough leverage at the negotiating table to move the process forward in a favorable direction. Reports of battles won or lost can also affect the psychosocial dimension, or morale. Battles are therefore hardly irrelevant. The extent to which they are decisive depends on the circumstances and the skills of those who make use of them, though Weigley and other scholars have attempted to argue otherwise.[14]

Ironically, the traditional paradigm of war's nature and its imperatives did not apply much beyond the winning of battles or campaigns, even though Summers chose to defend it. While he identified an important gap in the strategic responsibilities of military commanders and diplomats, he offered little to close it. That gap has been a persistent problem in US strategic thinking, as Osgood noted some two decades earlier. By comparison, Mahan and many of his successors assumed military commanders served diplomacy best by pursuing the most complete victory possible with the resources at hand. They also believed it was solely diplomacy's responsibility to exploit such victories to achieve the war's purposes. By most conventions of the day, both assumptions usually worked. In Vietnam they did not, for several reasons. Perhaps the most important of these was the fact that policymakers and military practitioners held incommensurable assumptions about war's nature, and thus rarely started from the same reference point.

The Insurrection of the Operational Artists

By the time Boyd, Lind, and Warden began developing their individual theories of operational maneuver, America had started to climb out of its post-Vietnam malaise. All three of these operational artists witnessed or participated in efforts to redirect US foreign policy and strategy, to rebuild American military power, and to restore public morale. All three also believed American operational thinking needed to be reformed to strengthen military technique, though new types of military hardware also reinforced the need for a conceptual upgrade. None of these theorists, moreover, heeded Summers's warning about the fallacy of assuming the winning of battles would lead to the winning of wars, though all were aware of it. At this point, a Schelling-like tacit agreement seems to have been in place, namely, that policymakers and scholars could have their way of policy, so long as military theorists and defense analysts could have their ways of battle.

Boyd and Lind, in effect, developed a theory of maneuver that contributed to the US military's way of battle, the doctrinal component of which was AirLand Battle. Under this doctrine, air elements were to extend the depth of the battlefield, disrupt enemy command elements, and attrite an opponent's follow-on forces; however, the full cooperation of the US Air Force was not assured. At the time, air officers like Warden believed air power could do much more than merely support ground maneuver, and his *Air Campaign* attempted to operationalize that belief. It combined the theories of Douhet, systems analysis, and long-range, precision-strike capabilities into a concept of air operational maneuver that did not reject the maneuver warfare concepts of Boyd and Lind so much as make them irrelevant. But Warden's theories were perhaps more significant since they laid the groundwork for other concepts, such as Effects-Based Operations, advanced by Lieutenant-General David Deptula.

For Boyd and Lind, maneuver theory primarily meant defeating a foe in combat, though it could easily apply to other forms of competition. Success was to be gained not by attrition, but by accruing positional and temporal advantages. One's opponent was to be outmaneuvered by moving adroitly to physical and psychological positions of advantage, which, combined with the pressure to adapt to changes in the situation caused by such movement, would lead to system failure on the part of the foe. Maneuver theory did not address how to use operational advantages to achieve policy objectives, and thus it did not close the gap in responsibility identified by Summers. To be sure, gaining certain advantages can prove instrumental to success in any form of competition. But an advantage is rarely more than a means to an end. In fact, an advantage in one environment can be a distinct disadvantage in another; having one's forces closely concentrated in a nuclear war, for instance, is a disadvantage. Unless the circumstances and ends are specified, therefore, any theory of success based primarily on accruing advantages must be considered incomplete.

Boyd's theories were inelegant and always evolving. They stressed creativity and innovation and could be applied readily beyond wartime situations. The US defense establishment's "Offset strategies" offer examples of this type of thinking. The implied aim of such strategies is to nullify an advantage an opponent has, such as numerical superiority, or to change the balance of power so quickly and so profoundly that one's rival must concede because it cannot compete on the new terms.

Aside from citing a host of scientists and accomplished scholars, however, Boyd's theories show little evidence of any scientific methodology recognizable to Mahan and Luce. Nor did he start with a falsifiable hypothesis. Science had become widely popularized, even fashionable, during Boyd's lifetime. Magazines, television series, and documentaries made complex concepts, such as Einstein's theory of relativity or Heisenberg's uncertainty principle, accessible to the public. But instead of building concepts on a version of the scientific method, Boyd's theory began and ended with the assumption that the decision-cycle of an individual in aerial combat shared universal characteristics – in observing, orienting, deciding, and acting – with decision-making in other fields. His method, therefore, was largely speculative or intuitive. He preferred to innovate and change rather than to establish or to verify. Despite what his supporters might claim, Boyd only marginally modified his intuitions in the process of evolving his thinking.

Moreover, science had by this point moved from explaining an outcome to increasing the odds of achieving it. While individual philosophers of science such as Karl Popper and Thomas Kuhn continued to express doubts about achieving scientific certainty, the marriage of science with information technology was systematically eliminating uncertainty with ever-increasing computational power. On May 11, 1997, for example, IBM's supercomputer "Big Blue" defeated chess grandmaster Garry Kasparov.[15] According to some pundits, the nature of science itself had changed with the victory, however controversial, by ushering in the age of artificial intelligence. Neither positivism nor antipositivism necessarily mattered; instead, with enough data and computational power, every solution to a problem could be evaluated in advance, thereby reducing the risk of failure.

Boyd, Lind, and other maneuver theorists modified the Mahanian model of war's nature by augmenting it with the concept of friction. Even though this concept appeared in US doctrine in the early years of the twentieth century, it did not become a central feature of American strategic thinking until the 1970s. Friction served maneuverists as a means of control. It allowed them to reject the concept of limited war as too abstract. But it also enabled them to posit a chaotic and highly lethal battlefield in which only the distinctive principles of maneuver theory – speed, decentralized operations, and initiative – would avail. While maneuver theory appeared sound, even alluring, on paper, friction worked against it as much as it did other theories. Military commanders too often hesitated to give their subordinates latitude to execute decentralized operations, the sine qua non of maneuver theory. In addition, the dogma that maneuver warfare was not just a better way to fight, it was the right way, tended to hamper the influence of policy. Incorporating the operational level of war into American doctrine was expected to remedy the problem of operationalizing policy's guidance, and it partially did so; but it also further enabled the decoupling of strategy from tactics. Maneuver theory, in other words, became a grammar and a logic.

Although most maneuverists confined their thinking to the realm of military operations, Boyd and Lind actively extended maneuver theory into war's psychosocial dimension. The idea that decisive advantages were to be gained by disrupting an adversary's psychological center of gravity was easily transferable to a society's collective willingness to fight. Rather than sources of strength, social divisions and cultural differences became weaknesses. An enemy could target and exploit those weaknesses and presumably bring a foe to its knees without firing a shot. In the eyes of Boyd, Lind, and other proponents of fourth-generation warfare, the culture wars of the 1990s and 2000s were real, and America was losing them.

Warden's *Air Campaign* also targeted an opponent's psychosocial dimension, among others, but did so mostly kinetically, not unlike the proposals of Douhet and Mitchell. Precision air strikes were expected to reduce the reciprocal dynamic of warfare by depriving an adversary of the capacity to launch a counterstrike. The fear of a devastating second strike, which had rendered Mahan's first principles obsolete, was theoretically gone. Once again, one could employ the core principles of concentration, offensive action, and decision by battle. Only with respect to attacks against other nuclear powers, which were not being contemplated in any case, would a second strike be of concern. Under Warden's scheme, air strikes were also to be scalable: one could dial up a limited strike merely to punish a foe or a more comprehensive attack to paralyze an opponent. The coercive value of the latter was not clear, since a paralyzed enemy, by definition, would be unable to comply with one's wishes.

Warden's theory also became the forerunner of a different model of war's nature, one that still assumed war was a violent extension of human competition, but which presumed to bypass the problem of human passions and to manipulate chance. Air power had positioned itself to be an almost trouble-free extension of policy. The passions of the friendly populace rarely need come into play. Chance, moreover, could be greatly reduced, or so it was promised. Air power, it seemed, had become the perfect weapon for a superpower. Claims of a "new American way of war," which combined air power with small-footprint special operations capabilities, soon followed.[16] The assumption that war's nature was manipulable certainly clashed with the model of the maneuverists, but it was attractive to America's way of policy.

Significantly, from the late 1970s onward, the Howard and Paret translation of Clausewitz's *On War* served as the authoritative source for what war's nature, in fact, was. It would be accurate to say the US military rarely articulated what it believed war's nature to be until Howard and Paret published their translation of *On War*. It was during this period, too, that the Clausewitzian expression "war was more than a true chameleon" came into vogue, as did the idea that war's trinitarian forces were always paradoxical. To many military and policy practitioners, such expressions meant war was always changing, but never changed.

War's Character and Military Strategy

America's foremost strategic thinkers also regarded war's character – the political, military, economic, and psychosocial dimensions of warfare – as of varying importance as well. Mahan gave prominence to the military and economic dimensions of warfare initially, and he appears to have only seriously considered the political dimension after confronting Corbett's *Principles of Maritime Strategy* and conducting at least a partial reading of Clausewitz. Mitchell focused primarily on the military dimension, specifically the military-technological component of warfare. He originally linked his argument for an independent air arm to the thriving economy of the 1920s; airpower could readily secure America's commerce, which he claimed was becoming increasingly airborne. But he was neither as consistent nor as persuasive as Mahan in this regard. With respect to US society, both authors held elitist views and imagined themselves, with some justification, to belong to America's more influential social classes. The concerns of servants, laborers, and shop owners mattered little, except as a cause for social programs that would draw funds away from the US defense budget. Hence, their neglect of war's psychosocial dimension is not surprising.

The views of Brodie, Osgood, and Schelling were decidedly elitist as well; they were not in the minority by any means. Their attitudes were shaped by several sociocultural factors, including their levels of education as well as the culture of academe. For them, public support was important. But the public itself represented passion and ignorance, which meant it could have little place in the formulation of a national strategy in the nuclear age. It is hardly surprising, therefore, that these authors chose to focus almost exclusively on the political and military dimensions of war. They also saw the US military as driven too much by instinctive reaction rather than rigorous analysis; hence, military thinking posed a threat to the rational conduct of any conflict short of an all-out war. Regrettably, their apprehensions of the military viewpoint were often justified. General Curtis LeMay's advocacy of direct military action during the Cuban Missile Crisis, for instance, was irresponsibly instinctive, driven by the three Jominian imperatives of concentration, offensive action, and seeking a decision by battle. Yet the unwillingness of the strategy intellectuals to incorporate sociocultural forces into their conceptions of strategy weakened their theories. The primacy of the political dimension of war would become the acknowledged standard for US military strategy. But its prominence led to difficulties in the twenty-first century when US strategists needed to turn to war's psychosocial dimension to craft counterinsurgency campaign plans.

Unlike Osgood, Brodie and Schelling understood the economic dimension of warfare. But they rightly considered the role it would play in a nuclear conflict to be negligible, though economic power became a useful tool under Kennan's scheme of measures short of war. Schelling's limited war framework, unlike that of Brodie and Osgood, was concerned with the psychological struggle that took place within the minds of opposing heads of state. For Schelling, belligerent parties followed the same mental process, regardless of social background and culture, when deciding whether to concede. Understanding that process and influencing it were the goals of his primary strategic works: *Strategy of Conflict* and *Arms and Influence*. Ultimately, however, he, like Brodie and Osgood, committed the cardinal sin of failing to reduce the space between theory and practice. Schelling rarely concerned himself with that problem after 1970, pouring most of his intellectual energies into expanding game theory into other realms. All three had certainly made themselves familiar with Clausewitz's theories. But none appreciated his emphasis on war's psychosocial dimension beyond understanding it as something to be controlled.

Kahn's writings did concentrate on the psychosocial as well as the political and military-technological dimensions of warfare. This broader focus was due partly to his charter to promote civil defense as a national program and partly the result of expanding his research agenda. His perspective served as something of a corrective to the assumptions of the limited war theorists, but it was too little too late. Kahn's analysis did not appear in time to prevent the problem of America's postwar malaise. But it did assist in diagnosing it. He showed little interest in the economic dimension of war, though the competition between the superpowers was becoming predominantly economic.

Eccles and Wylie concentrated largely on war's military and psychosocial dimensions. While they did not ignore the political dimension of war, they offered little in the way of new insights for aligning political and military objectives. Instead, their concerns were, first, to distinguish valid concepts from misleading ones for the sake of guiding military strategy and defense policy; second, to balance strategic choices not just against available ways and means, but against what the public might support. Public support was obviously difficult to measure. But for a democracy, unlike a totalitarian state, gaining a reliable sense of public opinion could prove critical, as remains the case in the twenty-first century. A genuine assessment had to go beyond opinion polls, which were of dubious reliability, to include some intuitive feel for the public's morale – not unlike a ship's commander might develop an intuitive sense for the crew's morale. Any objective analyst in the 1950s and 1960s ought to have been able to conclude the American public, particularly the portion consisting of males of fighting age, was distracted by socioeconomic events at home. Patriotism and the willingness to fight Communism, though real, were competing against other and in some cases stronger attitudes regarding the need for social and political equality. This was particularly true when the stakes were not clear or were muddled by the debates over where America's true interests were. America's policy-makers and key strategists remained sensitive to opinion polls, but they lacked sensitivity to the cultural symbols and signs that surrounded them every day.

Summers decried the loss of cultural sensitivity among America's leadership. His argument for mending American military strategy stressed closing the gap between US citizens and their leaders in Washington. He blamed the latter for not instilling a sufficient fighting spirit within the citizenry. To a degree this blame is justified. America's political (and military) leaders attempted to minimize the war's negative impact on US society, as Rostow revealed, to maintain public support. The media, on the other hand, took the opposite angle because that made for better copy. To an important extent, however, Summers's criticism was unjustified. Fighting a limited war should not have required militarizing one's society, or the manipulation of public support, though sometimes unavoidable. Instead it should have entailed protecting those allies that truly mattered and doing so where and in a manner that ensured the political, military, economic, and psychosocial odds were in America's favor. As the West's efforts in Iraq and Afghanistan through the first two decades of the twenty-first century have made clear, the psychosocial dimension of conflict is vitally important to a modern democracy, except in the cases of swift punitive strikes or humanitarian relief operations. Unfortunately, neither Summers nor the limited war theorists fully accounted for the psychosocial dimension of conflict with respect to the Vietnam War.

Conclusion

Boyd and Lind initially concentrated almost exclusively on the military dimension of conflict. But as the culture wars continued, each theorist devoted more attention to war's psychosocial dimension. Pundits have since described that dimension as decisive, and they consider it the preferred domain of terrorists, as well as insurgents and counterinsurgents. One emerging danger in that line of reasoning, however, is that it privileges that dimension over the others: victory comes either through creating social chaos or instituting social reform, depending upon which side of the struggle one supports. It also assumes the psychosocial and political dimensions are sufficiently connected so actions affecting the former will generate favorable outcomes in the latter.

Warden's ring theory, though centered on the military dimension of war, speculated about what might happen if one could strike all the dimensions of conflict simultaneously. For ethical reasons, he considered the psychosocial dimension off-limits to direct attack. But he made it the target of indirect attacks. For instance, an air commander would avoid bombing civilians directly but could attack them indirectly by bombing their infrastructure – roads, bridges, railways, and so on – which would disrupt the flow of food and other essentials, causing many to suffer or die. Here, again, the causal linkages between and among dimensions were assumed rather than proven.

In the years ahead, American strategic thought will surely develop other models of war's nature. One would like to believe it will find a way to synchronize war's logic and its grammar. But one thing is certain, if war is a continuation of politics by other means so, too, is thinking about war.

Notes

Introduction

1 C. von Clausewitz, *Vom Kriege*, 19th ed. (Bonn: Dümmlers, 1980), 991; hereafter VK; compare C. von Clausewitz, *On War*, trans. and ed. Michael Howard and Peter Paret (Princeton, NJ: Princeton University, 1976), 605; hereafter OW.
2 Russell Weigley, *The American Way of War* (Bloomington: Indiana University Press, 1973). For a summary of interpretations of the American way of war, see Antulio J. Echevarria II, *Reconsidering the American Way of War* (Washington, DC: Georgetown University Press, 2014), ch. 1.
3 These include the archives of William (Billy) Mitchell, Smedley Butler, Bernard Brodie, Robert Osgood, Herman Kahn, Henry Eccles, J. C. Wylie, Herbert Rosinski, Harry Summers, and John Boyd.
4 On tunnel history, see J. H. Hexter, *Reappraisals in History* 2d ed. (Chicago, IL: University of Chicago Press, 1979), 258; Jeremy Black, *Rethinking Military History* (London: Routledge, 2004) adds to the case for an interdisciplinary approach.
5 Mahan (1840–1914), Mitchell (1879–1936), and Eccles (1898–1986) belonged to three distinct generations. The four others are: (a) Brodie (1910–78) and Wylie (1911–93); (b) Osgood (1921–86), Schelling (1921–2016), and Kahn (1922–83); (c) Boyd (1927–97) and Summers (1932–99); and (d) Lind (1947–) and Warden (1943–).
6 Gen. Joseph F. Dunford, Jr., "The Character of War and Strategic Landscape Have Changed," *Joint Forces Quarterly* 89, 2 (2018): 2–3.
7 Adm. Bill Owens, *Lifting the Fog of War* (New York: Farrar, Straus, Giroux, 2000).
8 Michael I. Handel, *Masters of War: Classical Strategic Thought* (London: Frank Cass, 2001), 109–10.
9 Thomas S. Kuhn, *The Structure of Scientific Revolutions*, 2d ed. (Chicago, IL: University of Chicago Press, 1970), viii, 6.
10 Rosinski to Eccles, Sept. 7, 1959. Emphasis original. Naval War College Special Collections. Eccles Papers.

11 Cited from Walter R. Borneman, *The Admirals: Nimitz, Halsey, Leahy, and King – The Five-Star Admirals Who Won the War at Sea* (New York: Little, Brown, 2013), 207.
12 James Lacey, *The Washington War* (New York: Bantam, 2019), 130–33.
13 John I. Alger, *The Quest for Victory: The History of the Principles of War* (Westport, CT: Greenwood Press, 1982).
14 Bruce Kuklick, *Blind Oracles: Intellectuals and War from Kennan to Kissinger* (Princeton, NJ: Princeton University Press, 2007).
15 J. Kelly and M. J. Brennan, *Alien: How Operational Art Devoured Strategy* (Carlisle, PA: Strategic Studies Institute, 2009).
16 David H. Ucko, *The New Counterinsurgency Era: Transforming the US Military for Modern Wars* (Washington, DC: Georgetown University, 2009).

Chapter 1

1 Mahan published 20 books and 137 articles in his lifetime; J. B. Hattendorf and L. C. Hattendorf, eds., *A Bibliography of the Works of Alfred Thayer Mahan* (Newport, RI: Naval War College, 1986). Compare: W. D. Puleston, *The Life and Work of Captain Alfred Thayer Mahan* (New Haven, CT: Yale University, 1939); M. T. Sprout, "Mahan: Evangelist of Sea Power," in *Makers of Modern Strategy*, ed. Edward Mead Earle (Princeton, NJ: Princeton University, 1943), 415–45; Robert Seager II, *Alfred Thayer Mahan: The Man and His Letters* (Annapolis, MD: Naval Institute, 1977).
2 A. T. Mahan, *The Harvest Within: Thoughts on the Life of the Christian* (Boston, MA: Little, Brown, 1909); and Suzanne Geissler, *God and Sea Power: The Influence of Religion on Alfred Thayer Mahan* (Annapolis, MD: Naval Institute, 2015).
3 J. Simon Rofe, "'Under the Influence of Mahan': Theodore and Franklin Roosevelt and Their Understanding of American National Interest," *Diplomacy & Statecraft* 19 (2008): 732–45.
4 B. J. Armstrong, ed., *21st Century Mahan: Sound Military Conclusions for the Modern Era* (Annapolis, MD: Naval Institute, 2013); James Stavridis, *The History and Geopolitics of the World's Oceans* (New York: Penguin, 2017).
5 A. T. Mahan, *The Influence of Sea Power upon History, 1660–1783* (Boston, MA: Little, Brown, 1890), iii.
6 Mahan, *Influence of Sea Power upon History*; A. T. Mahan, *The Influence of Sea Power upon the French Revolution and Empire, 1793–1812* (Boston, MA: Little, Brown, 1892); *The Life of Nelson: The Embodiment of the Sea Power of Great Britain*, 2 vols. (Boston, MA: Little, Brown, 1897); *Sea Power in Its Relations to the War of 1812*, 2 vols. (Boston, MA: Little, Brown, 1905).
7 A. T. Mahan, "The United States Looking Outward," *Atlantic Monthly* 66 (Dec. 1890): 816–24; "Hawaii and Our Future Sea Power," *The Forum* 15 (Mar. 1893): 1–11.
8 Weigley, *American Way of War*, 178–79; Philip A. Crowl, "Alfred Thayer Mahan: The Naval Historian," in *Makers of Modern Strategy*, ed. Peter Paret (Princeton, NJ: Princeton University Press, 1986); and Robert Seager II, *Alfred Thayer Mahan: The Man and His Letters* (Annapolis, MD: Naval Institute Press, 1977).

9 A. T. Mahan, "Distinguishing Qualities of Ships of War," *Scripps-McRae Newspaper League*, Nov. 1898, in *Lessons of the War with Spain and Other Articles* (Boston, MA: Little, Brown, 1899), 257–73; "Sea Power in the Present European War," *Leslie's Illustrated Weekly* CXIX (Aug. 20, 1914), in *Letters and Papers of Mahan* III: 706–10.
10 A. T. Mahan, *From Sail to Steam: Recollections of a Naval Life* (New York: Harper, 1907), 287, 321–22; Letter to John Brown, Jan. 26, 1897, in *Letters and Papers of Alfred Thayer Mahan*, 3 vols., ed. Robert Seager II and Doris D. Maguire (Annapolis, MD: Naval Institute Press, 1975) II: 488.
11 Adm. S. B. Luce, "The Intellectual Focus: On the Study of Naval Warfare as a Science," and "Address Delivered at the United States Naval War College June 2, 1903," in *The Writings of Stephen B. Luce*, ed. J. D. Hayes and J. B. Hattendorf (Newport, RI: Naval War College, 1975), 54, 68.
12 Samuel P. Huntington, *The Soldier and the State: The Theory and Politics of Civil–Military Relations* (Cambridge, MA: Harvard University Press, 1957), 273–79.
13 Geissler, *God and Sea Power*, 50–54.
14 Benjamin L. Apt, "Mahan's Forebears: The Debate over Maritime Strategy, 1868–1883," *Naval War College Review* 50, 3 (Summer 1997): 86–111.
15 Lawrence Sondhaus, *Naval Warfare, 1815–1914* (London: Routledge, 2001), 161.
16 Arne Røksund, *The Jeune École: The Strategy of the Weak* (Leiden: Brill, 2007).
17 Letter to George Sydenham Clarke, May 24, 1898, in *Letters and Papers* II: 556.
18 Huntington, *Soldier and the State*, 20.
19 Richard W. Turk, *The Ambiguous Relationship: Theodore Roosevelt and Alfred Thayer Mahan* (New York: Greenwood, 1987), 101–07.
20 Matthew Oyos, *In Command: Theodore Roosevelt and the American Military* (Washington, DC: Potomac [Nebraska Imprint], 2018), 252–57.
21 Compare A. T. Mahan, "Some Reflections upon the Far-Eastern War," *National Review* 47 (May 1906): 383; William S. Sims, "The Inherent Tactical Qualities of All-Big-Gun, One-Caliber Battleships of High Speed, Large Displacement Gunpower," *Proceedings* (Sept. 1906), 1337–66; on Sims's errors see Wayne P. Hughes, "Mahan, Tactics and Principles of Strategy," in *The Influence of History on Mahan: The Proceedings of a Conference Marking the Centenary of Alfred Thayer Mahan's Influence of Sea Power upon History 1660–1783*, ed. John B. Hattendorff (Newport, RI: Naval War College, 1991), 25–36.
22 "Recollections of Ellen Kuhn Mahan," *Letters and Papers* III: 730; Lyle Mahan, "My Parents, Rear Admiral and Mrs. Alfred Thayer Mahan," in *Influence of History on Mahan*, 120.
23 Trent Hone, *Learning War: The Evolution of Fighting Doctrine in the US Navy from 1898 to 1945* (Annapolis, MD: Naval Institute Press, 2018); Scott Mobley, *Progressives in Navy Blue: Maritime Strategy, American Empire, and the Transformation of U.S. Naval Identity from 1873 to 1898* (Annapolis, MD: Naval Institute Press, 2018).

24 D. W. Knox, "Old Principles and Modern Applications," *Proceedings* 40, 3 (July–Aug. 1915): 1009–39.
25 Mahan, *From Sail to Steam*.
26 Crowl, "Mahan," 472.
27 Fred T. Jane, *Fighting Ships* (London: Sampson Low, Marston, 1912), 27.
28 John M. Cooper, Jr., *Pivotal Decades: The United States, 1900–1920* (New York: W. W. Norton, 1990), 132.
29 Alan Greenspan and Adrian Wooldridge, *Capitalism in America: A History* (New York: Penguin, 2018), 92.
30 R. Ohmann, *Selling Culture: Magazines, Markets, and Class at the Turn of the Century* (London: Verso, 1996), 62–80.
31 Robert J. Gordon, *The Rise and Fall of American Growth: The US Standard of Living since the Civil War* (Princeton, NJ: Princeton University Press, 2016), 62–204.
32 Woodrow Wilson, "Speech of Acceptance," Aug. 7, 1912, in *A Crossroads of Freedom: The 1912 Campaign Speeches of Woodrow Wilson*, ed. John W. Davidson (New Haven, CT: Yale University Press, 1956), 21.
33 Letter to Horatio G. Dohrman, Sept. 2, 1912, in *Letters and Papers* III: 476–78.
34 National Association for the Advancement of Colored People, *Thirty Years of Lynching in the United States* (New York: Lawbook Exchange, 2010 reprint), 5.
35 Letter to Silas McBee, Nov. 27, 1898, in *Letters and Papers* II: 617; emphasis original.
36 Frederick E. Hoxie, *A Final Promise: The Campaign to Assimilate the Indian, 1880–1920* (New York: Cambridge University Press, 1997).
37 Letter to the Editor of *The Times*, June 13, 1913, in *Letters and Papers* III: 499.
38 Joe Kraus, "How the Melting Pot Stirred America: The Reception of Zangwill's Play and Theater's Role in the American Assimilation Experience," *Melos* 24, 3 (1999).
39 Roger Daniels, "Immigration to the United States in the Twentieth Century," in The Cambridge Companion to Modern American Culture, ed. Christopher Bigsby (Cambridge: Cambridge University Press, 2006), 74; John M. Cooper, Jr., *Pivotal Decades: The United States, 1900–1920* (New York: W. W. Norton, 1990), 2.
40 US Congress, Report of the Commission on Industrial Relations (Chicago: Bernard & Miller, 1915), 28, 10.
41 Seager II, *Mahan*, 331.
42 Compare: Henry George, *Progress and Property* (New York: D. Appleton, 1879), which became a best-seller; and William Graham Sumner, *What Social Classes Owe Each Other* (New York: Harper, 1884).
43 John S. Gardner, ed., *The Company Town: Architecture and Society in the Early Industrial Age* (New York: Oxford University Press, 1992).
44 E. L. Bowers, *Is It Safe to Work? A Study of Industrial Accidents* (Boston, MA: Houghton Mifflin, 1930), 2; E. H. Downey, *History of Work Accident Indemnity in Iowa* (Iowa City, IA: State Historical Society, 1912), 5; M. Linder, "Fatal Subtraction: Statistical MIAs on the Industrial Battlefield," *Journal of Legislation* 20, 2 (1994): 99–145.

45 Richard Schneirov et al., *The Pullman Strike and the Crisis of the 1890s: Essays on Labor and Politics* (Urbana: University of Illinois Press, 1999); Scott Martelle, *Blood Passion: The Ludlow Massacre and Class War in the American West* (New Brunswick, NJ: Rutgers University Press, 2007).
46 Letter to William H. Henderson, Dec. 26, 1910, in *Letters and Papers* III: 371.
47 Letter to John Bassett Moore, April 20, 1905, in *Letters and Papers* III: 129, 150.
48 Robert Stern et al., *New York 1900: Metropolitan Architecture and Urbanism, 1890–1915* (New York: Rizzoli, 1983), 13–15.
49 "Recollections," in *Letters and Papers* III: 721–24.
50 George M. Beard, *American Nervousness: Its Causes and Cures* (New York: Putnam's, 1881), vi–viii, xiii.
51 "Recollections" and Letter to W. Henderson, Nov. 7, 1913, in *Letters and Papers* III: 721–24, 514 respectively.
52 A. T. Mahan, *Admiral Farragut* (New York: D. Appleton, 1893), 312–15; *Life of Nelson*, I: 32–33, 207–09, 295–97; II: 129, 139–41.
53 S. Crane, *The Red Badge of Courage* (New York: D. Appleton, 1895) was serialized in 1894; E. Wharton, *The House of Mirth* (New York: Macmillan, 1905), which *Scribner's Magazine* (Mar. 1905) advertised as "the book everyone is talking about," sold over 140,000 copies by the end of 1905. Upton Sinclair's *The Jungle* (New York: Doubleday, 1906) was a hit in serial form well before he finished the final chapters.
54 *The Jungle* may have persuaded Theodore Roosevelt to increase government controls over the meat-packing industry. Kevin Mattson, *Upton Sinclair and the Other American Century* (Hoboken, NJ: Wiley, 2006).
55 Letter to Stephen Luce, Nov. 18, 1907, in *Letters and Papers* III: 233–34.
56 Mahan, *Harvest Within*, 1; Reo N. Leslie, Jr., "Christianity and the Evangelist for Sea Power: The Religion of Alfred Thayer Mahan," in *Influence of History on Mahan*, 127–39; Geissler, *God and Sea Power*, 147–49, 177–78.
57 A. T. Mahan, "Women's Suffrage: A Speech," undated, in *Letters and Papers* III: 712–13.
58 Subscribers to each newspaper exceeded 800,000 by 1898. Marcus M. Wilkerson, *Public Opinion and the Spanish–American War: A Study in War Propaganda* (New York: Russell & Russell, 1967), 8, 42.
59 Seager II, *Mahan*, 329–30.
60 A. T. Mahan, *Lessons of the War with Spain and Other Articles* (Boston, MA: Little, Brown, 1899), 89, 130, 200; A. T. Mahan, "Current Fallacies upon Naval Subjects," *Harpers' New Monthly* 97 (June 1898): 42–53.
61 David R. Spencer, *Yellow Journalism: The Press and America's Emergence as a World Power* (Evanston, IL: Northwestern University Press, 2007); W. Joseph Campbell, *Yellow Journalism: Puncturing the Myths, Defining the Legacies* (Westport, CT: Praeger, 2003).
62 A. T. Mahan, "The Future in Relation to American Naval Power," *Harper's New Monthly* 91 (Oct. 1895): 767–75.
63 The League maintained a robust network that spanned the United States and remained active until November 1920. E. Berkeley Tompkins, Anti-Imperialism

in the United States: The Great Debate, 1890–1920 (Philadelphia: University of Pennsylvania, 1970), 122–33.
64 Letter to Bouverie Clark, July 23, 1909, *Letters and Papers* III: 308; emphasis original.
65 Letter to Ellen Kuhn Mahan, May 19, 1894, *Letters and Papers* II: 273.
66 Philip S. Foner, *Mark Twain as Social Critic* (New York: International Publishers, 1981), 315, 322.
67 Letters to Henry Cabot Lodge, Feb. 7, 1899, and John Long, June 27, 1899, *Letters and Papers* II: 627, 635–36.
68 Frederick W. Taylor, *The Principles of Scientific Management* (New York: Harper & Brothers, 1911).
69 Mary Pattison, *The Business of Home Management: The Principles of Domestic Engineering* (New York: R. McBride, 1915), 1.
70 Dale Carnagey, *Public Speaking and Influencing Men of Business* (n.p., 1913); it later became the bestseller *How to Win Friends and Influence People* (1936).
71 Frederick S. Calhoun, *Uses of Force and Wilsonian Foreign Policy* (Kent, OH: Kent State University Press, 1993).
72 A. T. Mahan, "The Practical Character of the United States Naval War College," in *Naval Administration and Warfare* (Boston: Little, Brown, 1908), 234.
73 Herbert Spencer, *A System of Synthetic Philosophy*, 10 vols. (New York: D. Appleton, 1862–93).
74 William James, *Principles of Psychology*, 2 vols. (New York: Henry Holt, 1890), I: 109.
75 Alfred Marshall, *Principles of Economics*, 2 vols. (London: Macmillan, 1890), I: 72–73.
76 Franklin H. Giddings, *Principles of Sociology* (New York: Macmillan, 1896), xvi–xvii, emphasis original.
77 H. Wager Halleck, *Elements of Military Art and Science* (New York: D. Appleton, 1846); James Mercur, *Elements of the Art of War*, 2nd ed. (New York: John Wiley, 1889); James S. Pettit, *Elements of Military Science*, rev. ed. (New Haven, CT: Tuttle, Morehouse & Taylor, 1895), 149, emphasis original.
78 D. W. Knox, "The Role of Doctrine in Naval Warfare," *Proceedings* 41, 2 (1915): 330ff.
79 Brian McAllister Linn, *The Echo of Battle: The Army's Way of War* (Cambridge, MA: Harvard University Press, 2007), 5.
80 Mahan, *Influence of Sea Power upon History*, 6–7; A. T. Mahan, *Naval Strategy Compared and Contrasted with the Principles and Practice of Military Operations on Land* (Boston, MA: Little, Brown, 1911), 299–300.
81 P. H. Colomb, *Naval Warfare: Its Ruling Principles Historically Treated* (London: W. H. Allen, 1891).
82 John B. Hattendorf, "The Idea of a 'Fleet in Being' in Historical Perspective," *Naval War College Review* 67, 1 (Winter 2014): 43–60.
83 Fred T. Jane, *Heresies of Sea Power* (New York: Longman, Green, 1906).
84 Julian S. Corbett, *Some Principles of Maritime Strategy* (London: Longman, Green, 1911).

85 Corbett, *Principles*, 13–27.
86 Bradley A. Fiske, *The Navy as a Fighting Machine* (New York: Scribner's, 1916), 170.
87 Luce, "Intellectual Focus," 53–60; James, *Psychology*, I: 185–94; Marshall, *Economics*, I: 60–77.
88 A. T. Mahan, "Subordination in Historical Treatment," in *Naval Administration* (Boston, MA: Little, Brown, 1908), 250.
89 A. T. Mahan, "The War on the Sea and Its Lessons: I. How the Motive of the War Gave Direction to Its Earlier Movements," *McClure's Magazine* (Dec. 1898): 114; "The War on the Sea and Its Lessons. III. The Reasons for Blockading Cuba," *McClure's Magazine* (Feb. 1899): 358.
90 Mahan, *Naval Strategy*, 17; *Influence of Sea Power upon History*, 13.
91 Mahan, *Sea Power in Its Relations to the War of 1812*, II: 299–309, 370–82; William S. Dudley, "Alfred Thayer Mahan on the War of 1812," *The Influence of History on Mahan*, ed. John B. Hattendorf (Newport, RI: Naval War College, 1991), 141–54.
92 Mahan, *Influence of Sea Power upon History*, 29–59.
93 Baron de Jomini, *Summary of the Art of War*, trans. O. F. Winship and E. E. McClean (New York: Putnam, 1854), 80–81.
94 Mahan, *Naval Strategy*, 6, 8, 32, 38.
95 A. T. Mahan, "The War on the Sea and Its Lessons IV. The Problems Presented to Our Navy by Cervera's Appearance in West Indian Waters and How They Were Solved," *McClure's Magazine* (Mar. 1899): 479–80.
96 Mahan, *Naval Strategy*, 6, 409, 416, 423; "Distinguishing Qualities of Ships of War," 259; *Sea Power in Its Relations to the War of 1812*, I: 316.
97 Jon Tetsuro Sumida, *Inventing Grand Strategy and Teaching Command: The Classic Works of Alfred Thayer Mahan Reconsidered* (Baltimore, MD: Johns Hopkins University Press, 1997).
98 Mahan, *Naval Strategy*, 36, 127; A. T. Mahan, "Some Considerations of the Principles Involved in the Current War," *National Review* 44 (Sept. 1904): 27–46, at 45–46.
99 Mahan, "Some Considerations of the Principles," esp. 45–46; "Some Reflections upon the Far-Eastern War."
100 A. T. Mahan, "Preparedness for Naval War," *Harper's New Monthly* 94 (Mar. 1897): 579–88, at 586.
101 A. T. Mahan, "The War on the Sea and Its Lessons. II. The Effect of Deficient Coast Defense on the Movements of the Navy," *McClure's Magazine* (Jan. 1899): 232–33, 235–36.
102 Mahan, "War on the Sea and Its Lessons IV," 480.
103 Mahan, *Naval Strategy*, 31–32.
104 Mahan, *Naval Strategy*, 81–82, 100.
105 A. T. Mahan, "A Twentieth-Century Outlook," *Harper's New Monthly* (Sept. 1897): 521–33.
106 A. T. Mahan, "The Moral Aspect of War," *North American Review* (Oct. 1899) in *Some Neglected Aspects of War* (London: Sampson Low, Marston, 1907), 36; "The Place of Force in International Relations," *North American Review* 195 (Jan. 1912): 28–39.

107 A. T. Mahan, "War from the Christian Standpoint," Nov. 15, 1900, in *Some Neglected Aspects of War* (London: Sampson Low, Marston, 1907), 108.
108 A. T. Mahan, "The Isthmus and Sea Power," *The Atlantic Monthly* 72 (Oct. 1893): 459–72; *Lessons of the War with Spain*, 34, 56–58, 64–67, 185.
109 N. Angell, *The Great Illusion* (New York: Putnam's, 1910); "The Great Illusion: A Reply to Rear-Admiral A. T. Mahan," *North American Review* 195 (Jan. 1912): 754–72. Mahan, "Place of Force in International Relations," 34; Letters to Joseph Choate, Mar. 15, 1912, and Leopold Maxse, Dec. 24, 1912, *Letters and Papers* III: 448–49, 486–87 resp.
110 Mahan, *Lessons of War with Spain*, 84–85, 163.
111 Mahan, "Preparedness for Naval War"; "The Future in Relation to American Naval Power."
112 Walter LaFeber, "A Note on the 'Mercantilistic Imperialism' of Alfred Thayer Mahan," *Mississippi River Valley Review* 48 (Mar. 1962): 674–85.
113 Capt. John Bigelow, *The Principles of Strategy: Illustrated Mainly from American Campaigns*, 2nd ed. (New York: J. B. Lippincott, 1894), 224–29.

Chapter 2

1 W. Mitchell, *Winged Defense: The Development and Possibilities of Modern Air Power – Economic and Military* (New York: G. P. Putnam's, 1925), 3–4.
2 Weigley, *American Way of War*, 136.
3 Compare Edward Warner, "Douhet, Mitchell, Seversky: Theories of Air Warfare," in *Makers of Modern Strategy: Military Thought from Machiavelli to Hitler*, ed. Edward Mead Earle (Princeton, NJ: Princeton University Press, 1943), 485–503; and David MacIsaac, "Voices from the Central Blue: The Air Power Theorists," in *Makers of Modern Strategy: From Machiavelli to the Nuclear Age*, ed. Peter Paret (Princeton, NJ: Princeton University Press, 1986), 624–47.
4 Calvin Coolidge, Address to American Society of Newspaper Editors, Jan. 17, 1925; www.presidency.ucsb.edu/documents/address-the-american-society-newspaper-editors-washington-dc
5 On the film's inaccuracies, see James J. Cooke, *Billy Mitchell* (Boulder, CO: Lynne Rienner, 2002), 3–5.
6 Emile Gauvreau and Lester Cohen, *Billy Mitchell: Founder of Our Air Force and Prophet without Honor* (New York: E. P. Dutton, 1942); I. D. Levine, *Mitchell: Pioneer of Air Power* (New York: Duell, Sloane & Pierce, 1943); see also Alexander P. Seversky's dedication to Mitchell in *Victory through Air Power* (New York: Simon & Schuster, 1942); Roger Burlingame, *General Billy Mitchell: Champion of Air Defense* (New York: McGraw-Hill, 1952); and A. P. Seversky, "I Remember Billy Mitchell," *Air Power Historian* (Oct. 1956): 179.
7 R. P. White, *Mason Patrick and the Fight for Air Service Independence* (Washington, DC: Smithsonian, 2001).
8 See C. von Clausewitz, *On War*, Bk I, Ch. 3.
9 Mitchell to his mother, dated 1891. Mitchell Papers.
10 Mitchell to his mother, Dec. 27, 1898. Mitchell Papers.
11 Cooke, *Billy Mitchell*, 33–34.

12 Cited from Cooke, *Billy Mitchell*, 71.
13 Cited from Levine, *Mitchell*, 36–37.
14 Report cards of W. Mitchell, Mar. 5, 1891; Nov. 18, 1892; and Dec. 23, 1893. Mitchell Papers.
15 Mr. Watson R. Hake to Mrs. Mitchell, Dec. 23, 1890. Mitchell Papers.
16 Alfred F. Hurley, *Billy Mitchell: Crusader for Air Power* (Bloomington: Indiana University Press, 1975), 5.
17 Mitchell to his mother, Dec. 27, 1898. Mitchell Papers.
18 Levine, *Mitchell*, 50–55.
19 George D. Hayworth, 51st Iowa Inf., to Mrs. J. B. Atkins, Mar. 8, 1899; and Corporal Frank M. Dickey, 1st Colo. Inf., to "Folks at Home," Jan. 4, 1899. Army Heritage Center Papers.
20 Dickey to "Folks at Home," Jan. 4, 1899. Army Heritage Center Papers.
21 W. Mitchell, "Building the Alaskan Telegraph System," *National Geographic Magazine* 14, 12 (1903): 357–61, here 360.
22 W. Mitchell, *Field Signal Communications*, 2nd Lecture (Ft. Leavenworth: Dept. Mil. Art, 1905). Mitchell Papers.
23 Gladys Hansen and Emmet Condon, *Denial of Disaster* (San Francisco: Cameron, 1989), 160ff.
24 Douglas Waller, *A Question of Loyalty: General Billy Mitchell and the Court-Martial That Gripped the Nation* (New York: HarperCollins, 2004), 101–02.
25 W. Mitchell, "Our Faulty Military Policy," 1915, Box 45, Mitchell Papers, Library of Congress.
26 Waller, *Question of Loyalty*, 103.
27 Tami Davis Biddle, *Rhetoric and Reality in Air Warfare: The Evolution of British and American Ideas about Strategic Bombing, 1914–1945* (Princeton, NJ: Princeton University Press, 2002), 52.
28 R. F. Futrell, *Ideas, Concepts, Doctrine: Basic Thinking in the United States Air Force*, vol. 1 (Maxwell AFB: Air University, 1989), 22.
29 W. Mitchell, "Air Service at St. Mihiel," *World's Work* 38 (Aug. 1919): 360–70.
30 W. Mitchell, "Air Service at the Argonne-Meuse," *World's Work* 38 (Sept. 1919): 552–60.
31 Thomas Wildenberg, *Billy Mitchell's War with the Navy: The Interwar Rivalry over Air Power* (Annapolis, MD: Naval Institute Press, 2013), 37.
32 Cited from G. Till, "Adopting the Aircraft Carrier: The British, American, and Japanese Case Studies," in *Military Innovation in the Interwar Period*, ed. W. Murray and A. Millett (Cambridge: Cambridge University Press, 1996), 209–10.
33 Hurley, *Billy Mitchell*, 44–45.
34 Mitchell to his mother, Feb. 20, 1920. Mitchell Papers.
35 G. Till, *Airpower and the Royal Navy 1914–1945: A Historical Survey* (London: MacDonald and Jane's, 1979), 158–59.
36 Jeremy Black, *Air Power: A Global History* (Lanham, MD: Rowman & Littlefield, 2016), 58–59.
37 David R. Mets, "The Influence of Aviation on the Evolution of American Naval Thought," in *The Paths of Heaven: The Evolution of Air Power*

Theory, ed. Phillip S. Meilinger (Maxwell AFB: Air University, 1997), 115–49.
38 Till, "Adopting the Aircraft Carrier"; John Kuehn, *America's First General Staff: A Short History of the General Board of the Navy, 1900–1950* (Annapolis, MD: Naval Institute Press, 2017).
39 M. Mauer and C. F. Senning, "Billy Mitchell, the Air Service, and the Mingo County War," *West Virginia Historian* 30 (Oct. 1968): 339–50.
40 Clayton D. Laurie, "The United States Army and the Return to Normalcy in Labor Dispute Interventions: The Case of the West Virginia Coal Mine Wars, 1920–1921," *West Virginia History* 50 (1991) 1–24.
41 W. Mitchell et al., *Report of Inspection Trip to France, Germany, Holland, and England Made During the Winter of 1921–1922* (Washington, DC: GPO, 1923).
42 "General Mitchell's Lecture to Army War College," dated Wed. Nov. 22, 1922, pp. 21–24. Army Heritage Center, Papers.
43 Waller, *Question of Loyalty*, 159.
44 W. Mitchell et al, *Report of Inspection of United States Possessions in the Pacific and Java, Singapore, India, Siam, China, and Japan* (Washington, DC: GPO, Oct. 24, 1924).
45 Steven T. Ross, *American War Plans 1890–1939* (London: Frank Cass, 2002), 79–86.
46 Wildenberg, *Mitchell's War*, 129–37.
47 Mitchell, *Winged Defense*, 102–05; Wildenberg, *Mitchell's War*, 131.
48 Waller, *Question of Loyalty*, 316–26; Ryan Wadle, *Selling Sea Power: Public Relations and the US Navy 1917–1941* (Norman: Oklahoma University Press, 2019).
49 Wildenberg, *Mitchell's War*, 147.
50 On Lindberg's later scandals see A. Scott Berg, *Lindberg* (New York: Penguin, 1999); Max Wallace, *The American Axis: Henry Ford, Charles Lindberg, and the Third Reich* (New York: St. Martin's Press, 2003).
51 Donald M. Pattillo, *A History in the Making* (New York: McGraw-Hill, 1998), 15–16; Stephen Budiansky, *Air Power* (New York: Viking, 2004), 155–57.
52 Susan Butler, *East to the Dawn: The Life of Amelia Earhart* (Cambridge, MA: Da Capo Press, 1997).
53 Cooke, *Billy Mitchell*, 264–65.
54 Aaron D. Purcell, ed., *The New Deal and the Great Depression* (Kent, OH: Kent State University Press, 2014), esp. 4–29.
55 G. M. Walton and H. Rockoff, *History of the American Economy*, 11th ed. (Mason, OH: Cengage, 2010), 418–19.
56 James S. Corum, "The Luftwaffe and Lessons Learned in the Spanish Civil War," in *Air Power History: Turning Points from Kitty Hawk to Kosovo*, ed. S. Cox and P. Gray (London: Frank Cass, 2002), 66–89.
57 M. Twain and C. D. Warner, *The Gilded Age: A Tale of Today* (Hartford, CT: American Publishers, 1873); Foner, *Twain as Social Critic*, 91–113.
58 Sec. of Treasury, *Statistical Abstract of the United States 1879* (Washington, DC: GPO, 1880), 146–47.

59 Donald Worster, *Dust Bowl: The Southern Plains in the 1930s* (Oxford: Oxford University Press, 2004), 5–7, 12.
60 Sec. of Commerce, *Statistical Abstract of the United States 1936* (Washington, DC: GPO, 1936), 1–2.
61 *Historical Statistics of the United States: Colonial Times to 1970* (Washington, DC: GPO, 1973), Ch. F, p. 224.
62 F. S. Fitzgerald, *The Great Gatsby* (New York: Scribner's, 1925), ch. IX; only 20,000 copies sold the first year.
63 Coolidge, "Address to Newspaper Editors," www.presidency.ucsb.edu/documents/address-the-american-society-newspaper-editors-washington-dc
64 Greenspan and Wooldridge, *Capitalism in America*, 194–95.
65 Walton and Rockoff, *History of the American Economy*, 400. Ford discontinued the Tin Lizzy in 1926 as his competitors began producing better alternatives.
66 Stanley Lebergott, *The American Economy: Income, Wealth, and Want* (Princeton, NJ: Princeton University Press, 1976), 248–99.
67 R. M. Coen, "Labor Force Unemployment in the 1920s and 1930s: A Reexamination Based on Postwar Experience," *Review of Economics and Statistics* 55 (1973): 46–55.
68 Martha Olney, *Buy Now Pay Later: Advertising, Credit, and Consumer Durables in the 1920s* (Chapel Hill: University of North Carolina Press, 1991).
69 J. Williamson and P. Lindert, *American Inequality: A Macroeconomic History* (New York: Academic, 1981); Walton and Rockoff, *History of American Economy*, 400.
70 Bowers, *Is It Safe to Work?*, 2; Linder, "Fatal Subtraction," 99–104.
71 https://annaleahmary.com/wordpress/wp-content/uploads/2015/09/MV-TRAFFIC-FATALITIES1899-2009.pdf
72 Mitchell, *Winged Defense*, 113, 171.
73 M. E. Parrish, *Anxious Decades: American Prosperity and Depression, 1920–1941* (New York: W. W. Norton, 1994), 30–31.
74 *New York Times*, Dec. 12, 1925; cited from Richard D. White, Jr., *Will Rogers: A Political Life* (Lubbock: Texas Tech University Press, 2011), 70.
75 White, *Will Rogers*, 284.
76 A. Harrison, *Black Exodus: The Great Migration from the American South* (Jackson: University of Mississippi Press, 1991).
77 C. M. Messer, T. E. Shriver, and Alison E. Adams, "The Destruction of Black Wall Street: Tulsa's 1921 Riot and the Eradication of Accumulated Wealth," *American Journal of Economics and Sociology* 77 (Oct. 2018): 789–819.
78 David M. Chalmers, *Hooded Americanism: The History of the Ku Klux Klan* (Durham, NC: Duke University Press, 1987).
79 Mitchell et al., *Report of Inspection of United States Possessions in the Pacific* (Washington, DC: War Dept., 1923).
80 W. Mitchell, "The Next War in the Air," *Popular Mechanics* 63 (Feb. 1935): 162–65, and 135A.
81 *Historical Statistics of United States: Colonial Times to 1970*, Series C89.
82 Elaine Showalter, "The Other Lost Generation," in *Sisters' Choice: Tradition and Change in American Women's Writing* (Oxford: Oxford University Press, 1991), 104–26.

83 Compare Nancy Cott, *The Grounding of Modern Feminism* (New Haven, CT: Yale University Press, 1988); W. L. O'Neill, *Feminism in America: A History*, 2nd ed. (New Brunswick, NJ: Rutgers University Press, 1989); William Chafe, *The Paradox of Change: American Women in the 20th Century* (New York: Oxford University Press, 1991).
84 Claudia Goldin, *Understanding the Gender Gap: An Economic History of American Women* (New York: Oxford University Press, 1990).
85 Linda Simon, *Lost Girls: The Invention of the Flapper* (London: Reaktion, 2017); Nancy Woloch, *Women and the American Experience*, 2nd ed. (New York: McGraw-Hill, 1994).
86 Ellen Wells Page, "A Flapper's Appeal to Parents," *The Outlook*, Dec. 6, 1922, p. 607.
87 Lisa McGirr, *The War on Alcohol: Prohibition and the Rise of the American State* (New York: W. W. Norton, 2015); G. Peck, *Prohibition in Washington, D.C.: How Dry We Weren't* (Charleston, SC: History Press, 2011); H. Abadinsky, *The Criminal Elite: Professional and Organized Crime* (Westport, CT: Greenwood Press, 1983).
88 Waller, *Question of Loyalty*, 161–62.
89 Series: Moving Images Relating to Military Aviation Activities, compiled 1947–84, documenting the period 1909–84; Record Group 342: Records of U.S. Air Force Commands, Activities, and Organizations, 1900–2003; https://unwritten-record.blogs.archives.gov/tag/billy-mitchell/
90 Cooke, *Billy Mitchell*, 257–59.
91 Mitchell, *Winged Defense*, 95.
92 Mitchell, *Winged Defense*, 140.
93 Mitchell, *Winged Defense*, 6.
94 W. Mitchell, "America in the Air: The Future of Airplane and Airship, Economically and as Factors in National Defense," *National Geographic* 39, 3 (Mar. 1921): 339–52; and "Some Considerations Regarding a Limitation of Armaments," *Annals of the American Academy of Political Social Sciences* 120 (1925): 87–89, here 87.
95 W. Mitchell, "Airplanes in National Defense," *Annals of American Academy of Political and Social Science* 131 (May 1927): 38–42.
96 Mitchell, "Airplanes in National Defense," 38; emphasis original.
97 Mitchell, "Airplanes in National Defense," 38.
98 W. Mitchell, "Has the Airplane Made the Battleship Obsolete?," *World's Work* (Apr. 1921), 552.
99 W. Mitchell, "Aviation over the Water," *American Review of Reviews* 62 (Oct. 1921): 391–98, here 392.
100 Mitchell, "Airplanes in National Defense," 42.
101 Mitchell, *Winged Defense*, 199.
102 W. Mitchell, "Look Out Below!," *Collier's, The National Weekly*, April 21, 1928, pp. 9, 41–42.
103 W. Mitchell, "Air Power vs. Sea Power," *American Review of Reviews* 58 (Mar. 21, 1921): 273–77, here 273.
104 Mitchell, *Winged Defense*, 24–25.
105 Mitchell, *Winged Defense*, 21.

106 Mitchell, "Air Power vs. Sea Power," 277; *Winged Defense*, 113–15.
107 Mark A. Clodfelter, "Molding Airpower Convictions: Development and Legacy of William Mitchell's Strategic Thought," in *The Paths of Heaven: The Evolution of Air Power Theory*, ed. Phillip S. Meilinger (Maxwell AFB: Air University, 1997), 79–114, esp. 95.
108 W. Mitchell, "General Mitchell's Lecture to Army War College," Nov. 22, 1922, pp. 21–24; *Winged Defense*, 164–71.
109 "Text of Air Report by Morrow Board," *New York Times*, Dec. 3, 1925.
110 Mitchell, *Winged Defense*, 139.
111 Harry Bruno, *Wings over America: The Story of American Aviation* (New York: Halcyon, 1944).
112 Mitchell, *Winged Defense*, 205–06.
113 W. Mitchell, "Anecdotes of the Air," [Part I] *Women's Home Companion* (Dec. 1930): 30–31; and [Part II] (Feb. 1931): 13–14, 67; "The World's Largest Airship," *Women's Home Companion* (Nov. 1931): 18–19, 57–58; and "The Automobile of the Air," *Women's Home Companion* (May 1932): 18–19, 126.
114 Mitchell, "Airplanes in National Defense," 38.
115 S. B. Luce, "The Benefits of War," *North American Review* (Dec. 1891): 672–73; B. Fiske, "Our Naval Profession," *Naval Institute Proceedings* (June 1907): 475–78; from Ronald Spector, *Professors of War: The Naval War College and the Development of the Naval Profession* (Newport, RI: Naval War College, 1977), 83.
116 S. Butler, "America's Armed Forces," *Common Sense* 4, 11 (1935): pt. 2; *War Is a Racket* (New York: Round Table Press, 1935).
117 Matheny, *Carrying the War to the Enemy*, 71.
118 Maj.-Gen. H. von Freytag-Loringhoven, *The Power of Personality in War* (Washington, DC: USAWC Hist. Section, 1938); reprinted in *Roots of Strategy: Book 3* (Harrisburg, PA: Stackpole, 1991).
119 Mitchell, *Winged Defense*, 3–4, xii; Phillip S. Meilinger, ed., *The Paths of Heaven: The Evolution of Air Power Theory* (Maxwell AFB: Air University, 1997), xi.
120 Panama (1903, 1918–20), Cuba (1906–09, 1917–20), Honduras (1912–19, 1924–25), Nicaragua (1912–25, 1926–33), Haiti (1915–34), Mexico (1914, 1916), Dominican Republic (1916–24), Russia and Siberia (1918–20), and China (1900, 1912–38).
121 Hans Schmidt, *Maverick Marine: General Smedley D. Butler and the Contradictions of American Military History* (Lexington: University Press of Kentucky, 1998). Butler evidently attempted to return the first medal, arguing he had not earned it. But the Dept. of the Navy sent it back with explicit instructions to wear it "proudly." Dwight S. Mears, *The Medal of Honor: The Evolution of America's Highest Decoration* (Lawrence: University Press of Kansas, 2018), 50.
122 Maj.-Gen. Smedley D. Butler, USMC, draft manuscripts, US Marine Corps Historical Center, Quantico, VA.
123 Linn, *Echo of Battle*, 127–28; M. Janowitz, *The Professional Soldier: A Social and Political Portrait* (New York: Free Press, 1964).

Part II

1. Weigley, *American Way of War*, 474.
2. Marc Trachtenberg, *History and Strategy* (Princeton, NJ: Princeton University, 1991), 261; Ken Booth, "The Evolution of Strategic Thinking," in *Contemporary Strategy I: Theories and Concepts*, 2nd Ed. (New York: Holmes & Meier, 1987), 44–60; for exceptions see Colin S. Gray, "What RAND Hath Wrought," *Foreign Policy* 4 (Autumn 1971): 111–29; Stephen Peter Rosen, "Vietnam and the American Theory of Limited War," *International Security* 7, 2 (Autumn 1982): 83–113.
3. B. Brodie, ed., *The Absolute Weapon: Atomic Power and World Order* (New York: Harcourt, Brace, 1946); it included two of his essays and four others: "The Common Problem" by Frederick S. Dunn, "The Atomic Bomb in Soviet–American Relations" by Arnold Wolfers, "Effect on International Organization" by Percy E. Corbett, and "International Control of Atomic Weapons" by William T. R. Fox.
4. Walter R. Borneman, *The Admirals: Nimitz, Halsey, Leahy, and King – The Five-Star Admirals Who Won the War at Sea* (New York: Little, Brown, 2012).
5. Cited from Steiner, *Brodie*, 269, n. 6.
6. Donald Stoker, *Why America Loses Wars: Limited War and US Strategy from the Korean War to the Present* (Cambridge: Cambridge University Press, 2019).

Chapter 3

1. T. C. Schelling, "A Tribute to Brodie and (Incidentally) to RAND" (Santa Monica, CA: P-6355, RAND, July 1979), 1.
2. Especially: Fawn McKay Brodie, *No Man Knows My History: The Life of Joseph Smith* (New York: Alfred A. Knopf, 1945); and *Thomas Jefferson: An Intimate History* (New York: W. W. Norton, 1974).
3. B. and F. Brodie, *From Crossbow to H-Bomb: The Evolution of the Weapons and Tactics of Warfare* (Bloomington: Indiana University Press, 1962); compare Melvin Kransberg and Carroll W. Pursell, Jr., eds., *Technology in Western Civilization*, 2 vols. (New York: Oxford University Press, 1967).
4. Brodie and Brodie, *Crossbow to H-Bomb*, 7.
5. B. Brodie, *Sea Power in the Machine Age* (Princeton, NJ: Princeton University Press, 1941); and *A Layman's Guide to Naval Strategy* (Princeton, NJ: Princeton University Press, 1942).
6. Schelling, "Tribute to Brodie," 1.
7. Letter from Datus C. Smith, Jr., June 22, 1942 to Rosinski, quoting Brodie. Rosinski Papers. Naval War College Archives.
8. For Brodie's chronology, see Barry H. Steiner, *Bernard Brodie and the Foundations of American Nuclear Strategy* (Lawrence: University Press of Kansas, 1991), 251–52; B. Brodie, *Strategy in the Missile Age* (Princeton, NJ: Princeton University Press, 1959); and *Escalation and the Nuclear Option* (Princeton, NJ: Princeton University Press, 1966).
9. B. Brodie, *War and Politics* (New York: Macmillan, 1973).

10 A. J. Echevarria II, "On the Clausewitz of the Cold War: Reconsidering the Primacy of Policy in *On War*," *Armed Forces & Society* 34, 1 (Oct. 2007): 90–108.
11 Barry Scott Zellen, *State of Doom: Bernard Brodie, the Bomb, and the Birth of the Bipolar World* (New York: Continuum International, 2012), 261.
12 Immigration and Naturalization Service, *2000 Statistical Yearbook of the Immigration and Naturalization Service*; and *2001 Statistical Yearbook of the Immigration and Naturalization Service* (Washington, DC: GPO, 2002 and 2003), table I, p. 15 and pp. 111–21, respectively.
13 Strikes took place from November 1945 to May 1946 and included 200,000 automobile workers, 300,000 meatpackers, 750,000 steelworkers, 180,000 electrical workers, and 400,000 coalminers. Melvin Dubofsky and Joseph A. McCartin, *American Labor: A History*, 9th ed. (Oxford: Wiley Blackwell, 2017), 295–300. The number would have been higher had not Truman preempted a looming railroad-workers' strike by federalizing the railroads in May 1946.
14 H. W. Brands, *American Dreams: The United States since 1945* (New York: Penguin, 2010), 68–99.
15 Gordon, *The Rise and Fall American Growth*, 379–81.
16 Greenspan and Wooldridge, *Capitalism in America*, 291–92.
17 Ellen Schrecker and Phillip Deery, *The Age of McCarthyism* (New York: St. Martin's, 2017).
18 Letter from John Higgins to Eccles, Dec. 6, 1954. Eccles Papers. Naval War College.
19 Executive Order 9981, July 26, 1948; Truman Library; https://trumanlibrary.org. The order paralleled the Democratic Party's 1948 national platform which emphasized racial and religious equality, a plank that caused many of the "Southern Dixiecrats" to bolt from the party. Kari Frederickson, *The Dixiecrat Revolt and the End of the Solid South, 1932–1968* (Chapel Hill: University of North Carolina Press, 2001).
20 Cited from Isaac Hampton II, *The Black Officer Corps: A History of Black Military Advancements from Integration through Vietnam* (New York: Routledge, 2013), 108.
21 B. Brodie, "The Influence of Mass Destruction Weapons on Strategy," Lecture to the US Army War College, Mar. 21, 1955, P-669.
22 John Howard Griffin, *Black Like Me* (New York: Signet, 1962); it appeared as a movie in 1964.
23 Terry H. Anderson, *The Movement and the Sixties: Protest in America from Greensboro to Wounded Knee* (New York: Oxford University, 1996), 43–44.
24 Paul J. Scheips, *The Role of Federal Forces in Domestic Disorders, 1945–1992* (Washington, DC: CMH, 2005), 101–36.
25 Taylor Branch, *Parting the Waters: America in the King Years, 1954–63* (New York: Simon & Schuster, 1988), 737–46, 876.
26 John H. Barnhill, "Watts Riots (1965)," in *Revolts, Protests, Demonstrations, and Rebellions in American History*, ed. Steven L. Danver, vol. 3 (Santa Barbara, CA: ABC-CLIO, 2011).
27 Gordon, *Rise and Fall of American Growth*, 415, 550.

28 Betty Friedan, *The Feminist Mystique* (New York: W. W. Norton, 1963).
29 Even the racial equality and antiwar movements of the 1960s marginalized women by discouraging them from assuming leadership roles within the movements. Susan M. Hartmann, *From Margin to Mainstream: American Women and Politics since 1960* (New York: Alfred Knopf, 1989).
30 In 1950, only 30 percent of undergraduates were women. S. J. Kleinberg, "Women in the Twentieth Century," in *The Cambridge Companion to Modern American Culture*, ed. Christopher Bigsby (Cambridge: Cambridge University Press, 2006), 205. As a whole, women in this period probably accomplished more new legislation, such as the Equal Rights Amendment, than feminists had collectively in the many decades beforehand; however, they also fought over whether to include minority women and gay women within their ranks. Sara M. Evans, *Tidal Wave: How Women Changed America at Century's End* (New York: Free Press, 2003), 61–97.
31 Kate Millett, *Sexual Politics* (Garden City, NY: Doubleday, 1970).
32 T. C. Schelling, "Strategic Analysis and Social Problems," *Social Problems* 12, 4 (Spring 1965): 367–79; "Models of Segregation," RAND RM-6014-RC, May 1969; and "Dynamic Models of Segregation," *Journal of Mathematical Sociology* 1, 2 (July 1971): 143–86.
33 Bill Warren, *Keep Watching the Skies: American Science Fiction Films of the Fifties*, 2 vols. (Jefferson, NC: McFarland, 2009); "Invasion of the Body Snatchers" was serialized in *Collier's* in 1954.
34 The title came from Robert Lindner's *Rebel Without a Cause: The Story of a Criminal Psychopath* (New York: Grune & Stratton, 1944), which defined criminal psychopaths as rebels without any cause but their own satisfaction (p. 2).
35 In 1958, Elvis was drafted into the US Army, served his obligation without major incident, and received an honorable discharge in 1960. Brian MacAllister Linn, *Elvis' Army: Cold War GIs and the Atomic Battlefield* (Cambridge, MA: Harvard University Press, 2016), 3–6, 293.
36 Adrian R. Lewis, *The American Culture of War: The History of US Military Force from World War II to Operation Enduring Freedom*, 3rd ed. (London: Routledge, 2018).
37 Timothy Leary, *Turn On, Tune In, Drop Out* (Oakland, CA: Ronin Publishing, 1965), 3–6.
38 James E. Perone, *The Music of the Counterculture Era* (Westport, CT: Greenwood Press, 2004).
39 George Q. Flynn, *The Draft, 1940–1973* (Lawrence: University Press of Kansas, 1993); Adam Garfinkle, *Telltale Hearts: The Origins and Impact of the Vietnam Antiwar Movement* (New York: St. Martin's, 1995).
40 Kyle Longley, *LBJ's 1968: Power, Politics, and the Presidency in America's Year of Upheaval* (Cambridge: Cambridge University Press, 2018); Lawrence O'Donnell, *Playing with Fire: The 1968 Election and the Transformation of American Politics* (New York: Penguin, 2017).
41 B. Brodie, ed., *The Absolute Weapon: Atomic Power and World Order* (New York: Harcourt, Brace, 1946).
42 Brodie, *Absolute Weapon*, 76.

43 Ken Booth, "Bernard Brodie," in *Makers of Nuclear Strategy*, ed. J. Baylis and J. Garnett (London: Pinters, 1991).
44 Cited from John Lewis Gaddis, *George F. Kennan: An American Life* (New York: Penguin, 2012), 233.
45 From the Latin: *Si vis pacem, para bellum*; usually attributed to the Roman military writer Flavius Vegetius Renatus.
46 Compare B. Brodie, "Impact of New Weapons on War," and "The Atomic Bomb as a Weapon," National War College Lectures, Sept. 4 and Sept. 6, 1946, respectively; "A-Bombs and Air Strategy"; "The Problem of Integrating the Factors of National Strategy"; "Air Power in an Overall Strategy"; and "Changing Capabilities in and War Objectives," Air War College Lectures, March 24, 1949; March 17, 1950; May 23, 1951; April 17, 1952; respectively. Air University Library, Maxwell AFB, Cat. Nos. M-33506-C; M-33507-C; K239.716250-12(R); K239.716251-26; and K239.716252-105, respectively. Also "Sea Power in the Atomic Age," Naval War College Lecture, Jan. 19, 1949, Cat. No. 6890-7770.
47 Brodie, "Problem of Integrating the Factors of National Strategy," 2–3.
48 Zellen, *State of Doom*, 96–97.
49 B. Brodie, "Must We Shoot from the Hip?" RAND Working Paper, Sept. 4, 1951.
50 B. Brodie, "Nuclear Weapons: Strategic or Tactical?," *Foreign Affairs* 32, 2 (Jan. 1954): 217–29 at 228.
51 Brodie, "Nuclear Weapons: Strategic or Tactical?"; and "Unlimited Weapons and Limited War," *The Reporter* 11 (Nov. 18, 1954): 16–21.
52 *Public Papers of the Presidents: Dwight D. Eisenhower, 1954* (Washington, DC: 1960), 326; www.presidency.ucsb.edu/ws/index.php?pid=10184
53 B. Brodie, *Possible U.S. Military Strategies*, Lecture Delivered at the US Army War College, March 30, 1954, published as RAND P-524, Santa Monica, April 7, 1954.
54 Brodie, "Unlimited Weapons and Limited War," 19.
55 US Congress Senate, Committee on Armed Services, *Report of Proceedings: Inquiry into the Military Situation in the Far East and the Facts Surrounding the Relief of General of the Army Douglas MacArthur from his Assignment in that Area* (Washington, DC: Ward & Paul, 1951).
56 B. Brodie, "Strategy Hits a Dead End," *Harper's Magazine* (May 1955): 33–37.
57 Brodie delivered the lectures at the Naval War College and the Army War College on Feb. 6 and Feb. 20, 1956, respectively, and at Dartmouth College in March 1956; compare B. Brodie, *Nuclear Weapons and Changing Strategic Outlooks* (Santa Monica, CA: RAND P-811, Feb. 27, 1956).
58 Brodie, *Nuclear Weapons and Changing Strategic Outlooks*, 3, 17.
59 Lecture delivered at the Command and General Staff College, Ft. Leavenworth, KS, on March 7, 1957, published as B. Brodie, *On the Worth of Principles of War* (Santa Monica, CA: RAND P-1092, May 21, 1957).
60 Published as B. Brodie, *The Meaning of Limited War* (Santa Monica, CA: RAND PM-2224, July 30, 1958).
61 Brodie, *Meaning of Limited War*, Summary.

62 Brodie, *Meaning of Limited War*, 8.
63 Michael Handel, "Clausewitz in the Age of Technology," in *Clausewitz and Modern Strategy*, ed. Michael Handel (Totowa, NJ: Frank Cass, 1986), 58–62.
64 Brodie, *War and Politics*, 1.
65 Barton C. Hacker, *Elements of Controversy: The Atomic Energy Commission and Radiation Safety in Nuclear Weapons Testing, 1947–1974* (Berkeley, CA: University of California Press, 1994).
66 Robert E. Osgood, *Limited War: The Challenge to American Strategy* (Chicago, IL: University of Chicago Press, 1957), vii. But Osgood did not consider Morgenthau's "prescriptions remotely adequate to the most serious problems of international conflict." Letter to Mr. Matthew Dever, Sept. 18, 1981. Johns Hopkins University Library Archives. Osgood Papers.
67 R. E. Osgood, *Ideals and Self-Interest in America's Foreign Relations* (Chicago, IL: University of Chicago Press, 1953); see Karl K. Schonberg, "Robert E. Osgood and the Origins of Social International Relations Theory," *International Journal* 64 (Summer 2009): 811–23.
68 B. Brodie, "Review: More About Limited War," *World Politics* 10, 1 (1957): 119.
69 Harold Stein, "Review of Robert E. Osgood, *Limited War: The Challenge to American Strategy*," *American Political Science Review* 52, 2 (June 1958): 534.
70 Albert Norman, "Review of Robert E. Osgood, *Limited War: The Challenge to American Strategy*," *Political Science Quarterly* 73, 2 (June 1958): 283.
71 Rosinski to Eccles, Sept. 5, 1958. Naval War College Special Collections.
72 Osgood, *Limited War*, 44.
73 Charles E. Heller and William A. Stofft, eds., *America's First Battles, 1776–1965* (Lawrence: University Press of Kansas, 1986).
74 Hugh Rockoff, *America's Economic Way of War: War and the US Economy from the Spanish–American War to the Persian Gulf* (Cambridge: Cambridge University Press, 2012), discusses how these costs are recouped.
75 Huntington, *Soldier and the State*; Janowitz, *The Professional Soldier*.
76 Osgood, *Limited War*, ix, 13, 28.
77 Osgood, *Limited War*, 2–3, 62–67.
78 Osgood, *Limited War*, 145, 178.
79 Compare D. Clayton James and Anne Sharp Wells, *Refighting the Last War: Command and Crisis in Korea 1950–1953* (New York: Free Press, 1993) and D. Stoker, *Why America Loses Wars: Limited War and US Strategy from the Korean War to the Present* (Cambridge: Cambridge University Press, 2019).
80 Osgood, *Limited War*, 2–3.
81 Osgood, *Limited War*, 88–95, 104, 111–13.
82 H. Kissinger, *Nuclear Weapons and Foreign Policy* (New York: Harper, 1957).
83 Kissinger, *Nuclear Weapons and Foreign Policy*, 134.
84 Kissinger, *Nuclear Weapons and Foreign Policy*, 140–41, 145.
85 Kissinger, *Nuclear Weapons and Foreign Policy*, 189–92.
86 Walter Millis, "Review of *Nuclear Weapons and Foreign Policy* by Henry A. Kissinger," *Political Science Quarterly* 72, 4 (Dec. 1957): 608.

87 Hans J. Morgenthau, "Review of *Nuclear Weapons and Foreign Policy* by Henry A. Kissinger," *American Political Science Review* 52, 3 (Sept. 1958): 842–44.
88 Brodie to Max Ascoli, editor of *The Reporter*, Sept. 6, 1957. UCLA Archives.
89 Niall Ferguson, *Kissinger 1923–1968: The Idealist* (New York: Penguin, 2015), makes this point about Kissinger's dissertation.
90 Kissinger was eventually made aware of Brodie's irritation and apologized. Kissinger to Brodie, April 25, 1958. UCLA Archives.
91 Kissinger, *Nuclear Weapons and Foreign Policy*, 440.
92 Robert McClintock, *The Meaning of Limited War: The Diplomacy of Force and the Force of Diplomacy under Pax Ballistica* (Boston, MA: Houghton Mifflin, 1967), xi.
93 McClintock, *Meaning of Limited War*, 196.
94 George K. Tanham, *Communist Revolutionary Warfare: From the Vietminh to the Viet Cong* (New York: Praeger, 1961), 121.
95 Peter Paret and John W. Shy, *Guerrillas in the 1960's*, Princeton Studies in World Politics, no. 1 (New York: Praeger, 1962), 19–20.
96 Maj.-Gen. Edward G. Lansdale, "Viet Nam: Do We Understand Revolution?" *Foreign Affairs* 43, 1 (Oct. 1964): 75–86. On Lansdale's role, see Max Boot, *The Road Not Taken: Edward Lansdale and the American Tragedy in Vietnam* (New York: W. W. Norton, 2018).
97 Lansdale, "Viet Nam," 76.
98 Douglas Pike, *Viet Cong: The Organization of the National Liberation Front of South Vietnam* (Cambridge, MA: MIT Press, 1966); and *War, Peace, and the Viet Cong* (Cambridge, MA: MIT Press, 1969).
99 George K. Tanham, *Communist Revolutionary Warfare: From the Vietminh to the Viet Cong*, 2nd ed. (New York: Praeger, 1967).
100 Lt. Col. John J. McCuen, *The Art of Counter-Revolutionary War: The Strategy of Counter-insurgency* (London: Farber, 1966).
101 McCuen, *Art of Counter-Revolutionary War*, 79–80.
102 Osgood, *Limited War*, 19–22, 15–18.
103 Osgood, *Limited War*, 24.
104 R. E. Osgood, *Limited War Revisited* (Boulder, CO: Westview, 1979).
105 Osgood, *Limited War Revisited*, iii. He addressed the four main explanations for US failure at the time: (1) politically and socially, the government in Saigon was too vulnerable to insurgency and could not be saved without the excessive costs of a massive intervention and the likelihood of turning Vietnam into a US protectorate; (2) the US military was not trained or equipped to fight an insurgency, and thus transformed the war into a conventional, attrition-based conflict the American public would not support; (3) incremental expansion of the war was inefficient militarily and fatal politically; and (4) US national interests were not compelling enough to justify the scale and duration of effort necessary to win. Osgood, *Limited War Revisited*, 34–37.
106 Brodie had debunked the domino theory in 1973. Brodie, *War and Politics*, 144–53.
107 Osgood, *Limited War Revisited*, 30.

108 Dominic Tierney, *How We Fight: Crusades, Quagmires, and the American Way of War* (New York: Little, Brown, 2010).
109 Kissinger, *Nuclear Weapons and Foreign Policy*, 171.

Chapter 4

1 Lawrence Freedman, ed., *Strategic Coercion: Concepts and Cases* (Oxford: Oxford University Press, 1998); and Daniel Byman and Matthew Waxman, *The Dynamics of Coercion: American Foreign Policy and the Limits of Military Might* (Cambridge: Cambridge University Press, 2002).
2 Letter to Faye B. Schmidt, Yale University Press, Feb. 14, 1966. Brodie Papers. UCLA Archives.
3 Schelling to Brodie, Dec. 18, 1964, and Sept. 12, 1965. Brodie Papers. UCLA Archives. T. C. Schelling, *Arms and Influence* (New Haven, CT: Yale University Press, 1966), preface.
4 On Schelling's use of memoirs, see Robert Ayson's definitive *Thomas Schelling and the Nuclear Age: Strategy as Social Science* (New York: Frank Cass, 2004).
5 Thomas C. Shelling, "An Essay on Bargaining," *American Economic Review* 46, 3 (June 1956): 281–301; and "Bargaining, Communication, and Limited War," *Journal of Conflict Resolution* 1, 1 (Mar. 1957): 19–36.
6 Colin S. Gray, "What RAND Hath Wrought," *Foreign Policy* 4 (Autumn 1971): 111–29.
7 Brodie's Letter to Schelling, dated Jan. 9, 1957. Brodie Papers. UCLA Archives.
8 Thomas C. Schelling, "Strategy of Conflict: Prospectus for a Reorientation of Game Theory," *Journal of Conflict Resolution* 2, 3 (Sept. 1958): 203–64; on game theory, see Lawrence Freedman, *The Evolution of Nuclear Strategy*, 3rd ed. (London: Palgrave Macmillan, 2003), 171–78.
9 Fred Kaplan, *Wizards of Armageddon* (New York: Simon & Schuster, 1983), 332–35. H. R. McMaster (*Dereliction of Duty: Lyndon Johnson, Robert McNamara, the Joint Chiefs of Staff, and the Lies that Led to Vietnam* [New York: Harper, 1998], 226–42) discusses the planning and goals of Rolling Thunder.
10 Robert A. Pape, *Bombing to Win: Air Power and Coercion in War* (Ithaca, NY: Cornell University Press, 1996), 177–95; Kaplan, *Wizards*, 460–61; and Fred Kaplan, "All Pain, No Gain," *Slate*, Oct. 11, 2005. Robert Dodge, in *The Strategist: The Life and Times of Thomas Schelling* (Hollis, NH: Hollis Publications, 2006), 115–21, challenges Kaplan's interpretation.
11 Nobel Prize Laureates, "Thomas C. Schelling – Biographical," www.nobelprize.org; and Dodge, *Strategist*, 157–58. Kissinger's biographer suggested the event served as an "insurance policy" for Schelling and others against Harvard reprisals; Ferguson, *Kissinger 1923–1968*, 16.
12 Interview in Richard Swedberg, *Economics and Sociology: Redefining their Boundaries: Conversations with Economists and Sociologists* (Princeton, NJ: Princeton University Press, 1990), 189.

13 T. C. Schelling, *The Strategy of Conflict* (Cambridge, MA: Harvard University Press, 1960); and *Arms and Influence*.
14 Roger B. Myerson, "Learning from Schelling's Strategy of Conflict," *Journal of Economic Literature* 47, 4 (Dec. 2009): 1109–25.
15 Osgood, *Limited War Revisited*, 110, n. 5.
16 Brodie to Schelling, Oct. 9, 1964. Brodie Papers. UCLA Archives.
17 Brodie to Schelling, Jan. 8, 1965. Brodie Papers. UCLA Archives.
18 Schelling to Brodie, Dec. 18, 1964. Brodie Papers. UCLA Archives.
19 Schelling, *Strategy of Conflict*, 5–6, 21–22, and 15; emphasis original. He was also rightly criticized for not considering decision logic in terms of organizational or social behavior. See Allan D. Coult, "Review of *The Strategy of Conflict* by Thomas C. Schelling," *American Anthropologist* 64, 3, Part 1 (June 1962): 686–87; Robert L. Bishop, "Review of *The Strategy of Conflict* by Thomas C. Schelling," *American Economic Review* 51, 4 (Sept. 1961): 674–76; and E. D. Carter "Review of *The Strategy of Conflict* by Thomas C. Schelling," *International Affairs* 38, 2 (Apr. 1962): 234.
20 Schelling, *Strategy of Conflict*, 22; T. C. Schelling, "The Reciprocal Fear of Surprise Attack," RAND P-1342, Apr. 16, 1958, p. 1.
21 Schelling, *Arms and Influence*, 215–19.
22 Schelling, *Arms and Influence*, 215–16.
23 Schelling, *Arms and Influence*, 2–3, 16, 34.
24 Schelling, *Arms and Influence*, 5; emphasis original.
25 Schelling, *Arms and Influence*, 80, 70–71; emphasis original.
26 Keith B. Payne, *The Great American Gamble: Deterrence Theory and Practice from the Cold War to the Twenty-first Century* (Fairfax, VA: National Institute, 2008); Lawrence Freedman, *Deterrence* (Cambridge: Polity, 2004); Patrick Morgan, *Deterrence Now* (Cambridge: Cambridge University Press, 2003).
27 T. C. Schelling, "Controlled Response and Strategic Warfare," *Adelphi Paper* 19 (London: Institute for Strategic Studies, 1965).
28 Brodie to Schelling, Oct. 9, 1964. Brodie Papers. UCLA Archives.
29 Succinctly captured in Freedman, *Deterrence*, 43–45.
30 T. C. Schelling, "Strategic Analysis and Social Problems," *Social Problems* 12, 4 (Spring 1965): 367–79.
31 Dodge, *The Strategist*, 121; cf. Robert S. McNamara, James Blight, Robert K. Brigham, Thomas J. Biersteker, and Col. Herbert Schandler, *Argument without End: In Search of Answers to the Vietnam Tragedy* (New York: Perseus Books, 1999), 170.
32 Schelling, *Arms and Influence*, 69–76; Peter Viggo Jakobsen, "The Strategy of Coercive Diplomacy: Refining Existing Theory to Post-Cold War Realities," in Lawrence Freedman, ed., *Strategic Coercion: Concepts and Cases* (Oxford: Oxford University Press, 1998), 66.
33 Compare James Gleick, *Chaos: Making a New Science* (New York: Penguin, 1988); M. Mitchell Waldrop, *Complexity: The Emerging Science at the Edge of Order and Chaos* (New York: Touchstone, 1993); Stephen F. Kellert, *In the Wake of Chaos* (Chicago, IL: University of Chicago Press, 1993). Newton himself was evidently opposed to the clockwork analogy: Jean F. Drew, "Newton vs. the Clockwork Universe," July 19, 2004; www.freerepublic.com/focus/f-news/1174268/posts

34 Compare T. C. Schelling, "Managing the Arms Race," in *Problems of National Security*, ed. H. Kissinger (New York: Praeger, 1965), 361–75; "The Role of Communication in Arms Control," in *First Steps to Disarmament*, ed. E. Luard (London: Thames & Hudson, 1965), 201–25; "A Framework of the Evaluation of Arms-Control Proposals," *Daedalus* 104, 3 (Summer 1975): 187–200; "What Went Wrong with Arms Control?" *Foreign Affairs* 64, 2 (Winter 1985/86): 219–33.
35 T. C. Schelling, "Strategic Analysis and Social Problems," *Social Problems* 12, 4 (1965): 367–79.
36 T. C. Schelling, "Economics and Criminal Enterprises," *The Public Interest* 7 (Spring 1967): 61–78.
37 T.C. Schelling, "What Is the Business of Organized Crime?" *The American Scholar* 40, 4 (Autumn 1971): 643–52.
38 T. C. Schelling, "The Cost of Combating Global Warming," *Foreign Affairs* 76, 6 (Nov./Dec. 1997): 8–14.

Chapter 5

1 Herman Kahn, *On Thermonuclear War* (Princeton, NJ: Princeton University Press, 1960); *Thinking about the Unthinkable* (Princeton, NJ: Princeton University Press, 1962); and *On Escalation* (New York: Praeger, 1965).
2 B. Bruce-Briggs, *Supergenius: The Mega-Worlds of Herman Kahn* (New York: North American Policy, 2000), 398, n. 1.
3 Bruce-Briggs, *Supergenius*, 12.
4 Fellow RAND employee, Andrew Marshall, one of the Pentagon's most iconic figures, was the best man at Kahn's wedding to Heilner; Bruce-Briggs, *Supergenius*, 31.
5 Herman Kahn and Irwin Mann, *Game Theory*, P-1166, RAND Corporation, July 30, 1957; *War Gaming*, P-1167, RAND Corporation, July 30, 1957; *Techniques of Systems Analysis*, RAND RM 1829-1, June 1957; and *Ten Common Pitfalls*, RAND RM 1937, July 17, 1957.
6 Sharon Gamrami-Tabrizi, "Simulating the Unthinkable: Gaming War in the 1950s and 1960s," *Social Studies of Science* 30, 2 (Apr. 2000): 163–223.
7 *Newsweek*, Oct. 9, 1961.
8 National Defense University Library, Herman Kahn Archives. Box 4.
9 Lewis Sorely, *A Better War* (New York: Harcourt Brace, 1999), 123.
10 W. B. McDermott, "Thinking about Herman Kahn," *Journal of Conflict Resolution* 15, 1 (Mar. 1971): 55–70.
11 Cited from Alex Abella, *Soldiers of Reason: The RAND Corporation and the Rise of the American Empire* (Orlando, FL: Mariner Books, 2009), 103.
12 Sharon Gamrami-Tabrizi, *The Worlds of Herman Kahn: The Intuitive Science of Thermonuclear War* (Cambridge, MA: Harvard University Press, 2005), 21.
13 Abella, *Soldiers of Reason*, interview of Roberta Wohlstetter, 101.
14 Ghamari-Tabrizi, *Worlds of Herman Kahn*, 208.
15 Kahn, *On Thermonuclear War*, 3.
16 Kahn, *On Thermonuclear War*, 126–27.

17 The term finite deterrence appears to have been first used in 1959; Paul Backus, Commander, USN, "Finite Deterrence, Controlled Escalation," *Proceedings* (Mar. 1959): 23–29; William Burr, ed., "How Much is Enough? The US Navy and 'Finite' Deterrence," May 1, 2009; https://nsarchive2.gwu.edu//nukevault/ebb275/index.htm
18 Gerard C. Smith, Director Policy Planning Staff, to John Foster Dulles, Secretary of State, Review of Strategic Concept, Memorandum, Jan. 20, 1959. Record Group 59, Dept. of State Participation in Operations Coordinating Board and National Security Council, 1947–63, Box 95, NSC 5810.
19 Kahn, *On Thermonuclear War*, 15; emphasis original.
20 Daniel Ellsberg, *Doomsday Machine: Confessions of a Nuclear War Planner* (New York: Bloomsbury, 2017).
21 Kahn, *On Thermonuclear War*, 556; emphasis original.
22 Albert Wohlstetter, "The Delicate Balance of Terror," P-1472 RAND, Nov. 6, 1958; rev. Dec. 1958; and "The Delicate Balance of Terror," *Foreign Affairs* 37, 2 (Jan. 1959): 211–34.
23 On the dispute between Brodie and Wohlstetter, see Ron Robin, *The Cold World They Made: The Strategic Legacy of Roberta and Albert Wohlstetter* (Cambridge, MA: Harvard University Press, 2016), 79–111.
24 Kahn, *On Thermonuclear War*, 560.
25 For more see Robert Zarate and Henry Sokolski, eds., *Nuclear Heuristics: Selected Writings of Albert and Roberta Wohlstetter* (Carlisle Barracks, PA: US Army War College, SSI, 2009).
26 Warren Kozak, *Curtis LeMay: Strategist and Tactician* (Washington, DC: Regnery, 2014), 311–12.
27 Christopher Hollis, "Dr. Strangelove and Dr. Kahn," *The Spectator* 28 (1964), 11, mocked the comparison and outlined the many ways in which the two differed.
28 Bruce-Briggs, *Supergenius*, 184.
29 For more on this genre see Si Sheppard, "Atomic Cinema: Nuclear Proliferation and Deterrence Theory as Refracted through the Camera Lens," 31–59; www.filmint.nu
30 Kahn, *On Escalation*, 47.
31 Cited from Freedman, *Evolution of Nuclear Strategy*, 227.
32 Kahn, *On Thermonuclear War*, 145; emphasis original.
33 Kahn, *On Thermonuclear War*, 148.
34 Kahn, *On Thermonuclear War*, 152.
35 Kahn, *On Thermonuclear War*, 285.
36 Kahn, *On Thermonuclear War*, 287.
37 Kahn, *Thinking about the Unthinkable*, 185.
38 Kahn, *Thinking about the Unthinkable*, 57.
39 Kahn, *Thinking about the Unthinkable*, NSPP-02-29 (p. 109).
40 Kahn, *Thinking about the Unthinkable*, 178.
41 Kahn, *Thinking about the Unthinkable*, 202.
42 Roberta Wohlstetter, *Pearl Harbor: Warning and Decision* (Stanford, CA: Stanford University Press, 1962); the book won the Bancroft Prize in 1963.

43 Wohlstetter, *Pearl Harbor*, 400–01.
44 Roberta Wohlstetter, "Cuba and Pearl Harbor: Hindsight and Foresight," *Foreign Affairs* 43, 4 (July 1965): 691–707.
45 Wohlstetter, "Cuba and Pearl Harbor," 707.
46 Kahn, *On Escalation*, 39.
47 Kahn, *On Escalation*, 3.
48 Kahn, *On Escalation*, 6–7; Morton H. Halperin, *Limited War in the Nuclear Age* (New York: John Wiley, 1963), 3.
49 Kahn, *On Escalation*, 38.
50 Kahn, *On Escalation*, 74.
51 Kahn, *On Escalation*, 40.
52 Brodie, *Escalation and the Nuclear Option*, 103–10.
53 Kahn, *On Escalation*, 45.
54 Schelling to Brodie, Dec. 18, 1964. Brodie Papers. UCLA Archives.
55 Kahn, *On Escalation*, 217.
56 Kahn and Mann, *Ten Common Pitfalls*.
57 Forrest E. Morgan, et al., *Dangerous Thresholds: Managing Escalation in the Twenty-First Century* (Santa Monica: RAND, 2008), 7.
58 H. Kahn, "If Negotiations Fail," *Foreign Affairs* 46, 4 (July 1968): 627–41; see also Frank E. Armbruster et al., *Can We Win in Vietnam? The American Dilemma* (London: Pall Mall, 1968).
59 Sir Robert Thompson, "Squaring the Error," *Foreign Affairs* 46, 3 (Apr. 1968): 442–53.
60 H. Kahn and Garrett N. Scalera, "A Strategy for Vietnamization: A Discussion Paper" (Croton-on-Hudson, NY: Hudson Institute, Aug. 5, 1969), 15.
61 Rita James Simon, *Public Opinion in America: 1936–1970* (Chicago, IL: Rand McNally, 1974), 179.
62 H. Kahn and Anthony Wiener, eds., *American Values: Past and Future*, vol. I, *Values, Attitudes, and Life-Styles in a Changing World* (Croton-on-Hudson, NY: Hudson Institute, Dec. 31, 1974).
63 Kahn and Wiener, *American Values*, "Chapter X Values and the Quality of American Life," 28–30.
64 W. W. Rostow, *The Stages of Economic Growth: A Non-Communist Manifesto* (Cambridge: Cambridge University Press, 1960).
65 Montgomery McFate, *Military Anthropology: Soldiers, Scholars and Subjects at the Margins of Empire* (London: Hurst, 2018), 279–83.
66 Osgood, *Limited War*, 25–26.

Chapter 6

1 H. E. Eccles, "Military Theory and Education: A Working Paper," Nov. 1, 1962.
2 Interview with Rear Adm. Henry E. Eccles, USN (Ret.) by Anthony Nicolosi, Oral History Program, Naval War College, Newport, RI, Part 2, Jan. 13, 1977, p. 3.

3 John B. Hattendorf, B. Mitchell Simpson III, and John R. Wadleigh, *Sailors and Scholars: The Centennial History of the US Naval War College* (Newport, RI: Naval War College, 1984), 186.
4 Evelyn M. Cherpak, Register of the Papers of Henry E. Eccles, Series No. 6, 2nd ed., Naval War College, Newport, RI, 1988, pp. 4–5; and Interview Eccles, Part 4, June 14, 1977, p. 28.
5 S. A. Boorman, "The Legacy of Henry Eccles," *Naval War College Review* 62, 2 (Spring 2009): 91–116; K. O'Brien, "Logistics Pioneer: Rear Admiral Henry E. Eccles," *Air Force Journal of Logistics* 34, 1–2 (2010): 74–77; C. Paparone and G. L. Topic, Jr., "The 'Clausewitz' of Logistics: Henry E. Eccles," *Army Sustainment* (Jan.–Feb. 2014): 9.
6 Eccles, "Military Theory and Education: A Working Paper," 10.
7 H. E. Eccles, *Operational Naval Logistics* (Washington, DC: Bureau of Naval Personnel, 1950); for his early thoughts see "Pacific Logistics" and "Basic Elements and Aspects of Logistics," lectures delivered at the Naval War College on Mar. 30, 1946, and Aug. 27, 1947, respectively.
8 H. E. Eccles, *Logistics in the National Defense* (Harrisburg, PA: Stackpole, 1959), 12.
9 Eccles, *Logistics in National Defense*, 13.
10 Eccles, *Logistics in National Defense*, 14–15.
11 Eccles, *Logistics in National Defense*, 15.
12 Gordon B. Turner, "The Nature of War, Lecture Delivered at the Naval War College on Oct. 17, 1955," *Naval War College Review* 8, 7 (Mar. 1956): 25–43; Turner had served in the US Army during the Second World War.
13 Hiram M. Stout, "The Nature of Military Strategy, Lecture Delivered at the Naval War College on October 18, 1955," *Naval War College Review* 8, 7 (Mar. 1956): 45–61; Stout had served in the G-2, War Department General Staff, during the Second World War.
14 J. A. Huston, "The Theory and Principles of War, Lecture Delivered at the Naval War College on Aug. 26, 1959," *Naval War College Review* 12, 4 (Dec. 1959): 19–35.
15 B. Brodie, "Strategy as an Art and a Science, Delivered at the Naval War College on Sept. 18, 1958," *Naval War College Review* 11, 6 (Feb. 1959): 1–20; R. E. Osgood, "Concepts of General and Limited War, Delivered at the Naval War College on Sept. 18, 1959," *Naval War College Review* 12, 4 (Dec. 1959): 1–18.
16 Richard H. Sanger, "The Age of Sociopolitical Change," *Naval War College Review* 22, 2 (Oct. 1969): 16.
17 Gregory A. Daddis, *Westmoreland's War: Reassessing American Strategy in Vietnam* (New York: Oxford University, 2014), 30–31.
18 Boyd L. Dastrup, *The US Army Command and General Staff College: A Centennial History* (Manhattan, KS: Sun Flower, 1982), 110.
19 US Army Command and General Staff College Circular No. 9, June 20, 1961. My thanks to Gregory Daddis for passing along this memo and other pertinent materials.

20 James K. Libbey, *Alexander P. De Seversky and the Quest for Air Power* (Washington, DC: Potomac, 2013); Phillip S. Meilinger, "Alexander P. De Seversky," *Air & Space Power Journal* 16, 4 (2002): 8–23.
21 Alexander P. de Seversky, "A Lecture on Air Power, Part I," *Air University Quarterly Review* 1, 2 (Fall 1947): 25–26, 40; "A Lecture on Air Power, Part II," *Air University Quarterly Review* 1, 3 (Fall 1947): 26–41; and *Air Power: Key to Survival* (New York: Simon and Schuster, 1950).
22 https://hrc.contentdm.oclc.org/digital/collection/p15878coll90/id/41/rec/4
23 LTC Joseph L. Dickman, USAF, "Douhet and the Future," *Air University Quarterly Review* 2, 1 (1948): 3–15; B. Brodie, "The Heritage of Douhet," *Air University Quarterly Review* 6, 2 (1953): 64–69.
24 Col. T. H. Curtis, USAF, "USAF Officer Education in Counterinsurgency," *Air University Review* 18, 2 (Jan.–Feb. 1967): 67–69.
25 Col. Albert P. Sights, Jr., "Limited War for Unlimited Goals," *Air University Quarterly Review* 13, 3 (Spring 1962): 38–48, which cited Brodie directly; Lt.-Col. T. C. Pinckney, "Thoughts on the Limitation of War," *Air University Review* 20, 2 (Jan.–Feb. 1969): 79–83.
26 H. E. Eccles, *Military Concepts and Philosophy* (New Brunswick, NJ: Rutgers University Press, 1965).
27 Eccles, *Military Concepts and Philosophy*, vi, 26–27.
28 H. E. Eccles, "Suez 1956 – Some Military Lessons," *Naval War College Review* 21, 7 (Mar. 1969): 28–55.
29 Eccles, *Military Concepts and Philosophy*, 18; a point he continued to emphasize years later: H. E. Eccles, "The Dangers of 'Weapons Strategy," *Christian Science Monitor*, Oct. 1, 1981.
30 Eccles, *Military Concepts and Philosophy*, 9, 8.
31 Capt. Robert P. Beebe, USN, "Military Decision from the Viewpoint of Game Theory," *Naval War College Review* 10, 2 (Oct. 1957): 27–56.
32 E[rwin] Baumgarten, "Game Theory: Lecture, 12 Dec. 1960," *Naval War College Review* 13, 9 (May 1961): 16–41; and "Strategic War Gaming: Lecture, 16 Feb. 1961," *Naval War College Review* 13, 10 (June 1961): 1–22.
33 Herbert Glazer, "Limited War Gaming: Lecture, 19 Jan. 1965," *Naval War College Review* 17, 7 (Mar. 1965): 29–44.
34 Eccles, *Military Concepts and Philosophy*, 314–15, n. 12.
35 Sir Solly Zuckerman, "Judgment and Control in Modern War," *Foreign Affairs* 40, 2 (Jan. 1962): 196–212.
36 Eccles, *Military Concepts and Philosophy*, 28; H. E. Eccles, "Logistics and Strategy: Lecture, 2 Jan. 1962," *Naval War College Review* 14, 6 (Mar. 1962): 15–30.
37 Eccles, *Military Concepts and Philosophy*, 83–94; Eccles, "Logistics and Strategy," 23–24.
38 H. E. Eccles, "Military Theory and Education: The Need for and Nature of," *Naval War College Review* 21, 6 (Feb. 1965): 70–79.
39 Nicholas Prime, "The Making of the Control School of Strategy: Joseph C. Wylie, Henry Eccles, and Herbert Rosinski at the US Naval War College 1950–1974," Diss. for Degree of Doctor of Philosophy, Kings College, London, 2017.

40 Evelyn M. Cherpak, Register of the Papers of Herbert Rosinski, Series No. 17 (Newport, RI: Naval War College, 1988), 1–4.
41 Prime, *Control School*, 49; Richard P. Stebbins, *The Career of Herbert Rosinski: An Intellectual Pilgrimage* (New York: Lang, 1989), 10.
42 H. Rosinski, "Scharnhorst to Schlieffen: The Rise and Decline of German Military Thought," *Naval War College Review* (1976): 83–103.
43 Eccles, *Military Concepts and Philosophy*, 46–47, 313, n. 4; emphasis original; H. E. Eccles, "Strategy: The Essence of Professionalism," *Naval War College Review* 24, 4 (Dec. 1971): 43–51.
44 Eccles, *Military Concepts and Philosophy*, 47–49.
45 Brodie, *Layman's Guide to Naval Strategy*, 4 emphasis original; 84.
46 H. E. Eccles, *Military Power in a Free Society* (Newport, RI: Naval War College, 1979).
47 Eccles, *Military Power in a Free Society*, vii–xv; H. E. Eccles, "Strategy – The Theory and Application," *Naval War College Review* 32, 3 (May–June 1979), 18–19, American Political Science Association Conference 1978.
48 Eccles, *Military Power in a Free Society*, 160–62.
49 Eccles, *Military Power in a Free Society*, 148–49, 158.
50 Lieut.-Cdr. Theodore T. Leber, Jr., USNR, "The Genesis of Antimilitarism on the College Campus: A Contemporary Case Study of Student Protest," *Naval War College Review* 23, 3 (Nov. 1970): 48–99.
51 Urban Research Corporation, *Student Protest 1969 Summary* (Chicago, IL, 1970).
52 Ens. William F. Averyt, USNR, "The Philosophy of the Counterculture," *Naval War College Review* 23, 7 (Mar. 1971): 17–25.
53 Leber, "Antimilitarism," 94.
54 Neil Sheehan, "The Role of the Press," *Naval War College Review* 23, 6 (Feb. 1971): 4–7, introductory remarks to a panel discussion on "Communication Media" at the Naval War College.
55 Neil Sheehan, "The Press and the Pentagon Papers," *Naval War College Review* 24, 6 (Feb. 1972): 8–12.
56 Eccles, *Military Power in a Free Society*, 164–66.
57 James Clodfelter, "Vacillation and Stability in American Public Opinion toward Military and Foreign Policy," *Naval War College Review* 23, 6 (Feb. 1971): 55–61.
58 Lloyd A. Free, "Political Beliefs and Public Opinion," *Naval War College Review* 23, 7 (Mar. 1971): 4–16.

Chapter 7

1 J. C. Wylie, *Military Strategy: A General Theory of Power Control* (New Brunswick, NJ: Rutgers University Press, 1967).
2 Wylie, *Military Strategy*, 124.
3 Cited from J. B. Hattendorf, "Introduction," in Wylie, *Military Strategy*, x.
4 Interview of Rear-Adm. Joseph C. Wylie, USN (Ret.) by Dr. Evelyn M. Cherpak, Oral History Program, Naval War College, Newport, RI, 4 Parts; Part 1, Nov. 21, 1985, pp. 1–5.

5 American Merchant Marine at War, www.usmm.org
6 Interview of Wylie, Part 2, Dec. 17, 1985.
7 Interview of Wylie, Part 3, Jan. 15, 1986.
8 Jeffery G. Barlow, *The Revolt of the Admirals: The Fight for Naval Aviation, 1945–1950* (Washington, DC: Potomac, 2001).
9 E. V. Converse III, *History of Acquisition in the Department of Defense*, vol. 1, *Rearming for the Cold War* (Washington, DC: Historical Office, OSD, 2012), 324. The B-36 become obsolete in the mid-1950s due to advances in jet propulsion and radar.
10 Letter from J. C. "Caldwell" Wylie to Rosinski, March 19, 1951. Rosinski Papers. Naval War College Archives.
11 Interview of Wylie, Part 3, pp. 148–51.
12 J. B. Hattendorf, "Introduction," in J. C. Wylie, *Military Strategy* (Annapolis, MD: Naval Institute, 1989), xxxi.
13 Interview of Wylie, Part 4, Jan. 22, 1986.
14 Interview of Wylie, Part. 4, pp. 205–06. Whether Wylie and Holtoner, in fact, made these recommendations is difficult to establish given the lack of documentary evidence.
15 Brodie, *War and Politics*, 5.
16 J. C. Wylie, "The Navy's Reasons for Being – An Abortive Effort to Evaluate," A-2; declassified in 1982. Naval War College Special Collections, Archives Division, Newport, RI.
17 Edward J. Marolda, ed., *The US Navy in the Korean War* (Annapolis, MD: Naval Institute Press, 2013).
18 Wylie, "Navy's Reasons for Being," K-2.
19 Wylie, "Navy's Reasons for Being," B-3.
20 www.trumanlibrary.org/whistlestop/study_collections/coldwar/documents/pdf/10-1.pdf; reprinted in S. Nelson Drew, ed., *NSC-68: Forging the Strategy of Containment*, analyses by Paul H. Nitze (Washington, DC: NDU, 1996); Paul Nitze in Record of the State-Defense Policy Group Meeting, March 10, 1950, *Foreign Relations of the United States*, vol. I (Washington, DC: GPO, 1977), 195; cited from Drew, *NSC-68*, 4.
21 J. C. Wylie, Jr., "Maritime Strategy," staff presentation, Sept. 11, 1952, Naval War College Special Collections, Archives Division; rev. and publ. as "On Maritime Strategy," *Proceedings* 79, 5 (May 1953): 467–77. Compare B. Brodie, "Characteristics of a Sound Strategy," *Naval War College Review* 4, 10 (June 1952): 65–82.
22 Wylie, "Maritime Strategy," 1.
23 Wylie, "Maritime Strategy," 3.
24 Wylie, "Maritime Strategy," 476.
25 J. C. Wylie, "Historical and Contemporary Theories of Strategy," Aug. 17, 1965. Naval War College Special Collection, Archives Division, Newport, RI.
26 Wylie, "Historical and Contemporary Theories of Strategy," 5, 8.
27 On the Strategic Hamlet Program, see Office of the Secretary of Defense, Vietnam Task Force, *United States–Vietnam Relations, 1945–67*, Part IV, B, 2; on its failure: Andrew F. Krepinevich, Jr., *The Army and Vietnam* (Baltimore, MD: Johns Hopkins, 1986), 66–69, 82–87, 90, 215–16.
28 Wylie, "Historical and Contemporary Theories of Strategy," 16, 20.

29 Wylie, *Military Strategy*, 72, italics original; 77–78.
30 Matheny, *Carrying the War to the Enemy*, 53–54.
31 Wylie, *Military Strategy*, 77.
32 J. C. Wylie, "Why a Sailor Thinks Like a Sailor," *Proceedings* 83, 8 (Aug. 1957): 811–17.
33 Wylie, "Why a Sailor Thinks Like a Sailor," 812–13.
34 Wylie, *Military Strategy*, 78–80; Wylie drew heavily from two of Liddell Hart's more problematic works: *A Greater than Napoleon: Scipio Africanus* (London: W. Blackwood, 1926); and *Sherman: Soldier, Realist, American* (New York: Dodd Mead, 1929); see Albert Castel, "Liddell Hart's Sherman: Propaganda as History," *Journal of Military History* 67, 2 (Apr. 2003): 405–26.
35 Wylie, *Military Strategy*, 117–21.
36 J. C. Wylie, "Reflections on the War in the Pacific," *Proceedings* 78, 4 (Apr. 1952): 351–61, esp. 360.
37 Wylie, *Military Strategy*, 22; Lawrence Freedman, *Strategy: A History* (New York: Oxford University Press, 2013), 195; L. Milevski, "Revisiting J. C. Wylie's Dichotomy of Strategy: The Effects of Sequential and Cumulative Patterns of Operations," *Journal of Strategic Studies* 35, 2 (2012): 223–42.
38 H. W. Brands, *The General vs the President: MacArthur and Truman at the Brink of Nuclear War* (New York: Anchor Books, 2016), 73–88.
39 Wylie, *Military Strategy*, 67–68.
40 Wylie, *Military Strategy*, 69–71.
41 Wylie, *Military Strategy*, 11, 29.
42 Wylie, *Military Strategy*, 31.

Chapter 8

1 H. G. Summers, *On Strategy: The Vietnam War in Context* (Carlisle, PA: SSI, 1981); reprinted one year later as *On Strategy: A Critical Analysis of the Vietnam War* (Novato, CA: Presidio, 1982); hereafter, *On Strategy*.
2 Summers, *On Strategy*, 1.
3 Converse III, *Rearming for the Cold War*, 138.
4 David T. Zabecki, "Harry Summers Obituary," www.clausewitz.com/readings/SummersObitText.htm
5 The conversation reportedly took place on April 25, 1975, with Col. Tu of the NVA. *On Strategy* 1, 7 n. 1.
6 *Study on Military Professionalism* (Carlisle Barracks, PA: US Army War College, 1970), v, 15.
7 R. M. Swain, "Filling the Void: The Operational Art and the US Army," in *The Operational Art: Developments in the Theories of War*, ed. B. J. C. McKercher and Michael A. Hennessy (Westport, CT: Praeger, 1996), 156–57.
8 LTG John H. Cushman, US Army (Ret.), *Oral History*, 6 vols., vol. 2, 1951–1963, p. 60.
9 Electronic interview with Col. R. M. Swain, US Army (Ret.), May 2018.
10 Memorandum from Col. Charles F. Kriete, Aug. 4, 1980. Summers Papers. AHEC Archives.

11 Summers, *On Strategy*, 13.
12 W. S. Lind to H. G. Summers, Jr., Oct. 3, 1980. Summers Papers. AHEC Archives.
13 H. G. Summers, Jr. to W. S. Lind, Oct. 27, 1980. Summer Papers. AHEC Archives.
14 Michael Howard to H. G. Summers, Jr., Nov. 3, 1980. Summers Papers. AHEC Archives.
15 Summers to Lind, Oct. 27, 1980. AHEC Archives.
16 David G. Marr, "Review of *On Strategy* by Harry G. Summers," *Pacific Affairs* 56, 3 (Autumn 1983): 594–95.
17 Eliot Cohen, "Review of *On Strategy*," *Commentary* 74, 1 (July 1982): 84–86.
18 Summers, *On Strategy*, 4.
19 Summers, *On Strategy*, 55, 57–59.
20 "Harry Summers Interview: Conversations with History;" Institute of International Studies, UC Berkeley, March 6, 1996, p. 2; http://globetrotter.berkeley.edu/conversations/Summers/summers1.html
21 Summers, *On Strategy*, 63; War Dept., *FM 100-5. Operations* (Washington, DC: GPO, 1939), 27; emphasis original.
22 Summers, *On Strategy*, 64–65; US Congress, Senate Committee on Armed Services, *Report of Proceedings: Inquiry into the Military Situation in the Far East and the Facts Surrounding the Relief of General of the Army Douglas MacArthur from his Assignment in that Area* (Washington, DC: Ward & Paul, 1951).
23 Summers, *On Strategy*, 66; Dept. Army, *FM 100-5: Operations* (Washington, DC: GPO, 1954), 7.
24 Summers, *On Strategy*, 68–69; compare Edward Luttwak, *Grand Strategy of the Roman Empire* (Baltimore, MD: Johns Hopkins, 1976), 41–42.
25 Maxwell Taylor, *The Uncertain Trumpet* (New York: Harper & Row, 1960), 26.
26 Ingo Trauschweizer, *Maxwell Taylor's Cold War: From Berlin to Vietnam* (Lexington: University Press of Kentucky, 2019), 88.
27 Cushman, *Oral History*, vol. 6, p. 11.
28 Dept. Army, *FM 100-5. Operations* (Washington, DC: GPO, 1962), 5–6; emphasis original.
29 *FM 100-5* (1962), 4–5.
30 Summers, *On Strategy*, 13.
31 Walter LaFeber, "The Rise and Fall of Colin Powell and the Powell Doctrine," *Political Science Quarterly* 124, 1 (Spring 2009): 71–93; J. J. Carafano, *The Army Reserves and the Abrams Doctrine: Unfulfilled Promise, Uncertain Future* (Washington, DC: Heritage, 2005).
32 VK, 212; OW, 88.
33 Summers, *On Strategy*, 83.
34 Summers, *On Strategy*, 71; compare Chalmers Johnson, *Autopsy on People's War* (Berkeley: University of California Press, 1973), 44.
35 "Harry Summers Interview," p. 3.
36 Summers, *On Strategy*, 84–85.
37 Summers, *On Strategy*, 90.
38 Edwin E. Moise, *The Myths of Tet: The Most Misunderstood Event of the Vietnam War* (Lawrence: University Press of Kansas, 2017), 164–78;

Gregory A. Daddis, *No Sure Victory: Measuring US Army Effectiveness and Progress in the Vietnam War* (Oxford: Oxford University Press, 2011), 175.
39 Sir Robert Thompson, "Squaring the Error," *Foreign Affairs* 46, 3 (Apr. 1968): 442–53.
40 Lien-Hang T. Nguyen, *Hanoi's War: An International History of the War for Peace in Vietnam* (Charlotte: University of North Carolina, 2016), 89–91.
41 Douglas Pike, "Guerrilla Warfare in Vietnam," in Interdoc Conference, *Guerrilla Warfare in Asia* (The Hague: International Documentation and Information Center, 1971), 82–83; Johnson, *Autopsy on People's War*, 51.
42 William J. Duiker, *Ho Chi Minh* (New York: Hyperion, 2000), 531–61.
43 "Harry Summers Interview," 1.
44 Letter from H. G. Summers Jr to R. S. LeVieux, July 8, 1982; LeVieux authored "Strategy Is What?" (found in the Summers archives).
45 *Dictionary of Military and Associated Terms*, JCS Pub 1 (Washington, DC: GPO, 1979), 217.
46 Summers, *On Strategy*, 91.
47 AHEC Archives.
48 Maj. Edward S. Johnston, "A Science of War," *Command and General Staff School Quarterly* XIV, 53 (June 1934): 91–124, 104–41, here 121. Johnston won three silver stars in the First World War, graduated from the Army War College in 1935, and served on the Army General Staff from 1936 to 1940.
49 Summers, *On Strategy*, 94; emphasis original.
50 Compare: US Dept. Army, *FM 100-1. The Army* (Washington, DC: GPO, 1978), 14; *FM 100-5* (1954), 25; *FM 100-5* (1962), 46.
51 Summers, *On Strategy*, 128; emphasis original.
52 Herbert E. Wolff, Student Papers. AHEC Archives.
53 Herbert E. Wolff, "9 + 1 = 10," *Infantry* 55, 2 (Mar.–Apr. 1965): 30–33.
54 H. E. Wolff, "Nine Plus One Equals Ten," draft essay, dated Nov. 16, 1964. Wolff Papers. AHEC Archives.
55 MG H. E. Wolff, "The Tenth Principle," introductory note to "Nine Plus One Equals Ten."
56 Cited from Susan A. Brewer, *Why America Fights: Patriotism and Propaganda from the Philippines to Iraq* (New York: Oxford University Press, 2009), 180–95.
57 Adam J. Berinsky, *In Time of War: Understanding American Public Opinion from World War II to Iraq* (Chicago, IL: University of Chicago Press, 2009), 115.
58 M. E. Roberts III, *The Psychological War for Vietnam, 1960–1968* (Lawrence: University Press of Kansas, 2018), 10–12.
59 John I. Alger, *The Quest for Victory: The History of the Principles of War* (Westport: Greenwood, 1982).
60 Alger, *Quest for Victory*, xxiii.
61 Summers, *On Strategy*, 47; compare Alain C. Enthoven and K. Wayne Smith, *How Much is Enough, Shaping the Defense Program 1961–1969* (New York: Harper & Row, 1979), 267.
62 Summers, *On Strategy*, 196.

63 Russell W. Glenn, "No More Principles of War?," *Parameters* 28, 1 (Spring 1998): 48–66.
64 Anthony D. McIvor, ed., *Rethinking the Principles of War* (Annapolis, MD: Naval Institute Press, 2005).
65 Brodie, *War and Politics*, 492–94.
66 H. G. Summers, Jr., *On Strategy II: A Critical Analysis of the Gulf War* (New York: Dell, 1992).
67 Summers, *On Strategy II*, 19.
68 Summers, *On Strategy II*, 139.
69 Summers, *On Strategy II*, 154.
70 Summers, *On Strategy II*, 156.
71 G. R. Nelson, "The Supply and Quality of First-Term Enlistees under the All-Volunteer Force," in *The All-Volunteer Force after a Decade*, ed. William Bowman et al. (Washington, DC: Brassey's, 1986), 31–32.
72 *Department of the Army Historical Summary: FY 1979* (Washington, DC: CMH, 1982), ch. 2, p. 5.
73 John L. Moore, ed., *U.S. Defense Policy: Weapons, Strategy and Commitments*, 2nd ed. (Washington, DC: Congressional Quarterly, 1980), 13–14.
74 William J. Lewis, *The Warsaw Pact: Arms, Doctrine, and Strategy* (New York: Macgraw Hill, 1983).
75 Summers, *On Strategy II*, 156.
76 *FM 100-5 Operations* (1982), 2–3.
77 *FM 100-5 Operations* (1982), 1–1.
78 *FM 100-5 Operations* (1986), 2–10.
79 W. Clark, *Waging Modern War: Bosnia, Kosovo, and the Future of Combat* (New York: PublicAffairs, 2001), 450–53.
80 Dept. Defense, *Joint Publication 3-07: Joint Doctrine for Operations Other Than War* (Washington, DC: GPO, 1995).
81 Boot, *The Road Not Taken*, 447–70.
82 E. N. Luttwak, "The Operational Level of War," *International Security* 5, 3 (Winter 1980–81): 61–79; for a rejoinder see Matheny, *Carrying the War to the Enemy*.
83 Col. Arthur F. Lykke, Jr., "Defining Military Strategy = E + W + M," *Military Review* 69, 5 (1989), 3.
84 Interview with the author at the US Army War College, March 2018.

Part IV

1 T. C. Schelling, "From an Airport Bench," *Bulletin of the Atomic Scientists* 45, 4 (May 1989): 29–31.
2 B. J. C. McKercher and M. A. Hennessy, eds., *The Operational Art: Developments in the Theories of War* (Westport, CT: Praeger, 1996).
3 Michael R. Matheny, *Carrying the War to the Enemy: American Operational Art to 1945* (Norman: University of Oklahoma, 2011).
4 J. A. Olsen and M. van Creveld, eds., *The Evolution of Operational Art: From Napoleon to the Present* (Oxford: Oxford University Press, 2011); M. D. Krause and R. C. Phillips, eds., *Historical Perspectives of the Operational Art* (Washington, DC: CMH, 2005).

Chapter 9

1. R. Coram, *Boyd: The Fighter Pilot Who Changed the Art of War* (New York: Little, Brown, 2002), 9.
2. W. S. Lind, *Maneuver Warfare Handbook* (New York: Westview, 1985); W. S. Lind and G. A. Thiele, *4th Generation Warfare Handbook* (Kouvola, Finland: Castalia, 2015).
3. M. van Creveld, *A History of Strategy: From Sun Tzu to William S. Lind* (Kouvola, Finland: Castalia, 2015), 121–22.
4. I. T. Brown, *A New Conception of War: John Boyd, the US Marines, and Maneuver Warfare* (Quantico, VA: USMC, 2018); Coram, *Boyd*; G. T. Hammond, *The Mind of War: John Boyd and American Security* (Washington, DC: Smithsonian, 2001).
5. D. M. Oshinsky, *Polio: An American Story* (Oxford: Oxford University Press, 2005); G. N. Grob, *The Deadly Truth: A History of Disease in America* (Cambridge, MA: Harvard University Press, 2002).
6. US Air Force Oral History Interview, K239, 0512-1066, Col. John R. Boyd, Jan. 28, 1977, Air Univ., 1.
7. Coram, *Boyd*, 16–29.
8. Scott E. McIntosh, "The Wingman-Philosopher of MiG Alley: John Boyd and the OODA Loop," *Air Power History* (Winter 2011): 24–33, offers a description of air combat in the Korean War.
9. J. A. Olsen warns that this ratio has been contested: "Boyd Revisited: A Great Mind with a Touch of Madness," *Air Power History* (Winter 2016): 7–16.
10. Hammond, *Mind of War*, 47–48; www.dnipogo.org/boyd/pdf/boydaerialattack.pdf
11. Hammond, *Mind of War*, 57–61.
12. John T. Correll, "The Reformers," *Air Force Magazine* (Feb. 2008): 40–44.
13. John R. Boyd Archives, USMC University, Testimony before the Aspen Committee, Apr. 1991.
14. J. Arthur Bloom, "William Lind's Way of War: Meet the Field Marshal of Military Reform and Cultural Conservatism," *The American Conservative* (Nov./Dec. 2016): 6–9.
15. Bloom, "William Lind's Way of War," 7.
16. W. Lind and G. Hart, *America Can Win: The Case for Military Reform* (Bethesda, MD: Adler, 1986), 3.
17. W. S. Lind and W. H. Marshner, *Cultural Conservatism: Toward a New National Agenda* (Lanham, MD: Free Congress Foundation, 1987).
18. W. S. Lind, "The Scourge of Cultural Marxism," *The American Conservative* (May/June 2018): 12.
19. W. S. Lind, "The New Separatism," *The American Conservative* (Jan./Feb. 2018): 14.
20. W. S. Lind, "Alternate History: The Right Needs a Narrative to Refute the Superstitions of Progress," *The American Conservative* (July 2011): 30–34.
21. W. S. Lind vs Daniel Smith, "Symposium: Q: Is Multiculturalism a Threat to the National Security of the United States?," *Insight on the News*, Dec. 31, 2001, pp. 40–43.

22 Thomas Hobbes [W. Lind], *Victoria: A Novel of 4th Generation War* (Kouvola, Finland: Castalia, 2014).
23 Reflected in 2018 dollars; US Bureau of Economic Analysis; www.bea.gov/data/gdp/gross-domestic-product#gdp
24 H. S. Klein, *A Population History of the United States*, 2d ed. (Cambridge: Cambridge University Press, 2012), 168.
25 US Dept. Education, National Center of Educational Statistics; http://nces.ed.gov/programs/digest/d10
26 Claudia Goldin, *Understanding the Gender Gap: An Economic History of American Women* (New York: Oxford University Press, 1990), 59–68.
27 Elaine T. May, *Homeward Bound: American Families in the Cold War Era*, 4th ed. (New York: Basic Books, 2017), 129–51.
28 Klein, *Population History of the United States*, 162.
29 Evans, *Tidal Wave*, 1, 6–7, 92; Joanna Russ, *The Female Man* (New York: Bantam, 1975).
30 [Lind], *Victoria*, ch. 10.
31 Paul Gilje, *Rioting in America* (Bloomington: Indiana University Press, 1996).
32 Conversation with Harry Summers, 2.
33 Kahn, "If Negotiations Fail," 627–28.
34 Eccles, *Military Power*, 148–49, 158.
35 Kahn and Wiener, *American Values*, I: 28–30.
36 Brands, *American Dreams*, 203–04.
37 Klein, *Population History*, 211, 227–28.
38 "A Framework," June 22, 1992, pp. 1, 11–13. Boyd Papers. USMCU Archives.
39 "In the Shadow of Doom: Social Disintegration in America," c. 1992, p. 11. Boyd Papers. USMCU Archives.
40 L. Boyd, "Abstract of the Discourse and Conceptual Spiral"; www.dnipogo.org/boyd/pdf/intro.pdf
41 "Patterns," slide 2.
42 "Patterns," slide 134.
43 "Patterns," slide 10.
44 "Patterns," slide 140.
45 Coram, *Boyd*, 329.
46 http://pogoarchives.org/m/dni/john_boyd_compendium/destruction_and_creation.pdf
47 Kuhn, *The Structure of Scientific Revolutions*; Kurt Gödel, "On Formally Undecidable Propositions of the Principia Mathematica and Related Systems," in *The Undecidable* (Hewlett, NY: Raven, 1965), 3–38; Werner Heisenberg, *Physics and Philosophy* (New York: Harper, 1962); Nicholas Georgescu-Roegen, *The Entropy Law and the Economic Process* (Cambridge, MA: Harvard University Press, 1971).
48 http://pogoarchives.org/m/dni/john_boyd_compendium/conceptual-spiral-20111100.pdf
49 http://pogoarchives.org/m/dni/john_boyd_compendium/revelation.pdf
50 Compare: Maj. I. T. Brown, "The 'Grand Ideal': John Boyd and America's Strategic Vision," *Marine Corps Gazette* 100, 2 (Feb. 2016): 55–58; Ensign

S. Mason, "John Boyd and Strategic Naval Air Power," *Proceedings* 129, 7 (July 2003): 76.
51 W. S. Lind, "John Boyd's Art of War: Why Our Greatest Military Theorist Only Made Colonel," *The American Conservative* (July/Aug. 2013): 9–10.
52 Karl Popper, *Logic of Scientific Discovery* (New York: Hutchison, 1959).
53 Coram, *Boyd*, 319–22.
54 James Hasik, "Beyond the Briefing: Theoretical and Practical Problems in the Works and Legacy of John Boyd," *Contemporary Security Policy* 34, 3 (2013): 583–99.
55 Frans Osinga, *Science, Strategy, and War: The Strategic Theory of John Boyd*, PhD Diss., University of Leiden, 2005, pp. 272–73; and "The Enemy as a Complex Adaptive System: John Boyd and Airpower in the Postmodern Era," *Airpower Reborn: The Strategic Concepts of John Warden and John Boyd*, ed. John Andreas Olsen (Annapolis, MD: Naval Institute, 2015), 92.
56 Terry Terriff, "'Innovate or Die': Organizational Culture and the Origins of Maneuver Warfare in the United States Marine Corps," *Journal of Strategic Studies* 29, 3 (June 2006): 475–503.
57 W. S. Lind, "Ready, Aim, Think," *The New Republic* 192 (Mar. 4, 1985): 40.
58 W. S. Lind, "Defining Maneuver Warfare for the Marine Corps," *Marine Corps Gazette* (Mar. 1980): 56.
59 Richard Betts, "Conventional Strategy: New Critics, Old Choices," *International Security* 7, 4 (Spring 1983): 140–62.
60 E. Luttwak, "Attrition, Relational Maneuver, and the Military Balance," *International Security* 8, 2 (Fall 1983): 176–79; R. Betts, "Thesis, Antithesis, Synthesis? Reply to Luttwak," *International Security* 8, 2 (Fall 1983): 180–82.
61 *Truppenführung: On the German Art of War*, ed. and trans. by Bruce Condell and David Zabecki (Boulder, CO: Lynne Rienner, 2001), 131ff.
62 W. S. Lind, "Some Doctrinal Questions for the United States Army," *Military Review* 77, 1 (Jan./Feb. 1997 [1977]): 135–43.
63 Benoit Lemay, *Erich von Manstein: Hitler's Master Strategist*, trans. Pierce Hayward (Philadelphia, PA: Casemate, 2010), 98–102.
64 Compare John Kiszely, *Anatomy of a Campaign: British Fiasco in Norway 1940* (Cambridge: Cambridge University Press, 2017); G. H. Haarr, *German Invasion of Norway 1940* (Barnsley: Seaforth, 2009).
65 Robert A. Doughty, "Myth of the Blitzkrieg," and James S. Corum, "Myths of Blitzkrieg" reprinted in Jeremy Black, ed., *The Second World War*, vol. I (Aldershot: Ashgate, 2007), 91–114, 115–19, respectively.
66 One such promise was P. Sweeney, "Maneuver Warfare Demands Logistics Based on a Foundation of [Radio Frequency Identification] 2.0," *Defense Transportation Journal* 65, 5 (Sept. 2009): 17–20.
67 E. Rommel, *The Rommel Papers*, trans. P. Findlay, ed. B. H. Liddell Hart (New York: Da Capo, 1953), 455.
68 Phillips P. O'Brien, *How the War Was Won: Air–Sea Power and Allied Victory in World War II* (Cambridge: Cambridge University Press, 2015), 316–17.
69 Capt. Wayne P. Hughes, Jr., USN, "Naval Maneuver Warfare," *Naval War College Review* 50, 3 (Summer 1997): 25–49.

70 Capt. T. E. Somes, USN, "Musing on Naval Maneuver Warfare," *Naval War College Review* 51, 3 (Summer 1998): 122–28.
71 R. D. Hooker, ed., *Maneuver Warfare: An Anthology* (Novato, CA: Presidio, 1993); R. Leonard, *The Art of Maneuver: Maneuver-Warfare Theory and AirLand Battle* (Novato, CA: Presidio, 1991).
72 R. Waddell, "Maneuver Warfare and Low-Intensity Conflict," in Hooker, ed., *Maneuver Warfare*, 119–37.
73 K. Allard, *Somalia Operations: Lessons Learned* (Washington, DC: NDU, 1995); US Forces, *Somalia after Action Report* (Washington, DC: GPO, 1995; repr. 2004).
74 "Patterns," slides 50–52.
75 "Patterns," slide 125.
76 "Patterns," slide 122.
77 "Patterns," slides 122–25.
78 W. S. Lind, K. Nightengale, J. F. Schmitt, J. W. Sutton, and G. Wilson, "The Changing Face of War: Into the Fourth Generation," *Marine Corps Gazette* (Oct. 1989): 22–26; and *Military Review* (Oct. 1989): 2–11; it was also reprinted in the August 2013 and March 2016 issues of the *Marine Corps Gazette*.
79 W. S. Lind, "Understanding Fourth Generation War," *Military Review* 84, 5 (Sept./Oct. 2004): 12–16.
80 W. S. Lind, "Fourth-Generation Warfare's First Blow: A Quick Look," *Marine Corps Gazette* 85, 11 (Nov. 2001): 72.
81 Lind, "Fourth-Generation Warfare's First Blow," 72.
82 Terry Terriff, Aaron Karp, and Regina Karp, eds., *Global Insurgency and the Future of Armed Conflict: Debating Fourth-Generation Warfare* (London: Routledge, 2008).
83 T. X. Hammes, *The Sling and the Stone: On War in the 21st Century* (St. Paul, MN: Zenith, 2004).
84 W. S. Lind, "The Will Doesn't Triumph," in Terriff et al., eds., *Global Insurgency*, 102–03.
85 "Patterns," slide 182–84.
86 W. S. Lind, "The Theory and Practice of Maneuver Warfare," in Hooker, ed., *Maneuver Warfare*, 13, 18, n. 17.
87 "Patterns," slide 10.
88 James Gleick, *Chaos: Making a New Science* (New York: Penguin, 1987); M. Mitchell Waldrop, *Complexity: The Emerging Science at the Edge of Order and Chaos* (New York: Touchstone, 1993); Stuart Kauffman, *At Home in the Universe: The Search for the Laws of Self-Organization and Complexity* (Oxford: Oxford University Press, 1995).
89 Qiao Liang and Wang Xiangsui, Chinese People's Liberation Army, *Unrestricted Warfare* (Beijing: PLA Literature and Arts Publishing House, 1999).
90 Maj. J. F. Schmitt, "Out of Sync with Maneuver Warfare," *Marine Corps Gazette* 78, 8 (Aug. 1994), 22.
91 W. J. Harkin, "Maneuver Warfare in the 21st Century," *Marine Corps Gazette* 92, 2 (Feb. 2011): 19–25; M. Morgan, S. Fugler, and C. Batson, "Maneuver

and the Information Battlespace," *Marine Corps Gazette* 94, 4 (Apr. 2010): 14–16.
92 Dept. of the Navy, MCDP-1 *Warfighting* (Washington, DC: HQ USMC, Aug. 1, 1997), 13–19.

Chapter 10

1 J. A. Warden III, *The Air Campaign: Planning for Combat* (Washington, DC: NDU, 1988).
2 Warden, *Air Campaign*, xix, xxiii, 6.
3 John A. Olsen, *John Warden and the Renaissance of American Air Power* (Washington, DC: Potomac, 2007), 7–12, 21.
4 J. A. Warden III, "The Grand Alliance: Strategy and Decision," master's thesis, Texas Technical University, 1975.
5 J. A. Warden III, Interview in *Desert Story Collection*, Oct. 22, 1991, 4; May 30, 1991, 35–36.
6 J. A. Warden III, email exchange with the author Aug. 22, 2018.
7 Shmuel L. Gordon, "Air Superiority in the Israel–Arab Wars, 1967–1982," and Lawrence Freedman, "Air Power and the Falklands, 1982," in *A History of Air Warfare*, ed. J. A. Olsen (Washington, DC: Potomac, 2010), 127–55; and 157–74.
8 Warden interview, *Desert Story Collection*, 53; emphasis original.
9 Lawrence Freedman and Efraim Karsh, *The Gulf Conflict, 1990–1991: Diplomacy and War in a New World Order* (Princeton, NJ: Princeton University Press, 1992), 318.
10 Olsen, *John Warden*, 164.
11 D. A. Deptula, "Effects-Based Operations: Change in the Nature of War" (Arlington, VA: Aerospace Education Foundation, 2001).
12 Black, *Air Power*, 248.
13 Warden, *Air Campaign*, 6–8.
14 Warden, *Air Campaign*, 13.
15 Warden, *Air Campaign*, 20–21.
16 Warden, *Air Campaign*, 9.
17 James J. Schneider and Lawrence Izzo, "Clausewitz's Elusive Center of Gravity," *Parameters* (Sept. 1987): 46–57.
18 Warden, *Air Campaign*, 40, 138–39.
19 J. A. Warden III, "Employing Air Power in the Twenty-first Century," in *The Future of Air Power in the Aftermath of the Gulf War*, ed. Richard A. Schultz, Jr. and Robert L. Pfaltzgraff, Jr. (Maxwell AFB, Montgomery, AL: Air University, 1992), 64–67.
20 Warden, "Employing Air Power," 67.
21 J. A. Warden III, "The Enemy as a System," *Airpower Journal* 9, 1 (Spring 1995): 40–55, at 42.
22 Warden, "Enemy as a System," 53.
23 Pape, *Bombing to Win*.
24 Pape, *Bombing to Win*, 212–13.

25 J. A. Warden III, "Success in Modern War: A Response to Robert Pape's Bombing to Win," *Security Studies* 7, 2 (Winter 1997/98): 172–90, at 178.
26 Cited from Air Force Doctrine Center White Paper, March 2004.
27 www.dodccrp.org/events/9th_ICCRTS/CD/presentations/8/092.pdf
28 Lee W. Wagenhals, Alexander H. Levis, and Maris McCrabb, "Effects-Based Operations: A Historical Perspective for a Way Ahead," System Architectures Library, C3I Center, George Mason University, Fairfax, VA, June 2003.
29 Paul K. Davis, *Effects-Based Operations: A Grand Challenge for the Analytical Community* (Santa Monica, CA: RAND, 2001).
30 Gen. James N. Mattis, Memorandum for US Joint Forces Command, Aug. 14, 2008; James N. Mattis, "USJFCOM Commander's Guidance for Effects-Based Operations," *Parameters* (Autumn 2008): 18–25. For a rebuttal published in the same issue, see Tomislav Z. Ruby, "Effects-Based Operations: More Important Than Ever," *Parameters* (Autumn 2008): 26–35.
31 John T. Correll, "The Assault on EBO," *Air Force Magazine* (Jan. 2013): 50–54, which argued that the cardinal sin of EBO was only that it threatened the traditional way of war.
32 Leonard D. Rickerman, Major, US Army, "Effects-Based Operations: A New Way of Thinking and Fighting," School of Advanced Military Studies, USGSC, Ft. Leavenworth, KS, 2002.
33 Annex 3-0 Operations and Planning, Nov. 4, 2016; file:///C:/Users/ajech/Desktop/EBO/3-0-D06-OPS-EBAO.pdf
34 J. A. Warden III, "The New American Security Force," *Airpower Journal* 13, 3 (Fall 1999): 75–83.
35 Warden, "New American Security Force," 76.
36 Warden, "Enemy as a System," 43.
37 Steven M. Rinaldi, "Complexity Theory and Air Power," in *Complexity, Global Politics, and National Security*, ed. David S. Alberts and Thomas J. Czerwinski (Washington, DC: National Defense University, 1997), 283–85.

Conclusion

1 For an excellent explication of that approach in the Antebellum era, see Ian C. Hope, *A Scientific Way of War* (Lincoln: University of Nebraska Press, 2015).
2 Giddings, *Principles of Sociology*, xvii.
3 Joint Chiefs of Staff, *Joint Vision 2010* (Washington, DC, 1995); *Joint Vision 2020* (Washington, DC, 2000).
4 Bernard and Fawn M. Brodie, *From Crossbow to H-Bomb: The Evolution of the Weapons and Tactics of Warfare* (Bloomington: Indiana University Press, 1973).
5 Brodie, *War and Politics*, 332.
6 Clausewitz, *Vom Kriege* I/1, 213; *On War*, 89.
7 Osgood, *Limited War*, 15–18.
8 For more, see Antulio J. Echevarria II, *Military Strategy: A Very Short Introduction* (Oxford: Oxford University Press, 2017).

9 George Kennan, *Measures Short of War: the George F. Kennan Lectures at the National War College, 1946–47*, ed. Giles D. Harlow [and] George C. Maerz (Washington, DC: National Defense University Press, 1991).
10 Richard Ned Lebow, "Reason Divorced from Reality: Thomas Schelling and Strategic Bargaining," *International Politics* 43 (2006): 429–52.
11 Brodie, *War and Politics*, 452.
12 Alger, *Quest for Victory*.
13 Franklin Mark Osanka, ed., *Modern Guerrilla Warfare: Fighting Communist Guerrilla Movements, 1941–1961* (New York: Glencoe, 1962 and 1964), xv–xvi.
14 Weigley, *Age of Battles*.
15 Michele Mcphee, K. C. Baker and Corky Siemaszko, "Deep Blue, IBM'S Supercomputer, Defeats Chess Champion Garry Kasparov in 1997," *New York Daily News*, May 10, 2015.
16 Max Boot, "The New American Way of War," *Foreign Affairs* 82, 4 (July/Aug. 2003): 41–58.

Select Bibliography

Unpublished Sources

John R. Boyd Papers, USMC University, Quantico, VA.
Bernard Brodie Papers. UCLA Library. Special Collections. Los Angeles, CA.
Smedley Butler Papers. USMC University, Quantico, VA.
Henry Eccles Papers. Naval War College Library, Special Collections. Newport, RI.
Herman Kahn Papers. National Defense University, Washington, DC.
William L. Mitchell Papers. Library of Congress, Special Collections. Washington, DC.
Robert E. Osgood Papers. Johns Hopkins University Library, Baltimore, MD.
Herbert Rosinski Papers. Naval War College Library, Special Collections. Newport, RI.
Harry G. Summers Papers. Army Historical and Education Center. Carlisle, PA.

Published Sources

Abadinsky, H. *The Criminal Elite: Professional and Organized Crime.* Westport, CT: Greenwood, 1983.
Alger, John I. *The Quest for Victory: The History of the Principles of War.* Westport, CT: Greenwood, 1982.
Allard, K. *Somalia Operations: Lessons Learned.* Washington, DC: NDU, 1995.
Anderson, Terry H. *The Movement and the Sixties: Protest in America from Greensboro to Wounded Knee.* New York: Oxford University Press, 1996.
Angell, N. *The Great Illusion.* New York: Putnam's, 1910.
Anon. "In the Shadow of Doom: Social Disintegration in America," c. 1992.
"Text of Air Report by Morrow Board," *New York Times*, Dec. 3, 1925.
Apt, Benjamin L. "Mahan's Forebears: The Debate over Maritime Strategy, 1868–1883," *Naval War College Review* 50, 3 (Summer 1997): 86–111.
Armbruster, Frank E. et al. *Can We Win in Vietnam? The American Dilemma.* London: Pall Mall, 1968.
Armstrong, B. J., ed. *21st Century Mahan: Sound Military Conclusions for the Modern Era.* Annapolis, MD: Naval Institute Press, 2013.
Averyt, William F. Ens. USNR, "The Philosophy of the Counterculture," *Naval War College Review* 23, 7 (Mar. 1971): 17–25.

Ayson, Robert. *Thomas Schelling and the Nuclear Age: Strategy as Social Science.* New York: Frank Cass, 2004.
Bacevich, Andrew J. *The Pentomic Era: The US Army between Korea and Vietnam.* Washington, DC: NDU, 1986.
Backus, Paul. "Finite Deterrence, Controlled Escalation," Proceedings 85, 3 (Mar. 1959): 23–29.
Barlow, Jeffery G. *The Revolt of the Admirals: The Fight for Naval Aviation, 1945–1950.* Washington, DC: Potomac, 2001.
Barnes, Joseph. "The Great Bolshevik Cleansing," *Foreign Affairs* 17, 3 (Apr. 1939): 556–68.
Barnhill, John H. "Watts Riots (1965)," in *Revolts, Protests, Demonstrations, and Rebellions in American History*, ed. Steven L. Danver, vol. 3. Santa Barbara, CA: ABC-CLIO, 2011.
Bassford, Christopher. *Clausewitz in English.* Oxford: Oxford University Press, 1994.
Baumgarten, E[rwin]. "Game Theory: Lecture, 12 Dec. 1960," *Naval War College Review* 13, 9 (May 1961): 16–41.
  "Strategic War Gaming: Lecture, 16 Feb. 1961," *Naval War College Review* 13, 10 (June 1961): 1–22.
Beard, George M. *American Nervousness: Its Causes and Cures.* New York: Putnam's, 1881.
Beebe, Robert P., Capt. USN. "Military Decision from the Viewpoint of Game Theory," *Naval War College Review* 10, 2 (Oct. 1957): 27–56.
Berg, A. *Scott Lindberg.* New York: Penguin, 1999.
Berinsky, Adam J. *In Time of War: Understanding American Public Opinion from World War II to Iraq.* Chicago, IL: University of Chicago Press, 2009.
Bernstein, Richard. *China 1945: Mao's Revolution and America's Fateful Choice.* New York: Alfred A. Knopf, 2014.
Betts, Richard. "Conventional Strategy: New Critics, Old Choices," *International Security* 7, 4 (Spring 1983): 140–62.
  "Thesis, Antithesis, Synthesis? Reply to Luttwak," *International Security* 8, 2 (Fall 1983): 180–82.
  "Is Strategy an Illusion?," *International Security* 25, 2 (Fall 2000): 5–50.
Biddle, Tami Davis. *Rhetoric and Reality in Air Warfare: The Evolution of British and American Ideas about Strategic Bombing, 1914–1945.* Princeton, NJ: Princeton University Press, 2002.
Bigelow, John. *The Principles of Strategy: Illustrated Mainly from American Campaigns*, 2nd ed. New York: J. B. Lippincott, 1894.
Bishop, Robert L. "Review of *The Strategy of Conflict* by Thomas C. Schelling," *American Economic Review* 51, 4 (Sept. 1961): 674–76.
Black, Jeremy. *Air Power: A Global History.* Lanham, MD: Rowman & Littlefield, 2016.
Bloom, J. Arthur. "William Lind's Way of War: Meet the Field Marshal of Military Reform and Cultural Conservatism," *The American Conservative* (Nov./Dec. 2016): 6–9.

Blum, John M., ed. *The Price of Vision: The Diary of Henry A. Wallace*. Boston, MA: Houghton Mifflin, 1973.
Bond, Brian and Ian Roy, eds. *War and Society*, 2 vols. New York: Holmes & Meier, 1975–77.
Boorman, S. A. "The Legacy of Henry Eccles," *Naval War College Review* 62, 2 (Spring 2009): 91–116.
Boot, Max. *The Road Not Taken: Edward Lansdale and the Tragedy in Vietnam*. New York: Liveright, 2018.
Booth, Ken. "Bernard Brodie," in *Makers of Nuclear Strategy*, ed. John Baylis and John Garnett. London: Pinters, 1991.
  "The Evolution of Strategic Thinking," in *Contemporary Strategy I: Theories and Concepts*, 2nd ed. New York: Holmes & Meier, 1987, 44–60.
Bostorff, Denise M. *Proclaiming the Truman Doctrine: The Cold War Call to Arms*. College Station: Texas A&M University Press, 2008.
Bowers, E. L. *Is It Safe to Work? A Study of Industrial Accidents*. Boston, MA: Houghton Mifflin, 1930.
Bowie, Robert R. and Richard H. Immerman. *Waging Peace: How Eisenhower Shaped an Enduring Cold War Strategy*. New York: Oxford University Press, 2000.
http://pogoarchives.org/m/dni/john_boyd_compendium/conceptual-spiral-20111100.pdf
http://pogoarchives.org/m/dni/john_boyd_compendium/destruction_and_creation.pdf
http://pogoarchives.org/m/dni/john_boyd_compendium/revelation.pdf
https://unwritten-record.blogs.archives.gov/2014/08/27/billy-mitchells-boozy-barbecue-send-off-1925/
www.dnipogo.org/boyd/pdf/boydaerialattack.pdf
Branch, Taylor. *Parting the Waters: America in the King Years, 1954–63*. New York: Simon & Schuster, 1988.
Brands, H. W. *American Dreams: The United States since 1945*. New York: Penguin, 2010.
Brewer, Susan A. *Why America Fights: Patriotism and Propaganda from the Philippines to Iraq*. New York: Oxford University Press, 2009.
Brodie, B. *Sea Power in the Machine Age*. Princeton, NJ: Princeton University Press, 1941.
  A Layman's Guide to Naval Strategy. Princeton, NJ: Princeton University Press, 1942 & 1944.
Brodie, B., ed. *The Absolute Weapon: Atomic Power and World Order*. New York: Harcourt, Brace, 1946.
  "Impact of New Weapons on War," National War College Lecture, Sept. 4, 1946.
  "The Atomic Bomb as a Weapon," National War College Lecture, Sept. 6, 1946.
  "Sea Power in the Atomic Age," Naval War College Lecture, Jan. 19, 1949, Cat. No. 6890-7770.
  "A-Bombs and Air Strategy," Air War College Lecture, March 24, 1949. Air University Library, Maxwell AFB; M-33506-C.

"The Problem of Integrating the Factors of National Strategy," Air War College Lecture, March 17, 1950. Air University Library, Maxwell AFB; M-33507-C.

"Air Power in an Overall Strategy," Air War College Lecture, May 23, 1951. Air University Library, Maxwell AFB; K239.716250-12(R).

"Changing Capabilities and War Objectives," Air War College Lecture, April 17, 1952. Air University Library, Maxwell AFB; K239.716251-26; and K239.716252-105.

"Characteristics of a Sound Strategy," *Naval War College Review* 4, 10 (June 1952): 65–82.

"The Heritage of Douhet," *Air University Quarterly Review* 6, 2 (1953): 64–69.

"Nuclear Weapons: Strategic or Tactical?" *Foreign Affairs* 32, 2 (Jan. 1954): 217–29.

Possible U.S. Military Strategies, Lecture Delivered at the US Army War College, March 30, 1954, published as RAND P-524, Santa Monica, CA, April 7, 1954.

"Unlimited Weapons and Limited War," *The Reporter* 11 (Nov. 18, 1954): 16–21.

"Strategy Hits a Dead End," *Harper's Magazine* (May 1955): 33–37.

Nuclear Weapons and Changing Strategic Outlooks, RAND P-811, Santa Monica, CA, Feb. 27, 1956.

On the Worth of Principles of War, Lecture Delivered at the Command and General Staff College, Ft. Leavenworth, KS, on March 7, 1957, published as RAND P-1092, Santa Monica, CA, May 21, 1957.

"Review: More About Limited War," *World Politics* 10, 1 (1957): 119.

The Meaning of Limited War, July 30, 1958, published as RAND PM-2224, Santa Monica, CA.

"Strategy as an Art and a Science, Delivered at the Naval War College on 18 September 1958," *Naval War College Review* 11, 6 (Feb. 1959): 1–20.

Strategy in the Missile Age. Princeton, NJ: Princeton University Press, 1959.

Escalation and the Nuclear Option. Princeton, NJ: Princeton University Press, 1966.

"Why Were We So (Strategically) Wrong?," *Foreign Policy* 4 (Autumn 1971): 151–62.

War and Politics. New York: Macmillan, 1973.

Brooks, Jennifer E. *Defining the Peace: World War II Veterans, Race, and the Remaking of Southern Political Tradition*. Chapel Hill: University of North Carolina Press, 2004.

Brown, I. T., Maj. "The 'Grand Ideal': John Boyd and America's Strategic Vision," *Marine Corps Gazette* 100, 2 (Feb. 2016): 55–58.

A New Conception of War: John Boyd, the US Marines, and Maneuver Warfare. Quantico, VA: USMC, 2018.

Brown, Seyom. *Faces of Power: Constancy and Change in United States Foreign Policy*. New York: Columbia University Press, 2015.

Bruce-Briggs, B. *Supergenius: The Mega-Worlds of Herman Kahn*. New York: North American Policy, 2000.

Bruno, Harry. *Wings over America: The Story of American Aviation*. New York: Halcyon, 1944.
Budiansky, Stephen. *Air Power*. New York: Viking, 2004.
Burlingame, Roger. *General Billy Mitchell: Champion of Air Defense*. New York: McGraw-Hill, 1952.
Burr, William, ed. "How Much Is Enough?: The US Navy and 'Finite' Deterrence," May 1, 2009; https://nsarchive2.gwu.edu//nukevault/ebb275/index.htm
Butler, S. "America's Armed Forces," *Common Sense* 4, 11 (1935): pt. 2.
East to the Dawn: The Life of Amelia Earhart. Cambridge: De Capo, 1997.
Calhoun, Frederick S. *Uses of Force and Wilsonian Foreign Policy*. Kent, OH: Kent State University Press, 1993.
Califano, Jr., Joseph A. *The Triumph & Tragedy of Lyndon Johnson: The White House Years*. New York: Simon & Schuster, 1991.
Campbell, W. Joseph. *Yellow Journalism: Puncturing the Myths, Defining the Legacies*. Westport, CT: Praeger, 2003.
Cantril, Hadley and Mildred Strunck, eds. *Public Opinion, 1935–1946*. Princeton, NJ: Princeton University Press, 1951.
Carafano, J. J. *The Army Reserves and the Abrams Doctrine: Unfulfilled Promise, Uncertain Future*. Washington, DC: Heritage, 2005.
Carnagey, Dale. *Public Speaking and Influencing Men of Business*. n.p., 1913.
Caro, Robert A. *The Passage of Power: The Years of Lyndon Johnson*, vol. 4. New York: Vintage, 2013.
Carter, E. D. "Review of *The Strategy of Conflict* by Thomas C. Schelling," *International Affairs* 38, 2 (Apr. 1962): 234.
Castel, Albert. "Liddell Hart's Sherman: Propaganda as History," *Journal of Military History* 67, 2 (Apr. 2003): 405–26.
Chafe, William. *The Paradox of Change: American Women in the 20th Century*. New York: Oxford University Press, 1991.
Chalmers, David M. *Hooded Americanism: The History of the Ku Klux Klan*. Durham, NC: Duke University Press, 1987.
Cherpak, Evelyn M. *Interview of Rear Admiral Joseph C. Wylie, USN (Ret.) Oral History Program*, Naval War College, Newport, RI, 4 Parts; Part 1, Nov. 21, 1985.
  Register of the Papers of Henry E. Eccles, Series No. 6, 2nd Ed., Naval War College, Newport, RI, 1988.
  Register of the Papers of Herbert Rosinski, Series No. 17, Naval War College, Newport, RI, 1988, pp. 1–4.
Clark, W. *Waging Modern War: Bosnia, Kosovo, and the Future of Combat*. New York: PublicAffairs, 2001.
Clodfelter, James. "Vacillation and Stability in American Public Opinion toward Military and Foreign Policy," *Naval War College Review* 23, 6 (Feb. 1971): 55–61.
Clodfelter, Mark A. "Molding Airpower Convictions: Development and Legacy of William Mitchell's Strategic Thought," in Meilinger, ed. *Paths of Heaven*, 79–114.

Select Bibliography

Coen, R. M. "Labor Force Unemployment in the 1920s and 1930s: A Reexamination Based on Postwar Experience," *Review of Economics and Statistics* 55 (1973): 46–55.
Cohen, Eliot. "Review of *On Strategy*," *Commentary* 74, 1 (July 1982): 84–86.
Colomb, P. H. *Naval Warfare: Its Ruling Principles Historically Treated*. London: W. H. Allen, 1891.
Converse III, Elliott V. *History of Acquisition in the Department of Defense, vol. 1, Rearming for the Cold War, 1945–1960*. Washington, DC: Historical Office, OSD, 2012.
Cooke, James J. *Billy Mitchell*. Boulder, CO: Lynne Rienner, 2002.
Coolidge, Calvin. "Address to Newspaper Editors"; www.presidency.ucsb.edu/documents/address-the-american-society-newspaper-editors-washington-dc
Address to American Society of Newspaper Editors, Jan. 17, 1925; www.presidency.ucsb.edu/documents/address-the-american-society-newspaper-editors-washington-dc
Cooper, Jr., John M. *Pivotal Decades: The United States, 1900–1920*. New York: W. W. Norton, 1990.
Coram, R. *Boyd: The Fighter Pilot Who Changed the Art of War*. New York: Little, Brown, 2002.
Corbett, Julian S. *Some Principles of Maritime Strategy*. London: Longman, Green, 1911.
Correll, John T. "The Reformers," *Air Force Magazine* 91 (Feb. 2008): 40–44.
Corum, James S. "The Luftwaffe and Lessons Learned in the Spanish Civil War," in *Air Power History: Turning Points from Kitty Hawk to Kosovo*, ed. S. Cox and P. Gray. London: Frank Cass, 2002, 66–89.
Cott, Nancy. *The Grounding of Modern Feminism*. New Haven, CT: Yale University Press, 1988.
Coult, Allan D. "Review of *The Strategy of Conflict* by Thomas C. Schelling," *American Anthropologist* 64, 3, Part 1 (June 1962): 686–87.
Craig, Campbell and Sergey Radchenko. "MAD, not Marx: Khrushchev and the Nuclear Revolution," *Journal of Strategic Studies* 41, 1–2 (Feb. 2018): 208–33.
Craig, Gordon. *The Politics of the Prussian Army*. New York: Oxford University Press, 1955.
Crowl, Philip A. "Alfred Thayer Mahan: The Naval Historian," in *Makers of Modern Strategy*, ed. Peter Paret. Princeton, NJ: Princeton University, 1986.
Curtis, T. H., Col. USAF, "USAF Officer Education in Counterinsurgency," *Air University Review* 18, 2 (Jan.–Feb. 1967): 67–69.
Cushman, John H., LTG, US Army (Ret.). *Oral History*, 6 vols., vol. 2, 1951–63.
Daddis, Gregory A. *No Sure Victory: Measuring US Army Effectiveness and Progress in the Vietnam War*. Oxford: Oxford University Press, 2011.
   Westmoreland's War: Reassessing American Strategy in Vietnam. New York: Oxford University Press, 2014.
Dalleck, Robert. *An Unfinished Life: John F. Kennedy, 1917–1963*. New York: Little & Brown, 2004.
   Harry S. Truman. New York: Times Books, 2008.

Select Bibliography 273

Daniels, Roger. "Immigration to the United States in the Twentieth Century," in *Cambridge Companion to Modern American Culture*, ed. Christopher Bigsby. Cambridge: Cambridge University Press, 2006, 73–954.
Dastrup, Boyd L. *The US Army Command and General Staff College: A Centennial History*. Manhattan, KS: Sun Flower, 1982.
Davis, Paul K. and John Arquilla. *Deterring or Coercing Opponents in Crisis: Lessons from the War with Saddam Hussein*. Santa Monica, CA: RAND, 1991.
De Jomini, Baron. *Summary of the Art of War*, trans. O. F. Winship and E. E. McClean. New York: Putnam, 1854.
Department of the Army Historical Summary: FY 1979. Washington, DC: CMH, 1982.
Dept. Army. *FM 100-5. Operations*. Washington, DC: GPO, 1954.
Dept. Army. *FM 100-5. Operations*. Washington, DC: GPO, 1962.
Dept. Defense. *Joint Publication 3-07: Joint Doctrine for Operations Other Than War*. Washington, DC: GPO, 1995.
De Seversky, Alexander P. *Victory Through Air Power*. New York: Simon & Schuster, 1942.
  "A Lecture on Air Power, Part I," *Air University Quarterly Review* 1, 2 (Fall 1947): 25–40.
  "A Lecture on Air Power, Part II," *Air University Quarterly Review* 1, 3 (Fall 1947): 26–41.
  Air Power: Key to Survival. New York: Simon and Schuster, 1950.
  "I Remember Billy Mitchell," *Air Power Historian* (Oct. 1956): 179.
Devine, Robert A. *Eisenhower and the Cold War*. New York: Oxford University Press, 1981.
Dickman, Joseph L., LTC USAF. "Douhet and the Future," *Air University Quarterly Review* 2, 1 (1948): 3–15.
Dictionary of Military and Associated Terms, JCS Pub 1. Washington, DC: GPO, 1979.
Dodge, Robert. *The Strategist: The Life and Times of Thomas Schelling*. Hollis, NH: Hollis Publ., 2006.
Doughty, Robert A. *The Evolution of US Army Tactical Doctrine, 1946–1976*. Ft. Leavenworth, KS: CSI, 1979.
Downey, E. H. *History of Work Accident Indemnity in Iowa* (Iowa City: State Historical Society, 1912.
Drew, S. Nelson, ed. *NSC-68: Forging the Strategy of Containment with analyses by Paul H. Nitze*. Washington, DC: National Defense University, 1996.
Dubofsky, Melvin and Joseph A. McCartin, *American Labor: A History*, 9th ed. Oxford: Wiley Blackwell, 2017.
Dudley, William S. "Alfred Thayer Mahan on the War of 1812," *The Influence of History on Mahan*, ed. John B. Hattendorf. Newport, RI: Naval War College, 1991, 141–54.
Duiker, William J. *Ho Chi Minh*. New York: Hyperion, 2000.
Eastman, Lloyd E. *Seeds of Destruction: Nationalist China in War and Revolution, 1937–1949*. Stanford, CA: Stanford University Press, 2002.
Eccles, H. E. "Pacific Logistics." Paper presented at the Naval War College, March 30, 1946.

"Basic Elements and Aspects of Logistics." *Lecture delivered at the Naval War College*, Aug. 27, 1947.
Operational Naval Logistics. Washington, DC: Bureau of Naval Personnel, 1950.
"Logistics and Strategy: Lecture, 2 Jan. 1962," *Naval War College Review* 14, 6 (Mar. 1962): 15–30.
"Military Theory and Education: A Working Paper," Nov. 1, 1962.
"Military Theory and Education: The Need for and Nature of," *Naval War College Review* 21, 6 (Feb. 1965): 70–79.
Logistics in the National Defense. Harrisburg, PA: Stackpole, 1959.
Military Concepts and Philosophy. New Brunswick, NJ: Rutgers University Press, 1965.
"Suez 1956 – Some Military Lessons," *Naval War College Review* 21, 7 (Mar. 1969): 28–55.
"Strategy: The Essence of Professionalism," *Naval War College Review* 24, 4 (Dec. 1971): 43–51.
Eccles, H.E. *Military Power in a Free Society*. Newport, RI: Naval War College, 1979.
"Strategy – The Theory and Application," *Naval War College Review* 32, 3 (May–June 1979), 18–19, American Political Science Association Conference, 1978.
"The Dangers of 'Weapons Strategy," *Christian Science Monitor*, Oct. 1, 1981.
Electronic interview with Col. R. M. Swain, US Army (Ret.), May 2018.
Ellsberg, Daniel. *Doomsday Machine: Confessions of a Nuclear War Planner*. New York: Bloomsbury, 2017.
Enthoven, Alain C. and K. Wayne Smith. *How Much Is Enough, Shaping the Defense Program 1961–1969*. New York: Harper & Row, 1979.
Evans, S. M. *Tidal Wave: How Women Changed America at Century's End*. New York: Free Press, 2003.
Ferguson, Niall. *Kissinger 1923–1968: The Idealist*. New York: Penguin, 2015.
Fiebeger, G. J., Col. *Elements of Strategy*. West Point, NY: US Military Academy, 1917.
Fiske, B. "Our Naval Profession," Naval Institute Proceedings (June 1907): 475–78.
Fiske, Bradley A. *The Navy as a Fighting Machine*. New York: Scribner's, 1916.
Fitzgerald, F. S. *The Great Gatsby*. New York: Scribner's, 1925.
Flynn, George Q. *The Draft, 1940–1973*. Lawrence: University Press of Kansas, 1993.
Foner, Philip S. *Mark Twain as Social Critic*. New York: International Publishers, 1981.
Frederickson, Kari. *The Dixiecrat Revolt and the End of the Solid South, 1932–1968*. Chapel Hill: University of North Carolina Press, 2001.
Free, Lloyd A. "Political Beliefs and Public Opinion," *Naval War College Review* 23, 7 (Mar. 1971): 4–16.
Freedman, Lawrence, ed. *Strategic Coercion: Concepts and Cases*. Oxford: Oxford University Press, 1998.

Select Bibliography

Freedman, Lawrence. *Kennedy's Wars: Berlin, Cuba, Laos, and Vietnam.* Oxford: Oxford University Press, 2000.
The Evolution of Nuclear Strategy, 3rd ed. London: Palgrave Macmillan, 2003.
Deterrence. Cambridge: Polity, 2004.
Futrell, R. F. *Ideas, Concepts, Doctrine: Basic Thinking in the United States Air Force*, vol. 1. Maxwell AFB: Air University, 1989.
Gabriel, R. and P. Savage, *Crisis in Command: Mismanagement in the Army.* New York: Hill & Wang, 1978.
Gaddis, John Lewis. *George F. Kennan: An American Life.* New York: Penguin, 2012.
Gamrami-Tabrizi, Sharon. "Simulating the Unthinkable: Gaming War in the 1950s and 1960s," *Social Studies of Science* 30, 2 (Apr. 2000): 163–223.
The Worlds of Herman Kahn: The Intuitive Science of Thermonuclear War. Cambridge, MA: Harvard University Press, 2005.
Gardner, John S., ed. *The Company Town: Architecture and Society in the Early Industrial Age.* New York: Oxford University Press, 1992.
Garfinkle, Adam. *Telltale Hearts: The Origins and Impact of the Vietnam Antiwar Movement.* New York: St. Martin's Press, 1995.
Gauvreau, Emile and Lester Cohen. *Billy Mitchell: Founder of Our Air Force and Prophet without Honor.* New York: E. P. Dutton, 1942.
Geissler, Suzanne. *God and Sea Power: The Influence of Religion on Alfred Thayer Mahan.* Annapolis, MD: Naval Institute Press, 2015.
Gentile, Gian. "The Chimera of Success: Pacification and the End of the Vietnam War," in *War Termination*, ed. Matthew Moten. Leavenworth, KS: CSI, 2011, 225–35.
George, Henry. *Progress and Property.* New York: D. Appleton, 1879.
Georgescu-Roegen, Nicholas. *The Entropy Law and the Economic Process.* Cambridge, MA: Harvard University Press, 1971.
Giddings, Franklin H. *Principles of Sociology.* New York: Macmillan, 1896.
Gilbert, James. *A Cycle of Outrage: America's Reaction to the Juvenile Delinquent in the 1950s.* New York: Oxford University Press, 1988.
Gilje, Paul. *Rioting in America.* Bloomington: Indiana University Press, 1996.
Glazer, Herbert. "Limited War Gaming: Lecture, 19 Jan. 1965," *Naval War College Review* 17, 7 (Mar. 1965): 29–44.
Glenn, Russell W. "No More Principles of War?," *Parameters* 28, 1 (Spring 1998): 48–66.
Glueck, Eleanor T. "Wartime Delinquency," *Journal of Criminal Law and Criminology* 33, 2 (1942–43): 119–35.
Glueck, Eleanor T. and Sheldon Glueck. *Unraveling Juvenile Delinquency.* Cambridge, MA: Harvard University Press, 1950.
Gödel, Kurt. "On Formally Undecidable Propositions of the Principia Mathematica and Related Systems," in *The Undecidable.* Hewlett, NY: Raven, 1965.
Goldin, Claudia. *Understanding the Gender Gap: An Economic History of American Women.* New York: Oxford University Press, 1990.
Goodwin, Doris Kearns. *Lyndon Johnson and the American Dream.* New York: St. Martin's Press, 1991.

Gordon, Robert J. *The Rise and Fall American Growth: The US Standard of Living since the Civil War*. Princeton, NJ: Princeton University Press, 2016.
Gray, Colin S. "What RAND Hath Wrought," *Foreign Policy* 4 (Autumn 1971): 111–29.
Greenspan, Alan and Adrian Wooldridge. *Capitalism in America: A History*. New York: Penguin, 2018.
Greenwood, Sean. "Frank Roberts and the 'Other' Long Telegram: The View from the British Embassy in Moscow, March 1946," *Journal of Contemporary History* 25 (1990): 103–22.
Griffin, John Howard. *Black Like Me*. New York: Signet, 1962.
Grob, G. N. *The Deadly Truth: A History of Disease in America*. Cambridge, MA: Harvard University Press, 2002.
Haarr, G. H. *German Invasion of Norway 1940*. Barnsley: Seaforth, 2009.
Hacker, Barton C. *Elements of Controversy: The Atomic Energy Commission and Radiation Safety in Nuclear Weapons Testing, 1947–1974*. Berkeley, CA: University of California Press, 1994.
Hahn, Peter L. "Securing the Middle East: The Eisenhower Doctrine of 1957," *Presidential Studies Quarterly* 36, 1 (2006): 38–47.
Halleck, H. Wager. *Elements of Military Art and Science*. New York: D. Appleton, 1846.
Halperin, Morton H. *Limited War: An Annotated Bibliography*. Cambridge, MA: Harvard University Press, 1962.
Limited War in the Nuclear Age. New York: John Wiley, 1963.
Hämäläinen, Pekka. *The Comanche Empire*. New Haven, CT: Yale University Press, 2008.
Hammes, T. X. *The Sling and the Stone: On War in the 21st Century*. St. Paul, MN: Zenith, 2004.
Hammond, Grant T. *The Mind of War: John Boyd and American Security*. Washington, DC: Smithsonian, 2001.
Hampton II, Isaac. *The Black Officer Corps: A History of Black Military Advancements from Integration through Vietnam*. New York: Routledge, 2013.
Handel, Michael. "Clausewitz in the Age of Technology," in *Clausewitz and Modern Strategy*, ed. Michael Handel. Totowa, NJ: Frank Cass, 1986, 58–62.
Hansen, Gladys and Emmet Condon. *Denial of Disaster*. San Francisco, CA: Cameron, 1989.
Harkin, W. J. "Maneuver Warfare in the 21st Century," *Marine Corps Gazette* 92, 2 (Feb. 2011): 19–25.
Harrison, A. *Black Exodus: The Great Migration from the American South*. Jackson: University of Mississippi Press, 1991.
Hasik, James. "Beyond the Briefing: Theoretical and Practical Problems in the Works and Legacy of John Boyd," *Contemporary Security Policy* 34, 3 (2013): 583–99.
Hattendorf, J. B. and L. C. Hattendorf, eds. *A Bibliography of the Works of Alfred Thayer Mahan*. Newport, RI: Naval War College, 1986.

Hattendorff, J. B., ed. *The Influence of History on Mahan: The Proceedings of a Conference Marking the Centenary of Alfred Thayer Mahan's Influence of Sea Power upon History 1660–1783*. Newport, RI: Naval War College, 1991.

Hattendorf, John B. "The Idea of a 'Fleet in Being' in Historical Perspective," *Naval War College Review* 67, 1 (Winter 2014): 43–60.

Hattendorf, John B., B. Mitchell Simpson III, and John R. Wadleigh. *Sailors and Scholars: The Centennial History of the US Naval War College*. Newport, RI: Naval War College, 1984.

Heisenberg, Werner. *Physics and Philosophy*. New York: Harper, 1962.

Heller, Charles E. and William A. Stofft, eds. *America's First Battles, 1776–1965*. Lawrence: University Press of Kansas, 1986.

Hermes, Walter. *Truce Tent and Fighting Front*. Washington, DC: CMH, 1992.

Herring, George. *LBJ and Vietnam: A Different Kind of War*. Austin: University of Texas Press, 1994.

Hollis, Christopher. "Dr. Strangelove and Dr. Kahn," *The Spectator* 28, 1964: 11.

Hooker, R. D., ed. *Maneuver Warfare: An Anthology*. Novato, CA: Presidio, 1993.

Hosmer, Stephen T. *The Conflict over Kosovo: Why Milosevic Decided to Settle When He Did*. Santa Monica, CA: RAND Project Air Force, 2001.

House, Jonathan M. *A Military History of the Cold War, 1944–1962*. Norman: University of Oklahoma Press, 2012.

Howard, Michael, ed. *Soldiers and Governments: Nine Studies in Civil-Military Relations*. Bloomington: Indiana University Press, 1959.

War and the Liberal Conscience. London: Maurice Temple Smith, 1978.

Hoxie, Frederick E. *A Final Promise: The Campaign to Assimilate the Indian, 1880–1920*. New York: Cambridge University Press, 1997.

Hughes, Wayne P. "Mahan, Tactics and Principles of Strategy," in *The Influence of History on Mahan: The Proceedings of a Conference, Marking the Centenary of Alfred Thayer Mahan's* The Influence of Sea Power upon History, 1660–1783, ed. John B. Hattendorf. Newport, RI: Naval War College Press, 1991, 25–36.

Hughes, Jr., Wayne P., Capt. USN. "Naval Maneuver Warfare," *Naval War College Review* 50, 3 (Summer 1997): 25–49.

Huntington, Samuel P. *The Soldier and the State: The Theory and Politics of Civil-Military Relations*. Cambridge, MA: Harvard University Press, 1957.

Hurley, Alfred F. *Billy Mitchell: Crusader for Air Power*. Bloomington: Indiana University Press, 1975.

Huston, J. A. "The Theory and Principles of War, Lecture Delivered at the Naval War College on 26 August 1959," *Naval War College Review* 12, 4 (Dec. 1959): 19–35.

James, D. Clayton and Anne Sharp Wells. *Refighting the Last War: Command and Crisis in Korea 1950–1953*. New York: Free Press, 1993.

James, William. *Principles of Psychology*, 2 vols. New York: Henry Holt, 1890.

Jane, Fred T. *Fighting Ships*. London: Sampson Low, Marston, 1912.

Jane, Fred. T. *Heresies of Sea Power*. New York: Longman, Green, 1906.

Janowitz, M. *The Professional Soldier: A Social and Political Portrait*. New York: Free Press, 1964.
Jensen, Kenneth M., ed. *Origins of the Cold War: The Novikov, Kennan, and Roberts "Long Telegrams" of 1946*, rev. ed. Washington, DC: Washington Institute of Peace, 1995.
Jervis, Robert. "Deterrence Theory Revisited," *World Politics* 31 (1979): 289–324.
Joint State Government Commission, *A Report of the Committee on Penal Code and Juvenile Delinquency*. Harrisburg, PA, Apr. 20, 1945.
Jones, Archer. *Elements of Military Strategy: An Historical Approach*. Westport, CT: Greenwood, 1996.
Kahn, H. *On Thermonuclear War*. Princeton, NJ: Princeton UniversityPress, 1960.
Thinking about the Unthinkable. New York: Horizon, 1962.
On Escalation: Metaphors and Scenarios. New York: Praeger, 1965.
"If Negotiations Fail," *Foreign Affairs* 46, 4 (July 1968): 627–41.
Kahn, H. and Irwin Mann, *Techniques of Systems Analysis*, RAND Research Memorandum RM 1829-1, June 1957.
Ten Common Pitfalls, RAND Research Memorandum RM 1937, July 17, 1957.
Game Theory, P-1166, RAND Corporation, July 30, 1957.
War Gaming, P-1167, RAND Corporation, July 30, 1957.
Kahn, H. and Anthony Wiener, eds. *American Values: Past and Future*, vol. I, *Values, Attitudes, and Life-Styles in a Changing World*. Croton-on-Hudson, NY: Hudson Institute, Dec. 31, 1974.
Kahn, H. and Garrett N. Scalera. "A Strategy for Vietnamization: A Discussion Paper," Croton-on-Hudson, NY: Hudson Institute, Aug. 5, 1969.
Kaplan, Fred. *Wizards of Armageddon*. New York: Simon & Schuster, 1983.
"All Pain, No Gain," *Slate*, Oct. 11, 2005.
Kennan, George] X, "The Sources of Soviet Conduct," *Foreign Affairs* 25, 4 (July 1947): 566–82.
Kissinger, H. *Nuclear Weapons and Foreign Policy*. New York: Harper, 1957.
Diplomacy. New York: Simon & Shuster, 1994.
Kiszely, John. *Anatomy of a Campaign: British Fiasco in Norway 1940*. Cambridge: Cambridge University Press, 2017.
Klein, H. S. *A Population History of the United States*, 2nd ed. Cambridge: Cambridge University Press, 2012.
Koistinen, Paul A. C. *State of War: The Political Economy of American Warfare, 1945–2011*. Lawrence: University Press of Kansas, 2012.
Kozak, Warren. *Curtis LeMay: Strategist and Tactician*. Washington, DC: Regnery, 2014.
Kraus, Joe. "How the Melting Pot Stirred America: The Reception of Zangwill's Play and Theater's Role in the American Assimilation Experience," *Melos* 24, 3 (1999): 3–19.
Krause, M. D. and R. C. Phillips, eds. *Historical Perspectives of the Operational Art*. Washington, DC: CMH, 2005.

Krepinevich Jr., Andrew F. *The Army and Vietnam* (Baltimore, MD: Johns Hopkins University Press, 1986).

Kuhn, Thomas S. *The Structure of Scientific Revolutions*. Chicago, IL: University of Chicago Press, 1970.

Kurlansky, Mark. *1968: The Year That Rocked the World*. New York: Random House, 2005.

LaFeber, Walter. "A Note on the 'Mercantilistic Imperialism' of Alfred Thayer Mahan," *Mississippi River Valley Review* 48 (Mar. 1962): 674–85.

"The Rise and Fall of Colin Powell and the Powell Doctrine," *Political Science Quarterly* 124, 1 (Spring 2009): 71–93.

Lansdale, Edward G. Maj.-Gen. "Viet Nam: Do We Understand Revolution?," *Foreign Affairs* 43, 1 (Oct. 1964): 75–86.

Laub, John H. and Jinney S. Smith. "Eleanor Touroff Glueck: Unsung Pioneer in Criminology," *Women & Criminal Justice* 6, 2 (1995): 1–22.

Laurie, Clayton D. "The United States Army and the Return to Normalcy in Labor Dispute Interventions: The Case of the West Virginia Coal Mine Wars, 1920–1921," *West Virginia History* 50 (1991) 1–24.

Leary, Timothy. *Turn On, Tune In, Drop Out*. Oakland, CA: Ronin Publishing, 1965.

Leber, Jr., Theodore T., Lieut.-Cdr., USNR. "The Genesis of Antimilitarism on the College Campus: A Contemporary Case Study of Student Protest," *Naval War College Review* 23, 3 (Nov. 1970): 48–99.

Lebergott, Stanley. *The American Economy: Income, Wealth, and Want*. Princeton, NJ: Princeton University Press, 1976.

Leighton, Richard M. *Strategy, Money, and the New Look, 1953–1956*. Vol. III, *History of Office of Secretary of Defense*. Washington, DC: Historical Office, OSD, 2001.

Lemay, Benoit. *Erich von Manstein: Hitler's Master Strategist*, trans. Pierce Hayward. Philadelphia, PA: Casemate, 2010.

Leonard, R. *The Art of Maneuver: Maneuver-Warfare Theory and AirLand Battle*. Novato, CA: Presidio, 1991.

Leslie, Jr., Reo N. "Christianity and the Evangelist for Sea Power: The Religion of Alfred Thayer Mahan," in Hattendorf, ed. *Influence of History on Mahan*, 127–39.

Levine, I. D. *Mitchell: Pioneer of Air Power*. New York: Duell, Sloane & Pierce, 1943.

Lewis, William J. *The Warsaw Pact: Arms, Doctrine, and Strategy*. New York: Macgraw Hill, 1983.

Libbey, James K. *Alexander P. De Seversky and the Quest for Air Power*. Washington, DC: Potomac, 2013.

Lind, W. and Thomas Hobbes. *Victoria: A Novel of 4th Generation War*. Kouvola, Finland: Castalia, 2014.

Lind, W. S. "Defining Maneuver Warfare for the Marine Corps," *Marine Corps Gazette* (Mar. 1980): 56.

Maneuver Warfare Handbook. New York: Westview, 1985.

"Ready, Aim, Think," *The New Republic* 192 (Mar. 4, 1985): 40.

"The Theory and Practice of Maneuver Warfare," in *Maneuver Warfare: An Anthology*, ed. R. D. Hooker, Jr. Novato, CA: Presidio, 1993.

"Some Doctrinal Questions for the United States Army," *Military Review* 77, 1 (Jan./Feb. 1997 <1977>): 135–43.

"Fourth-Generation Warfare's First Blow: A Quick Look," *Marine Corps Gazette* 85, 11 (Nov. 2001): 72.

"Understanding Fourth Generation War," *Military Review* 84, 5 (Sept./Oct. 2004): 12–16.

"The Will Doesn't Triumph," in *Global Insurgency and the Future of Armed Conflict: Debating Fourth-Generation Warfare*, ed. Terry Terriff, Aaron Karp, and Regina Karp. London: Routledge, 2008, 102–03.

"Alternate History: The Right Needs a Narrative to Refute the Superstitions of Progress," *The American Conservative* (July 2011): 30–34.

"John Boyd's Art of War: Why Our Greatest Military Theorist Only Made Colonel," *American Conservative* (July/Aug. 2013): 9–10.

"The New Separatism," *The American Conservative* (Jan./Feb. 2018), 14.

"The Scourge of Cultural Marxism," *The American Conservative* (May/June 2018): 12.

Lind, W. and Gary Hart. *America Can Win: The Case for Military Reform*. Bethesda, MD: Adler & Adler, 1986.

Lind, W. S. and G. A. Thiele. *4th Generation Warfare Handbook*. Kouvola, Finland: Castalia, 2015.

Lind, W. S., K. Nightengale, J. F. Schmitt, J. W. Sutton, and G. Wilson, "The Changing Face of War: Into the Fourth Generation," *Marine Corps Gazette* (Oct. 1989): 22–26.

Lind, W. S. and Daniel Smith. "Symposium: Q: Is Multiculturalism a Threat to the National Security of the United States?" *Insight on the News*, Dec. 31, 2001, pp. 40–43.

Lind, William S. and W. H. Marshner. *Cultural Conservatism: Toward a New National Agenda*. Lanham, MD: Free Congress Foundation, 1987.

Linder, M. "Fatal Subtraction: Statistical MIAs on the Industrial Battlefield," *Journal of Legislation* 20, 2 (1994): 99–145.

Lindner, Robert M. *Rebel Without a Cause: The Story of a Criminal Psychopath*. New York: Grune & Stratton, 1944.

Linn, Brian McAllister. *The Echo of Battle: The Army's Way of War*. Cambridge, MA: Harvard University Press, 2007.

Elvis' Army: Cold War GIs and the Atomic Battlefield. Cambridge, MA: Harvard University Press, 2016.

Lippmann, Walter. *The Cold War: A Study in US Foreign Policy*. New York: Harper, 1947.

"A Society Cannot Stand Still," *New York Herald Tribune*, Oct. 10, 1957.

The Coming Tests with Russia. Boston, MA: Little, Brown, 1961.

Longley, Kyle. *LBJ's 1968: Power, Politics, and the Presidency in America's Year of Upheaval*. Cambridge: Cambridge University Press, 2018.

Luce, S. B., Adm. "The Intellectual Focus: On the Study of Naval Warfare as a Science," and "Address Delivered at the United States Naval War College

June 2, 1903," in *The Writings of Stephen B. Luce*, ed. J. D. Hayes and J. B. Hattendorf. Newport, RI: Naval War College, 1975.

Luce, Stephen B. "The Benefits of War," *North American Review* (Dec. 1891): 672–73.

Luttwak, E. N. *Grand Strategy of the Roman Empire*. Baltimore, MD: Johns Hopkins University Press, 1976.

"The Operational Level of War," *International Security* 5, 3 (Winter 1980–81): 61–79.

"Attrition, Relational Maneuver, and the Military Balance," *International Security* 8, 2 (Fall 1983): 176–79.

Lykke, Jr., Arthur F., Col. "Defining Military Strategy = E + W + M," *Military Review* 69, 5 (1989): 3.

MacIsaac, David. "Voices from the Central Blue: The Air Power Theorists," in *Makers of Modern Strategy: From Machiavelli to the Nuclear Age*, ed. Peter Paret. Princeton, NJ: Princeton University Press, 1986, 624–47.

Mahan, A. T. *The Influence of Sea Power Upon History, 1660–1783*. Boston, MA: Little, Brown, 1890.

"The United States Looking Outward," *The Atlantic Monthly* 66 (Dec. 1890): 816–24.

The Influence of Sea Power Upon the French Revolution and Empire, 1793–1812. Boston: Little, Brown, 1892.

Admiral Farragut. New York: D. Appleton, 1893.

"Hawaii and Our Future Sea Power," *The Forum* 15 (Mar. 1893): 1–11.

"The Isthmus and Sea Power," *The Atlantic Monthly* 72 (Oct. 1893): 459–72.

"The Future in Relation to American Naval Power," *Harper's New Monthly* 91 (Oct. 1895): 767–75.

The Life of Nelson: The Embodiment of the Sea Power of Great Britain, 2 vols. Boston, MA: Little, Brown, 1897.

"Preparedness for Naval War," *Harper's New Monthly* 94 (Mar. 1897): 579–88.

"A Twentieth-Century Outlook," *Harper's New Monthly* (Sept. 1897): 521–33.

"Current Fallacies Upon Naval Subjects," *Harpers' New Monthly* 97 (June 1898): 42–53.

"The War on the Sea and Its Lessons. I. How the Motive of the War Gave Direction to Its Earlier Movements," *McClure's Magazine* (Dec. 1898): 114.

"Distinguishing Qualities of Ships of War," *Scripps-McRae Newspaper League, Nov. 1898*, in *Lessons of the War with Spain and Other Articles*. Boston, MA: Little, Brown, 1899, 257–73.

"The War on the Sea and Its Lessons. II. The Effect of Deficient Coast Defense on the Movements of the Navy," *McClure's Magazine* (Jan. 1899): 232–36.

"The War on the Sea and Its Lessons. III. The Reasons for Blockading Cuba," *McClure's Magazine* (Feb. 1899): 358.

"The War on the Sea and Its Lessons IV. The Problems Presented to Our Navy by Cervera's Appearance in West Indian Waters and How They Were Solved," *McClure's Magazine* (Mar. 1899): 479–80.

"Some Considerations of the Principles Involved in the Current War," *National Review* 44 (Sept. 1904): 27–46.

Sea Power in Its Relations to the War of 1812, 2 vols. Boston, MA: Little, Brown, 1905.

"Some Reflections Upon the Far-Eastern War," *National Review* 47 (May 1906): 383–405.

From Sail to Steam: Recollections of a Naval Life. New York: Harper, 1907.

"War from the Christian Standpoint," Nov. 15, 1900, in *Some Neglected Aspects of War*. London: Sampson Low, Marston, 1907.

"The Moral Aspect of War," North American Review (Oct. 1899) in *Some Neglected Aspects of War*. London: Sampson Low, Marston, 1907.

"The Practical Character of the United States Naval War College," in *Naval Administration and Warfare*. Boston, MA: Little, Brown, 1908.

The Harvest Within: Thoughts on the Life of the Christian. Boston, MA: Little, Brown, 1909.

Naval Strategy Compared and Contrasted with the Principles and Practice of Military Operations on Land. Boston, MA: Little, Brown, 1911.

"The Place of Force in International Relations," *North American Review* 195 (Jan. 1912): 28–39.

"Sea Power in the Present European War," *Leslie's Illustrated Weekly* CXIX (Aug. 20, 1914), in *Letters and Papers of Mahan* III, 706–10.

"Subordination in Historical Treatment," in *Naval Administration, and Warfare: Some General Principles*. Boston, MA: Little, Brown, 1918.

Letters and Papers of Alfred Thayer Mahan, 3 vols., ed. Robert Seager II and Doris D. Maguire. Annapolis, MD: Naval Institute Press, 1975.

Marolda, Edward J., ed. *The US Navy in the Korean War*. Annapolis, MD: Naval Institute, 2013.

Marr, David G. "Review of *On Strategy* by Harry G. Summers," *Pacific Affairs* 56, 3 (Autumn 1983): 594–95.

Marshall, Alfred. *Principles of Economics*, 2 vols. London: Macmillan, 1890.

Martelle, Scott. *Blood Passion: The Ludlow Massacre and Class War in the American West*. New Brunswick, NJ: Rutgers University, 2007.

Mason, Ensign S. "John Boyd and Strategic Naval Air Power," *Proceedings* 129, 7 (July 2003): 76.

Matheny, Michael R. *Carrying the War to the Enemy: American Operational Art to 1945*. Norman: University of Oklahoma Press, 2011.

Matray, James I. "Dean Acheson's Press Club Speech Reexamined," *Journal of Conflict Studies* 21, 1 (Spring 2002): 28–55.

Mattson, Kevin. *Upton Sinclair and the Other American Century*. Hoboken, NJ: Wiley, 2006.

Mauer, M. and C .F. Senning, "Billy Mitchell, the Air Service, and the Mingo County War," *West Virginia Historian* 30 (Oct. 1968): 339–50.

May, Elaine T. *Homeward Bound: American Families in the Cold War Era*, 4th ed. New York: Basic Books, 2017.

May, Ernest R. and Philip D. Zelikow, eds. *The Kennedy Tapes: Inside the White House during the Cuban Missile Crisis*. New York: W. W. Norton, 2002.

McCarthy, Sen. Joseph. *Speech, Congressional Record, Senate, 81st Congress, 2nd Session, entered into the record February 20, 1950.* Washington, DC: US Congress, 1957.
McClintock, Robert. *The Meaning of Limited War: The Diplomacy of Force and the Force of Diplomacy under Pax Ballistica.* Boston, MA: Houghton Mifflin, 1967.
McCuen, John J., Lt. Col. *The Art of Counter-Revolutionary War: The Strategy of Counter-Insurgency.* London: Farber, 1966.
McCullough, David C. *Truman.* New York: Simon & Schuster, 1993.
McDermott, W. B. "Thinking about Herman Kahn," *Journal of Conflict Resolution* 15, 1 (Mar. 1971): 55–70.
McFate, Montgomery. *Military Anthropology: Soldiers, Scholars and Subjects at the Margins of Empire.* London: Hurst, 2018.
McGinnis, Anthony R. "When Courage Was Not Enough: Plains Indians at War with the United States Army," *Journal of Military History* 76 (Apr. 2012): 455–73.
McGirr, Lisa. *The War on Alcohol: Prohibition and the Rise of the American State.* New York: W. W. Norton, 2015.
McIntosh, Scott E. "The Wingman-Philosopher of MiG Alley: John Boyd and the OODA Loop," *Air Power History* (Winter 2011): 24–33.
McIvor, Anthony D., ed. *Rethinking the Principles of War.* Annapolis, MD: Naval Institute, 2005.
McKercher, B. J. C. and M. A. Hennessy, eds. *The Operational Art: Developments in the Theories of War.* Westport, CT: Praeger, 1996.
McMaster, H. R. *Dereliction of Duty: Lyndon Johnson, Robert McNamara, the Joint Chiefs, and the Lies that Led to Vietnam.* New York: HarperCollins, 1997.
McNamara, R. S. *In Retrospect: The Tragedy and Lessons of Vietnam.* New York: Random House, 1995.
Mears, Dwight S. *The Medal of Honor: The Evolution of America's Highest Decoration.* Lawrence: University Press of Kansas, 2018.
Meilinger, Phillip S., ed. *The Paths of Heaven: The Evolution of Air Power Theory.* Maxwell AFB, AL: Air University, 1997.
  "Alexander P. De Seversky," *Aerospace Power Journal* 16, 4 (2002): 8–15.
Mercur, James. *Elements of the Art of War*, 2nd ed. New York: John Wiley, 1889.
Messer, C. M., T. E. Shriver, and Alison E. Adams. "The Destruction of Black Wall Street: Tulsa's 1921 Riot and the Eradication of Accumulated Wealth," *American Journal of Economics and Sociology* 77 (Oct. 2018): 789–819.
Milevski, L. "Revisiting J. C. Wiley's Dichotomy of Strategy: The Effects of Sequential and Cumulative Patterns of Operations," *Journal of Strategic Studies* 35, 2 (2012): 223–42.
Millen, Raymond. "Eisenhower and US Grand Strategy," *Parameters* 44, 2 (Summer 2014): 35–48.
Millett, Kate. *Sexual Politics.* Garden City, NY: Doubleday, 1970.
Millis, Walter. "Review of *Nuclear Weapons and Foreign Policy* by Henry A. Kissinger," *Political Science Quarterly* 72, 4 (Dec. 1957): 608.

Mitchell, W. "Building the Alaskan Telegraph System," *National Geographic Magazine* (1903): 357–61.
Field Signal Communications, 2nd Lecture. Ft. Leavenworth, KS: Dept. of Military Art, 1905.
"Our Faulty Military Policy," 1915, Box 45, Mitchell Papers, Library of Congress.
"Air Service at St. Mihiel," *World's Work* 38 (Aug. 1919): 360–70.
"Air Service at the Argonne-Meuse," *World's Work* 38 (Sept. 1919): 552–60.
"Air Power vs. Sea Power," *American Review of Reviews* 58 (Mar. 21, 1921): 273–77.
"America in the Air: The Future of Airplane and Airship, Economically and as Factors in National Defense," *National Geographic* 39, 3 (Mar. 1921): 339–52.
"Has the Airplane Made the Battleship Obsolete?," *World's Work* (Apr. 1921): 552.
"Aviation over the Water," *American Review of Reviews* 62 (Oct. 1921): 391–98.
"General Mitchell's Lecture to Army War College," dated Wed. Nov. 22, 1922, pp. 21–24.
Winged Defense: The Development and Possibilities of Modern Air Power – Economic and Military. New York: G. P. Putnam's, 1925.
"Some Considerations Regarding a Limitation of Armaments," *Annals of the American Academy of Political Social Sciences* 120 (1925): 87–89.
"Airplanes in National Defense," *Annals of American Academy of Political and Social Science* 131 (May 1927): 38–42.
"The Next War in the Air," *Popular Mechanics* 63 (Feb. 1935): 135–65.
Mitchell, W. et al. *Report of Inspection Trip to France, Germany, Holland, and England Made During the Winter of 1921–1922*. Washington, DC: GPO, 1923.
Mitchell, W. et al. *Report of Inspection of United States Possessions in the Pacific and Java, Singapore, India, Siam, China, and Japan*. Washington, DC: GPO, Oct. 24, 1924.
Moise, Edwin E. *The Myths of Tet: The Most Misunderstood Event of the Vietnam War*. Lawrence: University Press of Kansas, 2017.
Moore, John L., ed. *U.S. Defense Policy: Weapons, Strategy and Commitments*, 2nd ed. Washington, DC: Congressional Quarterly, 1980.
Morgan, Forrest E. et al. *Dangerous Thresholds: Managing Escalation in the Twenty-First Century*. Santa Monica, CA: RAND, 2008.
Morgan, M. S., and Fugler C. Batson. "Maneuver and the Information Battlespace," *Marine Corps Gazette* 94, 4 (Apr. 2010): 14–16.
Morgan, Patrick. *Deterrence Now*. Cambridge: Cambridge University Press, 2003.
Morgenthau, Hans J. "Review of *Nuclear Weapons and Foreign Policy* by Henry A. Kissinger," *American Political Science Review* 52, 3 (Sept. 1958): 842–44.
Myerson, Roger B. "Learning from Schelling's Strategy of Conflict," *Journal of Economic Literature* 47, 4 (Dec. 2009): 1109–25.
National Association for the Advancement of Colored People. *Thirty Years of Lynching in the United States*. New York: Lawbook Exchange, 2010 reprint.

Select Bibliography 285

National Security Council Report. Basic National Security Policy (NSC 162/2), Oct. 30, 1953; http://history.state.gov/historicaldocuments/frus1952-54v02p1/d100

Nelson, G. R. "The Supply and Quality of First-Term Enlistees Under the All-Volunteer Force," in *The All-Volunteer Force After a Decade*, ed. William Bowman et al. Washington, DC: Brassey's, 1986.

Nguyen, Lien-Hang T. *Hanoi's War: An International History of the War for Peace in Vietnam*. Charlotte: University of North Carolina Press, 2016.

Nichols, David A. *Eisenhower 1956: The President's Year of Crisis – Suez and the Brink of War*. New York: Simon & Schuster, 2011.

Nicolosi, Anthony. Interview of Rear Admiral Henry E. Eccles, USN (Ret.) Oral History Program, Naval War College, Newport, RI, Part 2, Jan. 13, 1977, p. 3.

Nitze, Paul. Record of the State-Defense Policy Group Meeting, March 10, 1950, *Foreign Relations of the United States*, vol. 1. Washington, DC: GPO, 1977.

Norman, Albert. "Review of Robert E. Osgood, *Limited War: The Challenge to American Strategy*," *Political Science Quarterly* 73, 2 (June 1958): 283.

Norman, Lloyd and John B. Spore. "Big Push in Guerrilla Warfare," *Army* (Mar. 1962): 34.

NSC 124/2, *United States Objectives and Courses of Action with Respect to Southeast Asia*, Washington, DC; June 25, 1952; General Considerations, Para. A.

O'Brien, K. "Logistics Pioneer: Rear Admiral Henry E. Eccles," *Air Force Journal of Logistics* 34, 1–2 (2010): 74–77.

O'Brien, Phillips P. *How the War Was Won: Air-Sea Power and Allied Victory in World War II*. Cambridge: Cambridge University Press, 2015.

O'Donnell, Lawrence. *Playing with Fire: The 1968 Election and the Transformation of American Politics*. New York: Penguin, 2017.

O'Neill, W. L. *Feminism in America: A History*, 2nd ed. New Brunswick, NJ: Rutgers University Press, 1989.

Office of the Secretary of Defense, Vietnam Task Force, *United States–Vietnam Relations, 1945–67*, Part IV, B, 2.

Ohmann, R. *Selling Culture: Magazines, Markets, and Class at the Turn of the Century*. London: Verso, 1996.

Olney, Martha. *Buy Now Pay Later: Advertising, Credit, and Consumer Durables in the 1920s*. Chapel Hill: University of North Carolina Press, 1991.

Olsen, John A. *John Warden and the Renaissance of American Air Power*. Washington, DC: Potomac, 2007.

"Boyd Revisited: A Great Mind with a Touch of Madness," *Air Power History* (Winter 2016): 7–16.

Olsen, J. A. and M. van Creveld, eds. *The Evolution of Operational Art: From Napoleon to the Present*. Oxford: Oxford University Press, 2011.

Orwell, George. *Animal Farm*. New York: Harcourt, Brace, 1946.

Osanka, Franklin Mark, ed. *Modern Guerrilla Warfare: Fighting Communist Guerrilla Movements, 1941–1961*. New York: Glencoe, 1962 and 1964.

Osgood, R. E. *Ideals and Self-Interest in America's Foreign Relations*. Chicago, IL: University of Chicago, 1953.

    Limited War: The Challenge to American Strategy. Chicago, IL: University of Chicago Press, 1957.
    "Concepts of General and Limited War, Delivered at the Naval War College on 18 September 1959," *Naval War College Review* 12, 4 (Dec. 1959): 1–18.
    Limited War Revisited. Boulder, CO: Westview, 1979.
Oshinsky, D. M. *Polio: An American Story*. Oxford: Oxford University Press, 2005.
Osinga, Frans. *Science, Strategy, and War: The Strategic Theory of John Boyd*. PhD Diss., University of Leiden, 2005.
    "The Enemy as a Complex Adaptive System: John Boyd and Airpower in the Postmodern Era," in *Airpower Reborn: The Strategic Concepts of John Warden and John Boyd*, ed. John Andreas Olsen. Annapolis, MD: Naval Institute Press, 2015.
Oyos, Matthew. *In Command: Theodore Roosevelt and the American Military*. Washington, DC: Potomac [Nebraska Imprint], 2018.
Page, Ellen Wells. "A Flapper's Appeal to Parents," *The Outlook*, Dec. 6, 1922: 607.
Paparone, C. and G. L. Topic, Jr. "The 'Clausewitz' of Logistics: Henry E. Eccles," *Army Sustainment* (Jan.–Feb. 2014): 9.
Pape, Robert A. *Bombing to Win: Air Power and Coercion in War*. Ithaca, NY: Cornell University Press, 1996.
Paret, Peter and John W. Shy. *Guerrillas in the 1960's*. Princeton Studies in World Politics, No. 1. New York: Praeger, 1962.
Parker, Christopher S. *Fighting for Democracy: Black Veterans and the Struggle against White Supremacy in the Postwar South*. Princeton, NJ: Princeton University Press, 2009.
Parrish, M. E. *Anxious Decades: American Prosperity and Depression, 1920–1941*. New York: W. W. Norton, 1994.
Pattillo, Donald M. *A History in the Making*. New York: McGraw-Hill, 1998.
Payne, Keith B. *The Great American Gamble: Deterrence Theory and Practice from the Cold War to the Twenty-first Century*. Fairfax, VA: National Institute, 2008.
Peck, G. *Prohibition in Washington, D.C.: How Dry We Weren't*. Charleston, NC: History Press, 2011.
Perone, James E. *The Music of the Counterculture Era*. Westport, CT: Greenwood, 2004.
Petersen, Walter J. "Deterrence and Compellence: A Critical Assessment of Conventional Wisdom," *International Studies Quarterly* 30, 3 (Sept. 1986): 269–94.
Pettit, James S. *Elements of Military Science*, rev. ed. New Haven, CT: Tuttle, Morehouse & Taylor, 1895.
Phillips, Kimberley L. *War! What Is It Good For? Black Freedom Struggles and the U.S. Military from World War II to Iraq*. Chapel Hill, NC: University of North Carolina Press, 2005.
Pike, Douglas. *Viet Cong: The Organization of the National Liberation Front of South Vietnam*. Cambridge, MA: MIT Press, 1966.
    War, Peace, and the Viet Cong. Cambridge, MA: MIT Press, 1969.

"Guerrilla Warfare in Vietnam," in *Interdoc Conference, Guerrilla Warfare in Asia*. The Hague: International Documentation and Information Center, 1971.

Pinckney, T. C., Lt.-Col. "Thoughts on the Limitation of War," *Air University Review* 20, 2 (Jan.–Feb. 1969): 79–83.

Popper, Karl. *Logic of Scientific Discovery*. New York: Hutchison, 1959.

Prime, Nicholas. *The Making of the Control School of Strategy: Joseph C. Wylie, Henry Eccles, and Herbert Rosinski at the US Naval War College 1950–1974*. PhD Diss., Kings College, London, 2017.

Proctor, Pat. *Containment and Credibility: The Ideology and Deception that Plunged America into the Vietnam War*. New York: Carrel, 2016.

Public Papers of the Presidents: Dwight D. Eisenhower, 1954. Washington, DC: 1960; www.presidency.ucsb.edu/ws/index.php?pid=10184

Puleston, W. D. *The Life and Work of Captain Alfred Thayer Mahan*. New Haven, CT: Yale University Press, 1939.

Purcell, Aaron D., ed. *The New Deal and the Great Depression*. Kent, OH: Kent State University Press, 2014.

Racine College, report cards of W. Mitchell dated March 5, 1891; Nov. 18, 1892; and Dec. 23, 1893.

Reed, William and Katherine Sawyer. "Bargaining Theory of War," *Oxford Bibliographies*; http://www.oxfordbibliographies.com.

Reiter, Dan. "Exploring the Bargaining Model of War," *Perspectives on Politics* 1, 1 (Mar. 2003): 27–43.

Roberts III, M. E. *The Psychological War for Vietnam, 1960–1968*. Lawrence: University Press of Kansas, 2018.

Robin, Ron. *The Cold World They Made: The Strategic Legacy of Roberta and Albert Wohlstetter*. Cambridge, MA: Harvard University Press, 2016.

Rockoff, H. and G. M. Walton. *History of the American Economy*, 11th ed. Mason, OH: Cengage, 2010.

Rockoff, Hugh. *America's Economic Way of War: War and the US Economy from the Spanish–American War to the Persian Gulf*. Cambridge: Cambridge University Press, 2012.

Rofe, J. Simon. "'Under the Influence of Mahan': Theodore and Franklin Roosevelt and their Understanding of American National Interest," *Diplomacy & Statecraft* 19 (2008): 732–45.

Røksund, Arne. *The Jeune École: The Strategy of the Weak*. Leiden: Brill, 2007.

Rommel, E. *The Rommel Papers*, trans. P. Findlay, ed. B. H. Liddell Hart. New York: Da Capo, 1953.

Rosen, Stephen Peter. "Vietnam and the American Theory of Limited War," *International Security* 7, 2 (Autumn 1982): 83–113.

Rosinski, H. "Scharnhorst to Schlieffen: The Rise and Decline of German Military Thought," *Naval War College Review* 27 (1976): 83–103.

Ross, Steven T. *American War Plans 1890–1939*. London: Frank Cass, 2002.

Rostow, W. W. *The Stages of Economic Growth: A Non-Communist Manifesto*. Cambridge: Cambridge University Press, 1960.

Roth, David. *Sacred Honor: A Biography of Colin Powell*. San Francisco, CA: Harper Collins, 1993.

Russ, Joanna. *The Female Man.* New York: Bantam, 1975.
Sanger, Richard H. "The Age of Sociopolitical Change," *Naval War College Review* 22, 2 (Oct. 1969): 3–16.
Scheips, Paul J. *The Role of Federal Forces in Domestic Disorders, 1945–1992.* Washington, DC: CMH, 2005.
Schelling, T. C. "An Essay on Bargaining," *American Economic Review* 46, 3 (June 1956): 281–301.
——. "Bargaining, Communication, and Limited War," *Journal of Conflict Resolution* 1, 1 (Mar. 1957): 19–36.
——. "Strategy of Conflict: Prospectus for a Reorientation of Game Theory," *Journal of Conflict Resolution* 2, 3 (Sept. 1958): 203–64.
——. "The Reciprocal Fear of Surprise Attack," RAND P-1342, April 16, 1958.
——. *The Strategy of Conflict.* Cambridge, MA: Harvard University Press, 1960.
——. "Strategic Analysis and Social Problems," *Social Problems* 12, 4 (Spring 1965): 367–79.
——. *Controlled Response and Strategic Warfare*, Adelphi Papers, no. 19. London: Institute for Strategic Studies, June 1965.
——. *Arms and Influence.* New Haven, CT: Yale University Press, 1966.
Schmidt, Hans. *Marine Maverik: General Smedley D. Butler and the Contradictions of American Military History.* Lexington: University Press of Kentucky, 1998.
Schmitt, J. F., Maj. "Out of Sync with Maneuver Warfare," *Marine Corps Gazette* 78, 8 (Aug. 1994): 22.
Schneider, James J. and Lawrence Izzo. "Clausewitz's Elusive Center of Gravity," *Parameters* (Sept. 1987): 46–57.
Schneirov, Richard, et al. *The Pullman Strike and the Crisis of the 1890s: Essays on Labor and Politics.* Urbana: University of Illinois Press, 1999.
Schonberg, Karl K. "Robert E. Osgood and the Origins of Social International Relations Theory," *International Journal* (Summer 2009): 811–23.
Schrecker, Ellen and Phillip Deery. *The Age of McCarthyism.* New York: St. Martin's, 2017.
Seager II, Robert. *Alfred Thayer Mahan: The Man and His Letters.* Annapolis, MD: Naval Institute, 1977.
Sec. of Commerce. *Statistical Abstract of the United States 1936.* Washington, DC: GPO, 1936, 1–2.
Sec. of Treasury. *Statistical Abstract of the United States 1879.* Washington, DC: GPO, 1880, 146–47.
Series: Moving Images Relating to Military Aviation Activities, compiled 1947–1984, documenting the period 1909–1984; Record Group 342: Records of U.S. Air Force Commands, Activities, and Organizations, 1900–2003.
Sheehan, Neil. "The Role of the Press," *Naval War College Review* 23, 6 (Feb. 1971): 4–7.
——. "The Press and the Pentagon Papers," *Naval War College Review* 24, 6 (Feb. 1972): 8–12.
Sheehan, Neil, et al. *The Pentagon Papers: The Secret History of the Vietnam War.* New York: Racehorse, 2017.

Sheppard, Si. "Atomic Cinema: Nuclear Proliferation and Deterrence Theory as Refracted through the Camera Lens"; www.filmint.nu, 31–59.
Showalter, Elaine. "The Other Lost Generation," in *Sisters' Choice: Tradition and Change in American Women's Writing*. Oxford: Oxford University Press, 1991.
Sights, Jr., Albert P., Col. "Limited War for Unlimited Goals," *Air University Quarterly Review* 13, 3 (Spring 1962): 38–48.
Simon, Linda. *Lost Girls: The Invention of the Flapper*. London: Reaktion, 2017.
Simon, Rita James. *Public Opinion in America: 1936–1970*. Chicago, IL: Rand McNally, 1974.
Sims, William S. "The Inherent Tactical Qualities of All-Big-Gun, One-Caliber Battleships of High Speed, Large Displacement Gunpower," *Proceedings* (Sept. 1906): 1337–66.
Smith, Gerard C. Director Policy Planning Staff, to John Foster Dulles, Secretary of State, Review of Strategic Concept, Memorandum dated January 20, 1959. Record Group 59, Dept. of State Participation in Operations Coordinating Board and National Security Council, 1947–63, Box 95, NSC 5810.
Somes, T. E., Capt. USN. "Musing on Naval Maneuver Warfare," *Naval War College Review* 51, 3 (Summer 1998): 122–28.
Sondhaus, Lawrence. *Naval Warfare, 1815–1914*. London: Routledge, 2001.
Spector, Ronald. *Professors of War: The Naval War College and the Development of the Naval Profession*. Newport, RI: Naval War College, 1977.
Spencer, David R. *Yellow Journalism: The Press and America's Emergence as a World Power*. Evanston, IL: Northwestern University Press, 2007.
Spencer, Herbert. *A System of Synthetic Philosophy*, 10 vols. New York: D. Appleton, 1862–93.
Sprout, M. T. "Mahan: Evangelist of Sea Power," in *Makers of Modern Strategy*, ed. Edward Mead Earle. Princeton, NJ: Princeton University Press, 1943, 415–45.
Stavridis, James. *The History and Geopolitics of the World's Oceans*. New York: Penguin, 2017.
Stebbins, Richard P. *The Career of Herbert Rosinski: An Intellectual Pilgrimage*. New York: Lang, 1989.
Stein, Harold. "Review of Robert E. Osgood, *Limited War: The Challenge to American Strategy*," *American Political Science Review* 52, 2 (June 1958): 534.
Steiner, Barry H. *Bernard Brodie and the Foundations of American Nuclear Strategy*. Lawrence: University Press of Kansas, 1991.
Stern, Robert, et al. *New York 1900: Metropolitan Architecture and Urbanism, 1890–1915*. New York: Rizzoli, 1983.
Stout, Hiram M. "The Nature of Military Strategy, Lecture Delivered at the Naval War College on 18 October 1955," *Naval War College Review* 8, 7 (Mar. 1956): 45–61.
Study on Military Professionalism. Carlisle Barracks, PA: US Army War College, 1970.

Sumida, Jon Tetsuro. *Inventing Grand Strategy and Teaching Command: The Classic Works of Alfred Thayer Mahan Reconsidered.* Baltimore, MD: Johns Hopkins University Press, 1997.

Summers, Jr., H. G. *On Strategy: The Vietnam War in Context.* Carlisle, PA: SSI, 1981.

— *On Strategy: A Critical Analysis of the Vietnam War.* Novato, CA: Presidio, 1982.

— *On Strategy II: A Critical Analysis of the Gulf War.* New York: Dell, 1992.

Sumner, William Graham. *What Social Classes Owe Each Other.* New York: Harper, 1884.

Swain, R. M. "Filling the Void: The Operational Art and the US Army," in *The Operational Art: Developments in the Theories of War,* ed. B. J. C. McKercher and Michael A. Hennessy. Westport, CT: Praeger, 1996.

Swedberg, Richard. *Economics and Sociology: Redefining their Boundaries: Conversations with Economists and Sociologists.* Princeton, NJ: Princeton University Press, 1990.

Sweeney, P. "Maneuver Warfare Demands Logistics Based on a Foundation of [Radio Frequency Identification] 2.0," *Defense Transportation Journal* 65, 5 (Sept. 2009): 17–20.

Tanham, George K. *Communist Revolutionary Warfare: From the Vietminh to the Viet Cong,* rev. ed. New York: Praeger, 1961 and 1967.

Taubman, William. *Khrushchev: The Man and His Times.* New York: Simon & Schuster, 2017.

Taylor, Maxwell. *The Uncertain Trumpet.* New York: Harper & Row, 1960.

Terriff, Terry, Aaron Karp, and Regina Karp, eds. *Global Insurgency and the Future of Armed Conflict: Debating Fourth-Generation Warfare.* London: Routledge, 2008.

Terriff, Terry. "'Innovate or Die': Organizational Culture and the Origins of Maneuver Warfare in the United States Marine Corps," *Journal of Strategic Studies* 29, 3 (June 2006): 475–503.

Thompson, Sir Robert. "Squaring the Error," *Foreign Affairs* 46, 3 (Apr. 1968): 442–53.

Thompson, Wayne. "Operations over North Vietnam, 1965–1973," in *A History of Air Warfare,* ed. John Andreas Olsen. Washington, DC: Potomac, 2010, 107–26.

Tierney, Dominic. *How We Fight: Crusades, Quagmires, and the American Way of War.* New York: Little, Brown, 2010.

Till, G. *Airpower and the Royal Navy 1914–1945: A Historical Survey.* London: MacDonald and Jane's, 1979.

— "Adopting the Aircraft Carrier: The British, American, and Japanese Case Studies," in *Military Innovation in the Interwar Period,* ed. W. Murray and A. Millett. Cambridge: Cambridge University Press, 1996.

Tompkins, E. *Berkeley Anti-Imperialism in the United States: The Great Debate, 1890–1920.* Philadelphia: University of Pennsylvania Press, 1970.

Trachtenberg, Marc. *History and Strategy.* Princeton, NJ: Princeton University Press, 1991.

Select Bibliography

Truman Papers – Family, Business, and Personal Affairs Papers; Truman Library; https://trumanlibrary.org
Turk, Richard W. *The Ambiguous Relationship: Theodore Roosevelt and Alfred Thayer Mahan.* New York: Greenwood, 1987.
Turner, Gordon B. "The Nature of War, Lecture Delivered at the Naval War College on 17 October 1955," *Naval War College Review* 8, 7 (Mar. 1956): 25–43.
Twain, M. and C. D. Warner. *The Gilded Age: A Tale of Today.* Hartford, CT: American Publishers, 1873.
United States–Vietnam Relations, 1945–1967, IV. A. 2, Vietnam Task Force, OSD, 1967–68.
Urban Research Corporation. *Student Protest 1969 Summary* (Chicago, 1970).
US Air Force Oral History Interview, K239, 0512-1066, Col. *John R. Boyd*, Jan. 28, 1977, Air University, 1.
U.S. Bureau of the Census. *Historical Statistics of the United States: Colonial Times to 1970.* Washington, DC: GPO, 1973.
US Bureau of Economic Analysis; www.bea.gov/data/gdp/gross-domestic-product#gdp
US Congress Senate, Committee on Armed Services. *Report of Proceedings: Inquiry into the Military Situation in the Far East and the Facts Surrounding the Relief of General of the Army Douglas MacArthur from his Assignment in that Area.* Washington, DC: Ward & Paul, 1951.
US Congress. *Report of the Commission on Industrial Relations.* Chicago, IL: Bernard & Miller, 1915.
US Congress, Senate Committee on Armed Services. *Report of Proceedings: Inquiry into the Military Situation in the Far East and the Facts Surrounding the Relief of General of the Army Douglas MacArthur from his Assignment in that Area.* Washington, DC: Ward & Paul, 1951.
US Dept. Army. *FM 100-1. The Army.* Washington, DC: GPO, 1978.
US Dept. Education, National Center of Educational Statistics; http://nces.ed.gov/programs/digest/d10
US Forces. *Somalia After Action Report.* Washington, DC: GPO, 1995; repr. 2004.
Van Creveld, M. *A History of Strategy: From Sun Tzu to William S. Lind.* Kouvola, Finland: Castalia, 2015.
Wagner, Arthur L., Col. *Strategy.* Kansas City: Hudson-Kimberly, 1904.
Wainwright, R. "Our Naval Power," Naval Institute Proceedings (Mar. 1898): 42.
Wallace, Max. *The American Axis: Henry Ford, Charles Lindberg, and the Third Reich.* New York: St. Martin's, 2003.
Waller, Douglas. *A Question of Loyalty: General Billy Mitchell and the Court-Martial That Gripped the Nation.* New York: HarperCollins, 2004.
War Dept. *FM 100-5. Operations.* Washington, DC: GPO, 1939.
Warden III, John A. "*The Grand Alliance: Strategy and Decision.*" Master's Thesis, Texas Technical University, 1975.
 The Air Campaign: Planning for Combat. Washington, DC: NDU, 1988.
 Interview in *Desert Story Collection*, Oct. 22, 1991, 4; May 30, 1991.

"Employing Air Power in the Twenty-first Century," in *The Future of Air Power in the Aftermath of the Gulf War*, ed. Richard A. Schultz, Jr. and Robert L. Pfaltzgraff, Jr. Maxwell AFB, AL: Air University, 1992, 64–67.

"The Enemy as a System," *Airpower Journal* 9, 1 (Spring 1995): 40–55.

"Success in Modern War: A Response to Robert Pape's Bombing to Win," *Security Studies* 7, 2 (Winter 1997/98): 172–78.

"The New American Security Force," *Airpower Journal* 13, 3 (Fall 1999): 75–77.

Warner, Edward. "Douhet, Mitchell, Seversky: Theories of Air Warfare," in Earle, ed., *Makers*, 485–503.

Warren, Bill. *Keep Watching the Skies: American Science Fiction Films of the Fifties*, 2 vols. Jefferson, NC: McFarland, 2009.

White, Jr., Richard D. *Will Rogers: A Political Life*. Lubbock: Texas Tech University Press, 2011.

White, R. P. *Mason Patrick and the Fight for Air Service Independence*. Washington, DC: Smithsonian, 2001.

Wildenberg, Thomas. *Billy Mitchell's War with the Navy: The Interwar Rivalry Over Air Power*. Annapolis, MD: Naval Institute, 2013.

Wilkerson, Marcus M. *Public Opinion and the Spanish-American War: A Study in War Propaganda*. New York: Russell & Russell, 1967.

Williams, Eddie. *Son of a Soldier*. Actworth, GA: E&M Consulting, 2013.

Williamson, J. and P. Lindert. *American Inequality: A Macroeconomic History*. New York: Academic, 1981.

Wilson, Woodrow. "Speech of Acceptance," Aug. 7, 1912, in *A Crossroads of Freedom: The 1912 Campaign Speeches of Woodrow Wilson*, ed. John W. Davidson. New Haven, CT: Yale University Press, 1956.

Wohlstetter, Albert. "The Delicate Balance of Terror," *Foreign Affairs* 37, 2 (Jan. 1959): 211–34; and "The Delicate Balance of Terror," P-1472 RAND, Nov. 6, 1958; rev. Dec. 1958.

Wohlstetter, Roberta. "Cuba and Pearl Harbor: Hindsight and Foresight," *Foreign Affairs* 43, 4 (July 1965): 691–707.

Pearl Harbor: Warning and Decision. Stanford, CA: Stanford University Press, 1962.

Wolff, H. E. "The Tenth Principle," introductory note to "Nine Plus One Equals Ten."

Col. "Nine Plus One Equals Ten," draft essay, dated Nov. 16, 1964.

Col. "9 + 1 = 10," *Infantry* 55, 2 (Mar.–Apr. 1965): 30–33.

Woloch, Nancy. *Women and the American Experience*, 2nd ed. New York: McGraw-Hill, 1994.

Worster, Donald. *Dust Bowl: The Southern Plains in the 1930s*. Oxford: Oxford University Press, 2004.

www.hrc.utexas.edu/multimedia/video/2008/wallace/seversky_alexander_de_t.html.

www.saferoads.org/federal/2004/TrafficFatalities1899-2003.pdf.

www.trumanlibrary.org/whistlestop/study_collections/coldwar/documents/pdf/10-1.pdf

Wylie, J. C. "The Navy's Reasons for Being – An Abortive Effort to Evaluate," A-2; declassified in 1982. Naval War College Special Collections, Archives Division, Newport, RI, 1950.
"Reflections on the War in the Pacific," *Proceedings* 78, 4 (Apr. 1952): 351–61.
"Maritime Strategy," staff presentation, Sept. 11, 1952, p. 1, Naval War College Special Collections, Archives Division; rev. and publ. as "On Maritime Strategy," *Proceedings* 79, 5 (May 1953): 467–77.
"Why a Sailor Thinks Like a Sailor," *Proceedings* 83, 8 (Aug. 1957): 811–17.
"Historical and Contemporary Theories of Strategy," Aug. 17, 1965. Naval War College Sp. Coll., Arch. Div., Newport, RI.
Military Strategy: A General Theory of Power Control. New Brunswick, NJ: Rutgers University Press, 1967.
Zabecki, David T. "Harry Summers Obituary"; www.clausewitz.com/readings/SummersObitText.htm
Zarate, Robert and Henry Sokolski, eds. *Nuclear Heuristics: Selected Writings of Albert and Roberta Wohlstetter*. Carlisle Barracks, PA: US Army War College, SSI, 2009.
Zellen, Barry Scott. *State of Doom: Bernard Brodie, the Bomb, and the Birth of the Bipolar World*. New York: Continuum International, 2012.
Zuckerman, Sir Solly. "Judgment and Control in Modern War," *Foreign Affairs* 40, 2 (Jan. 1962): 196–212.

Index

absolute weapon, 57
air operational art, 195
Air University Quarterly Review, 118
AirLand Battle, 160, 183
Angell, Norman, 2, 29
armed conflict
    four species of, 117
Atwood, Margaret, 174
    Handmaid's Tale (1985), 174

Beard, George, 208
Big Blue, 222
Bigelow, Captain John
    and political strategy, 29
    Principles of Strategy, 29
Blackett, P.M.S., 120
Boyd, John R., 1, 169
    Aerial Attack Study, 171
    Conceptual Spiral (1992), 178
    Destruction and Creation (1976), 178–79
    Discourse on Winning and Losing, 178
    energy maneuverability (EM) theory, 171
    first principles of, 188
    Organic Design for Command and Control (1987), 178
    Patterns of Conflict, 172, 177
    principles of war, his views of, 188
    Strategic Game of ? and ?, 178
    war's nature, his view of, 189
Bradley, Omar, 149
Brodie, Bernard, 1, 57, 133, 158, 167
    Absolute Weapon, 66–67
    and *On War*, 61
    Escalation and the Nuclear Option, 60
    Layman's Guide to Naval Strategy, 60, 124
    on LeMay, 57
    on limited war, 70
    on Mahan's principles, 69
    on Osgood's *Limited War*, 72
    on Schelling's *Arms and Influence*, 82
    on the principles of war, 70
    rugged friendship with Schelling, 84
    Sea Power in the Machine Age, 60
    slighted by Kissinger, 75
    "Strategy as an Art and a Science", 117
    Strategy in the Missile Age, 60
    War and Politics, 60, 212, 215
    war's nature, his concept of, 80
Brodie, Bernard (and Fawn)
    From Crossbow to H-Bomb, 211
broken-back wars, 216
Bronowski, Jacob, 180
brush-fire wars, 216
Burke, Arleigh, 99
Burke, James, 180
Butler, Smedley, 51, 54, 192

Carter, President Jimmy, 175
Cash, W.J.
    Mind of the South, 132
Cebrowski, Arthur, 201
center of gravity, 155
Civil Operations, Rural Development Support (CORDS), 163
Clausewitz, Carl von, 31, 33, 76
Cohen, Eliot, 147
Colomb, Admiral Philip
    Naval Warfare, 24
compellence
    shortcomings of, 124
Containment, 153, 163
Coolidge, President Calvin, 38, 40, 43
Corbett, Julian
    and Mahan, 24
    Principles of Maritime Strategy, 24, 224
cult of the rebel, 64, 213

Deptula, David, 195, 221
    and effects based operations (EBO), 200
Deutsch, Karl, 120
Domino theory, 211
Dulles, John Foster, 68, 96

Index

Eccles, Henry E., 1, 57, 111
  America's social divisions his views of, 125
  as a structuralist, 115, 128
  control, strategy of defined, 123
  deterrence as an incomplete strategy, 123
  limited war, his views of, 115
  media, his views of, 126
  Military Concepts and Philosophy, 119–20
  Military Power in a Free Society, 125, 143, 175
  on public support for military action, 128
  on the elements of power, 116
  on weapon strategy, 120
  theory, components of a comprehensive, 121
  theory, his concept of, 119
  US strategy in Vietnam, his views of, 125
  war's character, his conception of, 128
  war's nature, his conception of, 128
effects based approach to operations (EBAO), 202
effects based operations (EBO), 201, 221
Eisenhower, Dwight D., 30, 34, 158
  and Little Rock Nine, 62
  massive retaliation, doctrine of, 68

Fiske, Bradley, 17, 31, 209
  and root of conflict, 51
  Navy as a Fighting Machine, 25
  vs Billy Mitchell, 38
FM 100-5 Operations (1954), 149
FM 100-5 Operations (1962), 149, 154
FM 100-5 Operations (1976), 167
FM 100-5 Operations (1982), 160
FM 100-5 Operations (1986), 160
Friedan, Betty
  Feminine Mystique, 63

Giddings, Franklin, 209
  Principles of Sociology, 23
Gray, Colin, 95
Griffin, John, 62

Halperin, Morton, 103
Hammes, T.X., 187
Hansberry, Lorraine
  Raisin in the Sun, 64
Heisenberg, Werner, 178
Ho Chi Minh, 152
Holtoner, Stanley, 133
Howard, Sir Michael, 146, 224
Hughes, Wayne, 183

Huntington, Samuel, 214
  on military experts, 15–16
  on objective control, 73
  Soldier and the State, 65, 132
Huston, J.A., 117

imperatives, military. *See* first principles
improvised explosive devices (IEDs), 204
"In Shadow of Doom
  Social Disintegration in America", 176

James, William
  Principles of Psychology, 23
Jane, Frederick T., 17
  Heresies of Sea Power, 24
Jeune École (Young School), 16
Johnson, Chalmers, 152
Johnston, Edward S.
  "Science of War," 154
Jomini, Antoine, 13, 31

Kahn, Herman, 1, 57, 167, 215
  American Values Past and Future, 106
  countervalue vs counterforce, 96
  deterrence, his three types, 96
  Doomsday Machine, 98–99
  Dr Strangelove, 93
  Dr Strangelove, 98
  escalation and bargaining, 101
  Escalation Ladder, defects of, 104
  Fail Safe, 93
  Fail Safe, 98
  first principles of, 107
  "If Negotiations Fail," 105
  Ladder of Escalation, 99
  and LSD, 94
  on all-out war, 96
  On Escalation, 93
  On Thermonuclear War, 93, 95
  On Thermonuclear War and *On War*, 95
  Thinking about the Unthinkable, 93, 100
  war's character, his understanding of, 109
  war's nature, his concept of, 108
Kasparov, Gary, 222
Kennan, George, 66
  measures short of war, 74, 213
  political warfare, 213
Kennedy, John F., 63
Kennedy, Robert F., 66
Kennedy, John F., 63
Kent State massacre May 4, 1970, 66
Kerouac, Jack
  On the Road, 65
Khrushchev, Nikita, 63

Index

King Jr., Martin Luther, 63, 65
King, Ernest J., 7, 30, 57
Kissinger, Henry, 219
   limited war and nuclear weapons, 75
   limited war, his concept of, 75
   60 Minutes interview, 75
   Nuclear Weapons and Foreign Policy, 65, 75
   on all-out war, 80
   vs Schelling, 84
   war's nature, his concept of, 80
Knox, Dudley Wright, 17
   definition of principles, 24
Kuhn, Thomas, 178, 222
   definition of paradigm shift, 4

Lansdale, Edward, 77, 162, 219
Le Duan, 152
Leahy, Patrick, 30
Leary, Timothy, 65, 94
LeMay, Curtis, 30, 57, 225
   America is in Danger (1968), 159
Liddell Hart, B.H., 59
limited war in military instruction, 118
limited war theory, 207
Lind, William S., 1, 146, 169
   America Can Win, coauthor of, 172
   and US Sen. Gary Hart, 172
   Cultural Conservatism, coauthor of, 173
   first principles of, 189
   Fouth-Generation Warfare, his theory of, 186
   4th Generation Warfare Handbook, 169
   Maneuver Warfare Handbook, 169
   Multiculturalism, as a threat, 186
   Victoria (2014), 174
   war's nature, his view of, 190
Luce, Stephen B.
   and law of nature, 51
   on Mahan, 15
Luttwak, Edward, 149, 181
Lykke Jr, Arthur F., 5, 164

MacArthur, Douglas, 30, 149
   insubordination of, 69
Mahan, Alfred Thayer, 1, 52, 208
   and the guardian tradition, 24
   and war's character, 30
   definition of theory, 23
   first principles of, 25–26
   ideas compared to Mitchell's, 53
   naval strategy, definition of, 28
   on defensive war, 27
   on Woodrow Wilson, 18
   principles and history, 26
   science of naval warfare, 30
   secondary principles of, 28
   war's nature, concept of, 28
   writing style of, 14
maneuver theory, 181
maneuver warfare, 180, *See* maneuver theory
Manstein, Erich von, 182
Marshall, Alfred
   Principles of Economics, 23
Marshall, George C., 7, 30, 34
massive retaliation, 117
McCarthy, Senator Joseph, 62
McClintock, Robert
   Meaning of Limited War, 76
McCuen, John J.
   Art of Counter-Revolutionary War, 77
McNamara, Robert, 157
McNaughton, John, 83
Meredith, James, 63
Military Review, 117
Miller, Perry
   New England Mind, 132
Mitchell, William (Billy), 1, 209
   air power, definition of, 32
   and Caroline Stoddard, 36, 39
   and control of the air, 48–49
   and Franklin Delano Roosevelt, 41
   and George S. Patton Jr., 47
   and Hugh Trenchard, 37, 39
   and Jominian first principles, 53
   and President Coolidge, 33
   and similarity to Douhet's ideas, 48
   and Stock Market Crash of 1929, 46
   and the target ship Ostfriedland, 39
   and war's nature, 51
   and Will Rogers, 44
   Court Martial of Billy Mitchell (movie), 32
   exploits in First World War, 37
   exploits in Philippines, 35
   first principles of, 48
   flying lessons, 37
   lecture to US Army War College 1922, 50
   relationship to his mother, 34
Morgenstern, Oskar, 83
Morgenthau, Hans, 71
   contra Kissinger, 75
Morrow Board, 50
Mutual Agreed Assured Destruction (MAAD), 99
Mutual Assured Destruction (MAD), 99
Myerson, Roger, 84

Index

National Security Council Paper 68, 134
Naval Doctrinal Publication (1992), 183
Naval War College Review, 117, 127
Neumann, John von, 83
Nimitz, Chester, 30
Nitze, Paul, 134
Nixon, Richard M., 63, 69, 144

observe, orient, decide, act (OODA) loop, 169, 177
Operation Rolling Thunder, 121, 133
operational art, 164, 167
Operational Naval Logistics, 114
Osgood, Robert E., 57
   and the Communist way of war, 73
   cited favorably by Kissinger, 76
   "Concepts of General and Limited War," 117
   first principles of, 78
   Ideals and Self-Interest in America's Foreign Relations, 72
   Korean conflict as model of limited war, 74
   Limited War, 65, 71, 212
   Limited War Revisited, 79, 143
   limited war, his definition of, 74
   on disassociating power and policy, 72
   on human passions, 108
   on Schelling, 84
   on unconditional surrender, 74
   three categories of limited war, 79
   war's nature, his concept of, 80
Owens, William (Bill), 202

Pape, Robert
   Bombing to Win (1996), 199
   contra Douhet, Mtchell, and Warden, 200
   strategic paralysis, 200
Paret, Peter, 224
   Guerrillas in the 1960s, coauthor of, 77
Parks, Rosa, 62
Patrick, Major General Mason, 33
Patton, George S., 30
Pentagon Papers 1971, 127
Pike, Douglas, 77, 152
Popper, Karl, 179, 210, 214, 222
   Logic of Scientific Discovery (1959), 179
Powell, Colin, 195
Presley, Elvis, 65, 174, 213
principles of war, 219

principles, core. *See* first principles
principles, first
   defined, 7

revolt of the admirals, 131
Riper, Paul Van, 202
Rosinski, Herbert, 5, 58, 111, 122, 132, 179
   "Evolution of Warfare and Strategy," 123
   "New Thoughts on Strategy," 123
   on Osgood, 72
   strategy of control, as essence of, 123
   strategy, his definition of, 123
Rostow, Walt, 107, 156
Russ, Joanna, 174
   Female Man (1975), 174

Salinger, J.D.
   Catcher in the Rye, 64
Schelling, Thomas C., 1, 57
   and segregation, 64
   Arms and Influence, 75, 84, 86
   bargaining defined, 84
   brute force vs coercion, 86
   categories of tacit and explicit bargains, 85
   countervalue vs counterforce, 88
   first principle of, 89
   game theory as framework, 85
   his deduction vs Mahan's induction, 88
   on Brodie, 59
   Strategy of Conflict, 84
   vs Kissinger, 84
   war's nature, his concept of, 90
Schlaffley, Phyllis, 174
scientific conservatism, 209
sea power
   Mahan's definition of, 13
Seversky, Alexander de, 118
   60 Minutes interview of, 119
Sims, William S., 16, 31
Spencer, Herbert
   and positivism, 23
Sputnik I and II, 65, 174
Starry, Donn, 154
Steinem, Gloria, 174
Stout, Hiram, 116
Strategic Air Command, 211
strategy as ends, ways, means, 164
strategy of control, 217
   its relationship to compellence, 124
Summers, Harry G., 1, 57, 111, 113, 120, 140
   Clausewitz's trinity, his views of, 147
   dialogue with NVA Colonel Tu, 144
   first principles, 159, 161
   Jominian core principles, his revival of, 163

Index

Summers, Harry G., (cont.)
  nature of Vietnam War, his view of, 151
  on 1968 Tet Offensive, 151
  on peoples' war, 151
  On Strategy, 143, 145, 169, 184, 193, 218
  On Strategy II, 145
  principles of war, 154
  US definition of strategy, his view of, 154
  vs Brodie, 147
  war's nature, his confusion over, 162
synchronization, principle of, 183

Tanham, George
  Communist Revolutionary Warfare, 77
Taylor, Maxwell, 120, 133, 149, 164
Thompson, Sir Robert, 105, 152
Till, Emmitt, 62
Truman, President Harry S., 138

US Defense Transformation, 202

Vietnamization, policy of, 105

Wallace, Mike, 119
Wang, Gung-Hsing
  Chinese Mind, 132
War Department Training Regulations 10-5 (1921), 154
war, character of
  characteristics, 2
  defined, 2
war, nature of
  characteristics, 2
  defined, 2
war, paradigms of
  materialist, 3
  modern, 3, 112
  political, 3
  traditional, 3
Warden III, John, 1, 169, 193
  Air Campaign (1988), 193, 221, 223
  and nonlinear factors, 204
  center of gravity, his concept of, 196
  debate with Robert Pape, 200
  "Enemy as a System," 198–99, 203
  first principles, 203
  five rings, 197–98
  his views compared to Douhet's, 198
  Instant Thunder, 194
  limited war, his views of, 194
  operational level of war, his definition of, 196
  Prometheus Project, 195
  strategic paralysis, 200, 204
  war's character, his views of, 205

war's material factors as more important than morale, 204
war's nature, his views of, 194, 203, 205
Warner, Denis, 152
war's character, 207
war's nature, 216, 223
  modern paradigm of vs materialist, 202
  political paradigm, 207
  strategy intellectuals view of, 211
  traditional paradigm of, 207, 219
war's nature distinguished from its character, 192
war's nature, as chaotic, 190
war's nature, as generally controllable, 190
war's nature, four paradigms of, 207
war's nature, modern paradigm of, 191
Watts riots, 6, 63
Weigley, Russell, 162
  American Way of War, 1, 5, 167
  American way of war, interpretation of, 184
  on Billy Mitchell, 32
  on Mahan, 14
  on the strategy intellectuals, 57
Wilson, President Woodrow, 192
Woerner, Fred, 175
Wohlstetter, Albert
  balance of terror, 97
  vs Kahn, 97
Wohlstetter, Roberta, 102
Wolff, Herbert E., 156
Woodstock 1969, 66
Wylie, Joseph C., 1, 57, 111
  and US intervention in Dominican Republic, 136
  center of gravity, his definition of, 136
  control, his definition of, 136
  first principles of, 140
  "Maritime Strategy," 134
  military mind, his types of, 132
  Military Strategy, 119, 130
  "Navy's Reasons for Being," 133
  Navy's way of battle, 135
  policy and politics, his views of, 138
  praise of Rosinski, 132
  sequential and cumulative strategies, his definitions of, 137
  strategy, his theory of, 134
  war's character, his view of, 141
  war's nature, his view of, 140
Wyly, Michael, 172

Zangwill, Israel
  "The Melting Pot" (1908), 19
Zuckerman, Sir Solly, 120

Printed in Dunstable, United Kingdom